Britain's
Best**B&B**

AA

This product includes mapping data licensed from Ordnance Survey® with the permission of the Controller of Her Majesty's Stationery Office. © Crown copyright 2007. All rights reserved. Licence number 100021153.

Maps prepared by the Cartography Department of The Automobile Association.

Maps © Automobile Association Developments Limited 2007.

Advertising Sales:
advertisementsales@theAA.com

Editorial:
lifestyleguides@theAA.com

Typeset by AA Lifestyle Guides

Printed and bound by Graficas Estella, Spain

Editorial contributors: Apostrophe S, Penny Phenix and Pam Stagg

A CIP catalogue record for this book is available from the British Library

ISBN-10: 0-7495-5175-5
ISBN-13: 978-0-7495-5175-9

Published by AA Publishing, which is a trading name of Automobile Association Developments Limited, whose registered office is:
Fanum House, Basing View
Basingstoke
Hampshire RG21 4EA

www.theAA.com

Registered number 1878835

A02832

Britain's
Best**B&B**

Contents

3

Welcome

Britain's Best B&B is a collection of the finest Guest Houses, Farmhouses, Inns and Restaurants with Rooms offering bed and breakfast accommodation in England, Scotland, Wales, the Isle of Man and the Channel Islands.

A Place to Stay

This fully revised and updated guide makes it easy to find that special place to stay for a weekend or a longer break. There are more than 560 establishments to choose from, including smart town guest houses, contemporary city B&Bs, accessible country farmhouses and undiscovered gems in hidden-away locations.

Best Quality

Every establishment has received a top star or diamond rating following a visit by an AA inspector. This will help to ensure that you have a friendly welcome, comfortable surroundings, excellent food and great value for money. Further details about the AA scheme, inspections, awards and rating system can be found on pages 8–10 of this guide.

Before You Travel

Some places may offer special breaks and facilities not available at the time of going to press. If in doubt, it's always worth calling the establishment before you book.

4

Using the Guide

Britain's Best B&B has been designed to enable you to find an establishment quickly and efficiently. Each entry provides clear information about the type of accommodation, the facilities available and the local area.

Use the contents (page 3) to browse the main gazeteer section by county and the index to find either a location (page 486) or a specific B&B (page 492) by name.

Finding your way

The main section of the guide is divided into five main parts covering England, Channel Islands, Isle of Man, Scotland and Wales. The counties within each of these sections are ordered alphabetically as are the town or village locations (shown in capital letters as part of the address) within each county. Finally, the establishments are listed alphabetically under each location name. Towns names featured in the guide can also be located in the map section (page 471).

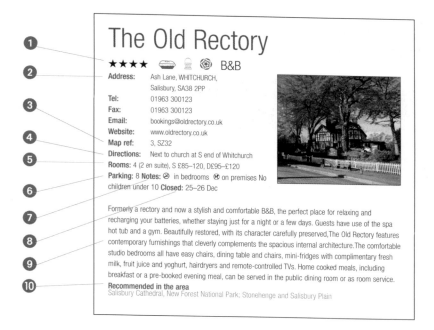

The Old Rectory

★★★★ ⬭ ☖ ☸ B&B

Address:	Ash Lane, WHITCHURCH, Salisbury, SA38 2PP
Tel:	01963 300123
Fax:	01963 300123
Email:	bookings@oldrectory.co.uk
Website:	www.oldrectory.co.uk
Map ref:	3, SZ32
Directions:	Next to church at S end of Whitchurch

Rooms: 4 (2 en suite), S £85–120, D£95–£120
Parking: 8 **Notes:** ⊘ in bedrooms ⊗ on premises No children under 10 **Closed:** 25–26 Dec

Formerly a rectory and now a stylish and comfortable B&B, the perfect place for relaxing and recharging your batteries, whether staying just for a night or a few days. Guests have use of the spa hot tub and a gym. Beautifully restored, with its character carefully preserved,The Old Rectory features contemporary furnishings that cleverly complements the spacious internal architecture.The comfortable studio bedrooms all have easy chairs, dining table and chairs, mini-fridges with complimentary fresh milk, fruit juice and yoghurt, hairdryers and remote-controlled TVs. Home cooked meals, including breakfast or a pre-booked evening meal, can be served in the public dining room or as room service.

Recommended in the area
Salisbury Cathedral, New Forest National Park; Stonehenge and Salisbury Plain

❶ Stars/Diamonds and Symbols

All entries in the guide have been inspected by the AA and, at the time of going to press, belong to the AA Guest Accommodation Scheme. Each establishment in the scheme is classified for quality with a grading of either one to five diamonds ◆ or stars ★. Each establishment in the Best B&B guide has three, four or five diamonds or stars. The majority of the establishments in this guide have been rated using the new system of common quality standards which awards stars. Establishments with a star rating have been given a descriptive category : B&B, GUEST HOUSE, FARMHOUSE, INN, RESTAURANT WITH ROOMS and GUEST ACCOMMODATION. See pages 8–10 for more information on the AA ratings and awards scheme.

Egg cups 🥚 and **Pies** 🥧 : These symbols denote where the breakfast or dinner has exceeded the quality level for the rating achieved by the establishment.

Rosette Awards ®: This is the AA's food award. See page 9 for further details.

❷ Contact Details

The establishment address includes a locator or place name in capitals (e.g. NORWICH). Within each county, entries are ordered alphabetically first by this place name and then by the name of the establishment.

Telephone and fax numbers, and e-mail and website addresses are given where available. See page 13 for international dialling codes. The telephone and fax numbers are believed correct at the time of going to press but changes may occur. The latest establishment details are on the B&B pages at www.theAA.com.

Website addresses have been supplied by the establishments and lead you to websites that are not under the control of Automobile Association Developments Ltd. AADL has no control over and accepts no responsibility or liability in respect of the material on any such websites. By including the addresses of third-party websites AADL does not intend to solicit business.

❸ Map reference

The map reference is composed of two parts. The first number shows the atlas map number (from 1–13) at the back of the guide (see pages 471 onwards). The second part is a National Grid reference. To find the town or village location on one of the maps, locate the lettered square and read the first figure across and the second figure vertically using the main gridlines to help guide you. For example, a map reference of '3, TQ28' refers to map 3 in the atlas section, grid square TQ on the map and a location of two across the grid square, running east-west, and eight in a north-south direction. The map section of this guide also provides road and county information.

Maps locating each establishment and a route planner are available at www.theAA.com.

❹ Directions

Where possible, directions have been given from the nearest motorway or A road. Distances are provided in miles (m) and yards (yds).

❺ Room Information

The number of letting bedrooms with a bath or shower en suite are shown. Bedrooms that have a private bathroom adjacent may be included as en suite. Further details on private bathroom and en suite provision may also be inlcuded in the description text (see ❾). Always telephone in advance and check to ensure that the accommodation has the facilities you require.

Prices: Charges shown are per night except where specified. S denotes bed and breakfast per person (single). D denotes bed and breakfast for two people sharing a room (double). In some cases prices are also given for twin (T), triple and family rooms, also on a per night basis. Prices are indications only, so check before booking.

❻ Parking

The number of parking spaces available. Other types of parking (on road or Park and Ride) may also be possible; check the descriptions for further information. Phone the establishment in advance of your arrival if unsure.

❼ Notes

This section provides details specific details relating to:

Smoking policy: The no smoking symbol by itself indicates a ban on smoking throughout the premises. If the establishment is only partly no smoking, the areas where smoking is not permitted are shown alongside the no smoking symbol.

The Smoking, Health and Social Care (Scotland) Act came into force in March 2006 (clearingtheairscotland.com). The law bans smoking in no-smoking premises in Scotland, which includes guest houses and inns with two or more guest bedrooms. The proprietor can designate one or more bedrooms with ventilation systems where the occupants can smoke, but communal areas must be smoke-free. Communal areas include the interior bars and restaurants in pubs and inns.

Similar laws covering England, Wales and Northern Ireland are due to come into effect during 2007. If the freedom to smoke or to be in a non-smoking atmosphere is important to you, we recommend that you check with the establishment when you book.

Dogs: Establishments that state no dogs may accept assist/guide dogs. Some places that accept dogs may restrict the size and breed and the rooms into which they can be taken. Always check the conditions when booking.

Children: No children means children cannot be accommodated, or a minimum age may be specified, e.g. No children under 4 means no children under four years old. The main description may also provide details about facilities available for children.

Establishments with special facilities for children may include additional equipment such as a babysitting service or baby-intercom system and facilities such as a playroom or playground, laundry facilities, drying and ironing facilities,

cots, high chairs and special meals. If you have very young children it as always wise to check before booking.

Other notes: Additional facilities, such as access for disabled people, or notes about other services (e.g. if credit card details are accepted), may be listed here.

⑧ Closed
Details of when the establishment is closed for business. Establishments are open all year unless Closed dates/months are shown. Please note that some places are open all year but offer a restricted service in low season. If the text does not detail the restricted services, check before booking.

⑨ Description
This is a general overview of the establishment and may include specific information about the various facilities offered in the rooms, a brief history of the establishment, notes about special features and descriptions of the food where an award has been given (see ❶ above).

⑩ Recommended in the area
This indicates places of interest, local sights to visit and potential day trips and activities.

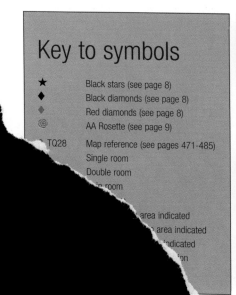

Key to symbols

★	Black stars (see page 8)
◆	Black diamonds (see page 8)
◆	Red diamonds (see page 8)
◉	AA Rosette (see page 9)
TQ28	Map reference (see pages 471-485)
	Single room
	Double room
	___ room
	___ area indicated
	___ area indicated
	___ indicated
	___ on

Best Quality

To obtain one of the highest ratings, an establishment must provide increased quality standards across all areas, with particular emphasis in five key areas: cleanliness, hospitality, breakfast, bedrooms and bathrooms.

The AA inspects and classifies more than 4,000 guest houses, farmhouses and inns for its Guest Accommodation Scheme. Establishments recognised by the AA pay an annual fee according to the rating and the number of bedrooms. This rating is not transferable if an establishment changes hands.

Common Standards

The AA has introduced new quality standards for inspected accommodation. This follows extensive consultation by the inspection organisations (the AA, VisitBritain, VisitScotland and Visit Wales) with consumers and the hospitality industry in order to make the rating systems for hotels and guest accommodation easier to understand.

Since January 2006, each inspection organisation has used the same standard procedures to determine the new Star rating of any inspected establishment. This replaces the previous Diamond rating, though the parallel one to five ratings indicate similar levels of quality. The new system of awards also uses six descriptive designators to classify the establishment (these are described on page 9).

Guests can now be confident that a guest house or a B&B anywhere in the UK and Ireland will offer consistent quality and facilities. The development of these new quality standards has received government support.

Stars & Diamonds

At the time of printing this edition of Britain's Best B&B Guide, not all establishments have been inspected under the new quality standards system and as a consequence many establishments are still rated with Diamonds. Check www.theAA.com for up-to-date information.

The AA Stars and Diamonds classify guest accommodation at five levels of quality, from one at the simplest, to five at the highest level of quality in the scheme.

Red Diamonds highlight the best within the three, four and five Diamond ratings. A similar method of highlighting the best establishments within each rating under the common standards Star rating system will be in place for 2008.

The Inspection Process

Establishments applying for AA recognition are visited by a qualified AA accommodation inspector as a mystery guest. Inspectors stay overnight to make a thorough test of the accommodation, food, and hospitality. After paying the bill the following morning they identify themselves and ask to be shown around the premises. The inspector completes a full report, resulting in a recommendation for the appropriate Star rating. After this first visit, the establishment will receive an annual visit to check that standards are maintained. If it changes hands, the new owners must re-apply for rating, as standards can change.

Guests can expect to find the following minimum standards at all levels:

■ Pleasant and helpful welcome and service, and sound standards of housekeeping and maintenance

■ Comfortable accommodation equipped to modern standards

■ Bedding and towels changed for each new guest, and at least weekly if the room is taken for a long stay

■ Adequate storage, heating, lighting and comfortable seating

■ A sufficient hot water supply at reasonable times

■ A full cooked breakfast. (If this is not provided, the fact must be advertised and a substantial continental breakfast must be offered.)

There are additional requirements for an establishment to achieve three, four or five Stars:

■ Three Stars and above - access to both sides of all beds for double occupancy.

■ Three Stars and above – bathrooms/shower rooms cannot be shared by the proprietor.

■ Three Stars and above (from January 1 2008) – a washbasin in every guest bedroom (either in the bedroom or the en suite/private facility).

■ Four Stars (from January 1 2008) – half of the bedrooms must be en suite or have private facilities.

■ Five Stars (from January 1 2008) – all bedrooms must be en suite or have private facilities.

Designators

All guest accommodation inspected under the new quality standards are given one of six descriptive designators to help the general public understand the different types of accommodation available in Britain and the facilities they can expect to find (see also ❶ on page 5). These descriptive designators are described in detail as follows:

B&B: Under the new Star rating, B&B accommodation is provided in a private house run by the owner and with no more than six guests. There may be restricted access to the establishment, particularly in the late morning and the afternoon, so do check this when booking.

GUEST HOUSE: A Star-rated Guest House provides for more than six paying guests and usually offers more services than a B&B, for example dinner, served by staff as well as the owner. Some Diamond-rated guest houses include the word 'hotel' in their name, though they cannot offer all the services required for the AA hotel Star rating (for example evening meals). London prices tend to be higher than outside the capital, and normally only bed and breakfast is provided, although some establishments do

AA Rosette Awards

Out of the many thousands of restaurants in the UK, the AA identifies some 1,800 as the best. The following is an outline of what to expect from restaurants with AA Rosette Awards. For a more detailed explanation of Rosette criteria please see www.theAA.com

◉ Excellent local restaurants serving food prepared with care, understanding and skill, using good quality ingredients.

◉ ◉ The best local restaurants, which aim for and achieve higher standards, better consistency and where a greater precision is apparent in the cooking. There will be obvious attention to the selection of quality ingredients.

◉ ◉ ◉ Outstanding restaurants that demand recognition well beyond their local area.

◉ ◉ ◉ ◉ Amongst the very best restaurants in the British Isles, where the cooking demands national recognition.

◉ ◉ ◉ ◉ ◉ The finest restaurants in the British Isles, where the cooking stands comparison with the best in the world.

provide a full meal service. Check on the service offered before booked as details may change during the currency of this guide.

FARMHOUSE: A farmhouse usually provides good value B&B or guest house accommodation and excellent home cooking on a working farm or smallholding. Sometimes the land has been sold and only the house remains, but many are working farms and some farmers are happy to allow visitors to look around, or even to help feed the animals. However, you should always take great care and never leave children unsupervised. The farmhouses are listed under towns or villages, but do ask for precise directions when booking.

INN: Traditional inns often have a cosy bar, convivial atmosphere, and good beer and pub food. Those listed in the guide will provide breakfast in a suitable room, and should also serve light meals during licensing hours. The character of the properties vary according to whether they are country inns or town

establishments. Check your arrival times as these may be restricted to opening hours.

RESTAURANT WITH ROOMS: These restaurants offer overnight accommodation with the restaurant being the main business and open to non-residents. The restaurant usually offers a high standard of food and service.

GUEST ACCOMMODATION: Within this edition of the Best B&B Guide this includes any establishment that meets the minimum entry requirements with a rating of three stars or more and outstanding results from an inspection visit.

■ A few entries in Britain's Best B&B do not have rating and designator information because the establishment changed ownership during the production of the guide. A rating is not transferable if an establishment changes hands. The new rating cannot be shown until a new inspection has taken place. For up-to-date information on these and other entries visit www.theAA.com.

Useful Information

There are so many things to remember when embarking on a short trip or weekend break. If you are unsure, always check before you book. Up-to-date information on contacting all B&Bs can be found at the travel section of www.theAA.com

Codes of practice

The AA encourages the use of The Hotel Industry Voluntary Code of Booking Practice in appropriate establishments. The prime objective of the code is to ensure that the customer is clear about the price and the exact services and facilities being purchased, before entering into a contractually binding agreement. If the price has not been previously confirmed in writing, the guest should be handed a card at the time of registration at the establishment, stipulating the total obligatory charge.

The Tourism (Sleeping Accommodation Price Display) Order 1977 compels hotels, motels, guest houses, farmhouses, inns and self-catering accommodation with four or more letting bedrooms to display in entrance halls the minimum and maximum prices charged for each category of room. This order complements the Voluntary Code of Booking Practice.

Fire precautions and safety

Many of the establishments listed in the guide are subject to the requirements of the Fire

www.theAA.com

Go to www.theAA.com to find more AA listed guest houses, hotels, pubs and restaurants – some 12,000 establishments.

Routes & Traffic on the home page leads to a route planner. Simply enter your postcode and the establishment postcode given in this guide and click Confirm. Check your details and then click GET MY ROUTE and you will have a detailed route plan to take you door-to-door.

Use the Travel section to search for Hotels & B&Bs or Restaurants & Pubs by location or establishment name. Scroll down the list of finds for the interactive map and local routes.

Postcode searches can also be made on www.ordnancesurvey.co.uk and www.multimap.com which will also provide useful aerial views of your destination.

Precautions Act 1971. This Act does not apply to the Channel Islands or the Isle of Man, where their own rules are exercised. All establishments should display details of how to summon assistance in the event of an emergency at night.

Licensed premises

Whereas inns hold a licence to sell alcohol, not all guest houses are licensed. Some may have a full liquor licence, or others may have a table licence and wine list. Licensed premises are not obliged to remain open throughout the permitted hours, and they may do so only when they expect reasonable trade.

Children

Restrictions for children may be mentioned in the description. Some establishments may offer free accommodation to children when they share their parents' room. Such conditions are subject to change without notice, therefore always check when booking.

Complaints

Readers who have cause to complain are urged to do so on the spot. This should provide an opportunity for the proprietor to correct matters. If this approach fails, please inform AA Hotel Services by writing to:

Fanum House, Basingstoke, Hampshire, RG21 4EA. The AA does not, however, undertake to obtain compensation for complaints.

Booking

Advance booking is always recommended to avoid disappointment. The peak holiday periods in the UK are Easter, and from June to September; public holidays are also busy times. In some parts of Scotland the winter skiing season is a peak holiday period. Some establishments may only accept weekly bookings from Saturday, and others require a deposit on booking. Please quote this guide in any enquiry. Guest houses may not accept credit or debit cards - ask when booking. VAT (Value Added Tax at 17.5%) is payable in the UK and in the Isle of Man, on basic prices and additional services. VAT does not apply in the Channel Islands. Always confirm the current price before booking; the prices in this guide are indications rather than firm quotations. It is a good idea also to confirm exactly what is included in the price when booking. Remember that all details, especially prices, may change without notice during the currency of the guide.

Cancellation

Advise the proprietor immediately if you must cancel a booking. If the room cannot be re-let you may be held legally responsible for partial payment. This could include losing your deposit or being liable for compensation. You should consider taking out cancellation insurance.

Bank and Public Holidays 2007	
New Year's Day	1st January
New Year's Holiday	2nd January (Scotland)
Good Friday	6th April
Easter Monday	9th April
May Day Bank Holiday	7th May
Spring Bank Holiday	28th May
August Holiday	1st August (Scotland)
Late Summer Holiday	27th August
Christmas Day	25th December
Boxing Day	26th December

International Information

If you're travelling from overseas, then the following information will provide some useful guidance to help you enjoy your stay in Britain. The individual entries in this book will also give you information regarding travel and the best routes to take.

Money

Some establishments may not accept traveller's cheques, or credit or debit cards, so ask about payment methods when you book. Most European and American credit and debit cards allow you to withdraw cash from British ATMs.

Driving

In the UK you drive on the left and overtake on the right. Seat belts are worn by every occupant of the car, whether they sit in the front or the rear. Speed limits are displayed in miles per hour.

Car rental

You will be rerquired to present your driving licence and credit or debit card. You can also provide an International Driving Permit along with your driving licence. Further identification, such as a passport, may also be required. A minimum age limit will apply.

Trains

The UK has an extensive rail network. To find out about routes, special offers or passes, contact National Rail (www.nationalrail.co.uk, tel: 08457 484950; from overseas +44 20 7278 5240, and international rates apply).or a travel agent.

Medical treatment & health insurance

Travellers who normally take medicines or carry an appliance, such as a hypodermic syringe, should ensure that they have sufficient supply for their stay and a doctor's letter describing the condition and treatment required.

Before travelling ensure you have insurance for emergency medical and dental treatment. Many European countries have reciprocal agreements for medical treatment and require EU citizens to obtain a European Health Insurance Card (EHIC) before travel.

Telephones

Many guest houses have direct dial telephones in the rooms. Always check the call rate before dialling. Payphones usually take cash, credit or debit cards, or phonecards. Phonecards can be purchased from newsagents and post offices.

The telephone and fax numbers in this guide show the area code followed by the subscriber number. When dialling from abroad first dial the international network access code, then the country code (44 for the UK). Omit the first digit of the area code then dial the subscriber number. For example:

From Europe   00 44 111 121212
From the US   011 44 111 121212

When dialling from the UK, dial the international network access code, then the country code.

Electrical appliances

The British electrical current is 220-240 volts and appliances have square three-pin plugs. Foreign appliances may require an adaptor for the plug, as well as an electrical voltage converter that will allow, for example, a 110-volt appliance to be powered.

ENGLAND

The valley of Borrowdale, Lake District National Park.

BERKSHIRE

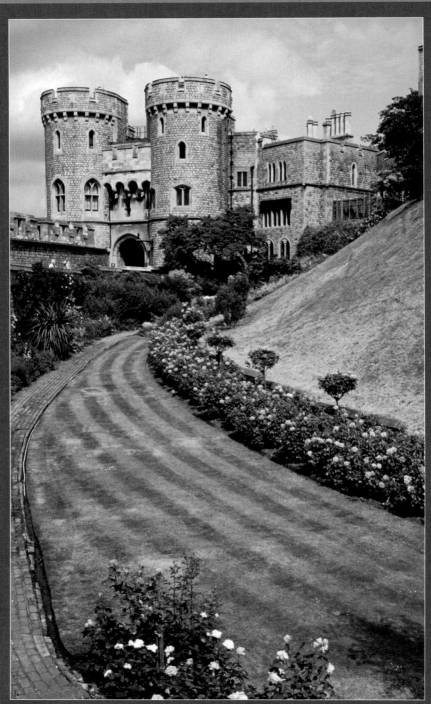

The rose gardens of Windsor Castle.

The Crown & Garter

★★★★ GUEST HOUSE

Address: Great Common, Inkpen,
HUNGERFORD RG17 9QR
Tel: 01488 668325
Email: gill.hern@btopenworld.com
Website: www.crownandgarter.com
Map ref: 3, SU36
Directions: 4m SE of Hungerford. Off A4 into Kintbury,
opp corner stores onto Inkpen Rd, straight for 2m
Rooms: 8 en suite, S £59.50 D £90 **Parking:** 40
Notes: ⊗ in bedrooms

Gillian Hern is the owner of this 16th-century inn set in the beautiful Kennet valley. The bar and restaurant are in keeping with the character of the building and real ales, spiced wine and a selection of malt whiskies are available. The restaurant offers an interesting range of country dishes prepared from local produce.The bedrooms are in a courtyard around a tranquil garden. Each room has a bath and power shower, a hairdryer, television and video, and tea and coffee facilities.

Recommended in the area

Historic Marlborough; Lambourn Downs; Salisbury Plain and Stonehenge

The Swan Inn

★★★★ INN

Address: Craven Road, Inkpen, HUNGERFORD RG17 9DX
Tel: 01488 668326
Fax: 01488 668306
Email: enquiries@theswaninn-organics.co.uk
Website: www.theswaninn-organics.co.uk
Map ref: 3, SU36
Directions: 3.5m SE of Hungerford. S on Hungerford High
St past railway bridge, left to Hungerford Common, right
signed Inkpen
Rooms: 10 en suite, S £60–70 D £80–95 **Parking:** 50 **Notes:** ⊗ on premises **Closed:** 25–26 Dec

The peaceful north Wessex downs provide an idyllic setting for this 17th-century inn. Outside it is a delightful picture, with white-painted walls, old tiled roof and pretty terraces. Inside there are oak beams, open fires and a warm welcome from the Harris family. The owners are organic farmers, and both the restaurant and an adjoining farm shop feature superb produce. The spacious en suite bedrooms are firmly rooted in the 21st century, with direct-dial and Internet connections.

Recommended in the area

Combe Gibbet; Kennet and Avon Canal; Avebury stone circle

Black Boys Inn

★★★★ ◉◉ RESTAURANT WITH ROOMS

Address: Henley Road, HURLEY SL6 5NQ
Tel: 01628 824212
Email: info@blackboysinn.co.uk
Website: www.blackboysinn.co.uk
Map ref: 3, SU88
Directions: 1m W of Hurley on A4130
Rooms: 8 en suite, D £65–75 **Parking:** 40
Notes: ⊘ on premises ⊗ on premises No children under 12 **Closed:** 24 Dec–9 Jan

This 16th-century inn, a five-minute walk from the River Thames, provides stylish accommodation in a lovely rural setting. With views across the Chiltern Hills the rooms are beautifully appointed, the furnishings complementing the original features of the building. The rooms have tea- and coffee-making facilities, TV with DVD player and Internet connection. Excellent modern British cooking features quality local produce.

Recommended in the area

Henley-on-Thames; Cliveden (NT); The Herb Farm, Sonning Common

Weir View House

★★★★ GUEST ACCOMMODATION

Address: 9 Shooters Hill, PANGBOURNE RG8 7DZ
Tel: 0118 984 2120
Fax: 0118 984 3777
Email: info@weirview.co.uk
Website: www.weirview.co.uk
Map ref: 3, SU67
Directions: A329 N from Pangbourne, after mini rdbt under rail bridge, opp Swan pub
Rooms: 9 en suite, D £75–90 **Parking:** 10 **Notes:** ⊘ on premises **Closed:** 23 Dec–1 Jan

In an enchanting setting beside the River Thames, this inviting guesthouse offers spacious en suite bedrooms (many with four-poster beds and river views) equipped with minibar, telephone with modem lines, tea and coffee facilities, hairdryer and trouser press. Continental breakfast is served in the bright dining room, and cooked meals can be delivered to your room from the pub across the road. During the day coffee and tea are served in the lounge, where Internet access is available free of charge.

Recommended in the area

Basildon Park (NT); Child Beale Wildlife Park; The Living Rainforest in Hampstead Norreys

Bull Inn

★★★★ INN

Address: High Street, SONNING RG4 6UP
Tel: 0118 969 3901
Fax: 0118 969 7188
Email: bullinn@accommodating-inns.co.uk
Website: www.accommodating-inns.co.uk/
              bullinn.html
Map ref: 3, SU77
Directions: From A4 (Maidenhead) junct for Sonning
Rooms: 5 en suite, S £85–125 D £85–125 Parking: 14

The 16th-century Bull Inn stands opposite the village church. Refurbished in keeping with the original character, its lovely bedrooms are individually furnished with high-quality fabrics and carpets, and their facilities include flat-screen televisions and DVDs. Jerome K Jerome mentions the Bull Inn in his comedy novel *Three Men in a Boat* and rooms are named from this book. Manager Dennis Mason is a real card and the epitome of a great barman. The bar blackboards display an extensive range of good pub grub and award-winning ales are sold.

Recommended in the area

River Thames; Windsor; Reading

The Old Manor

★★★★★ GUEST ACCOMMODATION

Address: Whitehouse Green,
              SULHAMSTEAD RG7 4EA
Tel: 0118 983 2423
Fax: 0118 983 6262
Email: rags-r@theoldmanor.fsbusiness.co.uk
Map ref: 3, SU66
Directions: M4 junct 12, A4 W, left for Theale Station,
over railway, over river, right after 0.4km. Continue for
1km and turn left at x-rds & Old Manor entrance on left
Rooms: 3 en suite S £40 D £80 Parking: 8 Notes: ⊗ on premises ⊗ on premises
No children under 8 Closed: 23 Dec–2 Jan

A haven for the discerning guest, this one-time manor house stands in 10 acres of well-kept grounds. You can relish being treated like a family friend by Rosemary and Peter Sanders-Rose. The elegant bedrooms include one with a four-poster bed and a spa bath. Good food and a complimentary glass of wine are served in the dining room, and afternoon tea is provided in the drawing room.

Recommended in the area

Basildon Park (NT); The Vyne (NT); Kennet and Avon Canal

BRISTOL

The River Avon.

Downlands House

★★★★ GUEST ACCOMMODATION

Address: 33 Henleaze Gardens, Henleaze,
BRISTOL BS9 4HH
Tel: 0117 962 1639
Fax: 0117 962 1639
Email: mjdownlands@blueyonder.co.uk
Website: www.downlandshouse.co.uk
Map ref: 2, ST57
Directions: 2m NW of city centre off A4018. M5 junct
17, signs Westbury-on-Trym/City Centre, pass private
girls schools, Henleaze Gdns on left
Rooms: 10 (7 en suite), S £38–52 D £60–75 **Notes:** ⊗ on premises ⌐ allowed in bedrooms

Combining Victorian elegance and the charm, atmosphere and comforts of a large family home,
Downlands House is the perfect place for both a weekend break or a longer holiday. The quiet setting
is not far from the centre of Bristol and the smart residential area of Clifton where you will find
Brunel's spectacular suspension bridge. It is also close to Bristol University and the Halls of Residence.
Downlands has plenty of pretty, well-equipped rooms to choose from – single, twin and double – and
one of the large double rooms is situated on the ground floor. There are smart facilities en suite, and
each room is thoughtfully supplied with a hairdryer, easy chair, a hospitality tray, colour TV and other
homely touches. Guests can relax in the comfortable lounge after a day spent exploring Bristol or its
environs. The day begins with a tasty cooked breakfast served either in the delightful conservatory
or the stylish dining room. In the garden, the patio is a charming place to enjoy the sun on warm days.
Free wireless broadband Internet access is available throught the hotel. If you don't want to drive
to the city for dinner there are a number of restaurants and local shops within a short walking distance
of Downlands House.

Recommended in the area

Durdham Downs; SS *Great Britain*; Clifton Suspension Bridge

The Clifton Suspension Bridge.

Downs Edge

★ ★ ★ ★ GUEST HOUSE

Address:	Saville Road, Stoke Bishop, BRISTOL BS9 1JA
Tel:	0117 968 3264
Fax:	0117 968 7063
Email:	welcome@downsedge.com
Website:	www.downsedge.com
Map ref:	2, ST57

Directions: M5 junct 17, onto A4018, 4th rdbt right onto B4054 Parrys Ln, 1st left onto Saville Rd, 3rd right onto Hollybush Ln, left after 2nd speed ramp

Rooms: 7 en suite, S £52–58 D £75–78 **Parking:** 8 **Notes:** ⊗ in bedrooms **Closed:** Xmas/New Year

Standing in glorious gardens, this lovely country house has a quiet countryside setting in the heart of the city, on the edge of Bristol's famous Durdham Downs. The comfortable, well-equipped bedrooms have sweeping views across the Downs and a thoughtful touch to each room is a basket full with life's little necessities. The drawing room has an open fire and is furnished with antiques and paintings. There's also a library with many books on Bristol. Breakfast is an impressive variety of hot and cold dishes.

Recommended in the area

Clifton Suspension Bridge; Bristol Zoo; Bristol city centre

Westfield House

★★★★   GUEST ACCOMMODATION

Address: 37 Stoke Hill, Stoke Bishop,
             BRISTOL BS9 1LQ
Tel: 0117 962 6119
Fax: 0117 962 6119
Email: admin@westfieldhouse.net
Website: www.westfieldhouse.net
Map ref: 2,ST57
Directions: 2m NW of city centre in Stoke Bishop
Rooms: 3 en suite, S £55–79 D £85–99 Parking: 5
Notes: ⊘ on premises ⊗ on premises
No children under 11

Set in 2.5 acres of private grounds, this large white-painted Georgian-style, family-run guesthouse makes an ideal retreat from Bristol's city lights. Westfield House is close to Durdham Downs – a vast expanse of open space which stretches from Bristol's suburbs to the cliffs of the Avon Gorge – and the Bristol University Halls of Residence. The very comfortable bedrooms (there is a choice of single and doubles) are well equipped with TV, tea- and coffee-making facilities, and are decorated in pastel shades. The living room centres round a cosy fireplace while large bay windows lead onto a spacious terrace. Owner Ann cooks more or less to order using quality local ingredients, and a typical meal may include dishes such as salmon en croute with pureed spinach and hollandaise sauce accompanied by potatoes dauphinoise, followed by a delicious home-made apple pie – all the better in the summer months when served on the patio overlooking the lovely rear garden. The grounds are also a haven for a variety of wildlife including owls, badgers, falcons and hedgehogs. If you still hanker for the the bright lights, Westfield House is just a short walk from Bristol city centre. There is ample off-street parking for guests.

Recommended in the area

Clifton Suspension Bridge; SS *Great Britain*; Bristol Zoo

CAMBRIDGESHIRE

The 'Backs' stretch of the River Cam.

A line of punts for hire on the willow tree lined River Cam, Cambridge

Rose Bungalow

★★★★ B&B

Address:	68 High Street, Great Wilbraham, CAMBRIDGE CB1 5JD
Tel:	01223 882385
Email:	rose.bungalow@btinternet.com
Website:	www.rosebungalow.co.uk
Map ref:	3, TL45
Directions:	6m E of Cambridge in Great Wilbraham centre

Rooms: 2 en suite, S £30–35 D £55–60
Parking: 2 (off-road) **Notes:** ⊘ on premises ⊗ on premises No children under 10

This attractive bungalow has the advantage of a quiet location yet is close to the park and ride for Cambridge with its many attractions. There are two well-equipped rooms, each with TV and hostess tray including fruit and chocolates. The full English breakfast is a speciality with Suffolk bacon and sausages, local eggs, home-made bread, fresh fruit and organic apple juice. A continental breakfast can be requested. Other meals can be taken at one of the two local pubs, one in walking distance.

Recommended in the area

Anglesey Abbey (NT); Wimpole Hall (NT); Cambridge; Duxford Imperial War Museum; Newmarket

CHESHIRE

Lyme Park gardens near Disley.

Sandhollow Farm B&B

★★★★ B&B

Address:	Harthill Road, BURWARDSLEY, Tattenhall,
	Chester CH3 9NU
Tel:	01829 770894
Email:	paul.kickdrum@tiscali.co.uk
Website:	www.sandhollowfarmbandb.co.uk
Map ref:	6, SJ55

Directions: A41 signs to Tattenhall and Burwardsley
Rooms: 3 en suite, S £50 D £70 **Parking:** 4
Notes: ⊘ on premises No children under 12
Closed: Xmas and annual holiday

Nestling in the sandstone ridge of the Peckforton Hills this lovely farmhouse, with spectacular views over the Cheshire Plain and Welsh hills, is very handy for Chester, Liverpool and Manchester. There are lovely views from the bedrooms, which also benefit from en suite bathrooms, and the public areas are comfortable and inviting. The dining room is the setting for hearty breakfasts that feature local, organic produce and home made preserves. Two acres of well-kept grounds complete the peaceful idyll.

Recommended in the area

Beeston Castle; Oulton Park; Chester

Rowton Poplars Hotel

◆◆◆◆

Address:	Whitchurch Road, Rowton,
	CHESTER CH3 6AF
Tel:	01244 333010
Fax:	01244 333020
Email:	val@rowtonpoplars.co.uk
Website:	www.rowtonpoplars.co.uk
Map ref:	5, SJ46

Directions: 2m SE of Chester. A55 onto A41 for Whitchurch, premises before filling station
Rooms: 8 en suite, S £55–65 D £65–75 **Parking:** 30 **Notes:** ⌁ allowed in bedrooms

Close to Chester and the M56, this stylish Victorian house is a friendly, family-run establishment. The en suite luxury bedrooms are furnished to a high standard and come with TV and tea and coffee facilities. The attractive lounge is the perfect place to unwind with a drink after a busy day sightseeing or shopping. Breakfast, and dinner by arrangement, is served in the pleasant dining room with individual tables. The property has secure parking and is close to Chester's park and ride.

Recommended in the area

Chester Zoo; Blue Planet Aquarium; Cheshire Oaks

Tatton Park gardens.

The manacle rocks, east of Lizard Point, make up the most hazardous area of the Cornish coast

Tolcarne House Hotel

♦♦♦♦

Address:	Tintagel Road, BOSCASTLE PL35 0AS
Tel/Fax:	01840 250654
Email:	crown@eclipse.co.uk
Website:	www.milford.co.uk/go/tolcarne.html
Map ref:	1, SX09

Directions: In village at junct B3266 & B3263
Rooms: 8 en suite, S £44–46 D £66–81 **Parking:** 15
Notes: 🐕 allowed in bedrooms No children under 10
Closed: Dec–Feb

Graham and Margaret Crown have lived and worked at Tolcarne House for over 11 years, providing friendly service in a beautiful environment. The house stands in an elevated position 800 yards from the sea amid delightful grounds. A short walk through the village takes you to the Elizabethan harbour, now a National Trust property. Bedrooms are individually decorated and offer sea or valley views. All have facilities en suite, hospitality trays, clock radios and hairdryers. Guests eat at individual tables in the dining room, where the home-cooked dinner is a choice of meat or fish dishes.

Recommended in the area

Tintagel Castle; Bodmin Moor; Pencarrow House

Bude Haven Hotel

★★★★ GUEST ACCOMMODATION

Address:	Flexbury Avenue, BUDE EX23 8NS
Tel:	01288 352305
Fax:	01288 352662
Email:	enquiries@budehavenhotel.com
Website:	www.budehavenhotel.com
Map ref:	1, SS20

Directions: 0.5m N of Bude in Flexbury village centre
Rooms: 10 en suite, S £26.50–35 D £53–70
Parking: 6 **Notes:** ⊗ on premises

Bude Haven is a charming building in a quiet residential area, with the town centre and two lovely beaches just a short walk away. Natural hosts Alison and Richard Long foster a friendly, homely atmosphere. They offer comfortable en suite bedrooms, each with a clock radio, hairdryer and a beverage tray. An inviting lounge features a television, video and DVD, music centre, books and games. There is a well-stocked bar and interesting meals are served in the evening. For complete pampering retreat to the hot tub in the secluded garden, or the services of the qualified masseuse.

Recommended in the area

South West Coast Path; Tintagel; The Eden Project

Carrek Woth

◆◆◆◆

Address: West Pentire Road, CRANTOCK,
Newquay TR8 5SA
Tel: 01637 830530
Map ref: 1, SW76
Directions: W from Crantock village towards
West Pentire
Rooms: 6 en suite, S £37 D £60 **Parking:** 6
Notes: ⊘ on premises ✛ allowed in bedrooms

The name Carrek Woth is Cornish for Goose Rock, which can be seen in Crantock Bay, and good Cornish hospitality and service are the keynotes here. This is an ideal base for enjoying the north Cornwall coast, particularly the popular resort of Newquay, and children of all ages are welcome. The neat and well-maintained bedrooms are all on the ground floor, and some have good views. There's a pleasant lounge that looks toward Newquay and the sea, and an attractive dining room where, in addition to the daily breakfasts Sunday lunch is also available. The pride that the Curtis family take in their establishment is evident throughout, and many guests return again and again.
Recommended in the area
Newquay; Penhale Sands; Trerice

Cotswold House Hotel

★★★★ GUEST ACCOMMODATION
Address: 49 Melvill Road, FALMOUTH TR11 4DF
Tel: 01326 312077
Email: info@cotswoldhousehotel.com
Website: www.cotswoldhousehotel.com
Map ref: 1, SW82
Directions: On A39 near town centre & docks
Rooms: 10 en suite, S £28–37 D £56–70 **Parking:** 10
Notes: ⊘ on premises ⊗ on premises

With Falmouth's superb sandy Gyllyngvase beach and the busy estuary, harbour and yachting marina just a short walk away, this small family-run hotel is ideal for both a holiday or a short break. The smart Victorian property is also close to the picturesque, cobbled town centre with its historic buildings and range of specialist shops. All the bedrooms have a bath or shower room en suite and hospitality trays; and many have lovely views of the sea and the River Fal. Well-cooked traditional cuisine is a feature of a stay here, and the friendly owners offer attentive service. The convivial bar is another plus at this relaxed house, and a popular place for socializing in the evening.
Recommended in the area
Falmouth National Maritime Museum; The Eden Project; Trebah and Glendurgan gardens

Dolvean House

◆◆◆◆◆

Address: 50 Melvill Road, FALMOUTH TR11 4DQ
Tel: 01326 313658
Fax: 01326 313995
Email: reservations@dolvean.co.uk
Website: www.dolvean.co.uk
Map ref: 1, SW83
Directions: On A39 near town centre and docks
Rooms: 10 en suite, S £35 D £70 Parking: 10
Notes: ⊘ on premises ⊗ on premises
No children under 12 Closed: Xmas

The Dolvean is a traditional Victorian residence situated between Falmouth's main golden sandy beach and its internationally renowned harbour which shelters all types of seagoing craft including tall ships and visiting cruise liners. In the main streets and narrow alleyways of the historic town you'll find restaurants, cafés and pubs situated alongside specialist antiques and arts shops – many exhibiting local works. Paul and Carol Crocker, resident proprietors of Dolvean House since 1994, are passionate collectors of antiques, curios, old books (on travel, cookery, remedies, household hints and woodwork), advertising memorabilia, sewing machines and sewing ephemera. These fascinating collections have spilled out of their home into every corner of Dolvean, and the Crockers enjoy sharing their interests with guests, some of whom have contributed to the collections. Pretty pictures and an abundance of lace and ribbon bring a special touch to the bedrooms, each of which has its own character. All the rooms have full facilities en suite with fluffy towels, luxury toiletries and wireless broadband access. Thoughtful extras include hospitality trays, Cornish mineral water and chocolates by your bed. The traditional English breakfast menu uses only the finest Cornish produce. There is an enclosed car park.

Recommended in the area

Pendennis Castle; Falmouth National Maritime Museum; Trebah Garden

Falmouth Bay.

Rosemullion

★ ★ ★ ★   GUEST ACCOMMODATION

Address:	Gyllyngvase Hill, FALMOUTH TR11 4DF
Tel:	01326 314690
Fax:	01326 210098
Email:	gail@rosemullionhotel.demon.co.uk
Map ref:	1, SW83

Directions: A39 to Port Pendennis. Turn right after bridge

Rooms: 13 (11 en suite), S £30–40 D £53–64

Parking: 18 Notes: ⊘ on premises ⊗ on premises
No children Closed: 23–29 Dec

This striking mock-Tudor hotel caters for the discerning
guest and its peaceful atmosphere draws people back
again and again. Bedrooms are beautifully decorated and
furnished, and some have glorious views over the bay
Breakfast is served in a smart wood-panelled dining room, and the drawing room is delightful for
relaxing. Rosemullion is a stroll from Falmouth's main beach, and handy for the town and harbour.

Recommended in the area

Gyllyngvase Beach and Pendennis Castle; Helford River and Trebah Garden; The Eden Project

The Old Quay House

★★★★★ ◉◉ RESTAURANT WITH ROOMS

Address: 28 Fore Street, FOWEY PL23 1AQ
Tel: 01726 833302
Fax: 01726 833668
Email: info@theoldquayhouse.com
Website: www.theoldquayhouse.com
Map ref: 1, SX15
Directions: M5 junct 31 onto A30 to Bodmin. Then A389 through town and take B3269 to Fowey
Rooms: 12 en suite, S £130–210 D £160–210
Notes: No children under 12

The Old Quay House is exactly what the name describes – a historic property idyllically set on the attractive waterfront at Fowey. Although it has a colourful history dating back to 1889, it is the more recent treatment of the interior that is most exciting. Architect designed, its contemporary styling is cleverly juxtaposed with traditional architecture, demonstrating a flair that is rarely seen outside the nation's capital. Every one of the 12 bedrooms has benefited from this approach, and seven of them have the extra attraction of a private patio with views down the estuary. It is clear that the owners are passionate about the Old Quay House, and this extends to the levels of service and attention to detail. First impressions here couldn't be more inviting. Guests are greeted by a view through to the Q restaurant, the sun terrace beyond and the glittering waters of the estuary in the background. The restaurant soon demands more than a cursory glance, for this is where head chef Ben Bass creates his innovative menus of modern European cuisine, which has brought many accolades, including two AA rosettes. It is fast becoming one of the places to eat in Cornwall. And what better, after a satisfying meal and perhaps a digestive by the waterside, than knowing that your bed is just a short walk away.

Recommended in the area

The Eden Project; Lost Gardens of Heligan; Lanhydrock House

Tregerrick Farm B&B

★★★★ 🏠 FARMHOUSE

Address:	GORRAN, St AustellPL26 6NF
Tel/Fax:	01726 843418
Email:	fandc.thomas@btconnect.com
Website:	www.tregerrickfarm.co.uk
Map ref:	1, SW94

Directions: 1m NW of Gorran. B3273 S from St Austell, right after Pentewan Sands campsite to The Lost Gardens of Heligan, continue 3m, farm on left

Rooms: 4 (2 en suite), **Parking:** 4 **Notes:** ⊘ on premises 🚫 on premises No children under 4

This is an interesting place to stay for anyone who is enthusiastic about ecological issues, as it is a working farm where sustainability and biodiversity are paramount. The varied and imaginative breakfasts, based on locally produced food, are served in the dining room or conservatory. The bedrooms, all with en suite bathrooms, are tastefully furnished in keeping with the age of the property and there's wireless internet in the main house. A delightful garden annexe can sleep up to five.

Recommended in the area

Lost Gardens of Heligan; South West Coast Path; The Eden Project.

Calize Country House

★★★★ 🏠 GUEST ACCOMMODATION

Address:	Prosper Hill, Gwithian, HAYLE TR27 5BW
Tel/Fax:	01736 753268
Email:	jilly@calize.co.uk
Website:	www.calize.co.uk
Map ref:	1, SW54

Directions: 2m NE of Hayle. B3301 in Gwithian at Red River Inn, house 350yds up hill on left

Rooms: 4 en suite, S £40–55 D £70–90 **Parking:** 6 **Notes:** ⊘ on premises No children under 12

Calize has superb views of the sea and countryside, and is close to the beaches and coves of West Penwith. Jilly and Nigel Whitaker are naturally friendly and their hospitality is outstanding (home-made cake and tea are offered on arrival). Guests are invited to share their comfortable lounge, which has a log-burning fire during colder months. Memorable breakfasts are served around a communal table with sea views – treats include home-made walnut bread and blackberry jelly, seeded toast, fresh fruit, creamy scrambled eggs and fresh smoked salmon. The local seals are also an attraction.

Recommended in the area

South West Coast Path; St Ives Bay; St Michael's Mount (NT); National Seal Sanctuary

Hurdon Farm

★★★★ ⬭ FARMHOUSE

Address: LAUNCESTON PL15 9LS
Tel: 01566 772955
Map ref: 1, SX38
Directions: A30 onto A388 to Launceston, at rdbt exit for hospital, 2nd right signed Trebullett, premises 1st on right
Rooms: 6 en suite, S £25–30 D £46–58 **Parking:** 10
Notes: ⊘ on premises **Closed:** Nov–Apr

Hurdon Farm is particularly appealing for its delightful setting and the high standard of accommodation provided in the 18th-century farmhouse. Fresh flowers and a well-stocked tea tray welcome guests to the individually decorated bedrooms. Single, double, triple and family rooms are available, all with bathrooms en suite and useful extras such as hairdryers. Evening meals are available by arrangement, using only the best of local produce – don't miss the home-made puddings and farm-fresh clotted cream – and special diets can be catered for. Hurdon Farm is a non-smoking house and children are welcome.

Recommended in the area

The Eden Project; South West Coast Path; Dartmoor and Bodmin Moor

Withnoe Farm

★★★★ FARMHOUSE

Address: Tavistock Road, LAUNCESTON PL15 9LG
Tel: 01566 772523
Map ref: 1, SX38
Directions: On A388 towards Plymouth, opp route sign Tavistock (B3362) 13, Liskeard (A390) 19 and Plymouth (A38) 24
Rooms: 3 (2 en suite), S £30–32 D £50–56 **Parking:** 6
Notes: ⊘ on premises **Closed:** Dec–Jan

Mrs Avril Colwill's bed and breakfast business has been established at Withnoe Farm for over 30 years, and she prides herself on her friendly and helpful service. Her spacious home is immaculately kept, set back from the Tavistock road in large gardens with far reaching views of the valley and grazing cattle. Accommodation is provided in double rooms, either en suite or with private facilities. A good breakfast is served in the dining room, from where the views are quite breathtaking. The farmhouse is convenient for the A30 and many attractions, and just 1 mile from the centre of Launceston. There is plenty of parking space.

Recommended in the area

The Eden Project; South West Coast Path; Dartmoor

Trecarne House

★★★★★ 🍵 🛏 GUEST ACCOMMODATION

Address: Penhale Grange, St Cleer,
LISKEARD PL14 5EB
Tel: 01579 343543
Fax: 01579 343543
Email: trish@trecarnehouse.co.uk
Website: www.trecarnehouse.co.uk
Map ref: 1, SX26
Directions: B3254 N from Liskeard to St Cleer.
Right at Post Office, 3rd left after church, 2nd right,
house on right
Rooms: 3 en suite, S £45–55 D £66–99 **Parking:** 6 **Notes:** ⊘ on premises ⓧ on premises

With Bodmin Moor right on the doorstep, this friendly guesthouse has beautiful rural views enjoyed in peace and quiet. The large garden is a haven for children, who are made to feel very welcome – there are plenty of toys for the younger members of the family and the paddock is the ideal place for ball games. A trampoline, outdoor table tennis and a pool table are provided, and indoors the atmosphere is very relaxed and informal. Breakfast can be taken at any time before 11.30 am, in either the smart dining room or a spacious conservatory, and there is a comfortable lounge with a large Cornish slate and stone fireplace. The individually named bedrooms have a Scandinavian feel with their stripped pine floors, and all come equipped with colour TV, hairdryers and tea and coffee facilities, plus many thoughtful extras such as videos. Some rooms have sofas, armchairs and French windows, and are either en suite or have a private bathroom. All are spacious and have extensive views across the beautiful countryside. Trecarne House is located at the end of a country lane, and the village with its shop, and pubs which serve evening meals, is just a short stroll away. Children are half price when sharing with their parents.

Recommended in the area

The Eden Project; The Hurlers Stone Circle; The Lost Gardens of Heligan

Looe harbour.

Barclay House

★★★★ ⬭ ▤ GUEST ACCOMMODATION

Address:	St Martin's Road, LOOE PL13 1LP
Tel:	01503 262929
Fax:	01503 262632
Email:	info@barclayhouse.co.uk
Website:	www.barclayhouse.co.uk
Map ref:	1, SX24

Directions: N of Looe bridge on junct A387 & B3253
Rooms: 10 en suite, S £40–67.50 D £80–130
Parking: 20 Notes: ⊘ on premises ⊗ on premises
Closed: 22–27 Dec, 2 wks mid-Jan

Perched on the hillside overlooking Looe harbour, Barclay House has captivating views over the water and countryside beyond. Originally a Victorian family home in 6 acres of grounds, the house has a spacious elegance and relaxed air about it. On the ground floor are a lounge bar and sitting room with panoramic terrace where you can enjoy an aperitif in summer. The bedrooms have modern facilities and are decorated in pastel shades. Take a day out from sightseeing and relax beside the heated pool.

Recommended in the area

Lost Gardens of Heligan; The Eden Project; Lanhydrock (NT)

Bay View Farm

★★★★ 🛏 FARMHOUSE

Address: St Martins, LOOE PL13 1NZ
Tel: 01503 265922
Fax: 01503 265922
Website: www.looedirectory.co.uk/bay-view-farm.htm
Map ref: 1, SX25
Directions: 2m NE of Looe. Off B3253 for Monkey Sanctuary, farm signed
Rooms: 2 en suite, S £27–30 D £50–55 **Parking:** 3
Notes: ⊘ on premises ⊗ on premises No children under 5

A genuine warm Cornish welcome, an air of tranquillity and great food are the hallmarks of Bay View Farm. Host Mrs Elford is a delightful lady and it's easy to see why her guests are drawn back to this special place again and again. The renovated and extended bungalow is situated in a truly spectacular spot with ever-changing views across Looe Bay, and is beautifully decorated and furnished throughout to give a light, spacious feel. The two en suite bedrooms each have their own very individual character – one is huge with comfy sofas and a spectacular view, the other smaller but still very inviting. Guests can relax at the end of the day either in the lounge or on the lovely patio and watch the sun set over Looe. Breakfasts at Bay View Farm are substantial and the evening meals feature home-made desserts accompanied by clotted cream. If you do choose to eat out there are numerous restaurants and pubs nearby. The coastal path outside the entrance takes you to Millendreath beach and on to Looe and Polperro. The old town of East Looe is a delight of tall buildings, narrow streets and passageways and the fishing industry brings a maritime bustle to the harbour and quayside. West Looe, the smaller settlement, has a lovely outlook across the harbour to East Looe.

Recommended in the area

The Lost Gardens of Heligan; The Eden Project; Looe

The Beach House

★★★★★ 🛏 GUEST ACCOMMODATION

Address: Marine Drive, Hannafore, LOOE PL13 2DH
Tel: 01503 262598
Fax: 01503 262298
Email: enquiries@thebeachhouselooe.com
Website: www.thebeachhouselooe.com
Map ref: 1, SX25
Directions: From Looe W over bridge, left to Hannafore & Marine Dr, on right after Tom Sawyer Tavern
Rooms: 5 (4 en suite), D £80–110 **Parking:** 6
Notes: ⊘ on premises ⊗ on premises No children under 16

This big, white-painted house is on the seafront at Hannafore, with the South West Coast Path running past the front gate. Huge windows make the most of the stunning views and create a lovely brightness in the interior. The bedrooms are equally light and many enjoy the sea views; two of the ground floor rooms have the use of the garden room. All rooms have quality linens, luxury towels and bathrobes, toiletries and TV. Breakfast is served in the balcony dining room. A particularly relaxing place to stay.
Recommended in the area
Eden Project; Lost Gardens of Heligan; walking the South West Coastal Path to Polperro.

Bucklawren Farm

★★★★ GUEST ACCOMMODATION

Address: St Martin-by-Looe, LOOE PL13 1NZ
Tel: 01503 240738
Fax: 01503 240481
Email: bucklawren@btopenworld.com
Website: www.bucklawren.com
Map ref: 1, SX25
Directions: 2m NE of Looe. Off B3253 to Monkey Sanctuary, 0.5m right to Bucklawren, farmhouse 0.5m on left
Rooms: 6 en suite, S £30–40 D £54–61 **Parking:** 6 **Notes:** ⊘ on premises ⊗ on premises No children under 5 **Closed:** Nov–Feb

With a lovely beach just a mile away, this spacious 19th-century farmhouse, set in 500 acres, is the perfect place for a holiday. Front-facing rooms have sea views, and all bedrooms are attractively furnished; one room is on the ground floor. The Granary restaurant in an adjacent converted barn is the setting for evening meals prepared from fresh local produce. Jean Henly is a charming hostess.
Recommended in the area
The Eden Project; fishing villages of Looe and Polperro; Lanhydrock (NT)

Looe harbour.

Coombe Farm

♦♦♦♦

Address:	Widegates, LOOE PL13 1QN
Tel:	01503 240223
Email:	coombe_farm@hotmail.com
Website:	www.coombefarmhotel.co.uk
Map ref:	1, SX25
Directions:	3.5m E of Looe on B3253 just S of Widegates

Rooms: 3 en suite, S £45–55 D £68–78 Parking: 20
Notes: ⊘ on premises 🐾 allowed in bedrooms

Coombe Farm offers distinctive accommodation and perfect solitude in 11 acres of lawns and woods with views down a valley to the sea. An additional bonus is the outdoor heated swimming pool. This appealing house has a warm, friendly atmosphere and is convenient for sandy beaches and glorious walks. Spacious garden rooms have beamed ceilings and stone features. Each has its own door into the gardens and a dining area with breakfast delivered to your room. Decorated in a fresh and cheerful fashion, they have shower rooms en suite, modern facilities, and one room is ideal for families.

Recommended in the area

The Eden Project; Bodmin Moor; West & East Looe

Polraen Country House

★★★★ 🚗 GUEST ACCOMMODATION

Address: Sandplace, LOOE PL13 1PJ
Tel: 01503 263956
Email: enquiries@polraen.co.uk
Website: www.polraen.co.uk
Map ref: 1, SX25
Directions: 2m N of Looe at junct A387 & B3254
Rooms: 5 en suite, S £45–76 D £64–76
Parking: 20 **Notes:** ⊘ on premises ⊗ on premises
Closed: 25–27 Dec

The friendly and attentive service at Polraen Country House earned it a place among the top twenty finalists in the 2006 AA Landlady of the Year Awards. Add to this the delicious food and the peaceful location close to one of Cornwall's most popular seaside towns and you have a place that is very special. Guests here warm to the country-house style of operation, which so admirably suits the fine old stone house and its lovely gardens. The house was actually built as a coaching inn around 1740 and a number of its original features remain – a lovely window seat in the dining room, a fine old fireplace in the lounge – with tasteful décor and furnishings completing the scene. The bedrooms are light and uncluttered, with modern en suite bathrooms, televisions, hair dryers and beverage-making facilities, and the radiators can be individually controlled. The lounge is bright and welcoming, with books, magazines, videos, board games and a toy box, and, along with the cosy bar, promotes a very sociable ambience. Dining is a treat here, too, with meals focussing on the finest local produce, but be aware that because each dish is so carefully prepared guests need to make reservations and menu choices by 11am. It is well worth the advance planning. Just a short drive away is the popular seaside resort and fishing port of Looe which has sandy beaches, a harbour and narrow streets lined with quaint buildings to explore.

Recommended in the area

Looe and Polperro; The Eden Project; The Lost Gardens of Heligan; Lanhydrock and Cotehele (NT)

Trehaven Manor Hotel

★★★★ 🛏 🏛 GUEST ACCOMMODATION

Address: Station Road, LOOE PL13 1HN
Tel: 01503 262028
Fax: 01503 265613
Email: enquiries@trehavenhotel.co.uk
Website: www.trehavenhotel.co.uk
Map ref: 1, SX25
Directions: In East Looe between railway station and bridge. Hotel drive adjacent to The Globe PH
Rooms: 7 en suite **Parking:** 8 **Notes:** ⊘ on premises ⊗ on premises

Neil and Ella Hipkiss, the enthusiastic owners of Trehaven Manor, are committed to providing the best service. Bedrooms provide a high level of comfort and style, with quality furnishings and thoughtful extras such as clocks and hairdryers; most overlook the estuary. Guests are welcomed on arrival with home-made scones and local clotted cream in the lounge. Fresh local produce again features at breakfast. Evening meals are available on request or Neil and Ella can recommend local restaurants.

Recommended in the area

Polperro; Looe town and beach; St Mellion Golf Course

Tremaine Farm

★★★★ FARMHOUSE

Address: Pelynt, LOOE PL13 2LT
Tel: 01503 220417
Email: rosemary@tremainefarm.co.uk
Website: www.tremainefarm.co.uk
Map ref: 1, SX15
Directions: 5m NW of Looe. B3359 N from Pelynt, left at x-rds
Rooms: 2 (1 family suite & 1 D), S £27–30 D £54–60 **Parking:** 6 **Notes:** ⊘ on premises No children under 4

This working farm is set within an area of outstanding natural beauty. The farmhouse retains original features such as beamed ceilings, inglenook fireplace and thick cob walls. The mature gardens provide a welcome haven of tranquillity and support plenty of wildlife. Accommodation consists of a luxury family suite comprising a king-sized double room with an adjoining twin room and a bathroom with power shower; and a luxury double suite with pretty furnishings and splendid bathroom. Each has a hospitality tray and TV. A hearty breakfast is served in the dining room and there is a pleasant lounge.

Recommended in the area

South West Coast Path; The Eden Project; The Monkey Sanctuary Trust

Woodlands

★★★★ 🛏 GUEST HOUSE

Address: St Martins Road,
             LOOE PL13 1LP
Tel: 01503 264405
Website: www.looedirectory.co.uk
Map ref: 1, SX25
Directions: 0.5m N of Looe bridge on B3253
Rooms: 5 (4 en suite), D £60–80 **Parking:** 6
Notes: ⊘ on premises ⊗ on premises
No children under 7 **Closed:** Dec–Jan

Woodlands is a lovely Victorian country house with stunning views over the peaceful Looe estuary and valley. An attractive wood borders one side of the property, and the shops, harbour and beaches of Looe are within walking distance. The well-appointed and comfortable bedrooms include double, twin and single rooms, all with en suite facilities; two rooms are easily adapted into accommodation suitable for families. All are equipped with hospitality tray, dressing gowns, TV and many other little luxuries. The front rooms have lovely views of the estuary. Wherever possible, local produce goes into the enjoyable breakfasts which include a well-regarded fruit compôte along with a cooked breakfast. Breakfasts are served at a relaxed pace in the elegant dining room. Woodlands also caters for vegetarians and other dietary needs. Delicious three-course dinners are available by arrangement. Woodlands has on-site parking. The area offers spectacular cliff and country walks but if you prefer to sit and relax while enjoying spectacular views then take a trip on the scenic Looe to Liskeard railway – the river views are best at high tide. Looe also offers shark and sea fishing, horse riding, tennis and several championship golf course within easy reach. Looe railway station is just a short walk from Woodlands.

Recommended in the area

The Eden Project; South West Coast Path; Lanhydrock (NT)

Degembris Farmhouse

★★★★ FARMHOUSE

Address:	St Newlyn East,
	NEWQUAY TR8 5HY
Tel:	01872 510555
Fax:	01872 510230
Email:	kathy@degembris.co.uk
Website:	www.degembris.co.uk
Map ref:	1, SW86

Directions: 3m SE of Newquay. A30 onto A3058 towards Newquay, 3rd left to St Newlyn East & 2nd left
Rooms: 5 (3 en suite), S £30 D £35 **Parking:** 8
Notes: ⊘ on premises ⊗ on premises **Closed:** Xmas

Degembris is a Grade II listed farmhouse, dating from the 16th to the early 17th century with 18th-century additions. The stone building, set in an attractive garden on a south-facing hillside, has an unusual slate-hung exterior. The Woodley family first owned the farm in 1893 and these days it is in the capable hands of Roger and Kathy Woodley. Their farm overlooks a wooded valley, where they have established a country trail to help preserve the wildlife and the bluebell walks in spring. A good choice of accommodation includes single, double, twin and family rooms, three with facilities en suite. The individually decorated bedrooms have attractive soft furnishings, and each one has a hairdryer, complimentary tea- and coffee-making facilities, electric blanket and heating. The comfortable sitting room, with a seasonal log fire, comes equipped with plenty of books and indoor games and there are local maps and booklets on interesting things to do and places to visit in Cornwall. Traditional farmhouse cooking is served at separate tables in the beamed dining room. Numerous attractions are within easy reach of Degembris – including the spectacular coastline, National Trust properties and famous Cornish gardens.

Recommended in the area

The Eden Project; Trerice (NT); The Lost Gardens of Heligan

Kallacliff

★★★★ GUEST ACCOMMODATION

Address: 12 Lusty Glaze Road, NEWQUAY TR7 3AD
Tel: 01637 871704
Email: kallacliffhotel@btconnect.com
Website: www.kallacliffhotel.co.uk
Map ref: 1, SW86
Directions: 0.5m NE of town centre. A3058 to
Newquay, right off Henver Rd onto Lusty Glaze Rd,
350yds on right
Rooms: 8 en suite, D £30–40 Parking: 10
Notes: ⊘ on premises ✸ on premises

Set on the cliff top above Lusty Glaze beach, with stunning sea views, this family-owned, guesthouse is in a peaceful location within walking distance of central Newquay. Guests can start the day enjoying the wonderful views over breakfast in the dining room, then return in the evening to watch the sun set over the sea in the conservatory or the lounge and bar (refreshments are available here throughout the day and evening). The bright bedrooms have en suite shower rooms, TV and hospitality trays.

Recommended in the area

Lusty Glaze beach; Blue Reef Aquarium; South West Coast Path.

Cross House Hotel

★★★★★ ⌂ GUEST ACCOMMODATION

Address: Church Street, PADSTOW PL28 8BG
Tel: 01841 532391
Fax: 01841 533633
Email: info@crosshouse.co.uk
Website: www.crosshouse.co.uk
Map ref: 1, SW97
Directions: A389 into town, one way past church, sharp
left 50yds
Rooms: 11 en suite, D £70–160 Parking: 4
Notes: ⊘ on premises ✸ on premises

Nestling in the heart of Padstow is Cross House, a delightful Grade II listed Georgian house formerly owned by John Tredwen, Padstow's last sailing ship builder. This friendly and relaxed house is just a short walk from the harbour and close to all amenities including some excellent restaurants. The elegant bedrooms and bathrooms are spacious, attractively furnished and complemented by an impressive range of accessories. There are two sumptuous lounges and a cosy dining room.

Recommended in the area

Camel Trail Cycle Path; Prideaux Place; Tintagel Castle

The Old Mill House

★★★★ ⬭ ⚏ GUEST HOUSE

Address: PADSTOW,
            Padstow PL27 7QT
Tel: 01841 540388
Fax: 01841 540406
Email: enquiries@theoldmillhouse.com
Website: www.theoldmillhouse.com
Map ref: 1, SW97
Directions: A389 between Wadebridge & Padstow,
in centre of Little Petherick
Rooms: 7 en suite, S £75–115 D £75–115
Parking: 20 Notes: ⊘ on premises No pets ⊗ on
premises No children under 14 Closed: Nov–Jan

You are assured of a warm welcome from the
enthusiastic owners Paul and Hanna Charlesworth at their Grade II listed Old Mill House which stands
next to a gentle stream in an Area of Outstanding Natural Beauty just 2 miles from the popular village
of Padstow. The idyllic converted corn mill and millhouse date from the 17th and 19th centuries and
have attractive secluded gardens next to a pretty stream with a variety of resident wildlife including
ducks and a pair of swans – you may even be lucky enough to spot a kingfisher here. The seven
comfortable bedrooms are individually decorated, well equipped and have tea- and coffee-making
facilities – all have good views, either over the picturesque garden or the village and bridge. An
extensive breakfast to set you up for the day – choices include a traditional full English, smoked
salmon and scrambled eggs or an omlette – is served in the original mill room where the mill wheel
still turns. The Old Mill House is licensed and offers a comprehensive wine list.

Recommended in the area

The Eden Project; The Lost Gardens of Heligan; Camel Trail Cycle Path

St Michael's Mount (NT)

Ennys

◆◆◆◆◆

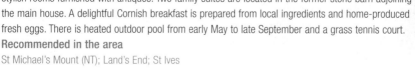

Address: Trewhella Lane, St Hilary,
PENZANCE TR20 9BZ
Tel: 01736 740262
Fax: 01736 740055
Email: ennys@ennys.co.uk
Website: www.ennys.co.uk
Map ref: 1, SW53
Directions: 1m N of B3280 Leedstown-Goldsithney road at end of Trewhella Ln

Rooms: 5 en suite, S £60–100 D £80–105 **Parking:** 8 **Notes:** ⊗ on premises ⊗ on premises
No children under 3 **Closed:** Nov–15 Mar

Set in the valley of the River Hayle, this 17th-century manor house offers a friendly welcome and stylish rooms furnished with antiques. Two family suites are located in the former stone barn adjoining the main house. A delightful Cornish breakfast is prepared from local ingredients and home-produced fresh eggs. There is heated outdoor pool from early May to late September and a grass tennis court.

Recommended in the area

St Michael's Mount (NT); Land's End; St Ives

The Summer House

★★★★★ ◎◎ GUEST ACCOMMODATION

Address: Cornwall Terrace, PENZANCE TR18 4HL
Tel: 01736 363744
Fax: 01736 360959
Email: reception@summerhouse-cornwall.com
Website: www.summerhouse-cornwall.com
Map ref: 1, SW43
Directions: A30 to Penzance, at railway station follow road along harbour front onto Promenade Rd, pass Jubilee Pool, right after Queens Hotel, Summer House 30yds on left
Rooms: 5 en suite, D £95–120 **Parking:** 6
Notes: ⊗ on premises No children under 13
Closed: Nov–Feb

The philosophy of the Summer House is great food, beautiful surroundings and a happy atmosphere making it the perfect seaside retreat for jaded townies. It is a stunning Grade II listed Regency house with bold decor and a curving glass-walled tower filling the building with light. Fresh flowers are among the thoughtful extras provided in the en suite bedrooms, and interesting family pieces and collectables enhance the individually decorated rooms. Fresh local food from the market as well as regional produce is simply prepared to provide memorable dining from a weekly changing menu. Dishes are distinctively Mediterranean, echoing the bistro food of France and Italy. Fish and shellfish always feature, and the rich Cornish puddings are hard to resist. The food is complemented by wines from the new breed of Italian vinters. The restaurant opens out on to a walled garden with terracotta pots, sub-tropical planting and attractive blue tables and chairs, where in warmer weather evening drinks and dinner can be enjoyed.

Recommended in the area

St Michael's Mount (NT); Land's End; The Minack Theatre

Ednovean Farm

★★★★★ 🏠 FARMHOUSE

Address: PERRANUTHNOE TR20 9LZ
Tel: 01736 711883
Email: info@ednoveanfarm.co.uk
Website: www.ednoveanfarm.co.uk
Map ref: 1, SW52
Directions: Off A394 Penzance-Helston towards
Perranuthnoe at Dynasty Restaurant, farm drive on left on
bend by post box
Rooms: 3 en suite, S £80 D £80–100 **Parking:** 4
Notes: ⊗ on premises No children under 16 **Closed:** 24–28 Dec and New Year

Spectacular sea views over St Michael's Mount and Mount's Bay are a delightful feature of this
converted 17th-century farmhouse which stands high above the village in beautiful grounds. The
stylish bedrooms are furnished with comfortable beds and quality pieces, chintz fabrics, and thoughtful
extras like flowers, magazines and fruit. Guests can relax in the elegant sitting room, the garden room
and on several sunny patios. The coastal footpath and the beach are just three minutes away.

Recommended in the area

St Michael's Mount (NT); Godolphin House; Penlee House Gallery (Newlyn School paintings)

Penryn House

◆◆◆◆ 🛏

Address: The Coombes, POLPERRO PL13 2RQ
Tel: 01503 272157
Fax: 01503 273055
Email: chrispidcock@aol.com
Website: www.penrynhouse.co.uk
Map ref: 1, SX25
Directions: A387 to Polperro, at mini-rdbt left down
hill into village (ignore restricted access). Hotel 200yds
on left
Rooms: 12 (11 en suite), S £31–35 D £62–80 **Parking:** 13 **Notes:** 🐕 allowed in bedrooms

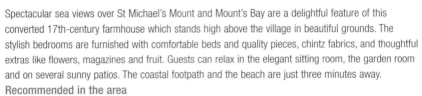

The fishing village of Polperro is a firm favourite with visitors to Cornwall, and this country hotel is
close to its centre. Wander through the narrow lanes among whitewashed cottages, and explore the
fishing harbour. Owners Anna and Chris Pidcock give a memorable welcome, and their neat en suite
bedrooms are equally hospitable, with well-stocked courtesy trays. In the evening relax in the licensed
bar, or enjoy a candlelit meal in the restaurant, where locally caught fish and fresh produce are stars.

Recommended in the area

The Eden Project; Lanhydrock (NT); Bodmin Moor

The Corn Mill

★★★★ B&B

Address: Port Isaac Road, Trelill,
PORT ISAAC PL30 3HZ
Tel: 01208 851079
Map ref: 1, SW09
Directions: Off B3314, between Pendoggett and Trelill
Rooms: 3 (2 en suite) D £70 **Parking:** 3 **Notes:** ⊘ on
premises ✝ allowed in bedrooms **Closed:** 24 Dec–5 Jan

Dating from the 18th century, this former mill has been
lovingly restored to provide a beautiful home packed with character. The delightful garden and
charming hostess add to the pleasure of a stay here. Bedrooms are individually styled, and personal
touches create a wonderfully relaxed and homely atmosphere. Most rooms have their own shower
room, while the twin room uses a bathroom with an enormous Victorian bathtub, and plenty of hot
water. Luxury extras such as huge towels and cotton bed linen are pampering touches. Delicious
breakfasts with home-made nutty bread are served in the farmhouse kitchen. The Eden Project
is only a half-hour drive away.
Recommended in the area
South West Coast Path; The Lost Gardens of Heligan; St Michael's Mount (NT)

Carradale

★★★★ B&B

Address: PORTLOE, TruroTR2 5RB
Tel: 01872 501508
Email: theguesthouse.portlow@virgin.net
Map ref: 1, SW93
Directions: Off A3078 into Portloe, B&B 200yds
from Ship Inn
Rooms: 2 en suite, S £30–35 D £55–60 **Parking:** 5
Notes: ⊘ on premises ⊗ on premises

The village of Portloe, on the Roseland Peninsula, is an idyllic place, and Carradale, a modern house
on the outskirts of the village, is an ideal place from which to explore its many delights. There are
extensive coastal walks just minutes away,along with sandy beaches and glorious countryside.
A stay here offers high levels of peace and comfort. There are just two bedrooms to choose from,
both are tastefully furnished and equipped with tea- and coffee-making facilities, and both have en
suite bathrooms. The room on the ground floor has its own south-facing patio area. The lounge, with
a television, is on the first floor and breakfasts are served at a communal table in the dining room.
Recommended in the area
The Eden Project; The Lost Gardens of Heligan; National Maritime Museum, Falmouth

Gwynoon Guest House

★★★★ 🏠 GUEST ACCOMMODATION

Address:	Chy-an-Dour Road, PRAA SANDS, PenzanceTR20 9SY
Tel:	01736 763508
Email:	enquiries@gwynoon.co.uk
Website:	www.gwynoon.co.uk
Map ref:	1, SW52

Directions: Off A394 at Germoe x-rds into village, 2nd left after Post Office, house on left

Rooms: 3 en suite, S £30 D £60 Parking: 6

Notes: ⊗ on premises 🚫 on premises

Beautifully positioned on Praa Sands, this seafront property has excellent views from its front rooms. The bedrooms are supplied with toiletries, tea and coffee facilities, Cornish spring water, biscuits and fruit. A first-floor balcony overlooks the bay and guests can bring their own wine to enjoy as they watch the sunset. The extensive breakfast features fresh local produce while cream teas, light snacks and drinks are served in the tea garden throughout the day.

Recommended in the area

St Michael's Mount (NT); Penzance; St Ives

The Gleneglos

★★★★ 🍴 GUEST ACCOMMODATION

Address:	Trewint Lane, ROCK, Wadebridge PL27 6LU
Tel:	01208 862369
Fax:	01208 862797
Email:	franklin.gleneglos@btopenworld.com
Website:	www.gleneglos.co.uk
Map ref:	1, SW97

Directions: Turn off main street in Rock at x-rds

Rooms: 6 en suite, D £62–69 Parking: 12 Notes: 🚫 on premises Closed: Dec

The popular village of Rock is tucked up the Camel estuary on the north Cornish coast. There are country views from every bedroom of this Edwardian house, with glimpses of the Atlantic here and there. The Gleneglos has spacious gardens in which to unwind when it is warm, and blazing fires to relax by on cooler days. The accommodation includes a four-poster bedroom and all rooms are en suite or have private bathrooms. Dinner in the pleasant dining room is a highlight, with local produce on the daily-changing menu. The licensed bar is a popular meeting place, before and after dinner.

Recommended in the area

Camel estuary; South West Coast Path; St Enedoc Golf Course

Anchorage House

★★★★★ 🛏 🍽 GUEST HOUSE

Address:	Nettles Corner, Tregrehan Mills, ST AUSTELL PL25 3RH
Tel:	01726 814071
Email:	info@anchoragehouse.co.uk
Website:	www.anchoragehouse.co.uk
Map ref:	1, SX05

Directions: 1m E of town centre off A390
Rooms: 4 en suite, S £85–115 D £110–140 Parking: 6
Notes: 🚭 on premises 🐾 on premises No children under 16 Closed: Dec–Feb

Jane and Steve Epperson have created a very special place to stay here, with the utmost luxury and pampering in a perfect location near the Cornish coast. Little wonder that it has been awarded "Britain's Best Bed and Breakfast" on two occasions – in 2003 and again in 2005. It has also been the AA's top-rated accommodation in Cornwall since 2002. The modern brick building has a charming conservatory at the rear, overlooking the good-sized outdoor swimming pool. The hospitality and delightful informality offered by this English/Texan couple is outstanding, the rooms are impeccably fitted out, with extra-large beds, satellite TV and lots of other extras, and the sparkling bathrooms have everything you would expect of such a highly-rated establishment. But that's not all. Facilities here include a spa with various treatments on offer, plus a hot tub, a lap pool and a small but well equipped gym. When guests have finished working out or being pampered in the spa, they can enjoy dinner (by arrangement 24 hours in advance), served house-party style, using the finest local fresh produce. Breakfast is also an occasion, with an extensive and delicious buffet to choose from. Anchorage House offers the luxury and facilities of a large hotel, without having to share it with a large guest list.

Recommended in the area

The Eden Project; Wheal Martin Hertitage Centre; The Lost Gardens of Heligan

ighland Court Lodge

◆◆◆◆◆

Address:	Biscovey Road, Biscovey, Par, ST AUSTELL PL24 2HW
Tel/Fax:	01726 813320
Email:	enquiries@highlandcourt.co.uk
Website:	www.highlandcourt.co.uk
Map ref:	1, SX05

Directions: 2m E of St Austell. A390 E to St Blazey Gate, right onto Biscovey Rd, 300yds on right
Rooms: 3 en suite, D £90–170 Parking: 12 Notes: ⊘ on premises ⊗ on premises

There is a definite "wow" factor to this excellent Cornish retreat, where an inspirational setting is combined with a truly relaxing atmosphere. The bedrooms are impressive, with quality furnishings, fresh flowers, a beverage tray, DVD and VCR players and broadband internet access. Each has a private patio and a spacious en suite bathroom, some with spa baths, where luxury toiletries are provided. There is a terrace with fine views, where dinner is served on summer evenings.

Recommended in the area

The Eden Project; The Lost Gardens of Heligan; South West Coast Path.

Hunter's Moon

◆◆◆◆

Address:	Chapel Hill, Polgooth, ST AUSTELL PL26 7BU
Tel/Fax:	01726 66445
Email:	enquiries@huntersmooncornwall.co.uk
Website:	www.huntersmooncornwall.co.uk
Map ref:	1, SX05

Directions: 1.5m SW of town centre. Off B3272 into Polgooth, pass village shop on left, 1st right
Rooms: 4 en suite, S £38–44 D £56–64 Parking: 5
Notes: ⊘ on premises ⊗ on premises No children under 14

A friendly welcome and pot of tea or coffee in the conservatory awaits you on arrival at Hunter's Moon. The guest rooms are decorated and furnished to a high standard and two of these have super king-size beds, which can be converted into twin beds. There is ample private car parking, and plenty of space to sit, relax and enjoy the garden and countryside views. The Polgooth Inn is five minutes' walk from Hunter's Moon and there are many more restaurants within a few miles.

Recommended in the area

The Eden Project; The Lost Gardens of Heligan; Charlestown harbour

Lower Barn

★★★★★ GUEST ACCOMMODATION

Address: Bosue, St Ewe, ST AUSTELL PL26 6EU
Tel: 01726 844881
Email: janie@bosue.co.uk
Website: www.bosue.co.uk
Map ref: 1, SX94
Directions: Follow A391 towards St Austell, turn right at
traffic lights onto A390 past Asda. At rdbt left onto B3273.
Pass Pentewan beach, turning r at x-rds and follow signs
Rooms: 3 en suite S £70 D £100–120 **Parking:** 7 **Notes:**
⊘ on premises **Closed:** Jan

Tucked away down a meandering country lane yet with easy access to local attractions, this converted barn has huge appeal and proprietors Mike and Janie Cooksley fully deserved the award AA Guest Accommodation of the Year for England 2005/2006. The warm colours and decoration create a Mediterranean feel that is complemented by informal and genuine hospitality. It is the attention to detail that places Lower Barn a cut above the rest. The three en suite bedrooms are equipped with a host of extras from daily fresh towels and fridges to tea- and coffee-making facilities. Breakfast is chosen from an extensive menu and served round a large table or on the patio deck overlooking the garden, which also has a luxurious hot tub. You can even collect your own free-range eggs for breakfast. A candlelit dinner, available most nights of the week, is served in the conservatory or on the terrace – and you can bring your own wine. After exploring the many attractions the area has to offer, including the fishing village of Mevagissey, where a bustling harbour shelters a fishing fleet and the narrow streets are lined with colour-washed old houses, galleries and gift shops, you can unwind with some gorgeous massage and therapy treatments to make your experience at Lower Barn memorable.

Recommended in the area

The Eden Project; The Lost Gardens of Heligan; Mevagissey; cliff walks; Roseland Peninsula

The Eden Project.

Sunnyvale Bed & Breakfast

◆◆◆◆

Address:	Hewaswater, ST AUSTELL PL26 7JF
Tel:	01726 882572
Email:	jmuden@aol.com
Website:	www.sunny-vale.co.uk
Map ref:	1, SX05

Directions: 4m SW of St Austell. Off A390 in Hewas Water

Rooms: 2 en suite, S £30–35 D £56–60 **Parking:** 4

Notes: ⊗ on premises ⊗ on premises No children under 16

The visitors' book tells it all: guests from near and far enthuse about the friendly atmosphere, impressively equipped bedrooms, and the delicious breakfasts. Judy and Richard Uden are natural hosts who have made their beautiful home a gem of a retreat. Privacy is a bonus as the en suite bedrooms are in an annexe, and include smart bathrooms, easy chairs and TVs, plus access to a hospitality tray and fridge. Sunnyvale also offers excellent facilities for disabled people.

Recommended in the area

The Eden Project; The Lost Gardens of Heligan; South West Coast Path

Wisteria Lodge

★★★★★ GUEST HOUSE

Address:	Boscundle, Tregrehan,
	ST AUSTELL PL25 3RJ
Tel:	01726 810800
Fax:	0871 661 6213
Email:	info@wisterialodgehotel.co.uk
Website:	www.wisterialodgehotel.co.uk
Map ref:	1, SX05
Directions:	1m E of town centre off A390

Rooms: 5 en suite, £90–160 Parking: 5 Notes: ⊘ on premises ⊗ on premises No children under 12

Stylish Wisteria Lodge, named after the plant which clambers all over the building, stands in lovingly tended gardens close to St Austell. Sally and James Wilkins offer high levels of personal service and a relaxed atmosphere at their delightful guesthouse. There are five stylish bedrooms available – one room comes complete with spa whirlpool bath and private lounge, or you can choose the opulent suite with four-poster bed. Complimentary chocolates, fluffy bathrobes and bath sheets are among the pampering touches found here. Skilfully prepared meals are served in the conservatory-dining room, which overlooks the large garden where you can take tea or enjoy a game of croquet. Breakfast is a triumph of full traditional British or a continental option and the candlelit dinner an absolute delight. The menu might feature dishes such as fried tiger prawns with chilli and lime leaf for starters, followed by black bean roasted sea bass with fresh ginger and spring onion or organic chicken breast stuffed with Bousin cheese and wrapped in smoked bacon, with poached pears, stilton, port and clotted cream for dessert. The menu also features vegetarian dishes. Wisteria Lodge is well placed to visit many attractions – the Eden Project is close by and there are a number of excellent beaches within a 20-minute walk.

Recommended in the area

The Eden Project; The Lost Gardens of Heligan; Lanhydrock (NT)

Penarwyn House

◆◆◆◆◆ 🏠

Address: ST BLAZEY, Par PL24 2DS
Tel: 01726 814224
Fax: 01726 814224
Email: mrussell@fsbdial.co.uk
Website: www.penarwyn.co.uk
Map ref: 1, SX05
Directions: A390 W through St Blazey, left at 2nd
speed camera, house past school
Rooms: 3 en suite, S £79–100 D £88–112 Parking: 6 Notes: ⊘ on premises
🚫 on premises No children under 10 Closed: 21 Dec–9 Jan

True Cornish hospitality and memorable breakfasts complement this spacious Victorian residence which is set in tranquil surroundings, yet close to main routes. Since 2003, owners Mike and Jan Russell – who have many years experience successfully running bed and breakfast establishments – have been painstakingly restoring Penarwyn House to its original glory. Many of the old features have been faithfully restored alongside luxury new en suites, which include a bath by candlelight for romantics and a separate shower. The bedrooms are most impressive, spacious, delightfully appointed, and equipped with a host of extras including tea and coffee facilities, hairdryers, flat-screen colour TV and DVD/CD player. Treffry is a kingsize double room, looking out over the front garden, with a large corner bath and fluffy bath sheets. Prideaux, the largest room, has large comfy chairs and an en suite with a slipper bath and a separate shower, while Caerhayes, although smaller than the other bedrooms, offers the same comfort and style. There is a panelled snooker room with a $^3/_4$ size snooker table and wireless Internet access is available for use on guest laptops. Breakfast is another highlight at Penarwyn House, and along with the friendly and attentive service, this all makes for a pleasurable stay.

Recommended in the area

The Eden Project; Lanhydrock (NT); The Lost Gardens of Heligan

Borthalan

★★★★ GUEST ACCOMMODATION

Address:	Off Boskerris Road, Carbis Bay, ST IVES TR26 2NQ
Tel:	01736 795946
Fax:	01736 795946
Email:	borthalanhotel@btconnect.com
Website:	www.borthalan-hotel.co.uk
Map ref:	1, SW54
Directions:	A3074 into Carbis Bay, right onto Boskerris Rd, 1st left onto cul-de-sac

Rooms: 7 en suite, D £75–90 **Parking:** 7 **Notes:** ⊘ on premises ⊗ on premises
No children under 12 **Closed:** 20–28 Dec

Lovely gardens and views over the glorious golden sands of Carbis Bay and St Ives Bay are among the attractions of this smart guesthouse set in its own grounds in a quiet secluded road. The friendly hosts – Margaret and Martin – take great pleasure in looking after their guests. Most of the well-appointed bedrooms have views over the coast, and with facilities en suite, courtesy trays, colour TV and thoughtful extras, you are promised a relaxing stay. All seven bedrooms are on the first and second floors. Traditional full English breakfasts are served in the sunny dining room looking out over the sea, and there is a small licensed bar and a cosy lounge. The pretty gardens are a treat to relax in on warm days and evenings. The picturesque fishing harbour of St Ives, with its magnificent beaches that offer both safe family bathing and ideal surfing conditions, is just a few minutes away, and can be reached by a short train journey or a breathtaking walk along the coastal path. Borthalan is an ideal base for walking, cycling, diving and fishing holidays. St Ives has long been famous for its artists and its narrow, winding lanes are lined with numerable galleries and craft shops to explore. Parking is available at the hotel.

Recommended in the area

Barbara Hepworth Museum; The Eden Project; Tate St Ives

Edgar's

★★★★ GUEST ACCOMMODATION

Address:	Chy an Creet, Higher Stennack, ST IVES TR26 2HA
Tel/Fax:	01736 796559
Email:	stay@chy.co.uk
Website:	www.chy.co.uk
Map ref:	1, SW53

Directions: 0.5m W of town centre on B3306, opp Leach Pottery

Rooms: 8 en suite S £39 D £58–90 Parking: 8 Notes: ⊘ on premises Closed: Nov–Feb

Also known as Chy an Creet, Edgar's was built in the 1920s and is today a family-run guest house with character and plenty of space. Away from = but within easy reach of – the bustling town centre, harbour and golden sandy beaches, the property nestles in its own gardens near to where the edge of town meets the Penwith Moors. Public areas are homely and include a well-stocked bar with a real fire and a lounge. Eight en suite bedrooms, some on the ground floor, are well equipped including TV and a complimentary drinks tray. Breakfast features home-made preserves.

Recommended in the area

Land's End; Penzance; Tate Gallery

The Mustard Tree

★★★★ GUEST HOUSE

Address:	Sea View Meadows, St Ives Road, Carbis Bay, ST IVES TR26 2JX
Tel:	01736 795677
Email:	enquiries@mustard-tree.co.uk
Website:	www.stivesbnb.co.uk
Map ref:	1, SW58

Directions: A3074 to Carbis Bay, The Mustard Tree on right opp Methodist church

Rooms: 7 (6 en suite), S £36 D £62–74 Parking: 7

Notes: ⊘ on premises ⊗ on premises

Set in delightful gardens and overlooking Carbis Bay, The Mustard Tree is a short drive from the centre of St Ives (alternatively the coastal path also leads from Carbis Bay to St Ives). The pleasant bedrooms, most with a sea view, are very comfortable and have many extra facilities. A splendid choice is offered at breakfast in a relaxed and friendly atmosphere. There is also a comfortable, modern lounge available for guests with a 42" plasma screen TV.

Recommended in the area

Tate St Ives; St Michael's Mount (NT); The Minack Theatre

The bay at St Ives.

Old Vicarage

★★★★ 🏨 GUEST HOUSE

Address:	Parc-an-Creet, ST IVES TR26 2ES
Tel:	01736 796124
Email:	stay@oldvicarage.com
Website:	www.oldvicarage.com
Map ref:	1, SW54

Directions: Off A3074 in town centre onto B3306, 0.5m right into Parc-an-Creet

Rooms: 7 en suite, S £54 D £72 Parking: 12

Notes: 🐕 allowed in bedrooms Closed: Oct–Etr

An atmospheric Victorian vicarage set in very attractive grounds in a peaceful part of St Ives. Dianne Sykes is an accomplished artist and textile designer whose work is showcased throughout the property. Jack Sykes, her father, has run the business for more than 30 years, and is a popular figure behind the welcoming Victorian bar where his many stories are legendary. The stylish bedrooms have hospitality trays and facilities en suite, and there is capacity for families in many cases. Breakfast is a feast of local and home-made produce, including yoghurt and preserves.

Recommended in the area

Porthmeor Beach; Tate St Ives; Bernard Leach Pottery

Porthglaze

◆◆◆◆◆

Address: Steeple Lane, ST IVES TR26 2AY
Tel: 01736 799409
Email: info@porthglaze.co.uk
Website: www.porthglaze.co.uk
Map ref: 1, SW54
Directions: A3074 to St Ives, left at Cornish Arms, left
onto Steeple Ln, Porthglaze 500yds on left
Rooms: 2 en suite Parking: 4 Notes: ⊘ on premises
⊗ on premises No children under 14

Porthglaze, which takes its name from a rugged cove located near the sleepy village of Zennor to the west, lies in a quiet lane just a stroll from the golden sands of Porthminster Beach. Both of the spacious bedrooms have a king-size double bed and are classically furnished with either Sanderson or Liberty fabrics. They each have bath-shower rooms en suite with luxury towels, bathrobes, hairdryers and a selection of toiletries. The Roseberry Suite, to the rear of the building, has large walk-in wardrobes and French doors which lead to the patio and pleasant garden. The Cornflower Suite is situated at the front of the property and has a fabulous antique bed made up with fine linen. Both suites have tea- and coffee-making facilities and colour TV. The cosy lounge is furnished with comfortable armchairs and a sofa – ideal for relaxing after a busy day exploring the surrounding area. The delicious continental breakfast, served in a sunny breakfast room, is an impressive choice using fresh local produce where possible and home-made jams and preserves. The menu could include fruit juice, croissants, toast, cereal, fruit, yoghurts, smoked salmon with scrambled egg or home cured ham with eggs of your choice. The nearby fishing village of St Ives has a strong artistic inheritance. Parking is available for guests. Porthglaze does not have faciltes for children under the age of 14.

Recommended in the area

Tate St Ives; Bernard Leach Pottery; Barbara Hepworth Museum

The Regent

★★★★ 🛏 GUEST ACCOMMODATION

Address:	Fernlea Terrace, ST IVES TR26 2BH
Tel:	01736 796195
Fax:	01736 794641
Email:	keith@regenthotel.com
Website:	www.regenthotel.com
Map ref:	1, SW54

Directions: In town centre, near bus & railway station
Rooms: 9 (7 en suite), S £32.50–33.50 D £70–95
Parking: 12 Notes: ⊘ on premises ⊗ on premises
No children under 16

The Regent Hotel was established 78 years ago when a local architect purchased Penwyn House from a retired sea captain and converted it to provide an interest for his wife and daughter. In 1972 the late Mr and Mrs SH Varnals bought the property and in due course passed it on to Keith and Sandi Varnals, the present proprietors. Sandi, a former lingerie designer, has worked her magic on the interior of the old building, while Keith, an engineer turned chef, has modernised the hotel's facilities to appeal to today's modern traveller. Bedrooms are well equipped with colour TV, radio alarm clocks and tea- and coffee-making facilities. Seven rooms have facilities en suite, and most benefit from spectacular sea views. The breakfast menu offers a good choice of hot dishes, cooked to order, and an extensive buffet of cereals, yoghurts, pastries, fruit and juice. The oak-smoked fish and bacon is sourced locally. Also on offer are espresso, cappuccino, and cafetière coffee, hot chocolate and a choice of teas. There is a lounge and bar for evening relaxation, and parking is provided for all rooms. If you prefer not to drive, the hotel is situated close to the local bus, coach and rail stations. The Regent Hotel is ideally located to explore the local area, being just a short stroll from the narrow cobbled streets and harbour in St Ives, where fishing boats unload their catches of fish and crabs.

Recommended in the area

South West Coast Path; Tate St Ives; Penzance on Cornwall's south coast

The Rookery

★★★★ GUEST ACCOMMODATION

Address: 8 The Terrace, ST IVES TR26 2BL
Tel: 01736 799401
Email: therookerystives@hotmail.com
Website: www.rookerystives.com
Map ref: 1, SW54
Directions: A3074 through Carbis Bay, right fork at
Porthminster Hotel, The Rookery 500yds on left
Rooms: 6 en suite, S £32.50–35 D £55–75 Parking: 6
Notes: ⊘ on premises ⊗ on premises No children
under 7

Ron and Barbara Rook's friendly establishment stands on an elevated position overlooking the harbour, sandy beaches and St Ives Bay, near the town's train and bus stations, and only a short walk to the shops, galleries and restaurants in St Ives. The rooms are attractively decorated, and are well equipped with considerate extras such as a chiller to keep soft drinks and wines cool. A choice of full English, continental or vegetarian breakfast is served in the dining room.

Recommended in the area

Tate St Ives; Barbara Hepworth Museum; The Minack Theatre

Treliska

★★★★ 🛏 GUEST ACCOMMODATION

Address: 3 Bedford Road, ST IVES TR26 1SP
Tel/Fax: 01736 797678
Email: info@treliska.com
Website: www.treliska.com
Map ref: 1, SW54
Directions: A3074 to St Ives, fork at Porthminster Hotel
into town, at T-junct facing Barclays Bank left onto
Bedford Rd, house on right
Rooms: 5 en suite S £30–35 D £56–70 Parking: 0
Notes: ⊘ on premises ⊗ on premises No children under 10

A warm welcome awaits you at this modern and friendly guesthouse located close to the shops, galleries and museums of this artistic town, and only a 2-minute walk from the harbour. It is furnished for a high degree of comfort with all modern amenities. Bedrooms are exceptionally well equipped with tea and coffee facilities, hairdryers, and bathrooms with very smart fittings. Breakfast is an enjoyable experience with a good choice and quality ingredients accurately cooked.

Recommended in the area

Tate St Ives; Bernard Leach Pottery; Paradise Park Wildlife Sanctuary, Hayle

Woodside Hotel

★★★★ GUEST ACCOMMODATION

Address:	The Belyars,
	ST IVES TR26 2DA
Tel:	01736 795681
Email:	woodsidehotel@btconnect.com
Website:	www.woodside-hotel.co.uk
Map ref:	1, SW54

Directions: A3074 to St Ives, left at Porthminster Hotel onto Talland Rd, 1st left onto Belyars Ln, Woodside 4th on right

Rooms: 10 en suite S £36–51 D £72–108 Parking: 12 Notes: ⊘ on premises ⊗ on premises No children under 5

Suzanne and Chris Taylor are welcoming hosts who diligently attend to their beautiful hotel. They promise personal attention, ensuring an enjoyable holiday here. Woodside stands in peaceful grounds above St Ives Bay, with fantastic views from most bedrooms and all of the public rooms. Just a 5-minute walk away in St Ives are lovely stretches of golden beaches for bathing and surfing, the picturesque harbour with its traditional fishing fleet, and the narrow cobbled streets lined with artists' studios, galleries and craft shops. The comfortable, spacious en suite bedrooms range from single, double and twin to family rooms, and all are well equipped with colour TV, a radio-alarm clock, hairdryer and a hospitality tray. Guests can relax in the comfortable lounge with a TV and games area, enjoy a drink at the bar, or relish the sea views from the attractive gardens or terrace. A heated outdoor swimming pool is open from May to September. Breakfast is another delight, you'll find a hearty choice of full English, continental or vegetarian dishes prepared from fresh local produce where possible. A short hole golf course and a leisure centre with a superb gym and indoor pool are both within a short distance of Woodside.

Recommended in the area

Tate St Ives; Land's End; The Eden Project

Port William Inn

★★★ INN

Address:	Trebarwith Strand, TINTAGEL PL34 0HB
Tel:	01840 770230
Fax:	01840 770936
Map ref:	1, SX08

Directions: From A39 follow signs to Tintagel

Rooms: 8 en suite, D £44.50–52.50 Parking: 45

Notes: 🐕 allowed in bedrooms

An old harbour master's property perched on the side of a cliff, The Port William Inn became a drinking establishment in 1974 and overlooks the cove and beach at Trebarwith Strand, one of Cornwall's loveliest and most unspoiled places. The incoming tide is a spectacular sight as the surf pounds the rocks, while low tide reveals a mile of gleaming sand. All bedrooms have breathtaking views over the sea and offer well-equipped accommodation. The nautically themed bar is furnished with old pews and large wooden tables and has a real fire. The popular restaurant in the conservatory dining room serves a wide range of dishes but with an emphasis on locally caught fish. Car parking is also available.

Recommended in the area

Tintagel Castle; Port Issac; the Tintagel and Port Issac walk

Bodrean Manor Farm

★★★★ FARMHOUSE

Address:	Trispen, TRURO TR4 9AG
Tel:	01872 273227
Fax:	01872 273225
Website:	www.bodreanmanorfarm.co.uk
Map ref:	1, SW84

Directions: 3m NE of Truro. A30 onto A39 towards Truro, left after Trispen village signed Frogmore & Trehane, farm driveway 100yds

Rooms: 3 (2 en suite), S £35–40 D £50–55 Parking: 6

Notes: ⊘ on premises ⊗ on premises

This friendly farmhouse lies in countryside with splendid views, yet is only minutes from the city of Truro. It has been restored to a high standard and the spacious, luxurious bedrooms, all with facilities en suite, are thoughtfully equipped. The bathrooms are well provisioned with soft towels and a host of toiletries. Original features in the dining room include a beamed ceiling and an inglenook fireplace, while the full English breakfast, using local and home-grown produce, is certainly not to be hurried.

Recommended in the area

The Eden Project; The Lost Gardens of Heligan; Trelissick Garden (NT)

CUMBRIA

Helvellyn Mountain rises above Thirlmere Lake.

Brathay Lodge

★★★★ GUEST ACCOMMODATION

Address:	Rothay Road, AMBLESIDE LA22 OEE
Tel:	015394 32000
Email:	brathay@globalnet.co.uk
Website:	www.brathay-lodge.com
Map ref:	5, NY30

Directions: One-way system in town centre, Lodge on right opp church

Rooms: 21 en suite, S £45–95 D £65–142 Parking: 23

Notes: ⊘ on premises ⌐ allowed in bedrooms

Combining traditional and contemporary styles, Brathay Lodge offers a chance to relax in impressive surroundings. The spacious bedrooms are fitted with enormous beds, and decorated and furnished in smart fabrics and woods. Each room has a Jacuzzi spa bath, and some have balconies with stunning Lakeland views. The informal atmosphere is conducive to unwinding, with the choice of enjoying an extensive continental breakfast in the privacy of your bedroom, or in the lounge. Brathay Lodge is over 110 years old, but offers accommodation to meet the most testing demands of the 21st century.

Recommended in the area

Windermere cruises; Hill Top, Beatrix Potter's house; Wordsworth's Dove Cottage

Elterwater Park

★★★★ GUEST HOUSE

Address:	Skelwith Bridge, AMBLESIDE LA22 9NP
Tel:	015394 32227
Email:	enquiries@elterwater.com
Website:	www.elterwater.com
Map ref:	5, NY30

Directions: A593 from Ambleside to Coniston, 1m past Skelwith Bridge Hotel, layby on right fronts estate road to Elterwater Park, signed at gate

Rooms: 5 en suite, S £40–46 D £60–72 Parking: 10

Notes: ⊘ on premises No children under 10

Set on the hills above Langdale, this stone house is full of traditional features. All the attractive bedrooms are en suite and are furnished with radios, hairdryers, hospitality trays and fresh flowers – one room has easier access. Breakfast and dinner are served in the spacious lounge-dining room. Your hosts hold a full residential licence with a wine list chosen for quality and value to go with the freshly prepared dinners. There is a terrace for fine days – and a drying room for those other days.

Recommended in the area

Ambleside; Coniston Water; Cumbrian Way

View over Ambleside from Loughrigg Fell.

Kent House

★★★★ 🏛 GUEST HOUSE

Address: Lake Road, AMBLESIDE LA22 0AD
Tel: 015394 33279
Email: mail@kent-house.com
Website: www.kent-house.com
Map ref: 1, NY30
Directions: Follow one-way system, 300mtrs from Ambleside post office, on left on terrace above Lake Rd
Rooms: 5 (4 en suite), S £40–50 D £56–90 **Parking:** 2
Notes: ⊘ on premises ✱ in bedrooms with prior notice

Kent House, an elegant Victorian Guest House retaining many original features, has offered a friendly welcome to guests from all over the world since the mid 1800s. Sandra and Simon continue this tradition offering spacious guest rooms (featuring Wi-fi access) and a full English Lakeland breakfast prepared using local produce. Breakfasts can be tailored from the extensive menu and breakfast in bed is also available.

Recommended in the area

Lake Windermere; Wordsworth's Dove Cottage; Beatrix Potter's home

Riverside

★★★★ GUEST HOUSE

Address:	Under Loughrigg, AMBLESIDE LA22 9LJ
Tel:	015394 32395
Fax:	015394 32440
Email:	info@riverside-at-ambleside.co.uk
Website:	www.riverside-at-ambleside.co.uk
Map ref:	5, NY30

Directions: A593 from Ambleside to Coniston, over stone bridge, right onto Under Loughrigg Ln, Riverside 150yds left

Rooms: 6 en suite S £50–60 D £66–96 Parking: 15 Notes: ⊗ on premises ⊗ on premises No children under 5 Closed: Xmas & New Year

Built in 1866 and situated on a quiet country lane, alongside the River Rothay, Riverside is an award-winning bed and breakfast in a beautiful rural riverside location. It lies within a 10-minute walk of Ambleside, a major touring and hiking centre on the northern tip of lake Windermere, and is one of the best locations to explore the whole of the Lake District National Park, either by car, bicycle or on foot. Both traditional English and vegetarian breakfasts are offered using local ingredients with freshly prepared home-made breads and preserves. Bedrooms, all with lovely views of either the river or garden, are very comfortable, stylishly furnished and feature homely extras such as hospitality trays and colour TV; some have luxurious spa baths. The house has extensive landscaped and fell gardens with views of the surrounding fells. Guests are welcome to use the garden with its lovely terrace and relax in the lounge which is warmed by a log burning stove in the winter months. Here you'll find a good collection of local maps, guides and books to help you discover all the area has to offer. There

is secure storage for bicycles and useful drying facilities for when the weather is wet.

A comfortable four person cottage is also available to let. There is ample parking in the grounds and from the house there is access nearby to Loughrigg Fell, which offers spectacular views of Windermere, Rydal Water, Grasmere and many of the high mountains. If you prefer to sit back and admire the scenery from the water, then it is just a short walk from the centre of Ambleside to Waterhead where the steamers from Coniston call in on their round-the-lake cruises.

Recommended in the area

Grasmere; Dove Cottage and the Wordsworth Museum; The World of Beatrix Potter; Ambleside; walk to the waterfall Stock Ghyll Force; Bridge House in Ambleside (NT information centre)

Hall Croft

★★★★ B&B

Address: Dufton, APPLEBY-IN-WESTMORLAND
CA16 6DB
Tel: 017683 52902
Email: r.walker@leaseholdpartnerships.co.uk
Map ref: 6, NY62
Directions: Dufton signed from A66 near Appleby, B&B
at bottom of village green
Rooms: 3 (2 en suite) S £30 D £50 **Parking:** 3
Notes: ⛔ in bedrooms **Closed:** 24–26 Dec

Located in a tranquil village, this large Victorian house stands at the foot of the Pennines with spectacular views in all directions. The substantial gardens are a joy to explore as are the surrounding network of paths and walks from the village. Proprietors Frei and Ray Walker provide high quality facilities that include two spacious bedrooms with en suite and a third that has a large private bathroom. Substantial cooked breakfasts include a varied range of home-made produce and are served in the period lounge/dining room. Afternoon tea and cakes and packed lunches are available.
Recommended in the area
North Pennines AONB; Northern Lake District; Appleby-in-Westmorland

The Wheatsheaf at Beetham

★★★★ INN

Address: BEETHAM, Milnthorpe LA7 7AL
Tel: 015395 62123
Fax: 015395 64840
Email: info@wheatsheafbeetham.com
Website: www.wheatsheafbeetham.com
Map ref: 6, SD47
Directions: Off A6 into village centre, next to parish
church
Rooms: 6 en suite, S £65 D £80 **Parking:** 40 **Notes:** ⊗
on premises ⊗ on premises **Closed:** Xmas & 8–18 Jan

A family-owned free house, the Wheatsheaf is very much a dining inn with accommodation. The six en suite bedrooms make it a perfect base for exploring the Lake District and Yorkshire Dales. The award-winning menu is served throughout with the option of dining in the bars or the dining rooms. Home-made dishes range from traditional Cumbrian bar snacks to gourmet meals such as breast of local pheasant with a wild mushroom farce. The Wheatsheaf is non-smoking throughout.
Recommended in the area
Levens Hall; Lakeland Wildlife Oasis; Holme Park Fell (NT)

Hazel Bank Country House

★★★★★ ❀ GUEST HOUSE

Address:	Rosthwaite, BORROWDALE, Keswick CA12 5XB
Tel:	017687 77248
Fax:	017687 77373
Email:	enquiries@hazelbankhotel.co.uk
Website:	www.hazelbankhotel.co.uk
Map ref:	5, NY21
Directions:	B5289 to Rosthwaite, signed opp village

Rooms: 8 en suite, S £65–95 (incl. dinner) Parking: 12
Notes: ⊘ on premises ⊗ on premises No children under 12

Set amid some of the Lake District's loveliest scenery, this Victorian house is the epitome of hospitality and comfort. Wander in the 4 acres of carefully-tended lawns and woodland, or relax in the sitting room where log fires cheer up colder days. Bedrooms have four-poster, king-size or double beds, and smart bathrooms en suite. Imaginative four-course dinners are served in the delightful dining room.

Recommended in the area

Honister Slate Mine; Keswick Pencil Museum; family of Ospreys, Bassenthwaite Lake

The Hill On The Wall

◆◆◆◆◆

Address:	Gilsland, BRAMPTON CA8 7DA
Tel/Fax:	016977 47214
Email:	info@hadrians-wallbedandbreakfast.com
Website:	http://hadrians-wallbedandbreakfast.com
Map ref:	6, NY56

Directions: A69 into Gilsland & follow brown tourist signs for Birdoswald, The Hill on the Wall 0.5m on right
Rooms: 3 (2 en suite) S £40–50 D £66 Parking: 8
Notes: ⊘ on premises ⊗ on premises No children under 10

This elegant farmhouse overlooks Hadrian's Wall. The Grade II listed former bastle (fortified house) dates from the 16th century, and has impressive accommodation. The cosy lounge is comfortably furnished, while the smart dining room is the setting for good home-cooked breakfasts and evening meals, using quality local produce whenever possible. The bedrooms, including one on the ground floor, are very large and have new bathrooms. Elaine and Dick Packer are friendly and obliging hosts.

Recommended in the area

Hadrian's Wall; Birdoswald Roman Fort; Housesteads Roman Fort

The Wheatsheaf

★★★★ 🛏 🍸 INN

Address: BRIGSTEER, Nr Kendal LA8 8AN
Tel: 015395 68254
Email: wheatsheaf@brigsteer.gb.com
Website: www.brigsteer.gb.com
Map ref: 6, SD48
Directions: Off A591 signed Brigsteer, Wheatsheaf at bottom of hill
Rooms: 3 en suite **Parking:** 25 **Notes:** ⊘ on premises ⊗ on premises

Lying in the peaceful little hamlet of Brigsteer, just 3 miles to the west of Kendal, the Wheatsheaf, which dates back to the mid-18th century, became an alehouse in the early 1800s. It is well placed for touring the Lakes, visiting gardens and country houses and is a popular base with walkers. Whatever you spend your day doing it is a relaxing and peaceful place to return to. Kendal, most famous for the renowned Kendal Mint Cake (a hard mint-flavoured sugar slab favoured by the climbing fraternity), is well worth a visit with its ruined castle, historic buildings, museums, art galleries, individual shops and restaurants. The exterior of the sturdy-looking Wheatsheaf is well maintained, as are the outdoor seating areas and the traditional interior. The bedrooms have all been refurbished to offer modern comforts and come well equipped, together with bathrooms of a high quality. There is a cosy, well-stocked bar and a spacious, charming dining room where delicious home-cooked food is served at individual tables, including the hearty breakfast – ideal to set you up for the day. The cuisine is classic British with a modern twist using the finest game, meat, fish and seafood sourced locally. There is the added advantage of a smoke free policy throughout the building including the bar and restaurant areas. Well-behaved children are welcome and there is a special child menu available.

Recommended in the area

Kendal; Levens Hall; Lake District National Park; Windermere; Sizergh Castle (NT)

Caldbeck village, Lake District National Park.

Swaledale Watch Farm House

★★★★ GUEST ACCOMMODATION

Address:	Whelpo, CALDBECK CA7 8HQ
Tel/Fax:	016974 78409
Email:	nan.savage@talk21.com
Website:	www.swaledale-watch.co.uk
Map ref:	5, NY33
Directions:	1m SW of Caldbeck on B5299

Rooms: 4 en suite, S £28 D £50 **Parking:** 8
Notes: ⊘ on premises ⊗ on premises
Closed: 24–26 Dec

This busy farm is set in idyllic surroundings, with views of the fells and mountains. Just a mile away is the village of Caldbeck, once renowned for its milling and mining, or take a walk through The Howk, a beautiful wooded limestone gorge with waterfalls. Nan and Arnold Savage work hard to make their hospitality seem effortless and to put you at ease. The lounges have TVs, books and games while the bedrooms have bath and shower en suite. Two bedrooms and a lounge are in the converted cowshed, ideal for a group of four. Nan's hearty Cumbrian breakfasts are delicious.

Recommended in the area

100-acre nature reserve on site; Northern Fells; Howk Walk to Caldbeck village

The Weary at Castle Carrock

★★★★ ◎ RESTAURANT WITH ROOMS

Address: CASTLE CARROCK
            CA8 9LU
Tel: 01228 670230
Fax: 01228 670089
Email: relax@theweary.com
Website: www.theweary.com
Map ref: 6, NY55
Directions: Turn off A69 onto B6143 immediate left.
Continue for 4m, T-junct turn left. Hotel 1m on right in
centre of village
Rooms: 5 en suite, S £65–85 D £95–145 Parking: 8

Almost 300 years old, The Weary has been transformed into a contemporary oasis amid the raw natural landscape of northeast Cumbria. It is billed as a "Restaurant with Rooms", but don't be misled by this into thinking that the rooms take second place to the food. The accommodation here has been designed with the utmost in chilled-out indulgence in mind, and the bedrooms are brimming with all kinds of modern gadgetry. The beds are huge with soft, plump pillows, and in-room amenities include flat screen TVs with satellite channels, DVD players, stereos with discreet speakers and telephones. Their en suite bathrooms are nothing short of stunning, with big glass washbasins, invigorating power showers, Jacuzzi baths and – the ultimate decadence – another television. Fluffy towels and brand-name luxury toiletries complete the picture. Food is, of course, of great importance here and there's a choice of a bar menu in the bar and à la carte in the conservatory restaurant. As much local seasonal produce as possible is used in the cooked-to-order dishes. Portions are hearty and presentation is appetising and attractive. The Weary is indeed a haven for weary travellers, who can be assured that their wellbeing is of paramount importance to the attentive management and staff.

Recommended in the area

Hadrian's Wall; Talkin Tarn; Carlisle cathedral and museums, Gelt Woods and Carrock Fell

Rose Cottage

♦♦♦♦

Address: Lorton Road, COCKERMOUTH CA13 9DX
Tel: 01900 822189
Fax: 01900 822189
Email: bookings@rosecottageguest.co.uk
Website: www.rosecottageguest.co.uk
Map ref: 5, NY12
Directions: A5292 from Cockermouth to
Lorton/Buttermere, Rose Cottage on right
Rooms: 7 en suite, S £40–60 D £60–90 Parking: 12
Notes: ⊘ on premises ⌇ allowed in bedrooms
Closed: 7–29 Feb

This former inn on the edge of town has been refurbished to provide attractive, modern accommodation. John and Susan Graham maintain Rose Cottage to a high standard and offer genuine hospitality for visitors to the interesting and beautiful north Lakeland area. For the energetic there are opportunities to fish, play golf or tennis, go pony trekking or walk in the fabulous countryside. The local leisure centre offers swimming and badminton, while Cockermouth, the birthplace of poet William Wordsworth, has a medieval castle and the Castle Brewery that produces the excellent Jennings beer. The smart, well-equipped, centrally heated bedrooms with facilities en suite include a self-contained studio room with external access. Two of the bedrooms are on the ground floor and two others are suitable for families. All have colour TV and facilites for making tea and coffee. There is a cosy lounge and a smart dining room where delicious home-cooked dinners are a highlight, accompanied by a good choice of wines. The full English breakfast is sure to please and most diets are catered for. Children are most welcome (cots are available), as are well-behaved dogs. Internet access is available for visitors' laptops.

Recommended in the area

Wordsworth House (NT); Buttermere; Solway coast

Crosthwaite House

★★★★ GUEST HOUSE

Address: CROSTHWAITE, KendalLA8 8BP
Tel/Fax: 015395 68264
Email: bookings@crosthwaitehouse.co.uk
Website: www.crosthwaitehouse.co.uk
Map ref: 6, SD49
Directions: A590 onto A5074, 4m right to Crosthwaite, 0.5m turn left
Rooms: 6 en suite, S £25–27.50 D £50–55 **Parking:** 10 **Notes:** ⊘ on premises ⊁ allowed in bedrooms
Closed: mid-Nov to Dec

A sturdy mid 18th-century house, this establishment is in the village of Crosthwaite, at the northern end of the Lyth valley, famous for its damson orchards. You can see across the valley from the lounge, and from the dining room, where an imaginative menu of traditional home cooking is freshly cooked on the kitchen Aga. The spacious bedrooms have showers and toilets en suite, plus tea and coffee facilities. The owners create a relaxed atmosphere in which it is easy to feel at home.

Recommended in the area

Lake Windermere; Sizergh Castle and Garden (NT); three golf courses within 4 miles

Grizedale Lodge The Hotel in the Forest

★★★★ GUEST ACCOMMODATION

Address: GRIZEDALE, Hawkshead,
Ambleside LA22 0QL
Tel: 015394 36532
Fax: 015394 36572
Email: enquiries@grizedale-lodge.com
Website: www.grizedale-lodge.com
Map ref: 5, SD39
Directions: From Hawkshead signs S to Grizedale, Lodge 2m on right
Rooms: 8 en suite, S £40–47.50 D £90–95 **Parking:** 20
Notes: ⊁ allowed in bedrooms

Set in the heart of Grizedale Forest, the lodge has superb countryside views from the balcony and patio. The well-appointed bedrooms are elegant, some have four-poster beds. Breakfasts are hearty – evening meals are not available, but guests can order sandwiches until the late evening.

Recommended in the area

Windermere cruises; Hawkshead; Grizedale Forest

Sawrey Ground

★★★★ GUEST ACCOMMODATION

Address: Hawkshead Hill,
HAWKSHEAD LA22 0PP
Tel: 015394 36683
Email: mail@sawreyground.com
Website: www.sawreyground.com
Map ref: 5, SD39
Directions: B5285 from Hawkshead, 1m to Hawkshead Hill, sharp right after Baptist chapel, signs to Tarn Hows for 0.25m. Sawrey Ground on right
Rooms: 3 en suite, D £60–70 **Parking:** 6
Notes: ⊘ on premises ⊗ on premises No children under 8

Built by Anthony Sawrey in 1627, this picturesque oak-beamed farmhouse has a magical setting on the edge of the Tarn Hows Forest, a peaceful location in the centre of the Lake District just above Hawkshead village. Mike and Gill O'Connell offer guests a warm welcome to their home, with its friendly, relaxed atmosphere and popular home-made cakes which are served each afternoon. They will do all they can to make your stay enjoyable and memorable. The centuries of occupation have created a comfortable and lived-in feeling, from the entrance hall, lounge and dining room, to the three attractive south-facing bedrooms – all are en suite with colour TV and tea-and coffee-making facilities. Many walks are possible from the front door, leading to Coniston, Windermere and Langdale, and including the beautiful lake of Tarn Hows. The area is good for birdwatching and wildlife, and also for cycling and fishing. The central location is ideal for touring the Lakeland region, and there are some excellent places to eat within easy driving distance. Gill was a runner up for AA Landlady of the Year 2005. This is a non-smoking establishment.

Recommended in the area

Great walks from the front door; Blackwell (The Arts & Crafts House), Bowness-on-Windermere; Brantwood (Ruskin's house), Coniston

West Vale Country House

★★★★★   GUEST HOUSE

Address: Far Sawrey, HAWKSHEAD,
Ambleside LA22 0LQ
Tel: 015394 42817
Fax: 015394 45302
Email: enquiries@westvalecountryhouse.co.uk
Website: www.westvalecountryhouse.co.uk
Map ref: 5, SD39
Directions: Cross Windemere by car ferry at Bowness, B5285 for 1.25m to Far Sawrey, West Vale on left leaving village
Rooms: 7 en suite, S £70–78 D £116–134 **Parking:** 8
Notes: ⊗ on premises ⊗ on premises No children under 12

West Vale is a lovely country house, built in the 1890s as a Victorian gentleman's residence, where you can forget all your cares. It is surrounded by stunning countryside on the edge of the pretty village of Far Sawrey, with views of Grizedale Forest and the Old Man of Coniston beyond the vale. Beautiful gardens have been cultivated around the property, and there is a delightful spot by the large pond to sit and soak up the sun. Yours hosts Dee and Glynn Pennington have left nothing to chance in their desire to create a perfect retreat. The bedrooms are impeccably decorated, furnished and equipped to a very high standard, and the bathrooms are also stylish. After a long journey you can anticipate a welcoming decanter of sherry in the bedroom. Elegant lounges, with a roaring log fire in the winter months, help you to unwind, and excellent dinners are served in the dining room which is also open to non-residents. The traditional breakfasts, there are also vegetarian and continental options, are equally delicious.

Recommended in the area

Hill Top, Beatrix Potter's home; Brantwood; Dove Cottage

Dalegarth House

★★★★ 🏠 🛏 GUEST ACCOMMODATION

Address:	Portinscale,
	KESWICK CA12 5RQ
Tel:	017687 72817
Fax:	017687 72817
Email:	allerdalechef@aol.com
Website:	www.dalegarth-house.co.uk
Map ref:	5, NY22
Directions:	Off A66 to Portinscale, pass Farmers Arms,

100yds on left

Rooms: 10 en suite, S £33–40 D £66–80 **Parking:** 14 **Notes:** ⊘ on premises ⊗ on premises No children under 5 **Closed:** 1 Dec–1 Mar

The views from this spacious Edwardian house, in the village of Portinscale, just south of Keswick, are nothing short of stunning. It sits on high ground, with a panoramic vista that takes in Derwent Water (just 400 metres from the door), Skiddaw, Catbells and the expanse of the fells of the northern Lakeland. It would be hard to find a better location for a walking holiday, and the full meal service here is a real bonus for hungry hikers. A full English breakfast starts the day, packed lunches are available on request and guests can return to a daily-changing four-course table d'hote dinner, prepared by the resident chef-proprietors Pauline and Bruce Jackson. Traditional and contemporary dishes feature, many of which have a regional emphasis, and there's an extensive wine list. Their appetites thus sated, guests can stroll in the gardens or relax in the comfortable lounge bar, furnished, like the rest of the house, with many antiques. The bedrooms at Dalegarth vary, with double, twin, family and single rooms all available. Each has an en suite bathroom, TV radio and tea- and coffee-making facilities. The Jacksons have also embued the house with a charming family atmosphere while providing the most professional of standards.

Recommended in the area

Cars of the Stars, Keswick; Theatre by the Lake, Keswick; Mirehouse

Catbells Fell and Derwent Water.

Howe Keld

★★★★ ≌ GUEST HOUSE

Address:	5/7 The Heads, KESWICK CA12 5ES
Tel:	017687 72417
Fax:	017687 72417
Email:	david@howekeld.co.uk
Website:	www.howekeld.co.uk
Map ref:	NY22

Directions: From town centre towards Borrowdale, right opp main car park, 1st on left

Rooms: 15 en suite, S 38 D £76 **Parking:** 9 **Notes:** ⊘ on premises 🐾 allowed in bedrooms

Closed: Xmas & Jan

This friendly establishment has a cosy first-floor lounge with spectacular fell views and easy access to the facilities in Keswick and to Derwent Water. Breakfast in the dining room is a delight, whether you stick to the impressive buffet or order from the varied cooked selection. The bedrooms are smartly decorated – the two ground floor rooms are particularly popular.

Recommended in the area

Keswick; walking in the fells; Castlerigg Stone Circle

New House Farm

★★★★★ 🛏 GUEST HOUSE

Address: LORTON, Cockermouth CA13 9UU
Tel: 01900 85404
Fax: 01900 85478
Email: hazel@newhouse-farm.co.uk
Website: www.newhouse-farm.co.uk
Map ref: 5, NY12
Directions: 6m S of Cockermouth on B5289 between Lorton and Loweswater
Rooms: 5 en suite, S £67–100 D £134–138
Parking: 30 Notes: ⊗ on premises 🐕 allowed in bedrooms No children under 6

Hazel Thompson bought New House Farm in 1990 and has completely renovated it to its present de luxe standard. Located in the north-west corner of the Lake District National Park, this Grade II listed house dates from 1650. The restoration discovered original oak beams and rafters, flagstone floors, and fireplaces where blazing log fires now crackle on colder days. There are lovely views from all the stylish rooms, and these views can also be enjoyed by taking a relaxing Hot Spring Spa in the beautifully maintained garden. The appealing en suite bedrooms are richly furnished and equipped with many thoughtful extras including home-baked biscuits or a champagne tray and flowers for special occasions – two rooms have a magnificent oak four poster. The delicious five-course dinner menu uses local ingredients whenever possible and changes daily – traditional puddings are a speciality. Hearty breakfasts are another highlight. Stabling is available for guests who wish to bring their own horses. Guests are welcome to wander around the 15 acres of open fields, woods, streams and ponds.

Recommended in the area

Keswick; Cockermouth; Buttermere lake

Winder Hall Country House

★★★★★ 🍽 🏛 GUEST ACCOMMODATION

Address:	LORTON CA13 9UP
Tel:	01900 85107
Fax:	01900 85479
Email:	nick@winderhall.co.uk
Website:	www.winderhall.co.uk
Map ref:	5, NY12

Directions: A66 W from Keswick, at Braithwaite onto B5292 to Lorton, left at T-junct signed Buttermere, Winderhall 0.5m on right

Rooms: 7 en suite, S £100–110 D £120–170 Parking: 10 Notes: ⊘ on premises ⊗ on premises Closed: 2–31 Jan

Winder Hall an impressive former manor house, set in a peaceful valley. The smart, individually styled bedrooms are thoughtfully equipped, and all are furnished with fine antiques or pine and have stunning fell views. Two rooms have beautiful four-poster beds. The oak-panelled dining room is the perfect setting for skilfully prepared meals using local seasonal produce.

Recommended in the area

Buttermere; Keswick; beaches of west Cumbria

Underwood Country Guest House

★★★★★ 🍽 GUEST HOUSE

Address:	The Hill, MILLOM LA18 5EZ
Tel:	01229 771116
Fax:	01229 719900
Email:	enquiries@underwoodhouse.co.uk
Website:	www.underwoodhouse.co.uk
Map ref:	5, SD18

Directions: A595 onto A5093 through village, The Green & The Hill, Underwood 0.5m after The Hill

Rooms: 5 en suite, S £40–60 D £80–120 Parking: 20 Notes: ⊘ on premises No children under 14

This beautiful Victorian vicarage stands in 8 acres of mature grounds overlooking the Duddon Estaury and Whicham Valley. The bedrooms feature a king-size bed and bathrooms with power shower, all have colour TV and bathrobes. Guests can relax in one of the two lounges, swim in the heated pool or play tennis. The food is of a high quality, using the best of local fresh produce.

Recommended in the area

Lake District National Park; Windermere; Muncaster Castle and Gardens

Ees Wyke Country House

★★★★★ ◉ ⓛ GUEST HOUSE

Address:	NEAR SAWREY, Ambleside LA22 0JZ
Tel:	015394 36393
Email:	mail@eeswyke.co.uk
Website:	www.eeswyke.co.uk
Map ref:	5, SD39
Directions:	On B5285 on W side of village

Rooms: 8 en suite, S £80–108 D £160–180
Parking: 12 Notes: ⊘ on premises ⌁ allowed in bedrooms No children under 12

A warm welcome awaits you at Ees Wyke, once the holiday home of Beatrix Potter. The Georgian house has a reputation for fine food, and the thoughtfully equipped bedrooms have been carefully furnished. After a day walking, fishing, sailing or riding in the surrounding countryside, come back to Ees Wyke to relax. The charming lounge has an open fire, and carefully prepared five-course dinners are served in the dining room to guests and non-residents. At breakfasts you can feast on Cumberland sausage, bacon and eggs, or choose a lighter option of fresh fruit, yoghurt and cereals.

Recommended in the area

Hill Top Farm (Beatrix Potter's house); Blackwell, The Arts & Crafts House; Brantwood (Ruskin's House)

Sawrey House Country Hotel & Restaurant

◆◆◆◆◆ ◉ ⌣

Address:	NEAR SAWREY, Ambleside LA22 0LF
Tel:	015394 36387
Fax:	015394 36010
Email:	enquiries@sawrey-house.com
Website:	www.sawrey-house.com
Map ref:	5, SO39
Directions:	On B5285 in village

Rooms: 12 en suite, S £75–80 D £150–210 Parking: 24 Notes: ⊘ on premises ⌁ allowed in bedrooms No children under 10 Closed: Jan

Built around 1830, the house retains many original features including the stained-glass window in the spacious hall. It also has an elegant lounge with deep sofas where a log fire burns on chilly nights. Bedrooms are en suite and many have views of the lake. The excellent food is imaginatively and stylishly presented, and breakfast is in the traditional style with a choice of lighter alternatives.

Recommended in the area

Hill Top Farm (Beatrix Potter's house); Windermere; many walks from hotel

The Knoll Country House

★★★★★ GUEST ACCOMMODATION

Address: Lakeside, NEWBY BRIDGE,
Ulverston LA12 8AU
Tel: 015395 31347
Fax: 015395 30850
Email: info@theknoll-lakeside.co.uk
Website: www.theknoll-lakeside.co.uk
Map ref: 5, SD38
Directions: A590 W to Newby Bridge, over rdbt, signed
right for Lake Steamers, house 0.5m on left
Rooms: 8 en suite S £0–0 D £0–0 **Parking:** 8 **Notes:** ⊗ on premises No children under 16
Closed: 24–26 Dec

Jenny Meads and Tracey Watson escaped from the daily commute and corporate life in 2001 and
found the Knoll, a small Victorian country house set in a leafy dell on the west side of Windermere.
They knew this was the place to create a tranquil oasis offering fabulous food and quality
accommodation. All rooms have been refurbished, including new bathrooms, and some are de luxe.
They are all well equipped with colour TV and video players, alarm clock radios and bath robes, while
hospitality trays provide fruit and leaf teas, coffee and hot chocolate, and hand-baked biscuits.
The beautifully furnished lounge is cosy and has an open fire for chillier evenings and there is a
well-stocked bar. Food is the real feature here. The girls passionately support local businesses, using
excellent Cumbrian produce including daily fresh fish and meat. The hot breakfast is a hearty
traditional affair complemented by a healthy buffet option and home-made preserves. If you are out
walking the fells, then a packed lunch can be provided. Jenny and Tracy also actively support local
conservation. Their formula for the Knoll clearly works – more than half of the bookings come from
people who have stayed here before.

Recommended in the area

Aquarium of the Lakes; World of Beatrix Potter; Holker Hall and Gardens

Brooklands Guest House

★★★★ GUEST HOUSE

Address: 2 Portland Place, PENRITH CA11 7QN
Tel: 01768 863395
Fax: 01768 863395
Email: enquiries@brooklandsguesthouse.com
Website: www.brooklandsguesthouse.com
Map ref: 6, NY53
Directions: From town hall onto Portland Place, 50yds on left
Rooms: 7 en suite, S £30–35 D £60–70 **Parking:** 2
Notes: ⊘ on premises ⊗ on premises

Charming and elegant, Brooklands Guest House is situated in the heart of the bustling market town of Penrith with its many attractions. This beautiful, refurbished Victorian terrace house is an excellent base for exploring the many delights of the Lake District National Park while convenient for the attractive Eden Valley. Debbie and Leon ensure you have a most enjoyable stay and that you will be keen to make a return visit. The traditional hearty breakfast, designed to satisfy the largest of appetites, offers a choice of fruit juices, fresh fruit, yogurt, cereals, oak cakes and cheese followed by such delights as Cumberland sausage, back bacon and eggs cooked to your liking; there's also a vegetarian option. All bedrooms are furnished to the highest standard and have nice touches such as colour television and tea- and coffee-making facilties. For a romantic escape with a touch of luxury, the Brooklands' suite has a locally handcrafted four-poster bed, a sofa, television, DVD, radio-alarm clock, hairdryer, luxury branded toiletries, bath robes and a choice of light refreshments in a mini-fridge. If you intend to explore the area on two wheels then Brooklands has secure storage for your bicycle. Ullswater, one of the areas lovliest lakes, is just a short distance southwest of Penrith and can be enjoyed at leisure aboard a 19th-century steamer.

Recommended in the area

Penrith; Coast to Coast cycle route; Ullswater lake; Rheged Discovery Centre

Brookfield Guest House

★★★★ GUEST HOUSE

Address: SHAP, Penrith CA10 3PZ
Tel: 01931 716397
Fax: 01931 716397
Email: info@brookfieldshap.co.uk
Website: www.brookfieldshap.co.uk
Map ref: 6, NY51
Directions: M6 junct 39, A6 towards Shap, 1st accommodation off motorway
Rooms: 4 (3 en suite) S £30–35 D £58–60 Parking: 20
Notes: ⊘ on premises ⊗ on premises No children under 12 Closed: Jan

Brookfield is a very well-maintained property, where refreshments on arrival are just part of the warm welcome. The pretty garden enhances the peaceful atmosphere, even though the motorway is just a short drive away. Home cooking is a speciality – substantial and enjoyable dinners and breakfasts are freshly prepared and served in the pleasant dining room. The en suite bedrooms are extremely well-appointed, and home comforts include radio alarms, hospitality trays and hairdryers.
Recommended in the area
Shap Abbey; Kendal; Penrith

The Coach House

★★★★ GUEST HOUSE

Address: Lake Road, WINDERMERE LA23 2EQ
Tel: 015394 44494
Email: enquiries@lakedistrictbandb.com
Website: www.lakedistrictbandb.com
Map ref: 6, SD49
Directions: M6 junct 36, A590 then A591. In Windermere House 0.5m on right opp St Herberts Church
Rooms: 5 en suite, S £35–60 D £48–70 Parking: 5
Notes: ⊘ on premises ⊗ on premises No children under 5 Closed: 24–26 Dec

The property was originally a Victorian coach house, but now the interior is more chic and minimalist, achieved through the bold use of bright colours and contemporary furnishings. The modern decor continues in the bedrooms, with stylish iron beds, showers, and a host of amenities such as radios, alarm clocks and hairdryers. The breakfasts are a special feature.
Recommended in the area
Windermere lake cruises; Blackwell (The Arts & Crafts House); Holehird Gardens

The Coppice

★★★★ ⊜ GUEST HOUSE

Address: Brook Road,
                     WINDERMERE LA23 2ED
Tel: 015394 88501
Fax: 015394 42148
Email: chris@thecoppice.co.uk
Website: www.thecoppice.co.uk
Map ref: 6, SD49
Directions: 0.25m S of village centre on A5074
Rooms: 9 en suite, S £40–45 D £62–80 Parking: 10
Notes: ⊘ on premises 🐾 allowed in bedrooms

This traditional Lakeland vicarage retains all its character and charm. Built of local stone, The Coppice sits in an elevated position between the villages of Windermere and Bowness, perfectly placed for touring or walking in the Lake District National Park. Hosts Chris and Barbara promise a memorable experience and can provide extras such as flowers, chocolates and champagne on arrival or the chance to upgrade to a four-poster bed. The en suite bedrooms, some with bath, some with shower, have been individually designed so each has its own distinctive feel. All have colour TV and complimentary tea and coffee trays. The renowned Lakeland breakfast and dinner are enjoyed in the light and airy dining room and a pre-dinner drink can be taken in the spacious lounge which has an open fire. Dinner is served most evenings and the restaurant has an excellent reputation in the area with locally sourced seasonal ingredients used in the dishes. This includes championship sausages and fine cured bacon, fell-bred beef, pork and lamb and fish from Fleetwood. The dinner menu also features vegetarian options, together with home-made bread and desserts. Additional facilities at The Coppice include private car park, local leisure club membership and fishing. Dogs are welcome in some of the rooms.

Recommended in the area

Hill Top Farm (Beatrix Potter's house); Wordsworth's homes Rydal Mount and Dove Cottage

The Fairfield Garden Guest House

★★★★ GUEST HOUSE

Address:	Brantfell Road, Bowness-on-Windermere, WINDERMERE LA23 3AE
Tel/Fax:	015394 46565
Email:	tonyandliz@the-fairfield.co.uk
Website:	www.the-fairfield.co.uk
Map ref:	6, SD49

Directions: Into Bowness town centre, turn opp St Martins Church & sharp left by Spinnery restaurant, house 200yds on right

Rooms: 10, S £30–37 D £60–94 **Parking:** 10 **Notes:** ⊘ on premises 🐕 allowed in some bedrooms by arrangement No children under 6

Genuine hospitality in a Lakeland country house – Tony and Liz Blaney offer a high standard of personal service at their 200-year-old home. Situated close to Bowness Bay, with its restaurants, shops, clubs, pubs, and, of course, Windermere lake. The Fairfield is perfect for a tranquil break. The bedrooms – there's a choice of single, twin, double, four-poster, deluxe and family rooms available – are well furnished with a host of thoughtful extras such as hospitality tray, assorted toiletries and a hairdryer. Guests can now ask for Fairfield's latest room which has a wooden four-poster bed and a wet room with heated floor. The power shower here is big enough for two and has body jets and massage pebbles on the floor. Special facilities are available for visitors with mobility requirements. Choose from either the hearty or the healthy breakfast options, both using the best of ingredients. There's no need to pre-order as breakfast options are chosen at the table. There is free internet access via a public terminal or you can make use of the wireless connection if you have bought your own laptop.

Recommended in the area

Blackwell (The Arts & Crafts House); Windermere lake steamers; Wordsworth House (NT)

Newstead

◆◆◆◆

Address:	New Road, WINDERMERE
	LA23 2EE
Tel:	015394 44485
Fax:	015394 88904
Email:	info@newstead-guesthouse.co.uk
Website:	www.newstead-guesthouse.co.uk
Map ref:	6, SD49
Directions:	0.5m from A591 between Windermere

and Bowness

Rooms: 7 en suite, S £40–80 D £50–90 **Parking:** 10 **Notes:** ⊘ on premises ⊗ on premises
No children under 7

This charming detached house, owned by June and Ross Nicolson, has been stylishly refurbished to blend Victorian elegance with modern comforts. Built in 1897 of traditional Lakeland stone it is situated between the villages of Windermere and Bowness – both offer a selction of pubs, restaurants, entertainment and shops. The spacious bedrooms, situated on the first and second floors, have bathrooms en suite, and coordinated decor and soft furnishings using stunning fabrics from the Arts and Crafts and art noveau periods. Beautiful original Victorian fireplaces and woodwork, and tea and coffee trays enhance the comfortable atmosphere. For that special occasion, one room has a deluxe four-poster king-size bed. All rooms have hairdryer and colour TV. There is a fine mahogany staircase and a splendid lounge, decorated in the Arts and Crafts style with William Morris prints, with a roaring log fire on cooler days. Delicious breakfasts include a vegetarian choice, and are served at separate tables in the large dining room. The garden is an ideal place to relax on summer days. Ask about free use of the local private leisure facilities – swimming pool, sauna, badminton and snooker are just some of the options – just a few minutes' drive away.

Recommended in the area

Hill Top Farm (Beatrix Potter's house); Wrynose Pass spectacular drive; Windermere lake steamers

The Willowsmere

★★★★ GUEST HOUSE

Address: Ambleside Road,
WINDERMERE LA23 1ES
Tel: 015394 43575
Fax: 015394 44962
Email: info@thewillowsmere.com
Website: www.thewillowsmere.com
Map ref: 6, SD49
Directions: On A591, 500yds on left after Windermere station, towards Ambleside
Rooms: 12 en suite, S £35–55 D £56–106 **Parking:** 15
Notes: ⊗ on premises ✶ allowed in bedrooms No children under 12

The imposing 1850s house offers a home from home atmosphere in the heart of the Lake District National Park and within easy walking distance of Windermere centre. Owners Martin and Sue have done lots of refurbishment at this large Lakeland stone building, set in a colourful, well-tended garden, with a patio and water feature to the rear. The large bedrooms have been upgraded, with luxury pocket-sprung beds and headboards in all rooms, and are equipped with thoughtful extras including tea and coffee facilities. hairdryer and colour TV. One ground-floor room has easier access. There is a choice of inviting lounges, a well-stocked bar, and a stylish dining room where delicious traditional English breakfasts are served at individual tables. The south-facing garden is the ideal place in which to relax and plan your stay. The large private car park can accommodate boat or glider trailers with ease. An added bonus to your stay at the Willowsmere is the free use of the leisure facilities – there's a swimming pool, a small gym and a sauna – at the nearby Windermere Manor Hotel.

Recommended in the area

Windermere Lake cruises; Windermere Steamboats and Museum; National Park Visitor Centre; Wrynose Pass spectacular drive

Whitehaven harbour.

Falconwood

★★★★★ ⬭ B&B

Address:	Moor Road, Stainburn, WORKINGTON CA14 1XW
Tel:	01900 602563
Email:	info@lakedistrict-bedandbreakfast.co.uk
Website:	www.lakedistrict-bedandbreakfast.co.uk
Map ref:	5, NY02

Directions: M6 Junct 40 to Keswick and Workington.
A595 to Whitehaven, turn right 1m to Stainburn (1.5m)
Rooms: 2 double en suite, S £50 D £70 Special breaks
available **Parking:** 6 **Notes:** ⊗ on premises No children under 14

Enjoying spectacular views over the Solway Firth to Scotland, Falconwood is a perfect base for exploring the Western Lake District. Ian and Dawn Lewis-Dalby are the hosts and Ian's gourmet dinners in the comfortable dining room are worth the trip alone. Pre-dinner drinks can be enjoyed in the relaxing lounge. The bedrooms complete the experience with their perfect combination of luxury with comfort. All, of course, have en suite bathrooms and nicely coordinated décor.

Recommended in the area

Wordsworth House, Cockermouth; Western Lakes; Whitehaven harbour

Cable car over Heights of Abraham, Peak District National Park.

St Oswald's Parish Church, Ashbourne.

Dove House B&B

★★★★ B&B

Address:	Bridge Hill, Mayfield,
	ASHBOURNE DE6 2HN
Tel:	01335 343329
Email:	dovehouse2000@yahoo.com
Map ref:	7, SK14

Directions: 1m W of Ashbourne. A52 onto B5032, B&B 300yds on right
Rooms: 1 en suite, £45–55 **Parking:** 1

Peacefully located in the village of Mayfield, close to the picturesque Georgian town of Ashbourne, this well-proportioned Victorian house is set in attractive gardens, perfect for a relaxed stay. Carefully chosen furnishings enhance the splendid original features throughout the property. There is just one bedroom with a spacious bathroom en suite, which is nicely decorated and equipped with all that is needed to ensure a comfortable stay. A pleasant lounge is available for your further comfort. The location of Dove House makes it a perfect spot for cycling and walking enthusiasts, as there is easy access to off-road cycle tracks as well as paths for numerous rewarding walks.

Recommended in the area

Chatsworth House; Peak District; Alton Towers; the Potteries

Dannah Farm Country House Ltd.

★★★★★ 🛏 ⌂ GUEST ACCOMMODATION

Address: Bowmans Lane, Shottle, BELPER DE56 2DR
Tel: 01773 550273
Fax: 01773 550590
Email: reservations@dannah.co.uk
Website: www.dannah.co.uk
Map ref: 8, SK35
Directions: A517 from Belper towards Ashbourne, 1.5m right into Shottle after Hanging Gate pub on right, over x-rds & right
Rooms: 8 en suite, S £65–100 D £100–170
Parking: 20 **Notes:** ⊗ on premises **Closed:** 24–26 Dec

Dannah is a Georgian farmhouse on a working farm on the Chatsworth Estate, and is home to Joan and Martin Slack and their collection of pigs, hens and cats, and Cracker the very good-natured English setter. The house is being upgraded to even higher standards while keeping many original features. Each bedroom has its own individual character, beautifully furnished with antiques and old pine and filled with a wealth of thoughtful extras. Some rooms have private sitting rooms, four-poster beds and amazing bathrooms featuring a double spa bath or Japanese-style tubs – the Studio Hideaway suite even has its own private terrace with hot tub. All the bedrooms look out onto green fields and open countryside. The two delightful sitting rooms have open fires on chilly evenings and views over the gardens. The English farmhouse breakfasts are a true delight, served in relaxed and elegant surroundings. Dinner is available by arrangement, alternatively there are excellent pubs and restaurants within easy reach. Footpaths criss-cross the surrounding area in the heart of the Derbyshire Dales, making it an ideal location for walking enthusiasts.

Recommended in the area

Chatsworth; Dovedale; Alton Towers

Buxton's Victorian Guest House

★★★★★ GUEST HOUSE

Address: 3A Broad Walk, BUXTON SK17 6JE
Tel: 01298 78759
Fax: 01298 74732
Email: buxtonvictorian@btconnect.com
Website: www.buxtonvictorian.co.uk
Map ref: 7, SK07
Directions: Signs to Opera House, proceed to Old Hall Hotel. Right onto Hartington Rd, car park 100yds on right
Rooms: 8 en suite, S £46–74 D £64–88 **Parking:** 8
Notes: ⊘ on premises ⊗ on premises No children under 4 **Closed:** 22 Dec–12 Jan

This Grade II listed house is only minutes from the famous Opera House and the town's amenities, and has great views over Buxton's renowned Pavilion Gardens. Attention to detail and high quality accommodation are hallmarks here and the hosts ensure your stay will be memorable. Luxury bedrooms are individually themed and have many thoughtful extras. A complimentary tray of tea or coffee and biscuits awaits you in the tranquil drawing room on arrival.

Recommended in the area

Poole's Cavern (Buxton Country Park); Peak District National Park; Chatsworth

Grendon Guest House

★★★★★ ⊖ ▦ GUEST HOUSE

Address: Bishops Lane, BUXTON SK17 6UN
Tel: 01298 78831
Email: grendonguesthouse@hotmail.com
Website: www.grendonguesthouse.co.uk
Map ref: 7, SK07
Directions: 0.75m from Buxton centre, along A53, turn right into Bishops Lane
Rooms: 5 (4 en suite) S £30–35 D £60–85 **Parking:** 8
Notes: ⊘ on premises No children under 10

Spaciousness distinguishes this detached property set in attractive gardens with glorious Peak District views. Coordinated design and antique furnishings characterise the interior, and is particularly evident in the four-poster suite. All rooms have easy chairs and hospitality trays. Homemade specialities are a feature of the memorable breakfasts and dinner is available by arrangement.

Recommended in the area

Walks to the Goyt Valley from the door; Peak District National Park; Chatsworth

Pavilion Gardens, Buxton.

Oldfield Guest House

★★★★ GUEST HOUSE

Address:	8 Macclesfield Road, BUXTON SK17 9AH
Tel:	01298 78264
Email:	avril@oldfieldhousebuxton.co.uk
Website:	www.oldfieldhousebuxton.co.uk
Map ref:	7, SK07
Directions:	On B5059 0.5m SW of town centre

Rooms: 5 en suite, £64–76 Parking: 7

Notes: ⊘ on premises ⊗ on premises

No children under 5 Closed: Xmas & New Year

A warm welcome awaits you at this Victorian stone house in a leafy residential avenue not far from Buxton's attractions. The large, carefully furnished bedrooms have luxurious king- or queen-size beds with crisp linens, are equipped with tea and coffee facilities, and have modern bath-shower rooms en suite. Choose between a full English or continental breakfast complimented by an array of cereals, fruit juices and fruits, served in the attractive dining room. The cosy lounge has French doors opening onto a patio and very pleasant grounds with ponds and a stream. Off-street parking is available.

Recommended in the area

Buxton Opera House and Pavilion Gardens; Chatsworth ; Peak District National Park

The Rising Sun Hotel

★★★★ GUEST ACCOMMODATION

Address:	Thornhill Moor, Bamford,
	CASTLETON S33 0AL
Tel:	01433 651323
Fax:	01433 651601
Email:	info@the-rising-sun.org
Website:	www.the-rising-sun.org
Map ref:	7, SK18
Directions:	On A625 from Sheffield to Castleton

Rooms: 12 en suite, S £49.50–69.50 D £60–140
Parking: 120 Notes: 🐕 allowed in bedrooms

Carefully restored and lovingly presented by Carole and Graham Walker, the 18th-century Rising Sun at Thornhill Moor lies within the Hope Valley in the heart of the Peak District National Park. This family-run inn offers spacious luxury bedrooms, ranging from doubles to sumptuous executive suites, all with quality furnishings and efficient modern bathrooms. Some rooms have stunning country views, and nice touches include fresh flowers and antique furniture. The friendly staff attend to your every need in an considerate manner making any stay here truly memorable. A highlight is the excellent and imaginative food served in the pleasant public areas. The lunch and dinner menus are created daily using fresh produce, offering a choice of traditional British food with modern European and Far Eastern influences. Guests can choose from buffet-style menus or individually prepared dishes such as lamb shank braised in onion, soya and red wine gravy or pheasant casserole in port wine jus with a side salad of buttered mash followed by Bakewell Tart and custard or melting chocolate pudding. The good food is complemented by an equally good selection of real ales and fine wines. Well-behaved dogs are welcome in some of the rooms. Weddings and receptions are held at the Rising Sun Hotel.

Recommended in the area

Chatsworth; Castleton Caverns; Peveril Castle; Bakewell ; Eyam; Derwent and Ladybower reservoirs

Hornbeam House

★★★★ B&B

Address: Mile Hill, Mansfield Road, Hasland,
CHESTERFIELD S41 0JN
Tel: 01246 556851
Fax: 0870 052 1647
Email: enquiries@hornbeamhouse4t.demon.co.uk
Website: www.hornbeamhouse.4t.com
Map ref: 8, SK37
Directions: M1 junct 29, A617 towards Chesterfield,
1.5m 1st exit turn left at top of slip road, 200yds turn
right towards Hasland. Hornbeam House 0.75m on right
Rooms: 2 en suite, S £40–53 D £60–76 **Parking:** 3 **Notes:** ⊘ on premises ⊗ on premises

This large Victorian house stands in substantial grounds not far from the M1. On the ground floor there is a magnificent lounge with views to the front and rear gardens. Attentive service is always evident here, and fresh and healthy cooking is enjoyed at breakfast (the excellent dinners are by arrangement). A cottage-style annexe is also available. There is an 18-hole golf course just minutes away.
Recommended in the area
Hardwick Hall (NT); Matlock; Chatsworth

Woodlands

★★★★★ B&B

Address: Woodseats Lane, Charlesworth,
GLOSSOP SK13 5DP
Tel: 01457 866568
Email: mairs@lineone.net
Website: www.woodlandshighpeak.co.uk
Map ref: 7, SK09
Directions: 3m SW of Glossop. Off A626, 0.5m from
Charlesworth towards Marple
Rooms: 3 (2 en suite) S £40–45 D £55–65 **Parking:** 6
Notes: ⊘ on premises ⊗ on premises No children under 12

Judy and Brian Mairs rate service, friendliness and hospitality as key to their success here. Judy was a top twenty finalist for AA Landlady of the Year in 2003, 2004 and 2006. Woodlands is a welcoming Victorian property with wonderful views in a handy location on the Trans-Pennine Trail. Breakfast in the conservatory is a memorable occasion and guests can plan their day in the comfortable lounge. The king-size and double rooms, en suite or with private facilities are well furnished and cosy.
Recommended in the area
Chatsworth; Lyme Park; Roman Spa at Buxton

Win Hill looking west over Hope Valley.

Underleigh House

★★★★★ 🏠 GUEST ACCOMMODATION

Address:	Off Edale Road, HOPE, Hope Valley S33 6RF
Tel:	01433 621372
Fax:	01433 621324
Email:	info@underleighhouse.co.uk
Website:	www.underleighhouse.co.uk
Map ref:	7, SK18

Directions: From village church on A6187 onto Edale Rd, 1m left onto lane

Rooms: 6 en suite, S £50–55 D £70–90 Parking: 6 Notes: ⊘ on premises No children under 12 Closed: Xmas, New Year & 8–31 Jan

Vivienne and Philip Taylor provide thoughtfully furnished bedrooms with facilities en suite, each with a hairdryer, radio alarm, and tea and coffee facilities. Some rooms have direct access to the gardens, one has its own lounge. Enjoy an evening drink on the terrace in summer, or by the log fire in the lounge in cooler weather. Breakfast is served around one large table in the dining room.

Recommended in the area

Castleton Caverns; Chatsworth; Eyam

Hearthstone Farm

★★★★ FARMHOUSE

Address: Hearthstone Lane, Riber,
MATLOCK DE4 5JW
Tel: 01629 534304
Fax: 01629 534372
Email: enquiries@hearthstonefarm.co.uk
Website: www.hearthstonefarm.co.uk
Map ref: 7, SK35
Directions: A615 at Tansley 2m E of Matlock, turn opp
Royal Oak towards Riber, at gates to Riber Hall left onto
Riber Rd and 1st left onto Hearthstone Ln, farmhouse on left
Rooms: 3 en suite, S £45 D £32.50pp **Parking:** 6 **Notes:** ⊗ on premises ⌂ allowed in bedrooms
Closed: Xmas & New Year

Set high on the hill above Matlock, this traditional farmhouse is a welcoming home in a lovely rural
area. The farm has unrivalled views of the historic village of Riber, dominated by Riber Castle.
Beautifully decorated in keeping with its age and character, the stone house has original exposed
stone walls and oak beams. The three charming bedrooms are equipped with a host of extras for
that home-from-home feel, and all rooms are en suite with modern bathrooms and have farm or
valley views. Unwind in the inviting sitting room after a day exploring the area, while the elegant dining
room is a stylish setting for breakfast. As a working farm producing eggs, vegetables and organic beef,
pork and lamb by traditional environmentally friendly methods, Hearthstone can offer delicious truly
local, fresh food, particularly the sausages and bacon that are produced on the premises. The farm
overlooks the popular tourist destination of Matlock Bath where a cable car ride to the Heights of
Abraham offers a birds eye view of the surrounding area.

Recommended in the area

Peak Railway; Chatsworth; Haddon Hall; Dovedale and the Manifold Valley; Tramway Museum, Crich;
Cromford Mill

Hodgkinsons Hotel

★★★★ 🛏 GUEST ACCOMMODATION

Address:	150 South Parade, Matlock Bath, MATLOCK DE4 3NR
Tel:	01629 582170
Fax:	01629 584891
Email:	enquiries@hodgkinsons-hotel.co.uk
Website:	www.hodgkinsons-hotel.co.uk
Map ref:	7, SK25
Directions:	On A6 in village centre

Rooms: 8 en suite, S £40–75 D £75–120 **Parking:** 5
Notes: 🐕 allowed in bedrooms **Closed:** 24–26 Dec

You will receive a warm welcome at this fine Grade II listed Georgian hotel which is well situated for exploring the lovely Derbyshire countryside. The bedrooms are equipped with fine antique furniture, sumptuous furnishings and a wealth of thoughtful extras. The elegant dining room is the venue for imaginative European cuisine using fresh local produce. Relax in the lounge, beside a real fire, or in summer in the terraced garden overlooking the steep wooded valley. Children and pets are welcome.

Recommended in the area

Heights of Abraham; Matlock Bath; Chatsworth

Yew Tree Cottage

★★★★ 🏠 B&B

Address:	The Knoll, Tansley, MATLOCK DE4 5FP
Tel:	01629 583862
Email:	enquiries@yewtreecottagebb.co.uk
Website:	www.yewtreecottagebb.co.uk
Map ref:	7, SK35
Directions:	1.2m E of Matlock. Off A615 into Tansley

Rooms: 3 en suite, D £65–80 **Parking:** 3
Notes: ⊘ on premises ⊗ on premises No children

This historic 18th century cottage, full of original character and charm and with stunning views, is set in pretty, tranquil gardens in the village of Tansley. The cottage is a true home away from home and ideally situated for all the Peaks and Dales. The Dornans, a well-travelled couple, use their experiences to provide outstanding service and hospitality. The elegantly furnished and decorated bedrooms have TV/radios, bath robes, hair dryers, toiletries and well-stocked refreshment trays. Breakfast is a memorable feast of both home-made and local produce. Home-made snacks and light refreshments are served in the beamed sitting room where log fires cheer up the cooler days.

Recommended in the area

Chatsworth; Crich Tramway Village; Heights of Abraham cable cars

The Smithy

★★★★★ 🍽 🏛 GUEST ACCOMMODATION

Address: NEWHAVEN, Biggin SK17 0DT
Tel: 01298 84548
Fax: 01298 84548
Email:
thesmithy@newhavenderbyshire.freeserve.co.uk
Website: www.thesmithybedandbreakfast.co.uk
Map ref: 7, SK16
Directions: On A515 10m S of Buxton. Adjacent to
Biggin Ln, entrance via private driveway opp Ivy House
Rooms: 4 en suite, S £40–50 D £65–85 **Parking:** 8 **Notes:** ⊗ on premises

Welcoming owners Lynn and Gary Jinks have restored this former drovers' inn and blacksmith's shop to a high standard with all modern comforts and a very personal service. The well-decorated good-sized bedrooms are all en suite with hospitality trays and many extras. Tasty breakfasts, including free-range eggs and home-made preserves, are served in the forge, which still has its vast open hearth, and is adjacent to a cosy lounge. The pleasant gardens are set within four acres of meadowland.
Recommended in the area
Chatsworth; Tissington and High Peak Trails (within walking distance); Peak District National Park

The Old Manor House

★★★★★ B&B

Address: Coldwell Street, WIRKSWORTH,
Matlock DE4 4FB
Tel: 01629 822502
Email: ivan@spurrier-smith.fsnet.co.uk
Map ref: 7, SK25
Directions: From Derby B5023 towards
Duffield/Matlock. Coldwell St turn right at Market Place
Rooms: 1, S £50 D £80 **Parking:** 1 **Notes:** ⊘ on
premises ⊗ on premises No children
Closed: Xmas & New Year

This impressive 17th-century house is located on the edge of the pleasant town of Wirksworth, which is well worth a visit for its period buildings, narrow streets and intricate alleyways. The house and the private bathroom and bedroom, with its four-poster bed and quality furnishings, retains many original features. A full, hearty breakfast is served in the elegant dining room and a spacious drawing room is available to relax in after a day out. There are good restaurants and pubs in the vicinity.
Recommended in the area
Peak District National Park; Chatsworth; Carsington Water

DEVON

Heddon's Mouth, nr Lynton, Exmoor National Park.

Gages Mill Country Guest House

★★★★ GUEST ACCOMMODATION

Address:	Buckfastleigh Road, ASHBURTON TQ13 7JW
Tel:	01364 652391
Fax:	01364 652641
Email:	richards@gagesmill.co.uk
Website:	www.gagesmill.co.uk
Map ref:	2, SX77

Directions: Off A38 at Peartree junct turn right, left before filling station, Gages Mill 500yds on left

Rooms: 7 en suite, S £32–35 D £64–70 Parking: 7 Notes: ⊗ on premises No children under 8 Closed: 23 Oct–1 Mar

Gages Mill is a Grade II listed former wool mill on the edge of Dartmoor National Park. Bedrooms are well equipped and have views of open countryside; there is a twin room on the ground floor. The large dining room has a well-stocked corner bar, and stone archways lead through to the cosy sitting room.
Recommended in the area
Buckfast Abbey; Dartmoor National Park; South Devon Steam Railway

Greencott

★★★★ GUEST ACCOMMODATION

Address:	Landscove, ASHBURTON TQ13 7LZ
Tel:	01803 762649
Map ref:	2, SX76

Directions: 3m SE of Ashburton. Off A38 at Peartree junct, Landscove signed on slip road, village green 2m on right, opp village hall

Rooms: 2 en suite, £23pppn Parking: 3 Notes: ⊗ on premises Closed: 25–26 Dec

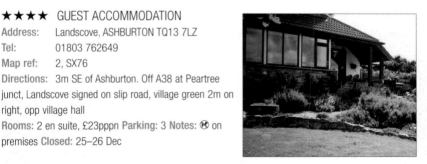

Modern facilities in a traditional atmosphere are offered at this renovated house in the village of Landscove, which is just 3 miles from Ashburton. Greencott stands in a garden with lovely country views. The bedrooms are carefully furnished and well equipped with baths and showers en suite, central heating, and tea and coffee amenities. Television, books, maps and local information are provided in the comfortable sitting room, and traditional country cooking is served around the oak dining table. The full English breakfast includes home-made bread, and dinner is available on request. Older children are welcome, but pets cannot be accommodated, with the exception of guide dogs.
Recommended in the area
Dartington; Buckfast Abbey; riding, fishing and golf nearby

The Rising Sun

★★★★ 🏨 INN

Address:	Woodland, ASHBURTON
	TQ13 7JT
Tel:	01364 652544
Fax:	01364 654202
Email:	risingsun.hazel@btconnect.com
Website:	www.risingsunwoodland.co.uk
Map ref:	2, SX77

Directions: Off A38 signed Woodland & Denbury, Rising Sun 1.5m on left

Rooms: 4 en suite, D £65 Parking: 30 Notes: 🐕 allowed in bedrooms

A fine example of the true West Country inn – the Rising Sun is a welcoming place that offers high quality accommodation, good home-cooked meals, an admirable selection of local beer, cider and wine and a jovial bunch of regulars to enliven the evenings, especially on the regular theme nights and quiz nights. It is also in a prime location, amid glorious Devon countryside, within easy reach of the Torbay resorts, Dartmoor and the cities of Exeter and Plymouth. This is a place to bring the kids and the dog – both are welcome, and children will especially enjoy the large garden and outdoor play area and the indoor family room with books and toys. The food here enjoys local renown, and the proprietors pride themselves on sourcing ingredients from the best local suppliers, including fish fresh from Brixham harbour or from the Dartmouth Smokehouse, a vast range of West Country cheeses, and vegetables and dairy produce from nearby farms. There's a varied and interesting menu, and home-made pies are a speciality. It can all be enjoyed in a totally smoke-free environment. The bedrooms are individually designed, well equipped and comfortable, with particularly good quality beds and bedlinens. Each has an en suite bath or shower room, television and beverage making facilities, and one is large enough for a family with three children.

Recommended in the area

Dartmoor National Park; Buckfast Abbey; South Devon Railway.

Kerrington House

★★★★★ 🛏 GUEST ACCOMMODATION
Address: Musbury Road, AXMINSTER EX13 5JR
Tel: 01297 35333
Fax: 01297 35345
Email: jreaney@kerringtonhouse.com
Website: www.kerringtonhouse.com
Map ref: 2, SY29
Directions: 0.5m from Axminster on A358 towards
Seaton, house on left
Rooms: 5 en suite, S £69–75 D £90–110 Parking: 6
Notes: ⊗ on premises

Be prepared for a very warm welcome and genuine pampering at this lovingly-restored period house set in landscaped gardens. Bedrooms are beautifully decorated and feature quality furniture, coordinated fabrics and many thoughtful extras while antique pieces and well-loved treasures create a personal atmosphere in the drawing room. Kerrington is renowned for its delicious food served at breakfast. Groups of families and friends are welcome to use the accommodation for small house parties.
Recommended in the area
Lyme Regis; Dorchester; East Devon Heritage Coast

The Bark House

★★★★★ 🛏 GUEST ACCOMMODATION
Address: Oakford Bridge, BAMPTON EX16 9HZ
Tel: 01398 351236
Website: www.barkhouse.co.uk
Map ref: 2, SS92
Directions: 2m W of Bampton on A396
Rooms: 5 (4 en suite), S £50–59.50 D £93–119
Parking: 15 Notes: ⊗ on premises 🐾 allowed in
bedrooms

Expect lots of character at this wisteria covered, cottagey hotel on the edge of Exmoor with a charming garden from where you can enjoy stunning views. There is strong emphasis placed on attention to detail: help with luggage, afternoon tea and cakes and early morning tea in the room. The cosy bedrooms have many thoughtful extras, including fresh flowers from the garden and a selection of magazines. For an extra charge, beautifully cooked dinners, preceded by canapés in the lounge by a real log fire, are served in a low-beamed candlelit dining room. Breakfast is taken very seriously, too, and all produce is sourced from the best West Country suppliers.
Recommended in the area
Exmoor National Park; Knightshayes Court (NT); Dulverton

Halmpstone Manor

♦♦♦♦♦ ⊛ ⊛

Address:	Bishop's Tawton, BARNSTAPLE EX32 0EA
Tel:	01271 830321
Fax:	01271 830826
Email:	jane@halmpstonemanor.co.uk
Website:	www.halmpstonemanor.co.uk
Map ref:	2, SS52

Directions: 3m SE of Barnstaple. Off A377 E of river & rail bridges

Rooms: 4 en suite, D £100–140 Parking: 12

Notes: 🐕 allowed in bedrooms Closed: Xmas & New Year

A place to seriously relax, this gracious 1700s house has its origins in the 12th century. It has been praised for its hospitality for hundreds of years, a tradition that owners Jane and Charles Stanbury happily continue. It stands in tranquil grounds, and offers a memorable stay with squashy sofas, crackling fires and quality bedrooms. One room has a four-poster bed – just the thing for a luxury break. Food is another high point, the excellent five-course dinner is based on the produce of Devon.

Recommended in the area

RHS Rosemoor and Marwood Hill; North Devon Heritage Coast; Tarka Trail

The Pines at Eastleigh

★★★★ GUEST ACCOMMODATION

Address:	The Pines, Eastleigh, BIDEFORD EX39 4PA
Tel:	01271 860561
Email:	pirrie@thepinesateastleigh.co.uk
Website:	www.thepinesateastleigh.co.uk
Map ref:	1, SS42

Directions: A39 onto A386 signed East-The-Water. 1st left signed Eastleigh, 500yds next left, 1.5m to village, house on right

Rooms: 6 en suite, S £35–45 D £75–90 Parking: 20

Notes: ⊗ on premises 🐕 allowed in bedrooms No children under 9

From its magnificent hilltop position overlooking the Torridge estuary and Lundy Island, this Georgian house is perfect for a relaxing break. It stands in 7 acres of pleasant gardens that guarantee peace and seclusion. Most of the comfortable bedrooms are in converted stables around a charming courtyard, each with independent ground-floor access – there are two rooms in the main house. The tasty breakfasts are made from local and home-made produce.

Recommended in the area

Instow and Clovelly; cycling and walking on The Tarka Trail; Hartland Heritage Coast

Hansard House

★★★★ GUEST ACCOMMODATION

Address:	3 Northview Road,
	BUDLEIGH SALTERTON EX9 6BY
Tel:	01395 442773
Fax:	01395 442475
Email:	enquiries@hansardhotel.co.uk
Website:	www.hansardhousehotel.co.uk
Map ref:	2, SY08
Directions:	B3178 to Budleigh Salterton

Rooms: 12 en suite, S £36–42 D £75–89
Parking: 11 Notes: ⌧ on premises

Set in an ideal situation a short walk from central Budleigh Salterton, Hansard House is just five minutes from the beach and the cliff path of this beautiful part of the East Devon coast. The tastefully decorated en suite bedrooms have TV, tea and coffee making facilities and hair dryers, and most have views across the town, to the countryside and estuary beyond. The hearty breakfast, and also dinner by arrangement, is served in the light and airy dining room. Children and pets are welcome.
Recommended in the area
Otter Estuary Bird Sanctuary; Bicton Park Gardens

Easton Court

★★★★ GUEST ACCOMMODATION

Address:	Easton Cross, CHAGFORD TQ13 8JL
Tel:	01647 433469
Fax:	01647 433654
Email:	stay@easton.co.uk
Website:	www.easton.co.uk
Map ref:	2, SX78
Directions:	Off A30 at Whiddon Down junction onto

A382 signed Moretonhampstead. After 0.5m, take 1st exit off minirdbt again onto A382 and signed Moretonhampstead. House 3.5m on left at x-rds for Chagford
Rooms: 5 en suite, S £45–60 D £62–75 Parking: 5 Notes: ⌧ ♤ in some bedrooms No kids under 10

Debra and Paul Witting's thatched Tudor farmhouse stands in acres of gardens and paddocks in the Teign valley. Evelyn Waugh was charmed by the place and wrote *Brideshead Revisited* here, and you too should find it inspiring. An Edwardian extension houses the en suite bedrooms with fabulous views of the countryside - four rooms are superior, and there is a mixture of showers and bathrooms.
Recommended in the area
Castle Drogo (NT); Fingle Bridge; Dartmoor National Park

Tor Cottage

◆◆◆◆◆ 🏠

Address: CHILLATON, Tavistock PL16 0JE
Tel: 01822 860248
Fax: 01822 860126
Email: info@torcottage.co.uk
Website: www.torcottage.co.uk
Map ref: 1, SX48
Directions: A30 Lewdown exit through Chillaton towards Tavistock, 300yds after Post Office right signed Bridlepath No Public Vehicular Access to end

Rooms: 4 en suite, S £94 D £140–150 **Parking:** 8 **Notes:** ⊘ on premises ⊗ on premises No children under 16 **Closed:** 17 Dec–7 Jan

This romantic cottage offers tranquillity and seclusion in 18 acres of grounds. Nothing is too much trouble for Maureen Rowlatt, who has equipped the en suite bed-sitting rooms with everything you could desire. Each one is individually designed, from the warmth and style of the Art Deco Room to the blue and cream elegance of The Craftman's Room – both converted from an original craftman's workshop. One room is in the cottage wing and the others are in converted barns – each has a private terrace/garden and a log fire. Laughing Waters, the garden retreat, is nestled in its own private valley and is also available on a self-catering basis during Christmas and New Year. Breakfast is an imaginative range of dishes, and can be taken in the conservatory-style dining room or on the terrace in fine weather. The gardens are a feature in their own right with many private corners, a stream, and in summer, a heated swimming pool. Woodlands cloaking the hillside behind the cottage are home to a variety of wildlife including badgers, pheasants and deer who enjoy the cover of the gorse, while buzzards and the occasional heron can be seen overhead. Children cannot be accommodated. Autumn and spring breaks are available – 3 nights for the price of 2.

Recommended in the area

Dartmoor; The Eden Project; National Trust houses and gardens

The beach at Beer on Lyme Bay.

Lower Orchard

★ ★ ★ ★   B&B

Address:	Swan Hill Road, COLYFORD EX24 6QQ
Tel:	01297 553615
Email:	robin@barnardl.co.uk
Map ref:	2, SY29

Directions: On A3052 in Colyford, between Lyme Regis & Sidmouth

Rooms: 2 (1 en suite), S £40–45 D £50–60 **Parking:** 3

Notes: ⊘ on premises ⌁ allowed in bedrooms
No children

The modern ranch-style family house has uninterrupted rural views across the Axe Valley. The two very spacious bedrooms are on the ground floor, one with a bathroom en suite and the other with adjacent private shower facilities. Breakfast is served in the lounge-dining room with patio doors leading to a sun terrace. A splash pool in the garden is tempting in warm weather. Lyme Regis only 6 miles away, and the unspoiled towns of Honiton and Sidmouth are also within easy reach. Owner Lorrie Barnard breeds Tibetan Terriers, so the establishment is pet friendly.

Recommended in the area

Forde Abbey and Gardens; Seaton Tramway; Jurassic Coast World Heritage Site

New Angel Rooms

◆◆◆◆

Address: 51 Victoria Road, DARTMOUTH TQ6 9RT
Tel: 01803 839425
Fax: 01803 839567
Email: reservations@thenewangel.co.uk
Website: www.thenewangel.co.uk
Map ref: 2, SX85
Directions: Located close to Dartmouth market place
Rooms: 6 en suite, S £90–120 D £110–140
Notes: ⊘ on premises Closed: Jan

Famous for many years as the Carved Angel, this superb restaurant situated on the waterfront in the heart of historic Dartmouth re-opened in 2004 as the New Angel, under the direction of one of Britain's top chefs, John Burton-Race, whose career has included a number of the finest hotels and restaurants in the country (notably his own L'Ortolan, near Reading in Berkshire), plus the TV series *French Leave* and *Return of the Chef*. In 2005 the New Angel was selected as AA Restaurant of the Year for England, and it was around the same time that John and his wife Kim opened the rooms (and a cookery school). A meal at the New Angel followed by a stay in one of the luxury suites or double rooms offers one of the best West Country experiences. Guests are greeted with a complimentary bottle of champagne in one of the stylish rooms, each with an en suite bathroom or shower room and all the comforts expected of a place of this calibre. The food, of course, is the highlight, but for all its renown, the restaurant is not in the least stuffy and guests can enjoy the top quality dishes amid a relaxed ambience. Breakfasts are wonderful too, featuring not only the traditional cooked breakfast, but also pastries freshly baked by a New Angel chef. Dartmouth, in an unrivalled setting at the mouth of the River Dart, has a network of cobbled streets which are a delight to explore; alternatively, take to the water on a river trip for a different view of this historic port.

Recommended in the area

Dartmouth Castle; Dartmouth Golf and Country Club; Blackpool Sands

Bayard's Cove, Dartmouth.

Nonsuch House

Address:	Church Hill, Kingswear,
	DARTMOUTH TQ6 0BX
Tel:	01803 752829
Fax:	01803 752357
Email:	enquiries@nonsuch-house.co.uk
Website:	www.nonsuch-house.co.uk
Map ref:	2, SX85

Directions: A3022 onto A379 2m before Brixham. Fork left onto B3205. Left up Higher Contour Rd, down Ridley Hill, house on bend

Rooms: 3 en suite, S £70–95 D £95–120 **Parking:** 3 **Notes:** ⊘ on premises No children under 10

Kit and Penny Noble's lovely Edwardian house is set on a south-facing hill in Kingswear, with a panoramic vista across the Dart estuary to Dartmouth in one direction and out to the open sea in the other. The accommodation here is of a very high quality – the spacious bedrooms are comfortable with lots of little extras. Meals are a highlight, prepared from fresh, local ingredients.

Recommended in the area

Dartmouth; Brixham; South West Coast Path

The Edwardian

★★★★ GUEST HOUSE

Address:	30-32 Heavitree Road, EXETER EX1 2LQ
Tel:	01392 276102
Fax:	01392 253393
Email:	michael@edwardianexeter.co.uk
Website:	www.edwardianexeter.co.uk
Map ref:	2, SX99

Directions: M5 junct 29, right at lights signed city centre, on left after Exeter University School of Education
Rooms: 12 en suite, S £55–60 D £70–80 Family £100
Parking: 2 Notes: ⊘ on premises ⇥ in bedrooms

Built in 1912, the Edwardian started life as two separate houses that were joined together in the 1970s. The property has been refurbished showing attention to detail, which is evident in the furnishings, and the antiques and china lovingly collected over the years. Situated in the city of Exeter and within easy access of the M5 motorway, the guest house is ideally located for both business and pleasure. The twelve bedrooms are decorated in different styles using original period furniture that complements the modern comforts. All are en suite and include telephone, TV, hair dryers and tea and coffee making facilities. The larger rooms have four-poster beds and two rooms have sleigh beds. Sofa beds in some rooms make them suitable for families. Other bedrooms have antique brass, wrought iron or period wooden bedsteads – one with a canopy over. Those south facing are bright with lovely views to the distant hills. A relaxing lounge provides the perfect place to unwind at the end of an exhausting day and the freshly prepared full English, vegetarian or continental breakfast is taken in a pretty dining room. Proprietors, Michael and Jackie Scott-Hake, are happy to advise on the abundance of excellent restaurants nearby.

Recommended in the area

Exeter Cathedral; Exeter quayside; Dartmoor National Park

Galley Fish & Seafood Restaurant with Rooms

★★★★★ ❀ RESTAURANT WITH ROOMS

Address:	41 Fore Street, Topsham,
	EXETER EX3 0HU
Tel:	01392 876078
Email:	fish@galleyrestaurant.co.uk
Website:	www.galleyrestaurant.co.uk
Map ref:	2, SX99

Directions: M5 junct 30, follow Topsham signs then Quay signs. Restaurant behind Lighter Inn by river

Rooms: 2 en suite, S £87.5–95 D £150–250 Parking: 4 Notes: ⊘ on premises ⊗ on premises No children under 12 Closed: Xmas–New Year

Quirky yet quaint, a stay at this part-restaurant part-guesthouse overlooking the Exe estuary is a magical experience. Reached by steep stairs, the bedrooms are in a 17th-century cottage with original features. A high point is dinner, when the restaurant serves imaginative fish and seafood dishes.

Recommended in the area

Historic Exeter; Dawlish Warren; Exmouth Beach

Mill Farm

★★★★ FARMHOUSE

Address:	Kenton, EXETER EX6 8JR
Tel:	01392 832471
Website:	www,millfarmstay.co.uk
Map ref:	2, SX99

Directions: A379 from Exeter towards Dawlish, over minirdbt by Swans Nest, farm 1.75m on right

Rooms: 5 en suite, S £32–35 D £48–50 Parking: 12 Notes: ⊘ on premises ⊗ on premises No children under 6 Closed: Xmas

Just a short drive from the Powderham Estate and outside the pretty village of Kenton, this charming working farmhouse is surrounded by peaceful pastureland and streams. Inside the decor is carefully coordinated, with stencil designs on the walls and lots of antique furniture. The spacious bedrooms are sunny with wide country views. Hearty farmhouse breakfasts served in the bright dining room are an appetising start to the day, and there are plenty of local places serving evening meals. There is also a lounge. The owner is very friendly, and keen to welcome you to her well-managed home.

Recommended in the area

Powderham Castle; Dartmoor; Exe Estuary Nature Reserve

The Barn Hotel

★★★★ GUEST ACCOMMODATION

Address:	Foxholes Hill, Marine Drive,
	EXMOUTH EX8 2DF
Tel:	01395 224411
Fax:	01395 225445
Email:	info@barnhotel.co.uk
Website:	www.barnhotel.co.uk
Map ref:	2, SY08

Directions: M5 junct 30, take A376 to Exmouth, then
signs to seafront. At rdbt last exit into Foxholes Hill,
Foxholes located on right

Rooms: 11 en suite, S £35–52 D £70–104 **Parking:** 30 **Notes:** ⊘ on premises
Closed: 23 Dec–10 Jan

Close to miles of sandy beaches, this Grade II listed establishment has a prime location. It is set in an impeccable and stunning 2-acre garden, which is sea facing, affording spectacular views of the East Devon Heritage Coast. There is pleasant terrace and a swimming pool for summer. The building is a leading example of the Arts and Crafts movement and was built in the early 1900s by Edward Prior, a contemporary of William Morris. The Barn has been sympathetically modernised and furnished in keeping with its architectural design and creates an atmosphere of country-house style. The public rooms and most of the bedrooms have outstanding sea views. The en suite bedrooms, attractively decorated in chintzy style, come with colour TV, hospitality tray, hairdryer and direct-dial telephone. Breakfast, featuring freshly squeezed juices and local produce, is served in the bright, airy dining room. Exmouth is fifteen minutes walk away along the tree-lined and landscaped Madeira Walk. There are also several rural and coastal walks in the area and the estuary of the River Exe offers opportunities for birdwatching, sailing, fishing and windsurfing.

Recommended in the area

Crealy Adventure Park; Exeter; Bicton Park Botanical Gardens

The Devoncourt Hotel

★★★★ GUEST ACCOMMODATION

Address: 16 Douglas Avenue, EXMOUTH EX8 2EX
Tel: 01395 272277
Fax: 01395 269315
Email: enquiries@devoncourt.com
Website: www.devoncourt.com
Map ref: 2, SY08
Directions: M5/A376 to Exmouth, follow seafront to
Maer Rd, right at T-junct
Rooms: 10 en suite, S £40–70 D £65–99 Parking: 50
Notes: ⊗ on premises

Subtropical gardens sloping gently towards the sea and sandy beaches give an appealing Mediterranean character to this smart seaside hotel. The Devoncourt has an outdoor pool with sun terrace and loungers or explore the 4 acres of landscaped grounds and find the private access to the beach, tennis courts, croquet, putting greens and golf nets. If it does rain, the leisure complex offers an indoor pool, spa, sauna, steam room, solariums and fitness centre. Another major attraction here is the the snooker room, opened by Ray Reardon, which contains a world championship standard table. The various, well-equipped bedrooms – single, double and spacious family suites – are light and simple, decorated in pastel tones and patterned fabrics. They have tea- and coffee-making facilities, clock radio, telephone and digital colour TV. Guests can choose between eating in the informal bar or in Avenues restaurant, where picture windows frame the fantastic sea views and the cuisine satisfies all tastes. Among the spacious public areas, the sun lounge is a particularly lovely spot to enjoy a pot of tea and while away the day. Or you may even venture out and stroll along the seafront promenade to the mouth of the River Exe.

Recommended in the area

Bicton Park Botanical Gardens; Crealy Adventure Park; Exeter with its cathedral and excellent Maritime Museum; Dartmoor National Park

Leworthy Farm House

◆◆◆◆

Address:	Lower Leworthy, Nr Pyworthy, HOLSWORTHY EX22 6SJ
Tel:	01409 259469
Fax:	01409 259469
Email:	leworthyfarmhouse@yahoo.co.uk
Website:	www.leworthyfarmhouse.co.uk
Map ref:	1, SS30

Directions: From Holsworthy onto Bodmin St towards North Tamerton, 4th left signed Leworthy/Southdown
Rooms: 7 en suite, S £35–45 D £60–65
Parking: 8 Notes: ⊗ on premises ⊗ on premises

Pat and Phil Jennings' passions for the countryside, collecting books, curios and classical music, and meeting new people come together wonderfully at Leworthy Farmhouse. Spacious public rooms include a softly lit dining room with an oak parquet floor and colourful displays of old china, a peaceful drawing room with comfortable old sofas and armchairs and more displays of pictures and china, and a warmly decorated conservatory. Bedrooms, some with window seats, are beautifully furnished with pine or antique pieces and thoughtfully equipped with radio alarms, hairdryers, electric blankets, books and magazines. Hospitality trays are set with bone china, fresh milk, a selection of teas, coffees and chocolate, biscuits and fresh flowers. All the rooms are en suite and have ample supplies of soft towels and toiletries. A good choice of dishes is served at breakfast, and picnics are available by arrangement. Evening meals are not served here, but there are plenty of cafés, pubs and restaurants to choose from in the area. Leworthy is an ideal base for exploring Dartmoor and Bodmin Moor and the lovely villages of Clovelly, Tintagel, Boscastle and Padstow. Bude and its wonderful four-mile sweep of golden sand is also within easy driving distance. No pets are allowed.

Recommended in the area

Rosemoor Gardens; South West Coast Path; Dartington Glass

Courtmoor Farm

★★★★ FARMHOUSE

Address:	Upottery, HONITON EX14 9QA
Tel:	01404 861565
Email:	courtmoor.farm@btinternet.com
Website:	www.courtmoor.farm.btinternet.co.uk
Map ref:	2, ST20

Directions: Off A30, 0.5m W of A30 & A303 junct,
4m from Honiton
Rooms: 3 en suite, S £33–35 D £53–56
Parking: 20 **Notes:** ⊘ on premises ⊗ on premises
Closed: 20 Dec–1 Jan

Rosalind and Bob Buxton welcome you to their spacious farmhouse with marvellous views over the Otter valley. The extensive grounds are home to a flock of sheep and three ponies. Accommodation is provided in a family room, double room and twin, all equipped with digital televisions, hairdryers, electric blankets, clock radios and tea and coffee facilities. Dinner is available by arrangement on weekdays. The full English breakfast should easily satisfy but special diets can be catered for.
Recommended in the area
Honiton antiques shops and Lace Museum; Lyme Regis; Forde Abbey and Gardens

West Colwell Farm

★★★★★ B&B

Address:	Offwell, HONITON EX14 9SL
Tel:	01404 831130
Fax:	01404 831769
Email:	westcolwell@tiscali.co.uk
Website:	www.westcolwell.co.uk
Map ref:	2, ST19

Directions: Off A35 to village, at church go downhill,
farm 0.5m on right
Rooms: 3 en suite, S £50 D £70–75 **Parking:** 3 **Notes:**
⊘ on premises ⊗ on premises No children under 12 **Closed:** Xmas

Frank and Carol Hayes are enthusiastic hosts who enjoy welcoming guests. Their farm has a glorious setting down a peaceful country lane, in an Area of Outstanding Natural Beauty. The stylish, spacious bedrooms are in converted stone barns; two rooms on the ground floor open on to their own terraces. Breakfast of home-baked bread, fresh coffee and the best local produce is taken overlooking a wooded valley and fields. Country walks start right at your door – ask for the farm's own walks guide.
Recommended in the area
East Devon Heritage Coast; Shute Barton (NT); Honiton

Norbury House

★★★★ GUEST ACCOMMODATION

Address:	Torrs Park, ILFRACOMBE EX34 8AZ
Tel:	01271 863888
Email:	info@norburyhouse.co.uk
Website:	www.norburyhouse.co.uk
Map ref:	2, SS54

Directions: A361 from Barnstaple, 1st lights turn left, 2nd lights over & left again into Torrs Park, Norbury House on right at top of hill

Rooms: 6 en suite, S £40 D £65–80 **Parking:** 6 **Notes:** ⊘ on premises 🐾 allowed in bedrooms **Closed:** Open all year

Norbury House stands in a quiet elevated position with views over the town and the sea in the distance. Andy and Carole Walters have transformed the property, bringing contemporary style to this traditional Victorian residence. Well-equipped bedrooms have generous hospitality trays, and there is a choice of suites, super kingsize, family and double rooms. Breakfast is served in the pleasant dining room and dinner is available by arrangement. Meals are freshly prepared, using local produce whenever possible.

Recommended in the area

Marwood Hill Gardens; Arlington Court (NT); Lundy Island

Strathmore

★★★★ GUEST ACCOMMODATION

Address:	57 St Brannock's Road,
	ILFRACOMBE EX34 8EQ
Tel:	01271 862248
Fax:	01271 862248
Email:	peter@small6374.fsnet.co.uk
Website:	www.strathmore.ukhotels.com
Map ref:	2, SS54

Directions: A361 from Barnstaple to Ilfracombe, Strathmore 1.5m from Mullacot Cross entering Ilfracombe

Rooms: 8 en suite, S £30–35 D £56–76 **Parking:** 7 **Notes:** ⊘ on premises 🐾 allowed in bedrooms

There is a warm atmosphere at this charming Victorian property within easy walking distance of Ilfracombe town centre and harbour. Cottage-style, en suite bedrooms with many thoughtful extras provide a restful night's sleep. Set yourself up for the day with a choice of either a light continental breakfast or a generous full English, both served in the relaxed setting of the elegant dining room

Recommended in the area

Bicclescombe Park; Cairn Nature Reserve; Lundy Island; South West Coast Path

Tinhay Mill Guest House and Restaurant

★★★★ ◉ ⬭ 🍽 RESTAURANT WITH ROOMS

Address:	Tinhay, LIFTON PL16 0AJ
Tel:	01566 784201
Fax:	01566 784201
Email:	tinhay.mill@talk21.com
Website:	www.tinhaymillrestaurant.co.uk
Map ref:	1, SX38

Directions: A30/A388 approach Lifton, Guest House at bottom of village on right

Rooms: 5 en suite, S £50–57.50 D £70–80 Parking: 18 Notes: No children under 12

Our inspectors continue to be impressed by the standards of comfort, quality and hospitality at this lovely guesthouse. It is located close to the A30 and perfectly placed for touring Dartmoor or hopping across the border into Cornwall. The former mill cottages offer a cosy charm, with open fireplaces and exposed beams, and everything is geared to ensure that guests enjoy a relaxed and comfortable stay. Food is taken very seriously here too, and the restaurant, which has earned an AA Rosette award, is another good reason to stay. The dinner menu features a selection of well-cooked dishes that use only the finest and freshest local ingredients. Guests who suffer from food allergies or have special dietary requirements will also be glad to know that these can be taken into account with a little bit of notice. Breakfasts are no less special, and the range of items available include freshly squeezed juices, fruit salad and local sausages. The bedrooms are elegant and spacious, with en suite shower rooms, television, hair dryer and other extra touches. One bedroom is situated on the ground floor, with easy access, and so is ideal for anyone with mobility problems. It is clear that the thoughtful owners have kept everyone in mind in the planning and running of their excellent accommodation.

Recommended in the area

Dartmoor National Park; Devon/Cornwall Coast; Tamar Valley

Becky Falls, nr Manaton, Dartmoor National Park.

Eastwrey Barton

★★★★ 🛏 GUEST ACCOMMODATION

Address:	Moretonhampstead Road, LUSTLEIGH, Newton AbbotTQ13 9SN
Tel:	01647 277338
Fax:	01647 277133
Email:	info@eastwreybarton.co.uk
Website:	www.eastwreybarton.co.uk
Map ref:	2, SX78
Directions:	On A382 between Bovey Tracey and Moretonhampstead, 4m from A38

Rooms: 5 en suite, S £47–53 D £64–76 **Parking:** 18 **Notes:** ⊗ on premises ⊗ on premises
No children under 10

This Georgian country house is set within the Dartmoor National Park with numerous outdoor pursuits available nearby. The bedrooms have TV, tea and coffee facilities, hair dryer and fine Egyptian linen; and offer views over the surrounding countryside while cosy sitting rooms provide ample space to relax. A full Devon breakfast is served in the dining room, plus afternoon tea and dinner by arrangement.

Recommended in the area

Dartmoor National Park; Castle Drogo (NT); Lustleigh village

Moor View House

★★★★★ ⬭ GUEST ACCOMMODATION

Address:	Vale Down,
	LYDFORD EX20 4BB
Tel:	01822 820220
Fax:	01822 820220
Map ref:	2, SX38
Directions:	1m NE of Lydford on A386

Rooms: 4 en suite, S £50 D £65–80
Parking: 15 **Notes:** ⊘ on premises No children under 12

Built in 1869, Moor View House is a small licensed Victorian country house situated in large mature grounds on the western slopes of Dartmoor, where guests have enjoyed hospitality for more than a hundred years. The house has a very interesting history: in around 1900 it changed hands over a game of cards whilst in Edwardian times, the writer Eden Phillpotts visited and wrote the famous play *A Farmer's Wife* and the novel *Widecombe Fair*. Today, David and Wendy Sharples offer first class accommodation and friendly hospitality. There are four en suite bedrooms, each with TV, radio, hospitality trays and bathrobes amongst other facilities. During 2006, a large conservatory was built, leading from the drawing room to the garden beyond and this offers lovely views towards Cornwall in the distance. Sunsets are a delight to behold. Guests to the house are offered accommodation and a choice of English or Continental breakfast. Dinner is available by prior arrangement and Wendy's award-winning cooking uses locally-produced meat, fish, game and vegetables. There are also fine, sensibly-priced wines to compliment the good food. Moor View House is an ideal base from which to tour Devon and Cornwall's heritage sites, coast and, of course, Dartmoor; after which it is a delight to return and relax in Moor View's garden on warm evenings, or, on cooler days, around a blazing log fire in the traditionally-furnished reception rooms.

Recommended in the area

Lydford Gorge (NT); Tavistock; Eden Project

Bonnicott House

★★★★★ GUEST HOUSE

Address: Watersmeet Road, LYNMOUTH EX35 6EP
Tel: 01598 753346
Email: stay@bonnicott.com
Website: www.bonnicott.com
Map ref: 2, SS74
Directions: A39 from Minehead over East Lyn River Bridge, left onto Watersmeet Rd, 50yds on right opp church
Rooms: 8 (7 en suite), S £46–86 D £64–96 **Notes:** ⊘ on premises No pets No children under 14

In the heart of the lovely village of Lynmouth, on a particularly scenic stretch of the north Devon coast, you will find Bonnicott House, a Grade II listed former rectory of the church opposite. It stands in an elevated location, which endows it with unparalleled panoramic views over the village, the East Lyn valley and the sea. This is a lovely house with beautiful terraced gardens, where guests can relax in the sun to the sound of the tinkling water feature. But you don't have to go outside to enjoy the views – inside each of the rooms the eye is drawn to the window and the stunning vista beyond. This house also boasts a beautiful lounge where guests can congregate to chat or quietly enjoy a book, take tea or light afternoon refreshments, or have a drink from the licensed bar. In cooler months, a crackling log fire makes it even more inviting. The dining room, where award-winning breakfasts and cooked-to-order evening meals are served, has a double aspect with more of those terrific views. The bedrooms, each with its own private bathroom, are luxurious and comfortable and guests are not only provided with complimentary tea- and coffee-making supplies, but also a decanter of sherry. It is very peaceful here (children under 14 and pets are not accommodated), and the hosts ensure a charming, homely atmosphere.

Recommended in the area

Cliff Railway, Lynmouth; Watersmeet Lodge and tea gardens; Valley of the Rocks, Lynton.

The Heatherville

★★★★★ 🍴 🏠 GUEST ACCOMMODATION

Address: Tors Park, LYNMOUTH EX35 6NB
Tel: 01598 752327
Fax: 01598 752634
Website: www.heatherville.co.uk
Map ref: 2, SS74
Directions: Off A39 onto Tors Rd, 1st left fork into Tors Park
Rooms: 6 en suite, D £60–86 Parking: 7
Notes: ⊗ on premises 🚭 allowed in bedrooms
No children under 16 Closed: Dec–Jan

Having a secluded and elevated south-facing position, Victorian Heatherville has splendid views over the River Lyn and surrounding woodland, yet is only a short walk from the heart of picturesque Lynmouth. Tea and coffee are served on arrival in the welcoming lounge, and the bedrooms with spectacular views are a pleasure, lovingly restored to a high standard. They combine luxury with the charm of a large country house, using fine coordinated fabrics – some have canopies over the bed and all have a shower or bath en suite. All bedrooms are equipped with a colour TV, tea- and coffee-making facilities and a hairdryer and all benefit from magnificent views. These views can also be enjoyed from the garden, an ideal place to relax on warm days. An appetising full English breakfast, featuring organic and free-range produce whenever possible, gets the day off to a good start. Evening meals, by arrangement, feature traditional dishes such as Exmoor leg of lamb served by candlelight in the elegant dining room. There is also an intimate bar for a relaxing pre-dinner drink. Superb walks lead from the front door. A waterpowered Victorian cliff railway connects Lymnouth to its clifftop twin village of Lynton with its cafés, tea rooms and shops. Not far from Lynton is the rugged Valley of the Rocks with its spectacular rock formations, weathered by the elements, and sea views.

Recommended in the area

Exmoor National Park; Lynton and Lynmouth Cliff Railway; Lynton

Lynmouth, Exmoor.

Rock House

★★★★ ➔ GUEST ACCOMMODATION

Address:	Manor Grounds, LYNMOUTH EX35 6EN
Tel:	01598 753508
Fax:	01598 753796
Email:	enquiries@rock-house.co.uk
Website:	www.rock-house.co.uk
Map ref:	2, SS74

Directions: On A39, at foot of Countisbury Hill right onto drive, pass Manor green/play area to Rock House
Rooms: 8 en suite, S £41 D £82–88 **Parking:** 8
Notes: ➔ allowed in bedrooms **Closed:** 24–25 Dec

Set at the harbour entrance, this Grade II listed building has stunning views whichever way you look. Each room has an alarm clock and hospitality tray. The restaurant looks out over the harbour, and meals are served either here or in the licensed bar. Regular boat trips from the harbour explore the cliffs with their colonies of razorbills, guillemots and kittiwakes.
Recommended in the area
Beautiful waterfalls in the Lyn Valley; Valley of the Rocks; scenic railway to Lynton

Sea View Villa

★★★★★  GUEST ACCOMMODATION

Address: 6 Summer House Path,
LYNMOUTH EX35 6ES
Tel: 01598 753460
Fax: 01598 753496
Email: reservations@seaviewvilla.co.uk
Website: www.seaviewvilla.co.uk
Map ref: 2, SS74
Directions: A39 from Porlock, 1st left after bridge, Sea View Villa on right 20yds along path opp church
Rooms: 5 (3 en suite), D £90–110 **Notes:** ⊘ on premises No children under 14
Closed: Jan

"Through Devonshire countryside we have roamed to Lynmouth, to find our palatial home. Tastefully wrapped in all shades of vanilla. We found our peace within Sea View Villa." So wrote one satisfied guest, referring to Chris Bissex and Steve Williams' luxurious Lynmouth guesthouse. Steve and Chris bought the house in 2002, moving from London, where Steve was a design director for a department store chain and Chris was a drama teacher, and where they were both involved in the arts as performers and directors. Their dream was to open a bijou hotel offering incredible customer service and many thoughtful extras. The interiors are supremely elegant, with en suite rooms, plentiful hot water, powerful showers, and Egyptian cotton bed linen and bath towels. All the rooms have stunning sea views. Walking and surfing are popular local pursuits; and wonderful walks, directly from the door, include the Two Moors Way and Lynton's Valley of the Rocks. Picnic lunches, one aptly named the Hikers Feast, are available on request. Home-made bread is a feature of the English breakfast, and interesting alternatives include a vegetarian option, eggs Benedict or smoked salmon. Sea View is licensed and optional evening meals are available.

Recommended in the area

The Valley of the Rocks; Exmoor National Park; Watersmeet Valley

Highcliffe House

★★★★★ 🛏 🔔 GUEST ACCOMMODATION

Address: Sinai Hill,
LYNTON EX35 6AR
Tel: 01598 752235
Fax: 01598 753815
Email: info@highcliffehouse.co.uk
Website: www.highcliffehouse.co.uk
Map ref: 2, SS74
Directions: Off A39 into Lynton, signs for Old Village, at pub turn right up steep hill, house 150yds on left
Rooms: 6 en suite, S £56–66 D £72–96 **Parking:** 7 **Notes:** ⊘ on premises ⊗ on premises No children under 14 **Closed:** Dec to mid-Feb

Once a private summer residence, this beautifully restored house is now more widely accessible, thanks to Karen and Michael Orchard. They aim to exceed all expectations of accommodation, facilities and service, and you are unlikely to be disappointed. Highcliffe House stands in grounds with stunning views over the Exmoor hills, and across Lynmouth, the coastline and the Bristol Channel towards South Wales. The elegant en suite bedrooms are very spacious, each one individual in design, and some have beautifully carved king-size beds. Fine furnishings, a welcoming decanter of sherry, and a hospitality tray and colour TV/DVD are among the extras provided for your comfort. There are two inviting lounges, one with a splendid view. There are also fine views from the candlelit conservatory restaurant where imaginative home cooking is served in the evening. This is also the setting for breakfast when the choice includes a West Country breakfast, smoked salmon, and pancakes with bacon and maple syrup – all accompanied by home-made preserves, local honey, fresh coffee and a selection of teas. Plenty of lovely walks begin from outside the house which is just a short walk from the waterpowered cliff railway which links Lynton with Lynmouth.

Recommended in the area

Exmoor National Park; cliff railway between Lynton and Lynmouth; South West Coast Path

The grass-covered cliffs at Lynton, Exmoor.

Pine Lodge

◆◆◆◆

Address: Lynway, LYNTON EX35 6AX
Tel: 01598 753230
Email: info@pinelodgelynton.co.uk
Website: www.pinelodgelynton.co.uk
Map ref: 2, SS74
Directions: 500yds S of town centre off Lynbridge Rd
opp Bridge Inn
Rooms: 6 en suite, S £25 D £50–56 Parking: 6
Notes: ⊘ on premises No pets on premises
No children under 12 Closed: Nov, Dec and Jan

Soak up the gorgeous views of the wooded West Lyn valley from the vantage point of this secluded old house. Set in an acre of peaceful landscaped gardens, Pine Lodge was built in the 19th century in the area nicknamed Little Switzerland by the Victorians. Hospitality trays make you feel at home in the bedrooms, which have a shower or bathroom en suite. This is a paradise for walkers, with Exmoor right on the doorstep and the coast nearby. There is a 10% discount on stays of three nights or more.

Recommended in the area

Watersmeet House (NT); Valley of the Rocks, Lynton; Arlington Court (NT)

Gate House

♦♦♦♦♦

Address:	North Bovey, MORETONHAMPSTEAD TQ13 8RB
Tel:	01647 440479
Fax:	01647 440479
Email:	srw.gatehouse@virgin.net
Website:	www.gatehouseondartmoor.com
Map ref:	2, SX78
Directions:	B3212 from Moretonhampstead to North Bovey

Rooms: 3 (2 en suite), S £48–50 D £70–72 **Parking:** 3 **Notes:** ⊘ on premises 🐕 allowed in bedrooms No children under 15

In a fast changing world it is good to know that some things stay the same, and John and Sheila Williams have succeeded in preserving a little bit of old Devon. Both gave up busy careers to retreat to this Grade II listed 15th-century thatched house, with quaint windows tucked under the eaves, and pursue their dream. The result is an idyllic hideaway filled with character, where you can savour the atmosphere and relax. Welcomed by a pot of tea and scrumptious home-made cake, guests are shown to bedrooms decorated in country style, with a view of the garden or the moors. Downstairs in the oak-beamed sitting room, the wood-burning stove, set in a huge granite fireplace, is a magnet on cooler days. Hearty breakfasts feature local produce, and Sheila's supper trays are available by arrangement. The outdoor swimming pool in the large garden is lovely in summer, and the beauty of Dartmoor is all around. Gate House, situated in the heart of the attractive conservation village of North Bovey, with its old granite pack horse bridges and thatched cottages, is in an ideal location to explore the surrounding countryside. You can hike over the moors, take a walk along the banks of the River Teign or take a waymarked route through woodland to the delightful Becky Falls.

Recommended in the area

Buckland Abbey (NT); Castle Drogo (NT); Saltram (NT)

Hazelcott Bed & Breakfast

★★★★ 🏛 B&B

Address:	Manaton, MORETONHAMPSTEAD, Newton Abbot TQ13 9UY
Tel:	01647 221521
Fax:	01647 221405
Email:	hazelcott@dartmoordays.com
Website:	www.dartmoordays.com
Map ref:	2, SX78
Directions:	A38 onto A382 through Bovey Tracey to Manaton. Pass Kestor Inn, right at x-rds, 0.5m past church

Rooms: 3 en suite, S £30–40 D £50–75 **Parking:** 6 **Notes:** ⊘ on premises ⌁ on premises

Standing on the edge of Dartmoor, this secluded home from home accommodation is an ideal spot for families, ramblers and cyclists alike. The best features of the house itself must be the delightful surroundings and the fantastic panoramic views. The bedrooms vary in size and style but all have bathrooms en suite. The Haytor suite offers a touch of luxury – with its spa bath, essential oils and candles it is ideal for a romantic break. It also benefits from a library, TV and VCR and a music centre and can be used by a family as there is a sofa bed in the private lounge. Houndtor, a double room on the ground floor with excellent moorland views, has a TV, radio and armchair, and is suitable for those with mobility difficulties. Horsham is a light double room with large south-facing windows from which to enjoy the views. All room have wireless Internet access on request. Breakfast is a real treat, using local produce and cooked to perfection in the Aga. Home-made preserves are a feature. Carole and Nigel, runners-up for AA Landlady of the Year 2005, are keen to ensure you are looked after and welcome everyone with tea and coffee and a slice of delicious home-made cake.

Recommended in the area

Becky Falls Woodland Park; Canonteign Falls and Country Park; Dartmoor National Park; Castle Drogo (NT)

Smeeton's Tower, Britain's first lighthouse, Plymouth.

Berkeley's of St James

◆◆◆◆

Address:	4 St James Place East, The Hoe, PLYMOUTH PL1 3AS
Tel/Fax:	01752 221654
Email:	enquiry@onthehoe.co.uk
Website:	www.onthehoe.co.uk
Map ref:	1, SX45

Directions: Off A38 towards city centre, left at sign The Hoe, over 7 sets of lights, left onto Athenaeum St, right to Crescent Av, 1st left

Rooms: 5 en suite, S £38–40 D £60–65 Parking: 3 Notes: ⊘ on premises ⊗ on premises
Closed: 23 Dec–1 Jan

This welcoming guesthouse lies in a quiet secluded square on Plymouth Hoe, just a short walk from the promenade and city centre. Bedrooms are decorated in pastel shades and pretty floral bedspreads, and equipped with a number of thoughtful extras; family rooms are available. The substantial traditional breakfast uses organic dry cure bacon and sausages and free-range eggs supplied by local farms.

Recommended in the area

National Maritime Museum; Historic Barbican; Dartmoor National Park

Avalon – A Haven for Non Smokers

★★★★ GUEST HOUSE

Address: Vicarage Road, SIDMOUTH EX10 8UQ
Tel: 01395 513443
Email: owneravalon@aol.com
Website: www.avalonsidmouth.co.uk
Map ref: 2, SY18
Directions: From Exeter take A3052 at Sidford lights turn right. B&B is 1.3m on left.
Rooms: 4 en suite, (3D & 1T) £54–58 **Parking:** 4
Notes: ⊘ on premises ⊗ on premises No children
Closed: 10 Dec–15 Jan

Avalon is an elegant Edwardian house with many character features of a bygone era and it's frontage has several times won first prize in its class in the Britain in Bloom competition. Conveniently situated, its location offers the best of both worlds – just five minutes level walk from the town centre and ten minutes from the seafront – and its spacious garden backs onto breathtaking scenery and stretches right down to the River Sid (known as The Byes). Just a few steps away from the garden is a delightful National Trust park with tame ducks, some of which will feed from your hand. The park was made famous by Edward, Duke of Kent, who used to walk here with his daughter, the future Queen Victoria. The house has been lovingly restored by its present owner to combine comfort with tasteful décor. This is a small, friendly, family-run business, providing a mixture of double and twin rooms, including the four-poster room for that special occasion. Generous and tasty breakfast options include an imaginative vegetarian menu. There are two separate parking areas. The owners do not knowingly accommodate smokers.

Recommended in the area

The World of Country Life, Exmouth; Branscombe Beach; Seaton Tramway

Glendevon Hotel

◆◆◆◆

Address:	Cotmaton Road, SIDMOUTH EX10 8QX
Tel:	01395 514028
Email:	enquiries@glendevon-hotel.co.uk
Website:	www.glendevon-hotel.co.uk
Map ref:	2, SY18

Directions: A3052 onto B3176 to minirdbt. Right, house 100yds on right

Rooms: 8 en suite, S £30 D £60 Notes: ⊘ on premises ⊗ on premises No children

This comfortable hotel is in a peaceful location on the western side of Sidmouth, just a short walk from the town's leisure facilities and Esplanade. The bedrooms are all neatly presented with bathrooms en suite. There is a spacious lounge and a sunny terrace, and full English breakfasts are served at individual tables in the dining room. Evening meals, prepared from fresh local produce, are available by arrangement.

Recommended in the area

Connaught Gardens; The Byes; Exeter

The Salty Monk

★★★★★ ⊛⊛ 🍴 🍽

RESTAURANT WITH ROOMS

Address:	Church Street, Sidford, SIDMOUTH EX10 9QP
Tel:	01395 513174
Email:	saltymonk@btconnect.com
Website:	www.saltymonk.biz
Map ref:	2, SY18

Directions: On A3052 in Sidford opp church

Rooms: 5 en suite, S £70–95 D £100–180 Parking: 20

Notes: ⊘ on premises 🐾 allowed in some bedrooms

Closed: 2wks Nov & 3wks Jan

The Salty Monk is an attractive 16th-century property set in lovely countryside inthe village of Sidford, just 2 miles from the coast. Some of the well-presented rooms feature spa baths, hydro massage showers or a king size water bed. The restaurant is decorated in country-house style and overlooks the lovely gardens. The menu consists of contemporary English cuisine, created with the freshest of ingredients using mainly local produce in season. There is a courtyard patio for summer drinks.

Recommended in the area

Exeter; The Donkey Sanctuary; South West Coast Path

Strete Barton Farmhouse

★★★★ B&B

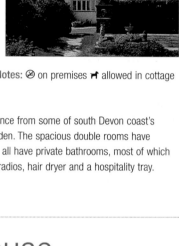

Address: Totnes Rd, STRETE, Dartmouth TQ6 0RN
Tel: 01803 770364
Fax: 01803 771182
Email: info@stretebarton.co.uk
Website: www.stretebarton.co.uk
Map ref: 2, SX84
Directions: From A38 take A384 to Totnes, onto A381/A3122 Dartmouth then A379 to Strete. B&B just below church.
Rooms: 6 (4 en suite), S £45–50 D £65–85 Parking: 4 Notes: ⊗ on premises 🐕 allowed in cottage No children under 2 Closed: 23–29 Dec

This beautifully refurbished farmhouse is only a short distance from some of south Devon coast's finest beaches – the coast path is 200 yards from the garden. The spacious double rooms have king-size beds (one has a super king-size four-poster) and all have private bathrooms, most of which are en suite. Rooms also have TV and DVD players, clock-radios, hair dryer and a hospitality tray.
Recommended in the area
Blackpool Sands; Woodlands Adventure Park; Dartmouth.

Thomas Luny House

★★★★★ 🏠 GUEST ACCOMMODATION

Address: Teign Street, TEIGNMOUTH TQ14 8EG
Tel: 01626 772976
Email: alisonandjohn@thomas-luny-house.co.uk
Website: www.thomas-luny-house.co.uk
Map ref: 2, SX97
Directions: A381 to Teignmouth, at 3rd lights turn right to quay, 50yds turn left onto Teign St, after 60yds turn right through white archway
Rooms: 4 en suite, S £65–70 D £80–92 Parking: 8
Notes: ⊗ on premises ⊗ on premises No children under 12

This delightful late 18th-century house is run by John and Alison Allan whose laid back yet attentive approach is appreciated by guests. The large drawing room and dining room are beautifully furnished while French doors open onto a walled garden. Home-made dishes and a full cooked breakfast are a speciality.
Recommended in the area
Tuckers Maltings; Powderham Castle; Cockington village

Colindale Hotel

★★★★★ ≗ GUEST ACCOMMODATION

Address:	20 Rathmore Road, Chelston,
	TORQUAY TQ2 6NY
Tel:	01803 293947
Email:	rathmore@blueyonder.co.uk
Website:	www.colindalehotel.co.uk
Map ref:	2, SX96

Directions: From Torquay station 200yds on left in Rathmore Rd

Rooms: 8 (6 en suite), S £35–40 D £60–75 Parking: 6

Notes: ⊗ on premises No children under 12 Closed: Dec

Barry Greenwood-Smith has worked as a butler for the rich and famous in Beverley Hills, Bermuda and Chelsea since the 1970s. Now he loves to share his home with visitors to Torquay. Well-kept grounds surround the elegant Victorian house set close to the sea. The bedrooms, some with views over Torbay, are mainly en suite and thoughtfully equipped to make you feel at home. Evening drinks are served in a snug bar, and there's a wonderful selection of books and videos in the pleasant sitting room.

Recommended in the area

Torre Abbey; Cockington village; Living Coasts Zoo

Crown Lodge

★★★★ GUEST ACCOMMODATION

Address:	83 Avenue Road, TORQUAY TQ2 5LH
Tel:	01803 298772
Fax:	01803 291155
Email:	john@www.crownlodgehotel.co.uk
Website:	www.crownlodgehotel.co.uk
Map ref:	2, SX96

Directions: A380 through Kingskerswell, over rdbt & 3 sets traffic lights, right at Torre Station

Rooms: 6 en suite, S £35 D £55–70 Parking: 7

Notes: ⊘ on premises ⊗ on premises No children under 12

This guest house is just a short, level walk from the seafront, shops and restaurants of Torquay's promenade. Inside, you'll find stylish and comfortable accommodation, with a ground floor room suitable for disabled guests. The level of comfort in the bedrooms is a particularly strong point. John and Lynda Leadbetter are affable hosts, and their diligent attention to detail makes for an enjoyable stay. Excellent home cooking ensures a satisfying breakfast and dinner (if required).

Recommended in the area

Paignton with its broad sandy beaches; Brixham harbour; South West Coast Path

Glenorleigh

★ ★ ★ ★ GUEST ACCOMMODATION

Address:	26 Cleveland Road, TORQUAY TQ2 5BE
Tel:	01803 292135
Fax:	01803 213717
Email:	glenorleighhotel@btinternet.com
Website:	www.glenorleigh.co.uk
Map ref:	2, SX96

Directions: A380 from Newton Abbot onto A3022, at Torre station lights right onto Avenue Rd & 1st left
Rooms: 15 (14 en suite), S £32–42 D £64–84
Parking: 10 **Notes:** ⊗ on premises

Set in a residential area, this family-run establishment has a range of smart bedrooms, a number of which are on the ground floor, some overlooking the garden. Other facilities including a solarium, a games room, and a heated outdoor swimming pool and terrace. All amenities are within walking distance, from shopping to water sports. The day starts with a hearty full English breakfast in the elegant dining room, while dinner is four courses of good home cooking with choices for vegetarian and special diets.
Recommended in the area
Living Coasts; Paignton Zoo; Babbacombe Model Village

Millbrook House Hotel

◆ ◆ ◆ ◆ ◆

Address:	1 Old Mill Road, Chelston,
	TORQUAY TQ2 6AP
Tel:	01803 297394
Fax:	01803 297394
Email:	jeffandmandyshatford@hotmail.com
Website:	www.millbrook-house-hotel.co.uk
Map ref:	2, SX96

Directions: A380 onto A3022, pass Torre station onto Avenue Rd, right at lights onto Old Mill Rd
Rooms: 9 en suite, S £25–30 D £50–70 **Parking:** 8 **Notes:** ⊘ on premises

Millbrook House is in a pleasing village location not far from the beaches and the centre of Torquay. Jeff and Mandy Shatford are enthusiastic hosts who offer attentive yet relaxed hospitality. Facilities here include a lovely lounge and conservatory and an elegant dining room overlooking the rear gardens and patio. There is also a well-stocked bar and a pool room. Bedrooms are all nicely decorated and well maintained, and include a four-poster room and a suite with its own lounge and patio.
Recommended in the area
Riviera Conference and Leisure Centre; Torre Abbey and Gardens; picturesque Cockington village

Mulberry House

Address:	1 Scarborough Road, TORQUAY TQ2 5UJ
Tel:	01803 213639
Fax:	01803 213639
Email:	stay@mulberryhousetorquay.co.uk
Website:	www.mulberryhousetorquay.co.uk
Map ref:	2, SX96

Directions: From Torquay seafront onto Belgrave Rd,
Scarborough Rd 1st right, house on corner
Rooms: 3 (2 en suite), S £40–52 D £60–80
Notes: ⊗ on premises ⊗ on premises

This Victorian gem, in the heart of Torquay, is just a short, level stroll to the seafront and the town centre. The young hostess Laura Wood is a natural, and helped by a friend she runs Mulberry House with great confidence and flair. The three spacious and immaculate bedrooms, The Tuckenhay, The Elberry and The Salcombe, are light and airy, and retain an abundance of original charm and character. Each room has either a private bathroom or an en suite, and is equipped with a colour TV, music system with a wake up alarm, luxury bathrobes, fresh flowers, fresh fruit, spring water and tea- and coffee-making facilities. Facilities for families include a cot, a childs' bed, games, books and teddy bears. Wiine, drinks and local and home-made produce are available for purchase from a cart on the landing. The food is a very important part of a stay here. Freshly prepared creative English cuisine, using the highest quality local seasonal produce is available in the licensed restaurant served at round tables with crisp white table cloths, fresh flowers and polished cutlery. On cooler evenings, a cosy log fire burns in the softly lit lounge, where you can enjoy a pre-diner drink while relaxing to gentle music. On Torquay's waterfront you'll find a promenade, seafront gardens, a harbour and an marina and close by are beautiful beaches.

Recommended in the area

Kent's Cavern; Cockington Forge; coastal walks

The Durant Arms

★★★★ 🛏 INN

Address: Ashprington, TOTNES TQ9 7UP
Tel: 01803 732240
Email: info@thedurantarms.com
Website: www.thedurantarms.com
Map ref: 2, SX85
Directions: A381 from Totnes for Kingsbridge,
1m left for Ashprington
Rooms: 7 (4 en suite) **Parking:** 8 **Notes:** ⊘ on premises
⊗ on premises No children **Closed:** Xmas and Boxing
Day evenings

Immaculate whitewashed walls and masses of well-tended shrubs and plants make this traditional country inn a focal point in the picturesque village of Ashprington, deep in the heart of Devon's South Hams district. Owners Eileen and Graham Ellis proudly offer their own brand of hospitality and provide attractive accommodation in either the main building or a refurbished annexe. The bedrooms are individually designed to a very high standard, using stylish furnishings, and include a host of thoughtful touches to help ensure a memorable stay. Each room has a luxurious well-appointed en suite bathroom that adds additional comfort. The inn is renowned locally for its delicious food. A blackboard menu of home-cooked food is available in the character bar or the smart dining room, both furnished in rich red velvets. All dishes are freshly cooked to order, offering fresh vegetables and a wide variety of meat and fish; seasonal local produce is used whenever possible. To compliment your meal there is a good choice of real ales, beers and wines, some from the local Sharpham Vineyard, just a 15-minute walk away and open to the public for visiting and wine tasting. There are stunning views of the River Dart from this delightful inn and a short walk from the village will take you directly alongside the riverbank. Packed lunches are available.

Recommended in the area

Historic Totnes; The Eden Project; Sharpham Vineyard

Eastacott Barton

◆◆◆◆◆

Address:	UMBERLEIGH EX37 9AJ
Tel:	01769 540545
Email:	stay@eastacott.com
Website:	www.eastacott.com
Map ref:	2, SS62

Directions: 1m E of Umberleigh. Off B3227 signed Eastacott, straight on at stone cross, Eastacott Barton 700yds on left
Rooms: 5 en suite, S £50–95 D £70–115 **Parking:** 8
Notes: ⊘ on premises 🐕 allowed in bedrooms

Sue and James Murray's peaceful stone farmhouse stands in 27 acres with stunning views over the Taw Valley. The bedrooms are generously appointed with stylish modern bathrooms, stereo systems and quality linen. Three rooms are in a converted barn just across a courtyard, and all rooms share the same magnificent views. Superb breakfasts offer considerable choice, including porridge, kippers and home-made croissants. Dinner is available for large parties only. A self-catering cottage is also available.
Recommended in the area
RHS Garden Rosemoor; Dartington Crystal; Arlington Court (NT)

Harrabeer Country House Hotel

★★★★ 🛏 GUEST ACCOMMODATION

Address:	Harrowbeer Lane,
	YELVERTON PL20 6EA
Tel:	01822 853302
Email:	reception@harrabeer.co.uk
Website:	www.harrabeer.co.uk
Map ref:	2, SX56

Directions: In village. Off A386 Tavistock Rd onto Grange Rd, right onto Harrowbeer Ln
Rooms: 6 (5 en suite), S £48–80 D £65–95 **Parking:** 10 **Notes:** ⊘ on premises 🐕 allowed in bedrooms **Closed:** 3rd wk Dec, 2nd wk Jan

This traditional Devon longhouse on the edge of Dartmoor has a relaxing lounge, a bar for a convivial evening drink and well-equipped comfortable bedrooms. Breakfast is a leisurely affair served in the dining room, and dinner can be served by arrangement. Self-catering accommodation is available.
Recommended in the area
The Garden House; The Eden Project; Dartmoor National Park

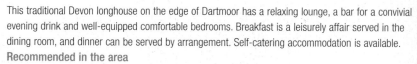

DORSET

Gold Hill, Shaftesbury.

Portman Lodge

★★★★★ B&B

Address: Whitecliff Mill Street,
             BLANDFORD FORUM DT11 7BP
Tel/Fax: 01258 453727
Email: enquiries@portmanlodge.co.uk
Website: www.portmanlodge.co.uk
Map ref: 2, ST80
Directions: On NW end of Blandford's one-way system,
follow signs from town centre to Shaftesbury & hospital
Rooms: 3 en suite, S £45–50 D £65 Parking: 6
Notes: ⊘ on premises No pets on premises No children under 10

Hospitable owners Barbara and Robin Wrigley have filled their Victorian home with mementoes of their extensive travels, including interesting artefacts, rugs and paintings. Relax and make yourself at home in the elegant accommodation, which includes a spacious lounge and bedrooms equipped with hairdryers and courtesy trays. Breakfast is a special occasion, using fresh local produce, while delicious dinners are produced with great skill from quality ingredients.
Recommended in the area
Georgian Blandford Forum; Monkey World; Jurassic Coast World Heritage Site

The Balincourt Hotel

★★★★★ GUEST ACCOMMODATION

Address: 58 Christchurch Road,
             BOURNEMOUTH BH1 3PF
Tel/Fax: 01202 552962
Email: rooms@balincourt.co.uk
Website: www.balincourt.co.uk
Map ref: 3, SZ09
Directions: On A35 between Lansdowne & Boscombe
Gardens, opp Lynton Court pub
Rooms: 12 en suite, S £40–70 D £70–80 Parking: 11
Notes: ⊘ on premises ⊗ on premises No children under 16 Closed: Xmas

Owners Alison and Nigel Gandolfi are natural hosts, and you will very quickly feel at home in their delightful establishment. It's an ideal touring base, and the beach and town centre are easily reached on foot. The wide choice of individual bedrooms includes two on the ground floor. Each of the en suite rooms features a hairdryer and a generous hospitality tray. The comfy armchairs in the bar-lounge are a magnet in the evenings, and traditional English cooking is served in the elegant dining room.
Recommended in the area
New Forest National Park; Bournemouth seafront; Poole Harbour and Brownsea Island

Cransley Hotel

★★★★ GUEST ACCOMMODATION

Address:	11 Knyveton Road, East Cliff,
	BOURNEMOUTH BH1 3QG
Tel:	01202 290067
Fax:	07092 381721
Email:	info@cransley.com
Website:	www.cransley.com
Map ref:	3, SZ09
Directions:	Off A338 at St Pauls rdbt by ASDA store,

over next rdbt, Knyveton Rd 1st left

Rooms: 11 (10 en suite), S £25–35 D £50–70 **Parking:** 8 **Notes:** ⊗ on premises ⊗ on premises
No children under 14

A quiet road in Bournemouth's East Cliff area is the setting for this comfortable property owned by Simon Goodwin and Jonathan Perry. The bedrooms are bright and welcoming, and most have bath or shower en suite. Patio doors lead from the sitting room to the south-facing garden, and the dining room, scene of traditional breakfasts (and evening meals by arrangement), is elegant and well furnished.

Recommended in the area

New Forest National Park; Thomas Hardy Country; Poole Harbour and Brownsea Island

Westcotes House Hotel

★★★★ GUEST HOUSE

Address:	9 Southbourne Overcliff Drive, Southbourne,
	BOURNEMOUTH BH6 3TE
Tel:	01202 428512
Website:	www.westcoteshousehotel.co.uk
Map ref:	3, SZ09
Directions:	2m E of town centre. A35 onto B3059

and seafront road, 1m E of pier

Rooms: 6 en suite, S £40–46 D £60–80 **Parking:** 6
Notes: ⊗ on premises No children under 10

Overlooking Poole Bay from the cliff top at Southbourne, this small establishment is elegantly decorated and has private parking. The conservatory-lounge leads onto a sunny sea-facing terrace, and a zigzag path and cliff lift give easy access to the promenade and sandy beach. All the rooms are en suite and your friendly hosts Brenda and Christopher Burrell have added numerous extras including bathrobes, tissues and toiletries. One of the bedrooms is on the ground floor. Excellent home cooking is served in the well-presented dining room, which has sea views. Dinner is available by arrangement.

Recommended in the area

Poole Harbour; Thomas Hardy Country; Bournemouth

The Roundham House

★★★★★ GUEST ACCOMMODATION

Address:	Roundham Gardens, West Bay Road, BRIDPORT DT6 4BD
Tel:	01308 422753
Fax:	01308 421500
Email:	cyprencom@compuserve.com
Website:	www.roundhamhouse.co.uk
Map ref:	2, SY49
Directions:	A35 into Bridport, at the Crown Inn rdbt take exit signed West Bay. Hotel 400yds on left

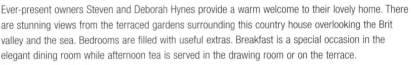

Rooms: 8 (7 en suite), S £49–57 D £77–115 **Parking:** 10 **Notes:** ⊘ on premises ⌇ allowed in bedrooms No children under 7 Snack and sandwiches available every evening **Closed:** Jan–Feb

Ever-present owners Steven and Deborah Hynes provide a warm welcome to their lovely home. There are stunning views from the terraced gardens surrounding this country house overlooking the Brit valley and the sea. Bedrooms are filled with useful extras. Breakfast is a special occasion in the elegant dining room while afternoon tea is served in the drawing room or on the terrace.

Recommended in the area

Abbotsbury Swannery and Gardens; Montacute House (NT); Forde Abbey and Gardens

---

Cashmoor House

★★★★ FARMHOUSE

Address:	CASHMOOR, Blandford DT11 8DN
Tel:	01725 552339
Email:	spencer@cashmoorhouse.co.uk
Website:	www.cashmoorhouse.co.uk
Map ref:	2, ST91
Directions:	On A354 Salisbury to Blandford, 3m S of Sixpenny Handley rdbt just past Inn on the Chase

Rooms: 4 en suite, S £30 D £45.50 **Parking:** 8
Notes: ⊘ on premises ⌇ allowed in bedrooms

Cashmoor House dates back to the 17th century and many original features can be seen throughout the farmhouse. Located in the village of Sixpenny Handley, halfway between Blandford and Salisbury, it is a perfect base for exploring the local countryside. The bedrooms have charming touches such as hand-embroidered quilts, tapestries and pretty furnishings. All rooms have TV and hot drink making facilities. The traditional breakfast is a treat, featuring home-made bread and preserves and eggs laid by the owners' hens, all served in the beamed dining room with its attractive open fireplace.

Recommended in the area

Salisbury Cathedral; Larmer Tree Pleasure Gardens; Cranborne Manor

Baytree House Dorchester

★★★★ B&B

Address: 4 Athelstan Road, DORCHESTER DT1 1NR
Tel: 01305 263696
Map ref: 2, SY69
Directions: Situated on S side of Dorchester, 0.5m from town centre.
Rooms: 3 en suite, S £27–30 D £53–60 **Parking:** 3
Notes: ⊘ on premises ⊗ on premises

In 2006 owners Nicola and Gary Cutler completely refurbished Baytree House, creating a stylish place to stay, with spacious and light rooms, contemporary décor and luxurious fittings. Although it is set in a quiet residential area, it's just a 10-minute stroll to the historic centre of Dorchester and a short drive to many of rural Dorset's attractions. The bedrooms offer either en suite shower room or a private bathroom, which has shower and bath. The Cutlers also own the Walnut Grove Restaurant and Coffee Shop in the town centre, and employ the same high standards of cooking at Baytree House. Guests are offered a 15 percent discount on meals at the Walnut Grove.

Recommended in the area

Thomas Hardy's Cottage; Monkey World; Dorset's Jurassic coastline.

The Casterbridge Hotel

★★★★★ ⌂ GUEST ACCOMMODATION

Address: 49 High East Street,
DORCHESTER DT1 1HU
Tel: 01305 264043
Fax: 01305 260884
Email: reception@casterbridgehotel.co.uk
Website: www.casterbridgehotel.co.uk
Map ref: 2, SY60
Directions: In town centre, 75yds from town clock
Rooms: 14 en suite, S £58–78 D £95–125 **Parking:** 2
Notes: ⊗ on premises **Closed:** 24–26 Dec

This well-run establishment provides a traditional English welcome, with cheerful attentive staff and a high standard of accommodation. Public rooms include an elegant dining room, drawing room, and a cosy bar-library. Breakfast in the conservatory is an extensive buffet or individually cooked breakfasts. All bedrooms are en suite with either bath or shower, tea and coffee facilities, direct-dial telephones, and one room is suitable for families. Children are welcome and high chairs are available.

Recommended in the area

Thomas Hardy Museum; Abbotsbury Swannery; Lulworth Cove

Little Court

★★★★★ 🏠 GUEST ACCOMMODATION

Address:	5 Westleaze, Charminster,
	DORCHESTER DT2 9PZ
Tel:	01305 261576
Fax:	01305 261359
Email:	info@littlecourt.net
Website:	www.littlecourt.net
Map ref:	2, SY69

Directions: A37 from Dorchester, 0.25m right at Loders Garage, Little Court 0.5m on right
Rooms: 8 en suite, S £69–89 D £69–89 Parking: 10 Notes: ⊘ on premises ⊗ on premises

A picture-postcard Edwardian house, Little Court nestles in 4 acres of beautiful grounds and gardens. The property has been refurbished to a very high standard and the proprietors are on hand to ensure you have a excellent stay. Bedrooms have a bath and shower en suite, and come with extras such as binoculars and even an umbrella. A delicious breakfast, including home-grown produce, is served in the dining room which adjoins a restful lounge with log fires. A pub nearby serves good food.
Recommended in the area
Jurassic Coast World Heritage Coast; Dorchester; Weymouth

Yalbury Cottage Hotel & Restaurant

★★★★★ 🏵🏵 🚼 GUEST HOUSE

Address:	Lower Bockhampton,
	DORCHESTER DT2 8PZ
Tel:	01305 262382
Email:	yalburyemails@aol.com
Website:	www.yalburycottage.com
Map ref:	2, SY69

Directions: Off A35 past Thomas Hardys cottage, over x-rds, 400yds on left, past telephone box, opp village pump
Rooms: 8 en suite, S £59–61 D £94–98 Parking: 16 Notes: 🐎 allowed in bedrooms

Situated in peaceful countryside, thatched Yalbury Cottage dates from the 17th century. The pretty restaurant serves excellent food, in an atmosphere enhanced by oak beams and inglenook fireplaces. The cosy lounge, the only part of the building where smoking is permitted, is also in the old part of the building. The spacious, well-equipped cottage-style bedrooms are in the modern annexe.
Recommended in the area
Thomas Hardy's birthplace; Athelhampton House; walks in a conservation area

Farnham Farm House

★★★★★ GUEST ACCOMMODATION

Address: FARNHAM, Blandford Forum DT11 8DG
Tel: 01725 516254
Fax: 01725 516306
Email: info@farnhamfarmhouse.co.uk
Website: www.farnhamfarmhouse.co.uk
Map ref: 2, SU84
Directions: Off A354 Thickthorn x-rds into Farnham, continue NW from village centre T-junct, 1m bear right
Rooms: 3 en suite, S £50 D £80 Parking: 7 Notes: ⊗ on premises ⊗ on premises Closed: 25–26 Dec

Farnham Farm House with its flagstone floors, open log fires and magnificent views dates back to the 1850s. Guests can walk around the 350-acre working farm, part of a private estate owned by the descendants of archaeologist General Pitt-Rivers. Facilities include a heated outdoor swimming pool, and the Sarpenela Treatment room for therapeutic massage and natural therapies. Delicious Aga-cooked breakfasts are served in the attractive dining room. Local produce is used whenever possible.
Recommended in the area
Cranborne Chase; Kingston Lacey (NT); Larmer Tree Gardens

Frampton House

◆◆◆◆◆

Address: FRAMPTON DT2 9NH
Tel: 01300 320308
Fax: 01300 321600
Email: maynardryder@btconnect.com
Map ref: 2, SY69
Directions: A356 into village, from green over bridge & left onto driveway past houses
Rooms: 2 en suite, S £65 D £85 Parking: 8
Notes: No children under 8

Georgina and Nicholas Maynard make you feel instantly at home when you enter their delightful property in this quiet village just outside Dorchester. Set back in landscaped grounds up a gravel drive, two Labradors run to greet you as you approach the Grade II listed building, which provides exceptionally high standards of quality and comfort throughout. One of the bedrooms is a double with a four-poster bed and the other is a twin room. Dinner by arrangement is highly recommended at Frampton House.
Recommended in the area
Weymouth; Cerne Abbas Giant; Dorchester

The Cricketers

◆◆◆◆◆

Address:	Main Street, IWERNE COURTNEY
	OR SHROTON, Blandford Forum DT11 8QD
Tel:	01258 860421
Fax:	01258 861800
Map ref:	2, ST68
Directions:	Establishment signed from A350

Blandford-Shaftesbury road, 0.25m on village green
Rooms: 1 en suite, S £45–50 D £70–75 Parking: 19
Notes: ⊗ on premises

The epitome of the best kind of English country pub, the creeper-clad Cricketers is across the road from the village green and is a social hub for the people who live here in the heart of Dorset's Cranborne Chase, officially designated an "Area of Outstanding Natural Beauty". The pub's cricket theme includes displays of sports memorabilia and hand pumps for the real ales which are shaped like cricket bats. And during the summer months the local cricket team really do frequent the establishment. Any concern that the peace might be disturbed by the lively discourse of the regulars in the bar can swiftly be set aside, since the accommodation is peacefully contained within an annexe garden room. Visitors can be sure of a degree of pampering here, too, because, with only one guest room, they are assured of all the attention they need. The friendly, personal service extended by proprietors is one of the hallmarks that have earned The Cricketers the AA's top quality rating. Naturally, the accommodation here is of a particularly high standard, too, with lots of thoughtful extras adding to guests' comfort. In addition to the en suite bathroom, the room is equipped with a TV and tea- and coffee-making facilities. Dinner is available in the pub's no-smoking dining room, with options ranging from a choice of bar snacks to a tempting range of interesting well-cooked daily specials from an extensive blackboard menu.

Recommended in the area

Poole and Brownsea Island; Bournemouth; Athelhampton House and Gardens

Ware Barn B&B

★ ★ ★ ★ ★ B&B

Address:	Ware Lane, Ware Cross, LYME REGIS DT7 3EL
Tel:	01297 442472
Fax:	01297 442472
Email:	info@kanta-enterprises.com
Website:	www.bedandbreakfasts-uk.co.uk/ submitbot.htm
Map ref:	2, SY39
Directions:	0.5m W of town centre off A3052

Rooms: 4 en suite, S £45–65 D £90–150 **Parking:** 12 **Notes:** ⊘ on premises ⊗ on premises

This newly converted barn sits in an area of outstanding natural beauty with views overlooking the sea and the famous Cobb, the setting for the film, *The French Lieutenant's Woman* (1981), starring Meryl Streep and Jeremy Irons. Just a short walk along Ware Lane is Lower Cliff, where there are paths to Lyme Regis, Seaton and other resorts along this fine stretch of coast. The house is well placed to visit both Dorset and Devon. Set in cleverly designed landscaping, peace and tranquility are the keynote of a stay at Ware Barn. An impressive wooden staircase leads up to the spacious en suite bedrooms attractive beamed ceilings, all of which are comfortably furnished and decorated to a high standard. One bathroom features a whirlpool bath. All rooms have tea and coffee making facilities, hairdryer and TV. The master bedroom, which also doubles as a family room, has a private dressing room. Downstairs there is a cosy sitting room with an inglenook fireplace, a pretty garden room and a separate TV room. Breakfast is served at individual tables in the oak panelled dining room. Dishes, including vegetarian options, are prepared using the best of local West Country produce and packed lunches are also available on request.

Recommended in the area

Seaton Tramway; Pecorama, Beer; Forde Abbey

The Poachers Inn

★★★★ INN

Address: PIDDLETRENTHIDE DT2 7QX
Tel: 01300 348358
Fax: 01300 348153
Email: thepoachersinn@piddletrenthide.
             fsbusiness.co.uk
Website: www.thepoachersinn.co.uk
Map ref: 2, SY79
Directions: 8m N from Dorchester on B3143, inn on left
Rooms: 21 en suite, S £52 D £74 Parking: 40
Notes: 🐕 allowed in bedrooms

The River Piddle flows gently through the garden of this delightful 17th-century family-run inn. Original features survive in the character bar and dining areas, and open fires and traditional pub games add to the atmosphere. The inn is known for its good home-cooked food – ranging from fish and seafood to game, pasta, steaks, vegetarian and traditional Dorset dishes – which can be served in the garden or next to the swimming pool on fine days. Snacks and cream teas are also available. The pool is heated during the summer, and set in an enclosed sun trap with parasols and padded sun recliners. Tasty traditional breakfasts are cooked to order, there's full Dorset breakfast or kippers to follow your choice from a table full of cereals, juices, yoghurts and fruit. The tastefully furnished bedrooms are in a modern extension surrounding the pool area, and are furnished with quality pieces. Some have baths in addition to showers, and each has a colour TV, hairdryer, hospitality tray, radio and direct-dial telephone. A suite with a king-size double bed, mini-fridge, Jacuzzi and wet room, and its own sitting room is a good choice for a special occasion. The village of Piddletrenthide lies in picturesque countryside within close proximity to the coast and the county town of Dorchester, with its wealth of museums.

Recommended in the area

Monkey World; Bovington Tank Museum; Thomas Hardy's Cottage (NT)

Munden House

Address: Munden Lane, Alweston,
SHERBORNE DT9 5HU
Tel: 01963 23150
Fax: 01963 23153
Email: admin@mundenhouse.demon.co.uk
Website: www.mundenhouse.co.uk
Map ref: 2, ST61
Directions: A3030 Sherborne to Sturminster Newton,
2nd left after post office
Rooms: 9 en suite, S £45–55 D £85–95
Parking: 13 **Notes:** ⊘ on premises

Munden House is everything you would expect of a rural
Dorset bed and breakfast. Its pleasing group of buildings,
arranged on two sides of a gravel courtyard, include a
pretty thatched cottage, with mellow tiled roofs stepping up and down on either side. From the house
and its well-tended grounds there are far reaching views across Blackmore Vale to the distant hills,
and the historic town of Sherborne is near by. Inside, each part of the house has retained its own
character, with exposed stone walls and a huge fireplace in the sitting room, an elegant breakfast
room, and individually styled bedrooms, some with antiques and others with more contemporary
furnishings. Each has an en suite bathroom and is equipped with TV, telephone, trouser press, hair
dryer and a generous hospitality tray. There are also three suites, complete with own kitchenette.
Proprietors Michael and Judith Rust have imbued Munden House with a great sense of style, and
their attention to detail reflects their enthusiasm and desire to offer the very best to their guests.
This extends to the delicious and satisfying breakfasts, which features locally sourced produce of
the highest quality.

Recommended in the area

Barrington Court (NT); Worldwide Butterflies; Fleet Air Arm Museum

Stourcastle Lodge

★★★★ GUEST HOUSE

Address: Goughs Close,
STURMINSTER NEWTON DT10 1BU
Tel: 01258 472320
Fax: 01258 473381
Email: enquiries@stourcastle-lodge.co.uk
Website: www.stourcastle-lodge.co.uk
Map ref: 2, ST71
Directions: Off town square opp cross
Rooms: 5 en suite, S £50–57 D £82–96 Parking: 8
Notes: ⊘ on premises ⊗ on premises No children

This splendid 18th-century family home is traditionally decorated and set in delightful cottage-style gardens. Jill and Ken Hookham-Bassett provide delicious meals, prepared from local produce, and served in the dining room which overlooks the picturesque gardens. For chillier evenings there is a cosy lounge complete with a log fire. The spacious bedrooms are furnished with antique brass bedsteads as well as modern conveniences such as bathrooms en suite with showers or whirlpool baths.
Recommended in the area
Stourhead (NT); Kingston Lacey (NT); Dorset country walks

Esplanade Hotel

★★★★ GUEST ACCOMMODATION

Address: 141 The Esplanade, WEYMOUTH DT4 7NJ
Tel/Fax: 01305 783129
Email: esplanadehotel@weymouth10.fsnet.co.uk
Website: www.theesplanadehotel.co.uk
Map ref: 2, SY67
Directions: E end of Esplanade, opp pier bandstand
Rooms: 11 en suite, S £30–42 D £50–72 Parking: 9
Notes: ⊘ on premises ⊗ on premises
No children under 4 Closed: Nov–Jan & 1st 2wks Feb

You are assured of a warm welcome from owners Colin and Brenda Jolliffe at this Georgian seafront terrace where the front-facing public rooms all have fabulous views of beautiful Weymouth Bay. The good-sized en suite rooms are particularly well furnished and attractively decorated, with many thoughtful extras – some have views over the sea. There are ground-floor bedrooms too and parking is available.
Recommended in the area
Abbotsbury Swannery; Dorset beaches; Sea Life Park

COUNTY DURHAM

Weardale Valley.

White water of Cauldron Snout.

Clow Beck House

★★★★★ 🛏 🍴 GUEST ACCOMMODATION

Address: Monk End Farm, Croft on Tees,
DARLINGTON DL2 2SW
Tel: 01325 721075
Fax: 01325 720419
Email: heather@clowbeckhouse.co.uk
Website: www.clowbeckhouse.co.uk
Map ref: 7, NZ21
Directions: 3m S of Darlington. In Croft-on-Tees on
A167 follow brown tourist signs to Clow Beck House
Rooms: 13 en suite, S £80 D £120 **Parking:** 15 **Notes:** Closed: Xmas & New Year

Clow Beck House gets its name from the beck that winds its way through the grounds of the farm to meet the River Tees, providing a perfect opportunity for trout fishing. The bedrooms, decorated to give a sense of period style, are in a cottage and in separate chalets in the gardens. The inviting lounge and the beamed dining room, where imaginative dishes and a good wine list are available, are in the house itself. Heather and David Armstrong are dedicated to making you feel at home.

Recommended in the area

Raby Castle; Beamish Open Air Museum; Yorkshire Dales and Moors

Hillrise Guest House

★ ★ ★   GUEST ACCOMMODATION

Address: 13 Durham Road West,
Bowburn,
DURHAM DH6 5AU
Tel: 0191 377 0302
Fax: 0191 377 0898
Email: enquiries@hill-rise.com
Website: www.hill-rise.com
Map ref: 7, NZ24
Directions: 4m SE of Durham. A1(M) junct 61 onto
A177, Hillrise 300yds on left
Rooms: 5 en suite, S £35 D £60–70
Notes: ⊘ on premises ⊗ on premises
No children under 5

Small and friendly, this guest house exudes hospitality and comfort. Durham city centre is just a few miles away, and the nearby A1(M) is an ideal transport link for visiting the many places of interest in the surrounding area. The bedrooms offer versatile accommodation that includes double, twin-bed and family rooms, all with private facilities. Furnishings and soft fabrics are smart and modern, and the rooms are equipped with colour TV and hospitality trays. The comfortable lounge with inviting leather seating has a television and a huge video collection. Hearty breakfasts are served in the bright and airy dining room, from where there is access to an enclosed garden terrace. Your host is George Webster, who has had long experience in the hotel trade and offers a warm welcome to all his guests. Although there is a no-smoking policy throughout the building, smokers can use the small patio area in the garden.

Recommended in the area

Beamish, The North of England Open Air Museum; Durham Cathedral and Castle; ruins of Finchale Priory; The Bowes Museum, Barnard Castle

The small signal box at Marley Hill.

Greenhead Country House Hotel

◆◆◆◆

Address: FIR TREE, Crook DL15 8BL
Tel/Fax: 01388 763143
Email: info@thegreenheadhotel.co.uk
Website: www.thegreenheadhotel.co.uk
Map ref: 7, NZ13
Directions: Off A68 at Fir Tree Inn E onto unclassified rd
Rooms: 8 en suite, S £60 D £75 **Parking:** 20
Notes: ⊘ on premises No children under 13

Greenhead is an extended early 18th-century property, just 500 yards from the A68, set in well-tended gardens at the foot of Weardale. It is convenient for Durham and the Durham Dales. The bedrooms are spacious and modern, one has a four-poster bed. The central stone arched lounge is a relaxed centre for planning excursions. There are three restaurants in Fir Tree, all serving dinner, and two are within easy walking distance. Menus are available to view in the house, no advance booking is required.

Recommended in the area

Durham Cathedral; Beamish Open Air Museum; Weardale Area of Outstanding Natural Beauty

Beth Chatto Gardens near Elmstead Market.

Chudleigh

★ ★ ★ ★   GUEST ACCOMMODATION

Address:	13 Agate Road, Marine Parade West, CLACTON-ON-SEA CO15 1RA
Tel:	01255 425407
Fax:	01255 470280
Email:	reception@chudleighhotel.com
Website:	www.tiscover.co.uk/chudleigh-hotel
Map ref:	4, TM11

Directions: Follow town centre/seafront & pier signs.
Right at seafront, after lights at pier right into Agate Road
Rooms: 10 en suite, S £41 D £60–62 Parking: 7
Notes: ✄ allowed in bedrooms

With its unique architecture, its front terrace with outdoor furniture and its masses of flowers spilling out of window boxes, tubs and hanging baskets, Chudleigh is a distinctive landmark near the Clacton sea front. The pier and the main shopping centre are both within a short distance, making this an ideal spot for both business and leisure visitors to the town, but it is nevertheless a peaceful place to stay. For more than three decades it has been run with dedication and enthusiasm by Carol and Peter Oleggini, who, as might be surmised from their name, can converse fluently with Italian-speaking guests. Service here is pleasantly informal, but attention to detail and high standards of housekeeping are paramount. It's a delicate balance, perfectly achieved, which brings many guests back time and time again. The bedrooms are very attractive, with coordinating décor, comfortable beds and chairs, en suite bathrooms and facilities such as televisions, direct-dial telephones and tea- and coffee-making supplies. There are also spacious family rooms. Downstairs there's a residents' lounge with a television, and an extensive breakfast menu is on offer in the dining room, where the separate tables are dressed with linen tablecloths.

Recommended in the area

Sandy beaches of the Essex coast; Colchester; Beth Chatto Gardens

The White House

★★★★ GUEST ACCOMMODATION

Address:	Smiths Green, TAKELEY CM22 6NR
Tel:	01279 870257
Fax:	01279 870423
Email:	enquiries@whitehousestansted.co.uk
Website:	www.whitehousestansted.co.uk
Map ref:	4, TL52

Directions: 400yds E of Takeley village x-rds on corner of B1256 & Smiths Green

Rooms: 3 (2 en suite), S £60 D £65 Parking: 6

Notes: ⊘ on premises ⊗ on premises

Closed: 24–25, 31 Dec & 1 Jan

This carefully refurbished family home displays many original 16th-century features alongside modern comforts. The Grade II listed building is close to Stansted Airport, but not on the flight path, and is enclosed by extensive gardens. Accommodation is stylish with large beds, and one room has a luxurious private Victorian bathroom with a roll top bath. All rooms have luxury bathrobes, radio alarm clocks, hairdryers, tea- and coffee-making facilities and colour TV/DVD. High speed wireless internet connection is available upon request. Served around one table in the farmhouse-style kitchen, the excellent traditional cooked breakfast is a wholesome start to the day. Evening meals are not available at the White House but a range of interesting dishes, using quality local ingredients, are served in the restaurant at the Lion and Lamb, a traditional English pub situated a mile up the road, which is owned by the same proprietors who offer free transport to and fro. The pub also serves a range of bar meals and has a beer garden with ample seating on wooden picnic benches.

Recommended in the area

Hatfield Forest (NT); Duxford Imperial War Museum; Newmarket Races

Colchester Castle Museum.

The Granary

★★★★ FARMHOUSE

Address:	Clarks Farm, Cranes Lane, Kelvedon, WITHAM CO5 9AY
Tel:	01376 570321
Fax:	01376 570321
Email:	enquiries@thegranary.me.uk
Website:	www.thegranary.me.uk
Map ref:	4, TL81
Directions:	3m N of Witham. A12 N onto B1024 towards Kelvedon, 1st left & follow signs

Rooms: 5 en suite, S £34–70 D £55–75 **Parking:** 10 **Notes:** ⊘ on premises ⊗ on premises

Set in the open countryside that surrounds Clarks Farm, The Granary consists of delightfully converted farm buildings adjacent to the main farmhouse – in all a pleasing ensemble in a neat well-tended grounds. An appropriate country theme is followed through in the bedrooms which have thoughtful homely touches, and three of them have room for an extra bed to be added for family stays. Guests go over to the farmhouse for Janet Cullen's delicious breakfasts, which are served at individual tables.

Recommended in the area

Colchester Castle and Zoo; Coggeshall barns; Constable country; Cressing Temple Barns

GLOUCESTERSHIRE

River Windrush, Bourton-on-the-Water.

Viney Hill Country Guesthouse

★★★★ GUEST HOUSE

Address:	Lower Viney Hill, BLAKENEY GL15 4LT
Tel:	01594 516000
Fax:	01594 516018
Email:	info@vineyhill.com
Website:	www.vineyhill.com
Map ref:	2, SO60

Directions: 2.5m from Lydney off A48 signed Viney Hill
Rooms: 7 en suite, D £50–70 Parking: 7
Notes: ⊘ on premises ⊗ on premises

The position of this period house on the fringes of the Forest of Dean makes it an excellent base for exploring the surrounding countryside. Mature well-tended gardens with wonderful views pay tribute to the high standard of accommodation found inside. Originally a working farm built in 1741, the property has been tastefully renovated throughout. Pretty en suite bedrooms with TV, hospitality trays and hairdryers provide a comfortable stay. There is a choice of lounges and a licensed dining room where breakfast is served.

Recommended in the area

Dean Forest Railway; Prinknash Abbey; Slimbridge Wildfowl Trust

Badger Towers

★★★★ GUEST ACCOMMODATION

Address:	133 Hales Road,
	CHELTENHAM GL52 6ST
Tel:	01242 522583
Fax:	01242 574800
Email:	MrBadger@BadgerTowers.co.uk
Website:	www.BadgerTowers.co.uk
Map ref:	2, SO92

Directions: Off A40 onto Hales Rd, 0.5m on right
Rooms: 7 en suite, S £45–55 D £65–120 Parking: 8
Notes: ⊘ on premises ↝ accepted by arrangement Closed: Xmas & New Year

A comfortable, relaxed atmosphere is felt as soon as you enter this impressive Victorian property, set in a quiet residential area. Owners Claire and Peter Christensen offer elegantly decorated and furnished bedrooms, including two on the ground floor. The breakfast room, where a full English breakfast is freshly cooked from locally sourced produce, is bright and cheerful, and there is a spacious sitting room.

Recommended in the area

Sudeley Castle; Prestbury Park; Cheltenham Promenade and Montpellier

Beaumont House

★★★★ GUEST ACCOMMODATION

Address:	56 Shurdington Road, CHELTENHAM GL53 0JE
Tel:	01242 223311
Fax:	01242 520044
Email:	reservations@bhhotel.co.uk
Website:	www.bhhotel.co.uk
Map ref:	2, SO92
Directions:	S side of town on A46 to Stroud

Rooms: 16 en suite, S £59–77 D £79–193
Parking: 16 Notes: ⊘ on premises ⊗ on premises
No children under 5

In a city noted for its fine Regency architecture, this former villa, built in the 1850s and converted into a hotel in the 1980s, is an ideal place to stay. It's just a pleasant 15-minute walk from the Montpelier area of the city centre and its many attractions, but is far enough from the hustle and bustle to offer a relaxed and peaceful atmosphere at the end of a busy day's sightseeing. Contributing greatly to the tranquillity are the beautiful gardens, where guests can enjoy drinks on fine summer evenings, and the ample car parking is another asset. The friendly Bishop family are now at the helm, and they have completely renovated the place over the last couple of years, including enhancements to the bedrooms – all of which have en suite bathrooms – and the creation of two stunning premier rooms (Asia and Africa) complete with luxury whirlpool baths, power showers and large flat screen televisions, set the scene for the further improvements that are in the pipeline. Public areas include a comfortable lounge, where guests can sink into a comfortable chair and enjoy a complimentary cappuccino or a drink from the "trust bar". Dinner is not served at Beaumont House, but there are a number of excellent restaurants within a short walk.

Recommended in the area

Cheltenham Art Gallery and Museum; Holst Birthplace Museum; Cotswold Way

Holly House

★★★★ B&B

Address: Ebrington, CHIPPING CAMPDEN GL55 6NL
Tel: 01386 593213
Email: hutsbybandb@aol.com
Website: www.hollyhousebandb.co.uk
Map ref: 3, SP13
Directions: B4035 from Chipping Campden towards
Shipston on Stour, 0.5m left to Ebrington & signed
Rooms: 3 en suite S £40–65 D £55–65 Parking: 5
Notes: ⊘ on premises ⊗ on premises
Closed: Xmas

A picturesque Cotswold village is the appealing setting for this Victorian guest house surrounded by quaint thatched cottages and close to the Norman village church. The en suite ground-floor bedrooms are in converted outbuildings around a courtyard – each room is thoughtfully equipped and has its own private entrance. Delicious Cotswold breakfasts are served in the cosy dining room. Parking spaces are plentiful, and the village pub serving traditional food is a short walk away.

Recommended in the area

Hidcote Manor Gardens (NT); Stratford-upon-Avon; Snowshill Manor (NT)

The Moda Hotel

★★★★ GUEST ACCOMMODATION

Address: 1 High Street,
CHIPPING SODBURY BS37 6BA
Tel: 01454 312135
Fax: 01454 850090
Email: enquiries@modahotel.com
Website: www.modahotel.com
Map ref: 3, ST78
Directions: In town centre
Rooms: 10 en suite, S £58.50–62 D £75–98
Notes: ⊘ on premises ⋔ allowed in bedrooms

This Grade II Georgian house has modern bedrooms and restful public areas while retaining original features. Jo and Duncan MacArthur offer a first-class personalised service and provide an excellent English breakfast sourced from local suppliers. Chipping Sodbury is an ideal base for exploration as well as offering pubs and restaurants within a short walk.

Recommended in the area

Bath; Westonbirt Arboretum; Dyrham Park (NT)

Hare & Hounds

★★★★ ☘ 🍵 INN

Address:	Fosse-Cross, Chedworth,
	CIRENCESTER GL54 4NN
Tel:	01285 720288
Fax:	01285 720488
Email:	stay@hareandhoundsinn.com
Website:	www.hareandhoundsinn.com
Map ref:	3, SP00
Directions:	A419/A417 onto A429 Stow Rd. B&B

by speed camera

Rooms: 10 en suite, S £60–80 D £65–85 **Parking:** 40 **Notes:** ⊘ on premises

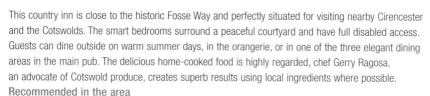

This country inn is close to the historic Fosse Way and perfectly situated for visiting nearby Cirencester and the Cotswolds. The smart bedrooms surround a peaceful courtyard and have full disabled access. Guests can dine outside on warm summer days, in the orangerie, or in one of the three elegant dining areas in the main pub. The delicious home-cooked food is highly regarded, chef Gerry Ragosa, an advocate of Cotswold produce, creates superb results using local ingredients where possible.

Recommended in the area

Chedworth Roman Villa (NT); Cheltenham; Cotswold Wildlife Park

Chapel Cottage

★★★★ GUEST ACCOMMODATION

Address:	3 Chapel Road, Berry Hill,
	COLEFORD GL16 7QY
Tel:	01594 836547
Email:	chapelcottagefod@btinternet.com
Website:	www.chapelcottagebedandbreakfast.co.uk
Map ref:	2, SO51
Directions:	Off A4136 at Five Acres onto Park Rd. 1st

left, B&B 200yds on left

Rooms: 3 en suite, D £60 **Parking:** 3

Notes: ⊘ on premises ⊗ on premises

The welcome at Chapel Cottage is very genuine and the friendly proprietor makes every effort to ensure you have a relaxing and comfortable stay. This lovely 19th-century cottage is well situated for exploring the The Forest of Dean, Chepstow, Monmouth and Ross-On-Wye. The attractive bedrooms are furnished to a high standard and come with a host of thoughtful extras – the stylish modern bathrooms are also of a high quality. Breakfast is a tasty event, served in the light and airy dining room.

Recommended in the area

Tintern Abbey; Forest of Dean; Wye Valley

The Plough Inn

★★★★ INN

Address:	FORD, Temple Guiting GL54 5RU
Tel:	01386 584215
Fax:	01386 584042
Email:	info@theploughinnatford.co.uk
Website:	www.theploughinnatford.co.uk
Map ref:	3, SP02
Directions:	On B4077 in village

Rooms: 3 en suite S £35 D £70 Parking: 50
Notes: ⊗ on premises

Here at the Plough you can find everything that is traditionally associated with an English inn – exposed beams, flagstone floors, solid wood furniture, and log fires lighting up many comfortable nooks and crannies. This charming 16th-century pub in the hamlet of Ford is popular for a drink (two traditional Donnington Ales are available along with Addlestones Cider and a select wine list) or a meal, and is a comfortable base for visiting the area. It offers accommodation in a converted stable block opening out onto a courtyard, next to the pretty beer garden. The inviting rooms are well equipped, and a good breakfast will set you up for the day. Home-cooked food is a feature of the bar and restaurant. A comprehensive blackboard menu features daily specials using seasonal local produce when available – fresh asparagus in season is a speciality. In addition to the blackboardd and set menu, a traditional roast is served all day on Sundays and Julian, the head chef, is happy to cater for special dietary needs such as gluten-free, dairy-free and vegetarian requirements. The nearby historic towns and villages of Stow-on-the-Wold, Broadway and Tewkesbury offer a variety of museums, antique and craft shops and other visitor attractions. There are fine walks (guides detailing local walks are available), cycling, fishing and golf in close proximity. For racing enthusiasts, the famous racing stables of Jackdaws Castle are opposite and Cheltenham, home of the National Hunt Festival, is nearby.

Recommended in the area

Sudeley Castle; Cotswold Farm Park; Birdland

Guiting Guest House

★★★★ 🍽 GUEST HOUSE

Address:	Post Office Lane, GUITING POWER, Cheltenham GL54 5TZ
Tel:	01451 850470
Email:	info@guitingguesthouse.com
Website:	www.guitingguesthouse.com
Map ref:	3, SP02
Directions:	In village centre

Rooms: 7 (5 en suite), S £38.50 D £72–77 Parking: 3
Notes: ⊘ on premises ⊗ on premises

Guiting is an engaging family home at one with its surroundings in a beautiful Cotswold village. Bedrooms are individually decorated and full of charm. Most have facilities en suite and four-poster beds, and all of them are equipped with hairdryers, bathrobes, quality toiletries, and hospitality trays with biscuits, fresh fruit and flowers. Exposed beams, inglenook fireplaces, solid elm floorboards and candlelight provide character in the inviting public rooms. Breakfast and evening meals, based on fresh local produce, are served in the dining room. Please give at least 24 hours notice for a dinner booking.

Recommended in the area

Cotswold Farm Park; Sudeley Castle; Blenheim Palace

Cambrai Lodge

★★★★ GUEST ACCOMMODATION

Address:	Oak Street, LECHLADE ON THAMES GL7 3AY
Tel:	01367 253173
Email:	www.cambrailodge@btconnect.com
Website:	www.cambrailodgeguesthouse.co.uk
Map ref:	3, SU29
Directions:	In town centre, off High St onto A361 Oak St

Rooms: 7 (5 en suite), S £30–45 D £50–75 Parking: 12 Notes: ⊘ on premises 🐕 allowed in bedrooms

This pleasant house, on the edge of the market town of Lechlade, is only a stroll from a number of pubs serving food – owner John Titchener will be happy to recommend places. The bedrooms are all carefully decorated and furnished. Some rooms are in a pretty cottage across the garden and include a four poster, and there are two ground-floor bedrooms. All the rooms have tea and coffee facilities and central heating. Hearty breakfasts are served in the conservatory overlooking the large gardens.

Recommended in the area

Cirencester; Oxford; The Cotswolds

Heavens Above at The Mad Hatters Restaurant

★★★★ ◉ ⇔ RESTAURANT WITH ROOMS

Address: 3 Cossack Square, NAILSWORTH GL6 0DB
Tel/Fax: 01453 832615
Email: mafindlay@waitrose.com
Map ref: 2, ST89
Directions: In town centre. Off A46 onto Spring Hill, left onto Old Market
Rooms: 3 (1 en suite), S £45 D £70
Notes: ⊘ on premises ⊗ on premises

Set in the heart of Nailsworth, with its individual shops and art galleries, this guest house is located above a delightful organic restaurant. The spacious bedrooms have the feel of a comfortable country home, complete with pine furniture and bay windows looking out onto the village street below. The intimate dining rooms are furnished in the style of a traditional parlour. The restaurant uses fresh, organic ingredients, many grown on the premises and simply prepared with love and care.

Recommended in the area

Ruskin Mill; Rivers Gallery; Ropestore Studio Gallery.

Highlands

◆◆◆◆

Address: Shortwood, NAILSWORTH, Stroud GL6 0SJ
Tel: 01453 832591
Fax: 01453 833590
Map ref: 2, ST89
Directions: Off A46 rdbt in Nailsworth onto Nympsfield road, turn left, pass bus station, fork left at Brittania Inn, follow signs for Wallow Green, Highlands opp church
Rooms: 3 en suite, S £30 D £55 **Parking:** 3
Notes: ⊘ on premises ⊗ on premises
No children under 8

Standing proud in an elevated position on the outskirts of this unspoilt town, Highlands is immaculately presented throughout, demonstrating great care and attention to detail. The bedrooms are comfortable, well co-ordinated with stylish furnishings and finished with considerate extras. There is a light and airy conservatory-lounge and breakfast is taken in the bright dining room. Nailsworth itself is in a superb location for easy access to the gentle hillsides and sleepy villages of the Cotswolds.

Recommended in the area

Stroud; Ruskin Mill; Westonbirt Arboretum

Northfield B&B

★★★★ GUEST ACCOMMODATION

Address:	Cirencester Road, NORTHLEACH GL54 3JL
Tel:	01451 860427
Fax:	01451 860427
Email:	nrthfield0@aol.com
Website:	www.northfieldbandb.co.uk
Map ref:	3, SP11

Directions: Signed off A429 Northleach-Cirencester road, 1m from Northleach lights

Rooms: 3 en suite, S £45–65 D £60–80 **Parking:** 10

Notes: ⊘ on premises ⊗ on premises **Closed:** 23–31 Dec

Animals graze in the fields around this Cotswold stone house set in immaculate gardens. Indoors there is a clear commitment to presentation and the bedrooms are a pleasure to stay in – two rooms have direct access to the gardens. The relaxing atmosphere extends to the lounge. The friendly dining room is the scene of delicious country breakfasts including eggs from the resident hens. Northleach is convenient for Cirencester and Gloucester.

Recommended in the area

Chedworth Roman Villa (NT); Keith Harding's Musical Museum; Cheltenham; Stow-on-the-Wold

Aston House

★★★★ B&B

Address:	Broadwell, STOW-ON-THE-WOLD GL56 0TJ
Tel:	01451 830475
Email:	fja@netcomuk.co.uk
Website:	www.astonhouse.net
Map ref:	3, SP12

Directions: A429 from Stow-on-the-Wold towards Moreton-in-Marsh, 1m right at x-rds to Broadwell, Aston House 0.5m on left

Rooms: 3 (2 en suite), D £58–60 **Parking:** 3

Notes: ⊘ on premises ⊗ on premises No children under 10 **Closed:** Nov–Feb

The enthusiastic owner ensures that the accommodation has every comfort, with armchairs in all the rooms, electric blankets and fans. Other amenities include quality toiletries in the en suite bathrooms, televisions, radios and hairdryers, tea-making facilities and bedtime drinks and biscuits. Although rooms are not suitable for wheelchair-bound visitors, the stair lift is a boon for those with limited mobility. A full English breakfast is served and there is a good pub within walking distance.

Recommended in the area

Cotswolds villages; Blenheim Palace; Hidcote Manor Gardens

Kings Head Inn & Restaurant

★★★★ 🍴 INN

Address: The Green,
Bledington,
STOW-ON-THE-WOLD OX7 6XQ
Tel: 01608 658365
Fax: 01608 658902
Email: kingshead@orr-ewing.com
Website: www.kingsheadinn.net
Map ref: 3, SP12
Directions: 4m SE off B4450

Rooms: 12 en suite, S £55–60 D £70–125 **Parking:** 24 **Notes:** ⊗ on premises
Closed: 25–26 Dec

Located next to the picturesque village green with a brook running past, this classic English country pub is well worth seeking out. In the 16th century it was used as a cider house, and its timeless interior, full of charm and character, has low ceilings, beams, exposed stone walls and open fires. Nicola Orr-Ewing was once a milliner in London, and she has used her creative talents to transform the accommodation. Husband Archie, born in the next village, helps to maintain a relaxed but efficient atmosphere. The stylish bedrooms are individually decorated and each has a modern bathroom. Some rooms are above the inn (these are full of character and have standard double beds), while others are in a quiet courtyard annexe set well back from the pub. These annexe rooms have king-size beds and are more spacious than those in the main building. All rooms have wireless Internet access and televisions. Tasty meals, using locally sourced and organic produce where possible, are served in the smart restaurant. The Aberdeen Angus beef comes from the family's own farm in a neighbouring village and the vegetables from the Vale of Evesham. The interesting breakfast menu offers a choice of delicious and sustaining dishes.

Recommended in the area

Blenheim Palace; Cotswold Farm Park; Cheltenham Races

Pittville Park, Cheltenham.

Rectory Farmhouse

♦♦♦♦♦

Address:	Lower Swell, STOW-ON-THE-WOLD, Cheltenham GL54 1LH
Tel:	01451 832351
Email:	rectory.farmhouse@cw-warwick.co.uk
Map ref:	3, SP12

Directions: B4068 from Stow-on-the-Wold signed Lower Swell, left before Golden Ball Inn onto private road, farmhouse at end of gravel driveway

Rooms: 2 en suite, D £85–90 **Parking:** 6

Notes: ⊘ on premises ⊗ on premises No children under 16

Discerning guests will love this Grade II listed 17th-century former farmhouse set in the pretty hamlet of Swell. Robert and Sybil Gisby enjoy having guests and not surprisingly have many return visits. Bedrooms are full of thoughtful extras, and have superb bathrooms with immaculate fittings. The spacious lounge with wood-burning stove is full of charm, while tasty country breakfasts are served in the elegant dining room. The excellent restaurants and inns nearby are further advantages.

Recommended in the area

Hidcote Manor Garden (NT); Stunning country walks; Stratford-upon-Avon theatre

Wesley House

★★★★ ◉◉ RESTAURANT WITH ROOMS

Address: High Street,
              WINCHCOMBE GL54 5LJ
Tel: 01242 602366
Fax: 01242 609046
Email: enquiries@wesleyhouse.co.uk
Website: www.wesleyhouse.co.uk
Map ref: 3, SP02
Directions: On High Street – B4632 between
Cheltenham and Broadway
Rooms: 5 en suite, S £65 D £80–95 (dinner B&B only
on Sat nights) **Notes:** ⊘ on premises ⊗ on premises
Closed: 25–26 Dec

At the heart of Winchcombe, one of the prettiest little
towns in the Cotswolds, Wesley House is an old timber-framed house that has been sympathetically
restored. Its name recalls the fact that John Wesley, the leader of the Methodist movement, stayed
at the house in 1755 and 1779 while he was preaching in the town (one of the bedrooms is called
"The Preacher's Room"). The double rooms are named after the fields surrounding nearby Sudeley
Castle and one has a private terrace overlooking the North Cotswold Edge. All of the bedrooms are
individually designed and combine the charm of exposed beams and antique furniture with a stylish
décor that features richly coloured fabrics and modern comforts such as en suite bathrooms, TV and
telephones. The public areas, too, are pleasing and harmonious, with a unique lighting system that
changes colour to suit the mood and stunning floral arrangements created by a world-renowned flower

arranger. Another contemporary touch is the
air-conditioned glass atrium that now covers the
terrace, from where there are lovely Cotswold
views. The food served at Wesley House has
won a well-deserved reputation that extends far
beyond the bounds of the town. The menu
is varied and exciting, featuring such complex
dishes as grilled noisette of Cornish lamb,
merguez, sweet potato purée, piquillo pepper and
coriander jus, and the excellent award-winning
wine list has a bias towards South Africa. There's
also a trendy wine, tapas bar and grill. Wesley
House is an ideal base from which to explore
the local area.

Recommended in the area

Sudeley Castle and Gardens; Broadway;
Cotswold Heritage Centre, Northleach;
Cheltenham Racecourse; Gloucester; Cotswold
Way; Hailes Abbey (NT); Snowshill Manor (NT)

Dobcross, Pennine hills.

Dunham Massey Hall, Altrincham.

Ash Farm Country House

♦♦♦♦♦

Address:	Park Lane, Little Bollington, ALTRINCHAM WA14 4TJ
Tel:	0161 929 9290
Fax:	0161 928 5002
Email:	jan@ashfarm97.fsnet.co.uk
Website:	www.ashfarm.co.uk
Map ref:	6, SJ78
Directions:	Off A56 beside Home (pub)

Rooms: 3 (2 en suite), S £51–58 D £69–82 **Parking:** 6

Notes: ⊗ on premises ⊗ on premises No children under 12 **Closed:** 22 Dec–5 Jan

An appealing 18th-century farmhouse with country views, Ash Farm is full of character and extends a warm welcome. Situated in a quiet village at the heart of National Trust countryside, the property is a short walk from Dunham Deer Park and the Bridgewater Canal. Several rooms have antique beds and all provide facilities en suite. Finishing touches include bathrobes, fresh fruit, mineral water, biscuits and toiletries. There is an attractive lounge and a breakfast room with views over the valley.

Recommended in the area

Manchester city centre; Dunham Massey (NT); Tatton Park (NT)

The Moorfield Arms

★★★★ INN

Address:	Shiloh Road, MELLOR, Stockport SK6 5NE
Tel:	0161 427 1580
Fax:	0161 427 1582
Email:	info@moorfieldarms.co.uk
Website:	www.moorfieldarms.co.uk
Map ref:	7, SJ98

Directions: 1m NE of Mellor. Off A6015 towards Mellor, right onto Shiloh Rd, B&B 0.3m on left

Rooms: 4 en suite, D £70–90
Parking: 100

This 400-year-old farmhouse is located in an elevated position on the border of Cheshire and Derbyshire and benefits from stunning views over the surrounding countryside and Kinder Scout. It has been renovated and extended to provide spacious, comfortable public areas and carefully furnished modern bedrooms in a converted barn. The Moorfield Arms is perfectly placed for visiting the nearby Peak District National Park, for superb walking and for the numerous attractions in the area. The en suite boutique bedrooms are equipped with tea-and coffee-making facilities and have a flat screen colour TV. One room has a four-poster bed and there is also a family room. There is a choice of a traditional full English or continental breakfast to set you up for the day. The excellent restaurant, a combination of traditional country inn and gastropub, is open seven days a week, 365 days a year. During the summer months the garden terrace with fine views is the perfect place to have your meal. Diners can choose from an extensive à la carte menu, a regularly changing specials board and a lunchtime three-course board. Fresh local ingredients are used in the preparation of meals where possible. On Sundays a carvery is set up in the function room. This room is also used for private parties, conferences and special occasions.

Recommended in the area

Pennine Way; Blue John Cavern and Mine, Castleton; Chatsworth House; Lyme Park (NT); Buxton

New and renovated buildings beside the canal basin in Manchester

Brooklands Luxury Lodge

★★★★ GUEST ACCOMMODATION

Address: 208 Marsland Road, SALE M33 3NE
Tel: 0161 973 3283
Map ref: 6, SJ79
Directions: M60 junct 6, 1.5m on A6144 near
Brooklands tram station
Rooms: 5 (4 en suite), S £30–45 D £50–60
Parking: 7 **Notes:** ⊗ on premises ⊗ on premises
No children under 5

This is a most unusual brick building, dating from the Victorian era but constructed to an Austrian design. The lovely Cheshire countryside is close at hand, and it's just a short walk to the tram station for easy access into central Manchester. Brooklands' imposing entrance leads into a home that provides a high standard of accommodation and plenty of privacy. The comfortable studio bedrooms all have easy chairs, dressing/writing tables, mini-fridges with complimentary fresh milk, yoghurt and fruit juice, remote-controlled TVs and hairdryers. Home cooked meals are served in the room, including continental or full cooked breakfast and an early evening meal (if booked in advance).

Recommended in the area

Trafford Shopping and Leisure Centre; Lowry Centre; Lancashire County Cricket Ground

HAMPSHIRE

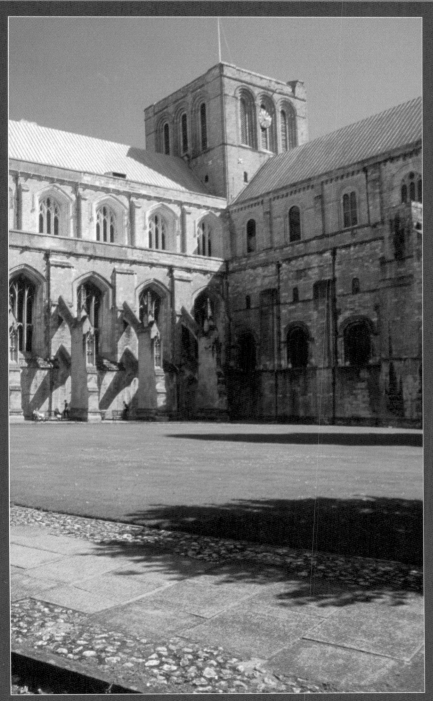

Winchester Cathedral.

Beech Barns Guest House

★★★★ GUEST HOUSE

Address:	61 Wellhouse Road, Beech,
	ALTON GU34 4AQ
Tel:	01420 85575
Fax:	01420 85575
Email:	timsiggs@yahoo.com
Website:	www.beechbarns.co.uk
Map ref:	3, SU73

Directions: A339 towards Beech. Take 2nd right, Wellhouse Rd, continue for 0.5m, on left

Rooms: 9 en suite, S £55–80 D £80–110 **Parking:** 12 **Notes:** 🖝 allowed in bedrooms

This rambling house and barn conversion, believed to date from the early 18th century, is set in its own grounds on the outskirts of Alton, where there are plenty of opportunities for walking and cycling in glorious countryside. The en suite bedrooms are attractively decorated with a blend of contemporary and traditional styles. There is a games and TV room and a separate lounge. Outside a large patio area is perfect for relaxing when enjoying tea and home-made cakes. Dinner is available on request.

Recommended in the area

Jane Austen's House; Gilbert White's House and The Oates Museum; Winchester

The Cottage Hotel

◆◆◆◆◆

Address:	Sway Road, BROCKENHURST SO42 7SH
Tel:	01590 622296
Fax:	01590 623014
Email:	enquiries@cottagehotel.org
Website:	www.cottagehotel.org
Map ref:	3, SU30

Directions: Off A337 opp Careys Manor Hotel onto Grigg Ln, 0.25m over x-rds, cottage next to war memorial

Rooms: 9 en suite, S £50–120 D £50–170 **Parking:** 14

Notes: ⊘ on premises No children under 10 **Closed:** Xmas and New Year

Owners David and Christina welcome guests to the cosy 17th-century Cottage Hotel with tea or coffee, served in front of the roaring fire in the Snug Bar. The village of Brockenhurst is one of the few New Forest settlements where grazing ponies and cattle still have right of way. The hotel is a short walk from the railway station and only 200 yards from the high street, cycle hire, and the open forest. The individually furnished bedrooms are en suite and a local New Forest breakfast is served.

Recommended in the area

National Motor Museum, Beaulieu; Exbury Gardens; walking, cycling and horse riding

36 on the Quay

★★★★　◎◎◎　RESTAURANT WITH ROOMS

Address:　47 South Street, EMSWORTH PO10 7EG
Tel:　01243 375592
Website:　www.36onthequay.co.uk
Map ref:　3, SU70
Directions:　On A259. From A3(M) take junct 2
Rooms: 5 en suite, S £70–90 D £95–150 **Parking:** 6
Notes: 🐾 allowed in bedrooms **Closed:** 3wks Jan,
1wk Oct

Located in a picturesque fishing village, this 16th-century house occupies a prime position with far-reaching views over the bay. It is the ideal setting to experience some accomplished and exciting cuisine. The stylish en suite rooms are a joy to relax in with their muted colours and sense of space. Charmingly named Nutmeg, Vanilla, Clove and Cinnamon they have great views and come equipped with colour TV, bathrobes, hospitality tray and toiletries. The lounge and summer terrace are perfect for breakfast or a drink. Centre stage goes to the elegant restaurant with its peaceful pastel shades where you can enjoy expertly cooked dishes, using fresh produce to create flavoursome, quality cuisine.
Recommended in the area
Chichester; Weald and Downland Open Air Museum; Portsmouth Historic Dockyard

Tudorwood Guest House

★★★★　GUEST HOUSE

Address:　164 Farnborough Road,
　　　　　　FARNBOROUGH GU14 7JJ
Tel:　01252 541123
Email:　info@tudorwood.net
Website:　www.tudorwood.net
Map ref:　3, SU85
Directions:　Off A325 Farnborough Rd onto Sycamore
Rd, next 3 left turns onto Cedar Rd, right onto Old
Farnborough Rd
Rooms: 6 en suite, S £40–55 D £60–70 Family room £65–90 **Parking:** 7 **Notes:** ⊗ on premises ⊗
on premises **Closed:** 24–29 Dec

Melanie and Peter offer a warm, welcome tot their 1920s Tudor character property in the centre of town. All rooms have en suite bathrooms, tea and coffee facilities, fridge, hair dryer and TV with video or DVD. Apart from the great breakfast, a wide variety of evening meals or snacks are served in the dining room on request. There is wireless Internet available free of charge.
Recommended in the area
London; Farnborough Air Show; RHS Garden Wisley; Thorpe Park

Alderholt Mill

★★★★ 🛏 GUEST ACCOMMODATION

Address:	Sandleheath Road,
	FORDINGBRIDGE SP6 1PU
Tel:	01425 653130
Fax:	01425 652868
Email:	alderholt-mill@zetnet.co.uk
Website:	www.alderholtmill.co.uk
Map ref:	3, SU11
Directions:	1m W from Fordingbridge, left at x-rds in

Sandleheath, 0.5m over bridge on right

Rooms: 5 (4 en suite), S £28–32 D £56–70 **Parking:** 10 **Notes:** ⊘ on premises 🐾 allowed in bedrooms No children under 8

This picturesque group of brick buildings beside a working watermill, is perfectly placed for exploring the New Forest. The rooms all have en suite bathrooms, television, tea- and coffee-making facilities and there's a residents' lounge. Delicious home-cooked dinners are served and breakfasts feature bread that's freshly baked using flour from the mill. Three self-catering apartments are also available.

Recommended in the area

Rockbourne Roman Villa; Breamore House; Salisbury Cathedral

Ravensdale

★★★★ B&B

Address:	19 St Catherines Road,
	HAYLING ISLAND PO11 0HF
Tel:	023 9246 3203
Fax:	023 9246 3203
Email:	phil.taylor@tayloredprint.co.uk
Website:	www.ravensdale-hayling.co.uk
Map ref:	3, SU70
Directions:	A3023 at Langstone, cross Hayling Bridge &

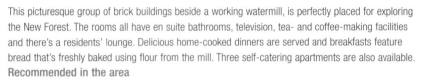

continue 3m until mini-rdbt, right onto Manor Rd. After 1m, right by Barley Mow onto Station Rd & 3rd left onto St Catherines Rd

Rooms: 3 (2 en suite), S £36–40 D £56–66 **Parking:** 4 **Notes:** ⊘ on premises ⊗ on premises No children under 8 **Closed:** last 2 wks of Dec

A relaxed and friendly environment is created here by hosts Jane and Phil Taylor. The attractive bedrooms are very comfortable and have thoughtful extras. Food is a highlight, the breakfast is excellent and you can book a delicious evening meal. Ravensdale is not far from the beach and golf course.

Recommended in the area

Chichester Cathedral; HMS *Victory* and the *Mary Rose*, Portsmouth; walking on the South Downs

Alma Mater

★ ★ ★ ★   B&B

Address: 4 Knowland Drive, MILFORD ON SEA,
                 Lymington SO41 0RH
Tel: 01590 642811
Email: bandbalmamater@aol.com
Website: www.newforestalmamater.co.uk
Map ref: 3, SZ29
Directions: A337 at Everton onto B3058 to Milford on
Sea. Pass South Lawn Hotel, right onto Manor Rd, 1st left
onto Knowland Dr
Rooms: 3 en suite, S £40 D £60–64 **Parking:** 4 **Notes:** ⊘ on premises No children under 15

Eileen and John Haywood enjoy welcoming guests to their beautifully kept home overlooking
landscaped gardens in a quiet residential area. It is a good base for exploring the New Forest and
coast, the yachting centre of Lymington is close by and the village and the beach are just a walk away.
A full four-course or continental breakfast is served in the dining room. The bedrooms are centrally
heated and have extras such as radios, tea and coffee provisions, toiletries and bathrobes.
Recommended in the area
Hurst Castle; Exbury Gardens; National Motor Museum, Beaulieu

Quinhay Farmhouse

◆ ◆ ◆ ◆

Address: Alton Road, Froxfield,
                 PETERSFIELD GU32 1BZ
Tel: 01730 827183
Fax: 01730 827184
Email: janerothery@hotmail.com
Website: www.quinhaybandb.co.uk
Map ref: 3, SU72
Directions: 4m NW of Petersfield. Off A3 at A272 junct
towards Petersfield, at rdbt exit signed Froxfield/Steep,
3.5m on right
Rooms: 2 (1 en suite), S £30–40 D £60–70 **Parking:** 10 **Notes:** ⊘ on premises No children under
12 **Closed:** 15 Dec–15 Jan

Jane Rothery takes great delight in welcoming you to her delightful farmhouse set in rolling
countryside outside Petersfield. The spacious bedrooms have a wealth of thoughtful extras, and the
large lounge has comfy sofas and access to a terrace. Quinhay is popular with walkers and cyclists.
Recommended in the area
Winchester; Portsmouth Historic Dockyard; Jane Austen's House, Chawton

Ponies in the New Forest.

Amberwood

♦♦♦♦

Address: 3/5 Top Lane, RINGWOOD BH24 1LF
Tel/Fax: 01425 476615
Email: maynsing@aol.com
Website: www.amberwoodbandb.co.uk
Map ref: 3, SU10
Directions: A31 onto B3347, over rdbt, left onto
School Ln, left onto Top Ln
Rooms: 2 en suite, D £50 (£35 single occ) Parking: 2
Notes: No children under 12 Closed: Xmas & New Year

With the New Forest and the sea right on the doorstep, this delightful Victorian property is well located for a holiday. Amberwood stands in pretty gardens in a quiet residential area, and is within walking distance of the attractive town of Ringwood. The two bedrooms – an en suite double and a twin with large private bathroom – are equipped with hospitality trays and are carefully maintained. A generous breakfast is served around one large table in the conservatory, and there is also a lounge. The nearby River Avon is a haven for anglers, and various lakes are also close by.

Recommended in the area

New Forest; Exbury Gardens; Moors Valley Country Park

Moortown Lodge Hotel

★ ★ ★ ★ GUEST ACCOMMODATION

Address: 244 Christchurch Road,
           RINGWOOD BH24 3AS
Tel: 01425 471404
Fax: 01425 476527
Email: enquiries@moortownlodge.co.uk
Website: www.moortownlodge.co.uk
Map ref: 3, SU10
Directions: 1m S of Ringwood. Off A31 at Ringwood
onto B3347, signs to Sopley, Lodge next to David Lloyds
Health Club
Rooms: 7 en suite, D £80–90 Parking: 9
Notes: ⊘ on premises 🐕 allowed in bedrooms

Moortown Lodge is a small, inviting hotel in the attractive market town of Ringwood, the western gateway to the New Forest, where there is a wide range of unusual shops, traditional pubs and lovely restaurants. Set in unspoilt countryside where wild ponies and deer roam, it provides the perfect setting for those keen on walking, horse riding, angling and cycling. Water sports are on hand, too, on the coast just a short drive away. The seven light and airy bedrooms all have en suite facilities, are beautifully decorated and finished to a very high standard – with digital TV, high-speed broadband, tea- and coffee-making facilities, direct dial telephones and hairdryers in each room. Every room is unique in style and design; two bedrooms are easily accessible on the ground floor, one is suitable for families and another features a four-poster bed. In the mornings a generous fresh cooked breakfast is taken in the smart lounge/dining room at separate tables. Arrangements can be made for guests wishing to use the facilities at the adjacent private David Lloyd Leisure Club, which has a bar, restaurant, gym, swimming pool and racquet sports. There is safe well-lit parking available.

Recommended in the area

Bournemouth; New Forest; Stonehenge

The Old Cottage

★ ★ ★ ★ B&B

Address: Cowpitts Lane, North Poulner,
RINGWOOD BH24 3JX
Tel/Fax: 01425 477956
Email: forestgatewines@btinternet.com
Map ref: 3, SU10
Directions: A31 E, 0.75m E of Ringwood left to
Hangersley, 1st right, 0.5m to x-rds & over, cottage
100yds on right
Rooms: 3 en suite, S £40–45 D £60–64 **Parking:** 3
Notes: ⊗ on premises ⊗ on premises No children under 10 **Closed:** Nov–Dec

This 300-year-old thatched cottage, standing in a beautiful garden in the New Forest, is full of
character – original beams and an inglenook fireplace blend with contemporary comforts. Mr and Mrs
Theobald are very hospitable, greeting their guests with offers of refreshment. The bedrooms are well
equipped – one has a four-poster bed. The market town of Ringwood, where you'll find a good choice
of pubs and restaurants for an evening meal, is 1.5 miles away.
Recommended in the area
New Forest National Park; Bournemouth and south coast beaches; Salisbury

Valley View

★ ★ ★ ★ B&B

Address: Cowpits Lane, North Poulner,
RINGWOOD BH24 3JX
Tel: 01425 475855
Fax: 01425 472542
Email: edward_brown@tinyworld.co.uk
Map ref: 3, SU10
Directions: A31 Poulner exit, N onto Gorley Rd, right
onto Cowpitts Ln
Rooms: 2, S £30–32 D £56–60 **Parking:** 5
Notes: ⊗ on premises

This modern establishment has easy access to the New Forest and the coast. The nearby town
of Ringwood is attractive with a lively Wednesday street market and many restaurants and pubs.
The house has just two rooms, with only one room let at a time; each is well furnished and decorated.
The breakfast, featuring delicious home-made preserves, is served in the family dining room. A home-
cooked dinner is available by arrangement and should be ordered before 4pm.
Recommended in the area
New Forest National Park; Salisbury Cathedral; Dorset Heavy Horse Centre

Greenvale Farm

★★★★ B&B

Address:	Melchet Park, Sherfield English,
	ROMSEY SO51 6FS
Tel:	01794 884858
Website:	www.greenvalefarm.com
Map ref:	3, SU32

Directions: 5m W of Romsey. On S side of A27 through red-brick archway for Melchet Court, Greenvale Farm 150yds on left, left at slatted barn

Rooms: 1 en suite, S £35 D £65 **Parking:** 10 **Notes:** ⊘ on premises ⊗ on premises No children under 14

This well-planned property is on a working farm close to the northern edge of the New Forest. The accommodation is modern and self-contained, and offers spacious twin or double rooms with showers en suite and plenty of homely extras. Dawn is often heralded by the cock crowing, and eggs from the farm hens feature in the delicious breakfasts, along with bacon from a local farm shop, and honey from the New Forest. Winchester and Salisbury are within easy reach and Mottisfont Abbey is nearby.

Recommended in the area

Eling Tide Mill; Florence Nightingale's grave, East Wellow; Hillier Arboretum

Dormy House

★★★★ GUEST ACCOMMODATION

Address:	21 Barnes Lane, Sarisbury, WARSASH,
	Southampton SO31 7DA
Tel:	01489 572626
Fax:	01489 573370
Email:	dormyhousehotel@warsash.globalnet.co.uk
Website:	www.dormyhousehotel.net
Map ref:	3, SU40

Directions: Off A27 at Sarisbury Green onto Barnes Ln, house 1m on right

Rooms: 12 en suite, S £52–56 D £64–75 **Parking:** 18

Notes: ⊗ on premises

Situated not far from the River Hamble and the Solent, this tranquil Victorian house has a pretty garden and patio, while indoors are all the expected comforts. All the bedrooms have hospitality trays and some have spacious seating areas. The rooms on the ground floor have access to the garden.

Recommended in the area

New Forest National Park; Isle of Wight; Southampton Boat Show

The River Test at Chilbolton.

Orchard House

★★★★★ 🛏 B&B

Address:	3 Christchurch Gardens, St Cross, WINCHESTER SO23 9TH
Tel:	01962 861544
Fax:	01962 861988
Email:	hopefamily@hotmail.co.uk
Map ref:	3, SU42

Directions: M3 jnct 3, follow signs to Winchester B3335. After 2nd trfc light, L into Barnes Close, R then R again

Rooms: 1 en suite, S £50–55 D £80–85 **Parking:** 2

Notes: ⊘ on premises ⊗ on premises No children under 6

At the heart of the historic St Cross area of Winchester, this stylish and well maintained house offers just one suite, but what a suite it is – extensive and luxurious. The twin or double bedroom features top quality beds and bedding, a bathroom with superior toiletries, a sitting room and a study area. Facilities include satellite television and broadband (high speed) Internet access. In addition guests have the benefit of free private parking within walking distance of the city centre.

Recommended in the area

Winchester – the Cathedral, Great Hall and many museums; New Forest; Southampton

Goodrich Castle.

Linton Brook Farm

◆◆◆◆

Address:	Malvern Road, Bringsty,
	BROMYARD WR6 5TR
Tel:	01885 488875
Fax:	01885 488875
Map ref:	2, SO65

Directions: Off A44 1.5m E of Bromyard onto B4220 signed Malvern. Farm 0.5m on left

Rooms: 3 (2 en suite), S £27.50–40 D £60–80

Parking: 12 **Notes:** ⊗ on premises

Closed: Xmas & New Year

Sheila and Roger Steeds's 400-year old farmhouse stands on an ancient site. With such a history behind it, this charming house is filled with atmosphere, fostered by the inglenook fireplace and enormous beam in the dining room, and the wood-burning stove in the sitting room. Bedrooms are spacious and homely. At breakfast, enjoy Sheila's tasty home-smoked food, and afterwards wander through the 68-acre grassland farm with access to wonderful scenic walks.

Recommended in the area

Brockhampton Estate (NT); Elgar Birthplace Museum; Berrington Hall (NT)

Little Hegdon Farm House

★ ★ ★ ★ B&B

Address:	Hegdon Hill, Pencombe,
	BROMYARD HR7 4SL
Tel:	01885 400263
Email:	howardcolegrave@hotmail.com
Website:	www.bedandbreakfastherefordshire.com
Map ref:	2, SO65

Directions: Between Pencombe & Risbury, at top of Hegdon Hill down farm lane for 500yds

Rooms: 2 en suite, S £35 D £60 **Parking:** 4

A 17th-century former farmhouse, Little Hegdon lies in the heart of Herefordshire with clear views over farmland, cider orchards and hop yards to the Malvern and Cotswold hills. Restored to provide high standards of comfort, the period character of the house survives in the open fires and plenty of exposed oak beams. Facilities include a drawing room and attractive garden. There is one double and one twin room, en suite or with a private bathroom, and they have hairdryers and tea and coffee facilities. Children and pets are welcome.

Recommended in the area

Lower Brockhampton Estate (NT); historic towns of Hereford and Ledbury; Worcester

Granton House B&B

★★★★ B&B

Address: GOODRICH, Ross-on-Wye HR9 6JE
Tel: 01600 890277
Email: info@grantonhouse.co.uk
Website: www.grantonhouse.co.uk
Map ref: 2, SO51
Directions: A40 S from Ross-on-Wye, 2nd Goodrich exit into village, near church
Rooms: 3 en suite, S £45–55 D £60–80
Parking: 4 **Notes:** ⊘ on premises No children
Closed: 18 Dec–2 Jan

This is a great place for people who enjoy country walks and exploring the beautiful Wye Valley. The River Wye is less than half a mile away. Granton House is an elegant 17th-century country house with a relaxing ambience and bedrooms furnished with antiques. The lounge has an interesting library of books, and the terrace is perfect for watching the sun go down. Delicious breakfasts featuring local produce and home-made bread and preserves are served around a large oak table.

Recommended in the area

Wye Valley; Symond's Yat; Ross-on-Wye; Forest of Dean

The Vauld House Farm

★★★★ FARMHOUSE

Address: The Vauld, Marden, HEREFORD HR1 3HA
Tel: 01568 797347
Fax: 01568 797366
Email: wellsthevauld@talk21.com
Map ref: 2, SO53
Directions: 6m N of Hereford. Off A49 onto A417, right at Englands Gate Inn, Bodenham. 2m turn right for The Vauld and Litmarsh, at junct farm opp
Rooms: 2 en suite, S £50 D £70 **Parking:** 20
Notes: ⊘ on premises ⊗ on premises **Closed:** Dec–Feb

Vauld House is set in beautifully landscaped grounds with ponds, a moat and wooded gardens, beyond which is the family-run stock farm and the hamlet of The Vauld. Guests have their own lounge with open log fire and television. The spacious suites retain many original features and are thoughtfully equipped. Start the day with a full traditional breakfast served family style in the beamed dining room overlooking the gardens. For dinner there are good eating establishments within easy reach.

Recommended in the area

Hampton Court Gardens; Hereford Cathedral; Broadfield Vineyard, Bodenham

Ford Abbey

★★★★★ 🍽 GUEST ACCOMMODATION

Address: Pudleston, LEOMINSTER HR6 0RZ
Tel: 01568 760700
Fax: 01568 760264
Email: info@fordabbey.co.uk
Website: www.fordabbey.co.uk
Map ref: 2, SO45
Directions: A44 Leominster towards Worcester,
turn left to Pudleston
Rooms: 6 en suite, D £125–180 Parking: 20
Notes: ⌘ allowed in bedrooms

An absolutely stunning guesthouse where quality, character and comfort are ever present. Ford Abbey nestles in a sheltered valley surrounded by 320 acres, and was once a sanctuary for Benedictine monks. Drafty corridors and spartan sleeping arrangements have given way to pure luxury, with blazing log fires and delicious food for the lucky traveller. Weathered stone, timber ceilings and inglenook fireplaces are found in the comfortable drawing room and cosy study, and the farmhouse kitchen is the scene of wonderful breakfasts and dinners using fresh local produce. Across the courtyard, the converted farm buildings house four self-catering units and an indoor swimming pool complex. In the main house, six luxury suites have stylish bathrooms and every conceivable comfort. One suite is on the ground floor for ease of access, and the landscaped gardens beyond are delightful for strolling in at any time. An impressive covered barbecue area overlooking the gardens and the main abbey building is the ideal place to gather on summer evenings and enjoy Ford Abbey steaks and a glass of wine. The wooded grounds offer plenty of places for a picnic – a hamper can be prepared on request. For a romantic weekend or a complete break, this place is hard to beat.

Recommended in the area

Croft Castle (NT); Hergest Croft Gardens; Berrington Hall (NT); Ludlow; Hereford Cathedral; Lower Brockhampton (NT)

Hills Farm

★★★★★ 🍽 🏆 FARMHOUSE

Address: Leysters, LEOMINSTER HR6 0HP
Tel: 01568 750205
Email: conolly@bigwig.net
Website: www.thehillsfarm.co.uk
Map ref: 2, SO45
Directions: Off A4112 Leominster to Tenbury Wells, on edge of Leysters
Rooms: 3 en suite, S £32–45 D £64–72 **Parking:** 8
Notes: ⊗ on premises ⊗ on premises No children under 12 **Closed:** Nov–Feb

On high ground, with panoramic views over the Teme Valley, this 15th-century farmhouse is a splendid base for exploring the Welsh Marches. The accommodation is located in beautifully converted barns; each room has its own front door, en suite bathroom, TV, radio and hospitality tray. Guests head to the main farmhouse for breakfast, which is served at separate tables. There's also a pleasant sitting room with lots of reading matter, including maps and guidebooks for planning the next day out.

Recommended in the area

Berrington Hall (NT); Hereford Cathedral and city; Burton Court

---

Cwm Craig Farm

★★★★ FARMHOUSE

Address: LITTLE DEWCHURCH HR2 6PS
Tel: 01432 840250
Fax: 01432 840250
Map ref: 2, SO53
Directions: Off A49 into Little Dewchurch, turn right in village, Cwm Craig 1st farm on left from Ross-On-Wye
Rooms: 3 en suite, S £26 D £50-52 **Parking:** 6
Notes: ⊗ on premises ⊗ on premises

Cwm Craig Farm is midway between Hereford and Ross-on-Wye and stands on the edge of a village surrounded by superb countryside. The Georgian property retains many original features and offers spacious accommodation furnished with fine period pieces. The bedrooms are all en suite and include two doubles and a family room. Guests have access to their rooms all day, and hospitality trays are provided. Home-cooked breakfasts are served in the dining room and morning room around large tables, and you can relax in the sitting room or the games room with its three-quarter-size snooker/pool table and dartboard. Pets cannot be accommodated.

Recommended in the area

Hereford Cathedral and city; Forest of Dean; Wye Valley

Moccas Court

★★★★★ 🛏 🏛 GUEST ACCOMMODATION

Address:	MOCCAS,
	Hereford HR2 9LH
Tel:	01981 500019
Fax:	01981 500095
Email:	bencmaster@btconnect.com
Website:	www.moccas-court.co.uk
Map ref:	2, SO34

Directions: A438, after Staunton, left towards Hay-on-Wye & on to Bredwardine, left after Red Lion Hotel to Moccas, left at memorial, left again, Moccas Court is signed at gatehouse

Rooms: 5 (4 en suite), S £112–156 D £140–195 **Parking:** 35 **Notes:** ⊘ on premises ⊗ on premises

At Moccas Court you can dwell in the lap of luxury looked after by charming and genial hosts. If you are seeking unique and memorable bed and breakfast accommodation you need look no further than this grand Grade I Georgian listed house perched above terraced banks over the River Wye. The country house has such historic interest that it is open to the public. If a little imposing on the outside, the atmosphere inside is warm and welcoming, and family portraits and restrained furnishings echo the period style of the house. The generously sized en suite bedrooms each have their own appeal and extraordinary vistas over the grounds. The largest room, often chosen by honeymooners, includes a dramatic oak armoire and contemporary works of art. It enjoys stunning views south over the parkland at the front of the house, designed by "Capability" Brown and Humphrey Repton, and towards the deer park to the hills beyond. Guests are welcome to use the sitting room that overlooks the gardens and pre-dinner drinks are offered in the elegant library. Not be missed is the delicious dinner, prepared from fresh and often organic produce, and served around a large circular mahogany table in the splendid candlelit dining room designed by Robert Adam.

Recommended in the area

Hay-on-Wye; Black Mountains; Brecon Beacons National Park; Hereford Cathedral; River Wye

Bridge House

★★★★ ◉◉ ⟶ RESTAURANT WITH ROOMS

Address:	Wilton, ROSS-ON-WYE HR9 6AA
Tel:	01989 562655
Fax:	01989 567652
Email:	info@bridge-house-hotel.com
Website:	www.bridge-house-hotel.com
Map ref:	2, SO52
Directions:	Off junct A40 & A49 into Ross, 300yds on left

Rooms: 9 en suite, S £65 D £96–110 **Parking:** 20

Notes: ⊘ on premises ✪ on premises No children under 14

This Georgian house stands beside the River Wye, just a stroll across the bridge to Ross-on-Wye. Mike and Jane Pritchard have created an establishment with real character and contemporary design. Standards are impressive and the bedrooms offer space, comfort and genuine quality. Period features in the public areas add to the stylish ambience. The highly acclaimed restaurant serves tempting dishes such as Welsh salt-marsh lamb with aubergine and tomato timbale and fondant potato.

Recommended in the area

Ross-on-Wye; Symonds Yat; Forest of Dean

Lumleys

★★★★ B&B

Address:	Kern Bridge, Bishopswood,
	ROSS-ON-WYE HR9 5QT
Tel:	01600 890040
Fax:	0870 706 2378
Email:	helen@lumleys.force9.co.uk
Website:	www.lumleys.force9.co.uk/
Map ref:	2, SO52
Directions:	Off A40 onto B4229 at Goodrich, over

Kern Bridge, right at Inn On The Wye, 400yds opp picnic ground

Rooms: 3 en suite, D £60–70 **Parking:** 15 **Notes:** ⊘ on premises ⛨ allowed in bedrooms

Its setting, on the banks of the River Wye, makes Lumleys a favourite with those who appreciate the unspoilt countryside of this corner of Herefordshire. The mellow stone Victorian house retains much of its original character, aided by the period pieces and ornaments that adorn the public areas. These include two sitting rooms and a dining room where breakfasts and early evening meals are served.

Recommended in the area

Symonds Yat; Forest of Dean; Goodrich Castle

Thatch Close

★★★★ GUEST ACCOMMODATION

Address:	Llangrove, ROSS-ON-WYE HR9 6EL
Tel:	01989 770300
Email:	info@thatchclose.co.uk
Website:	www.thatchclose.com
Map ref:	2, SO52

Directions: Off A40 at Symonds Yat West/Whitchurch junct to Llangrove, right at x-rds after Post Office, Thatch Close 0.6m on left

Rooms: 3 en suite, S £30–40 D £55–60 Parking: 8
Notes: ⊘ on premises ⊗ on premises

The sturdy farmhouse, dating from 1760, is full of character and has a welcoming atmosphere. It stands in 13 acres of colourful gardens, ancient hedges and mature trees, the habitat of badgers, foxes, owls and an African Grey parrot named Aku. The homely bedrooms are individually furnished, two rooms are en suite and one has a private bathroom. A wholesome breakfast and dinner are served in the dining room, and the leather sofas in the lounge are a pleasant place to retire after dinner.

Recommended in the area

Symonds Yat; Forest of Dean; Monmouth

Trecilla Farm

★★★★★ 🏛 B&B

Address:	Llangarron, ROSS-ON-WYE HR9 6NQ
Tel:	01989 770647
Email:	info@trecillafarm.co.uk
Website:	www.trecillafarm.co.uk
Map ref:	2, SO52

Directions: A40 onto A4137 to Hereford. 2m x-rds, left signed Llangarron. 1m Llangarron sign, Trecilla Farm 2nd drive on right

Rooms: 3 en suite, S £45–50 D £65–90 Parking: 7
Notes: ⊘ on premises ⊗ on premises No children under 13 Closed: 23 Dec–2 Jan

This lovely 16th century farmhouse lies in a rural location close to Ross-on-Wye. It oozes character with exposed beams and an inglenook fireplace, and stands in picturesque gardens with a spring-fed stream. Excellent breakfasts feature home-grown and local produce, and are served in the elegant dining room. The spacious bedrooms are furnished with fine period pieces including a four-poster bed. Fishing is available on nearby Garron Brook. There is a garden hideaway with snooker table.

Recommended in the area

Symonds Yat; Wye Valley; Forest of Dean

The River Wye at Symonds Yat.

Norton House

Address:	Whitchurch, Symonds Yat,
	SYMONDS YAT [WEST] HR9 6DJ
Tel:	01600 890046
Fax:	01600 890045
Email:	su@norton.wyenet.co.uk
Website:	www.norton-house.com
Map ref:	2, SO51
Directions:	0.5m N of Symonds Yat. Off A40 into
Whitchurch village	

Rooms: 3 en suite, S £40–45 D £60–75 **Parking:** 5 **Notes:** ⊘ on premises ⌁ allowed in bedrooms No children under 12 **Closed:** 25 Dec

Norton House is just a short walk from the River Wye and close to all the opportunities for outdoor pursuits that the area has to offer. The 16th-century house retains some exposed beams and has a generous range of extra facilities to enhance a stay here. The cooking at both dinner and breakfast is a particular strength, with accomplished skills making the best of fresh local produce.

Recommended in the area

Symond's Yat; Goodrich Castle; Forest of Dean

ISLE OF WIGHT

Deckchairs at Sandown, Isle of Wight

Blandings

★★★★ B&B

Address:	Horringford, ARRETON, Nr Newport PO30 3AP
Tel:	01983 865720
Fax:	01983 862099
Email:	robin.oulton@horringford.com
Website:	www.horringford.com/bedandbreakfast.htm
Map ref:	3, SZ58
Directions:	S through Arreton (B3056), pass Stickworth

Hall on your right, 300yds on left farm entrance signed
Horringford Gardens. Take U turn to left, drive to end of poplar trees, turn right. Blandings on left
Rooms: 1 en suite, D £60 **Parking:** 3 **Notes:** ⊘ on premises ⋔ allowed in bedrooms

Set within a small group of farm buildings, Blandings has a delightful rural setting with pleasant views of the downs. On warm sunny days its wooden sun deck is a good place to enjoy breakfast or relax with an evening sundowner. The cycle route from Cowes to Sandown (A23) runs past the front gate and cycles and equipment are available for hire in the village and can be delivered ready for use.
Recommended in the area
Osborne House; beaches at Sandown, Shanklin and Ryde; Bembridge; Newport

Chale Bay Farm

★★★★★ GUEST ACCOMMODATION

Address:	Military Road, CHALE PO38 2JF
Tel:	01983 730950
Fax:	01983 730395
Email:	info@chalebayfarm.co.uk
Website:	www.chalebayfarm.co.uk
Map ref:	3, SZ47
Directions:	By A3055 Military Rd in Chale, near Church

Rooms: 8 en suite, S £50 D £100 **Parking:** 50
Closed: November to March

Situated on National Trust coastline with uninterrupted views of the Needles and Tennyson Downs, Chale Bay Farm is a tranquil place to unwind. The spacious bedrooms are all on the ground floor, around a courtyard with a floodlit Japanese-style water garden. The rooms are all en suite with king-size beds, and equipped to a high standard including tea and coffee facilities and hairdryers, several have their own private patio. Before setting off to explore the island, enjoy a hearty home-cooked breakfast, served at individual tables dressed with fresh flowers in the pleasant dining room.
Recommended in the area
Blackgang Chine; Freshwater Bay; Dinosaur Farm

Newport.

Braunstone House Hotel

Address:	33 Lugley Street, NEWPORT PO30 5ET
Tel:	01983 822994
Fax:	01983 526300
Email:	lugleys@uwclub.net
Website:	www.isleofwight.com/braunstonehouse
Map ref:	3, SZ58
Directions:	Just off Newport High Street

Rooms: 5 (4 en suite), S £65–80 D £85–95

The renovation of this Grade II listed building, just a stone's throw from Newport town centre, has carefully retained its original Georgian charm. The dedicated staff do an excellent job, and the elegant, good-size bedrooms have individual character and are equipped with many extras. The building houses a popular brasserie, Lugley's, where flagstone floors and a modern aspect set the scene for a choice of tasty, well-prepared meals – there's a bar lounge where you can sit while you make your choice. In summer, meals can be served in the sheltered gardens.

Recommended in the area

Carisbrooke Castle; Robin Hill; Osborne House

Bedford Lodge Hotel

★★★ B&B

Address: 4 Chine Avenue, SHANKLIN PO37 6AQ
Tel: 01983 862416
Fax: 01983 868704
Email: aa@bedfordlodge.co.uk
Website: www.bedfordlodge.co.uk
Map ref: 3, SZ58
Directions: A3055 onto Chine Av, Lodge opp Tower Cottage Gardens
Rooms: 12 en suite, D £54–80 **Parking:** 8
Notes: No children under 3 **Closed:** Jan

The Lodge stands proud over sloping lawns, mature trees and flowering shrubs, a secluded haven in a sunny elevated spot. A licensed bar and breakfast room on the ground floor lead to the lounge, gardens and sun terrace where you can enjoy a drink and the fine views. All bedrooms are equipped with modern amenities and comfy duvets on the beds. The lodge is in the village of old Shanklin, an ideal place to relax in a pretty tea room or a traditional coaching inn. Ferry crossings can be arranged.
Recommended in the area
Ventnor; Sandown; Godshill

The Belmont

♦♦♦♦

Address: 8 Queens Road, SHANKLIN PO37 6AN
Tel: 01983 867875
Email: enquiries@belmont-iow.co.uk
Website: www.belmont-iow.co.uk
Map ref: 3, SZ58
Directions: From Sandown, left at Fiveways lights signed Ventnor. Hotel 400mtrs on right opp St Saviour's Church
Rooms: 13 en suite, S £27–61 D £50–82 **Parking:** 9
Notes: ⊗ on premises No children under 3 **Closed:** Nov–Feb

The Belmont offers friendly personal service and a relaxing atmosphere close to the pretty thatched old village, Shanklin Chine and the beach. The secluded garden is an attractive suntrap with a heated swimming pool, available from late May to early September. The bedrooms mostly face the sea or the garden and are well equipped, some having king-size or four-poster beds. Full English or continental breakfasts are served in the elegant dining room and an evening bar opens onto the veranda.
Recommended in the area
Shanklin old village; Osborne House; The Needles

Foxhills

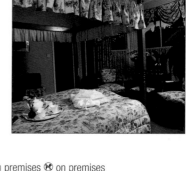

★★★★★ GUEST ACCOMMODATION

Address:	30 Victoria Avenue,
	SHANKLIN,
	Isle of Wight PO37 6LS
Tel:	01983 862329
Fax:	01983 866666
Email:	info@foxhillshotel.co.uk
Website:	www.foxhillshotel.co.uk
Map ref:	3, SZ58

Directions: A3020 from Shanklin centre towards Newport, Foxhills 450yds on left

Rooms: 8 en suite, D £78–98 Parking: 13 Notes: ⊘ on premises ⊗ on premises No children under 16 Closed: 3–31 Jan

Every effort is made to pamper guests at this superbly refurbished establishment. It is set in beautiful gardens just a short walk from Shanklin Chine and the town centre. Hospitality is exemplary, and you are welcomed with tea and chocolates on arrival. There are high levels of comfort in the en suite bedrooms, where DVD and CD players (there is a large library of up-to-date DVDs for guests' use), direct-dial telephones and modem, hairdryers and refreshment trays are all provided. For that special occasion the four-poster suite has a touch of modernised Victorian luxury. Bathrooms are beautifully fitted with quality units, and furnished with luxury towels, dressing gowns and toiletries. A whirlpool bath and beauty treatments are relaxing options, or else take a drink or afternoon tea in front of the log fire. Guests can use a neighbouring swimming pool, sauna and a gym for a small additional cost. There is also plenty of tourist and other information about the area – routes for walking and cycling, and car tours are available, and route maps are supplied free of charge. Picnic lunches can be prepared for those days out.

Recommended in the area

Shanklin Chine; Rhylstone Gardens; Osborne House; Bembridge Down

The Grange

★★★★ GUEST ACCOMMODATION

Address:	9 Eastcliff Road,
	SHANKLIN PO37 6AA
Tel:	01983 867644
Fax:	01983 865537
Email:	hotel@thegrangebythesea.com
Website:	www.thegrangebythesea.com
Map ref:	3, SZ58

Directions: A3055 to Shanklin. The Grange is on left just before old village.

Rooms: 17 (14 en suite), S £65 D £80–96

Parking: 8 **Notes:** ⊘ on premises

Nestled in the heart of Shanklin's Old Village on the Isle of Wight, and only moments from its long, sandy beach, The Grange is the perfect retreat from the hectic pace of modern life. It enjoys a tranquil yet convenient setting and its atmosphere is friendly and relaxed. Built in the 1820s and recently renovated throughout, The Grange has original features such as the ornate, carved fireplace in the lounge which is now complemented by a collection of paintings and sculptures ranging in style from bold and striking to classic and elegant. The beautifully presented bedrooms are decorated in natural tones that mirror the surrounding environment and newly fitted power showers and complementary luxury toiletries ensure a great start to each day. In addition, there are a wide range of inspirational courses and activities available including yoga, massage and beauty treatments, coastline walks, creative writing and art. The Grange meets high standards of cuisine, using the freshest ingredients, local and organic where possible. Breakfast and morning coffee can be taken outside in the garden in fine weather.

Recommended in the area

Shanklin Chine, Tiger Sanctuary in Sandown, Brading Roman Villa

Freshwater Bay.

The Hoo

★★★★ B&B

Address:	Colwell Road, TOTLAND BAY PO39 0AB
Tel/Fax:	01983 753592
Email:	jerjohnston@btinternet.com
Website:	www.thehoo.co.uk
Map ref:	3, SZ58

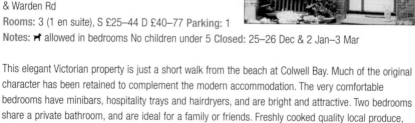

Directions: From Yarmouth ferry right onto A3054, 2.25m enter Colwell Common, The Hoo on corner Colwell & Warden Rd

Rooms: 3 (1 en suite), S £25–44 D £40–77 **Parking:** 1

Notes: ✝ allowed in bedrooms No children under 5 **Closed:** 25–26 Dec & 2 Jan–3 Mar

This elegant Victorian property is just a short walk from the beach at Colwell Bay. Much of the original character has been retained to complement the modern accommodation. The very comfortable bedrooms have minibars, hospitality trays and hairdryers, and are bright and attractive. Two bedrooms share a private bathroom, and are ideal for a family or friends. Freshly cooked quality local produce, including farm eggs, sausages and smoked salmon, makes breakfast a pleasure.

Recommended in the area

The Needles; Yarmouth Castle; Freshwater Bay

St Maur Hotel

★★★★ GUEST ACCOMMODATION

Address:	Castle Road,
	VENTNOR PO38 1LG
Tel:	01983 852570
Fax:	01983 852306
Email:	sales@stmaur.co.uk
Website:	www.stmaur.co.uk
Map ref:	3, SZ57

Directions: Exit A3055 at the end of Park Ave onto Castle Rd, premises 150 yards on the left

Rooms: 9 en suite, D £90–120 **Parking:** 9 **Notes:** ⊘ on premises No children under 5
Closed: Please enquire

Built in 1876, this Victorian villa has been run by the Groocock family since 1966, and they have continued to affectionately refurbish the property. St Maur is set in an elevated position overlooking a bay in one of the prettiest areas of the island, where you will discover sandy beaches, idyllic countryside, quaint villages and a variety of entertainment to suit every mood. The large sub-tropical gardens are a delight; there is a profusion of colour year round and fragrant scents greet you as you walk up the path to the front door. In summer the lawn provides a lovely spot to soak up the sun. The ample bedrooms all have large en suite bathrooms and are well equipped. Most rooms (there's a mix of double, twin and family rooms, some with queen-size beds) have recently been upgraded with pine-style furniture and have views over the park and sea beyond from pine decked verandas. A spacious lounge with Victorian grandeur overlooks the garden – this is a quiet place to sit and read or enjoy your coffee and mints after dinner. There is also a cosy licensed bar to occupy your evenings.
A comprehensive full English breakfast gets the day off to a satisfying start and at dinner a six-course menu is on offer.

Recommended in the area

Ventnor Botanical Gardens; Shanklin Chine; Carisbrooke Castle

KENT

St Margaret's Bay.

Chislet Court Farm

★★★★ FARMHOUSE

Address: Chislet, CANTERBURY CT3 4DU
Tel: 01227 860309
Fax: 01227 860444
Email: kathy@chisletcourtfarm.com
Website: www.chisletcourtfarm.com
Map ref: 4, TR15
Directions: Off A28 in Upstreet, farm on right
100yds past church
Rooms: 2 en suite, S £45 D £70 **Parking:** 4
Notes: ⊘ on premises ⊗ on premises No children under 12 **Closed:** Xmas

Chislet Court is an 800-acre arable farm, with an 18th-century farmhouse, set in mature gardens
overlooking the village church and surrounding countryside. There are two spacious double bedrooms,
each with modern bath and shower rooms, and tea and coffee facilities. You are welcome to relax
in the garden and in the conservatory dining room where breakfast is served. There is a good choice
of pubs and restaurants in the area for lunch and dinner. Guests are asked not to smoke in the house.
Recommended in the area
Canterbury Cathedral; Sandwich; Howletts Zoo Park

Magnolia House

◆◆◆◆◆

Address: 36 St Dunstan's Terrace,
CANTERBURY CT2 8AX
Tel/Fax: 01227 765121
Email: info@magnoliahousecanterbury.co.uk
Website: www.magnoliahousecanterbury.co.uk
Map ref: 4, TR15
Directions: A2 E onto A2050 for city centre, 1st rdbt
left signed University of Kent, St Dunstans Ter 3rd right
Rooms: 7 en suite, S £60 D £100–135
Parking: 5 **Notes:** ⊘ on premises ⊗ on premises No children under 12

This attractive Georgian house stands in a quiet residential street just a short walk from the city
centre. The property is beautifully maintained and exudes hospitality. Bedrooms are equipped with
plenty of useful features, including a fridge, and guests are provided with their own key. A cosy lounge
looks across the front garden, while the dining room looks onto the walled garden at the rear. Delicious
evening meals are served by arrangement, and in the morning breakfast offers plenty of choice.
Recommended in the area
Canterbury Cathedral; St Augustine's Abbey; Canterbury Tales Museum

Yorke Lodge

★★★★ GUEST ACCOMMODATION

Address: 50 London Road, CANTERBURY CT2 8LF
Tel: 01227 451243
Fax: 01227 462006
Email: enquiries@yorkelodge.com
Website: www.yorkelodge.com
Map ref: 4, TR15
Directions: 750yds NW of city centre. Arriving in Canterbury via M2, A2 take 1st signposted exit for Canterbury. At 1st rdbt turn left into London Rd
Rooms: 8 en suite, S £45–55 D £80–110 **Parking:** 5 **Notes:** 🐾 allowed in bedrooms

In a leafy street in north Canterbury, this Victorian town house is a 10-minute walk from the city centre, with all its historic and cultural attractions. It is also just 5 minutes from Canterbury West station, making it perfectly feasible to arrive by public transport. However, there is parking here, and it's just a 15-minute drive to the Kent coast. Decked on the outside with colourful window boxes and canopies, the interior also exudes a sense of style and elegance, with light, contemporary furniture and restful coordinating fabrics. Bedrooms are individually styled – twin-bedded, double-bedded and triple rooms are available – and the superior rooms have queen-sized four-poster beds that are sparingly draped to maintain the spacious feel of the room. All rooms have colour TV, a radio/alarm, a hairdryer and tea- and coffee-making facilities. There are several areas where guests can relax: a light and cosy conservatory; a sunny terrace of wooden decking overlooking the garden; and the library, with a large selection of books and several board games to suit adults or children. The spacious dining room is the setting for breakfast, which might be a traditional English breakfast or a lighter selection of cereals, yoghurts, fruits and seasonal compotes. It also houses the family's interesting collections of toys, household items, tobacco memorabilia and royal family mementoes.

Recommended in the area

Canterbury Cathedral; North Downs Way; Howletts Wild Animal Park, Bekesbourne

Waterside Guest House

★★★★ GUEST ACCOMMODATION

Address: 15 Hythe Road, DYMCHURCH,
Romney Marsh TN29 0LN
Tel: 01303 872253
Fax: 01303 872253
Email: info@watersideguesthouse.co.uk
Website: www.watersideguesthouse.co.uk
Map ref: 4, TR12
Directions: M20 junct 11 onto A259 follow signs for
Hythe then Dymchurch, 0.5m past village sign
Rooms: 5 en suite, S £35–60 D £50–60 **Parking:** 7 **Notes:** ⊘ on premises ⊗ on premises

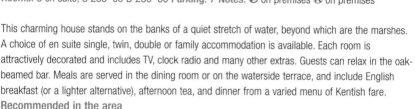

This charming house stands on the banks of a quiet stretch of water, beyond which are the marshes. A choice of en suite single, twin, double or family accommodation is available. Each room is attractively decorated and includes TV, clock radio and many other extras. Guests can relax in the oak-beamed bar. Meals are served in the dining room or on the waterside terrace, and include English breakfast (or a lighter alternative), afternoon tea, and dinner from a varied menu of Kentish fare.
Recommended in the area
Romney, Hythe and Dymchurch Railway; Port Lympne Animal Park; Dover Castle and the White Cliffs

Beesfield Farm

★★★★★ FARMHOUSE

Address: Beesfield Lane, FARNINGHAM DA4 0LA
Tel: 01322 863900
Fax: 01322 863900
Email: kim.vingoe@btinternet.com
Website: www.beesfieldfarm.co.uk
Map ref: 4, TQ56
Directions: From village centre S onto Beesfield Ln,
farm 0.5m on left
Rooms: 3 en suite, S £65–70 D £75–90 **Parking:** 10

Notes: ⊘ on premises ⊗ on premises No children under 12 **Closed:** 8 Dec–Jan

Doug and Kim Vingoe's farm is part arable and part dairy, but Doug's extensive record collection is more likely to engage the attention of guests. The attractive house is set in mature gardens and surrounded by open farmland yet close to major roads. Bedrooms are beautifully presented and fitted with many thoughtful touches while bathrooms are luxurious with quality towels. Satisfying breakfasts are served from a wide choice and enjoyed around a large polished table in the dining room.
Recommended in the area
Bluewater Shopping Mall; Brands Hatch; Eagle Heights Birds of Prey

Hotel Relish

◆◆◆◆◆

Address: 4 Augusta Gardens,
            FOLKESTONE CT20 2RR
Tel: 01303 850952
Fax: 01303 850958
Email: reservations@hotelrelish.co.uk
Website: www.hotelrelish.co.uk
Map ref: 4, TR23
Directions: Off A2033 Sandgate Rd
Rooms: 10 en suite, S £59–120 D £85–130 Parking: 2
Notes: ⊗ on premises 🐾 allowed in bedrooms Closed: 24 Dec–2 Jan

You will get a warm welcome from Sarah and Chris at this stylish Victorian property overlooking Augusta Gardens in the fashionable West End of town. On arrival you will be greeted with a complimentary glass of wine or beer and fresh coffee, tea and home-made cakes are available throughout your stay. The bedrooms feature lovely coordinated fabrics, great showers and the majority have DVD players. Public rooms include a modern lounge-dining room and a terrace where breakfast is served during summer.

Recommended in the area

Dover Castle; Romney, Hythe and Dymchurch Railway; Canterbury

Seabrook House

★★★★ GUEST ACCOMMODATION

Address: 81 Seabrook Road, HYTHE CT21 5QW
Tel: 01303 269282
Fax: 01303 237822
Email: info@seabrook-house.co.uk
Website: www.seabrook-house.co.uk
Map ref: 4, TR13
Directions: 0.9m E of Hythe on A259
Rooms: 13 en suite, S £35–45 £65–75 Parking: 13

This striking Victorian property, easily recognised by the heavily timber-framed frontage and pretty gardens, is conveniently located for the M20 and Eurotunnel and is also close to beach at Hythe. Many of the art-deco style bedrooms have lovely sea views. These spacious en suite rooms, with their attractive decor and furnishings, also have hospitality trays, TV and hairdryers. A memorable full English breakfast sets you up for the ferries from Folkestone or Dover or for sightseeing in the local area, and there are plenty of comfortable places for relaxation, including a sunny conservatory and an elegant lounge.

Recommended in the area

Romney, Hythe and Dymchurch Railway; Dover Castle; Port Lympne Animal Park; Royal Military Canal

The Black Horse Inn

★★★★ INN

Address:	Pilgrims Way, Thurnham,
	MAIDSTONE ME14 3LD
Tel:	01622 737185
Fax:	01622 739170
Email:	info@wellieboot.net
Website:	www.wellieboot.net/home_blackhorse.htm
Map ref:	4, TQ75
Directions:	M20 junct 7, N onto A249. Right into

Detling, opp pub onto Pilgrims Way for 1m

Rooms: 16 en suite, S £60–65 D £75–80 **Parking:** 40 **Notes:** 🐕 allowed in bedrooms

Tucked beneath the steep face of the North Downs on the Pilgrims Way, this 17th-century inn has public areas with oak beams adorned with hops, exposed brickwork and open fireplaces. The thoughtfully equipped bedrooms are in a courtyard annexe behind the premises, and each room is stylishly furnished. The inn's popular restaurant is open all day, and is candlelit in the evening. On the doorstep is a network of paths frequented by walkers and cyclists, and bikes can be hired.

Recommended in the area

Leeds Castle; Huckling Woodland Trust Estate; Museum of Kent Life

Langley Oast

★★★★ GUEST ACCOMMODATION

Address:	Langley Park, Langley,
	MAIDSTONE ME17 3NQ
Tel:	01622 863523
Fax:	01622 863523
Email:	margaret@langleyoast.freeserve.co.uk
Map ref:	4, TQ75
Directions:	2.5m SE of Maidstone off A274. After

Parkwood Business Estate lane signed Maidstone Golf Centre

Rooms: 3 (2 en suite), S £35–50 D £50–85 **Parking:** 5 **Notes:** ⊘ on premises **Closed:** Xmas

This is an authentic Kentish oasthouse, built in 1873 and originally used for drying hops used in the making of local beer. The interior has been the subject of a tasteful conversion, with exposed brick, clean white walls and period furniture, and the distinctive shape of the oast towers adds extra interest to the two 24-ft diameter "roundel" bedrooms, which include sofas and en suite bathrooms, one of which has a Jacuzzi bath. Breakfasts are served in an elegant dining room around a single table.

Recommended in the area

Leeds Castle; Sissinghurst Castle Gardens; Canterbury.

Ringlestone House

♦♦♦♦♦

Address:	Ringlestone Hamlet, Harrietsham, MAIDSTONE ME17 1NX
Tel:	01622 859911
Fax:	01622 859740
Email:	bookings@ringlestone.co.uk
Website:	www.ringlestonehouse.co.uk
Map ref:	4, TQ85

Directions: M20 junct 8, A20, at rdbt opp Ramada Hotel left to Hollingbourne, through village, right at x-rds at top of hill

Rooms: 3 en suite, S £75–135 D £95–165 Parking: 40 Closed: 25 Dec

Situated in tranquil grounds on the North Downs facing the famous Ringlestone Inn, this charming farmhouse provides luxury accommodation. Upstairs there are three large comfortable en suite bedrooms furnished in oak furniture, one with a canopied four-poster bed. There are exclusive facilities for private functions and Ringlestone Inn opposite is ideal for candlelit suppers or fireside lunches.

Recommended in the area

Leeds Castle; Cobtree Museum of Kent Life; Canterbury Cathedral

Merzie Meadows

♦♦♦♦♦

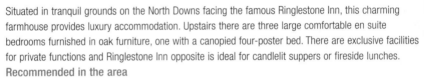

Address:	Hunton Road, MARDEN TN12 9SL
Tel/Fax:	01622 820500
Email:	pamela@merziemeadows.co.uk
Website:	www.merziemeadows.co.uk
Map ref:	4, TQ74

Directions: A229 onto B2079 for Marden, 1st right onto Underlyn Ln, 2.5m Large Chainhurst sign, right onto drive

Rooms: 2 en suite, S £60–65 D £70–85 Parking: 4

Notes: ⊘ on premises ⊗ on premises No children under 15 Closed: mid-Dec to mid-Feb

Merzie Meadows is set in 20 acres in the Kent countryside and the grounds are made up of conservation areas for wildlife, woodland, and an environment for waterfowl. The generously proportioned bedrooms are housed in two wings. The ground-floor location makes for easy access, and one room is a suite with its own terrace. Rooms are carefully decorated and furnished. The breakfast room has superb garden views.

Recommended in the area

Sissinghurst Castle Garden (NT); Leeds Castle; The Hop Farm Country Park, Yalding Organic Gardens

Sunset overt the Ashdown Forest.

Danehurst House

★★★★★ GUEST ACCOMMODATION

Address:	41 Lower Green Road, Rusthall, ROYAL TUNBRIDGE WELLS TN4 8TW
Tel:	01892 527739
Fax:	01892 514804
Email:	info@danehurst.net
Website:	www.danehurst.net
Map ref:	4, TQ53

Directions: 1.5m W of Tunbridge Wells in Rusthall.
Off A264 onto Coach Rd & Lower Green Rd

Rooms: 4 en suite, S £50–69.50 D £69.50–95 **Parking:** 6 **Notes:** ⊘ on premises ⊗ on premises No children under 8 **Closed:** Xmas

Angela and Michael Godbold's spacious Victorian home stands just west of the historic spa town of Tunbridge Wells. There is a baby grand piano in the drawing room, and the Victorian-style conservatory is a delightful setting for breakfast, whether full English, fish, cold meats or continental. The four cosy bedrooms are en suite, and have a wealth of thoughtful extras and notably comfortable beds. No pets.

Recommended in the area

Groombridge Place; Hever Castle; Chartwell (NT)

LANCASHIRE

The Bridestones.

The Park Restaurant Hotel

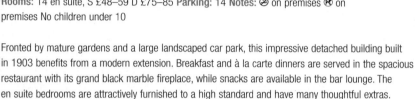

Address:	209 Tulketh Road, Ashton-On-Ribble, PRESTON PR2 1ES
Tel:	01772 726250
Fax:	01772 723743
Email:	parkrestauranthotel@hotmail.com
Website:	www.theparkpreston.com
Map ref:	6, SD52
Directions:	1m NW of town centre off A5085 Blackpool Rd

Rooms: 14 en suite, S £48–59 D £75–85 **Parking:** 14 **Notes:** ⊘ on premises ⊗ on premises No children under 10

Fronted by mature gardens and a large landscaped car park, this impressive detached building built in 1903 benefits from a modern extension. Breakfast and à la carte dinners are served in the spacious restaurant with its grand black marble fireplace, while snacks are available in the bar lounge. The en suite bedrooms are attractively furnished to a high standard and have many thoughtful extras.

Recommended in the area

Riversway Business Village and marina; National Football Museum; Harris Museum

The Bower

★★★★★ B&B

Address:	YEALAND CONYERS LA5 9SF
Tel/Fax:	01524 734585
Email:	info@thebower.co.uk
Website:	www.thebower.co.uk
Map ref:	6, SD57
Directions:	M6 junct 35, A6 towards Milnthorpe for 0.75m, under narrow bridge, take next left onto Snape Ln & bear left at end

Rooms: 2 (1 en suite), S £44–54 D £68–78 **Parking:** 6 **Notes:** ⊘ on premises ⊗ on premises No children under 12

The Bower, run by affable hosts Michael and Sally-Ann, is in a beautiful village setting with views of Ingleborough and surrounding hills just 10 minutes from the M6. This modernised property retains many original features and provides stylish accommodation in spacious bedrooms and opulent public rooms. There are two double rooms, one en suite and with an additional single bed, and the other with a private bathroom.

Recommended in the area

Leighton Hall; RSPB Reserve, Leighton Moss; Sizergh Castle (NT)

The Grand Union Canal.

Kegworth House

★★★★★ GUEST HOUSE

Address:	42 High Street, KEGWORTH, Derby DE74 2DA
Tel:	01509 672575
Fax:	01509 670645
Email:	info@kegworthhouse.co.uk
Website:	www.kegworthhouse.co.uk
Map ref:	3, SK42

Directions: From Birmingham M42/A42 follow signs for Airport, then Kegworth; M1 jnct 24, A6 to Loughborough 0.5m 1st r onto Packington Hill. L at jnct, house on left

Rooms: 11 en suite, S £75–135 D £95–195 **Parking:** 20 **Notes:** ⊘ on premises No children under 12

From the moment of arrival, it is abundantly clear that Kegworth House is a very superior and luxurious place to stay. Parts of the building are more than 300 years old with the elegant façade a Georgian addition. Many original features enhance the ambience, including beautiful fireplaces in the lounge, dining room and some of the larger bedrooms. Each of the bedrooms has been individually styled and furnished with pieces sourced from across Europe – some have brass bedsteads, others have a four-poster or sumptuous Empire style sleigh bed – and great care has gone into the choices of colours, fabrics and bedlinens. Bathrooms, too, are exceptional and individual, some with power showers, corner baths or Victorian-style roll-top tubs. Each room comes with a range of extras that include fluffy dressing gowns, trouser press, television with DVD player, CD player and broadband Internet connection, not to mention the well-stocked hospitality tray. There is a relaxing drawing room, where guests can sink into the cosy sofas and easy chairs, and a delightful garden. Full English or continental breakfasts are served around a large refectory table in the family-style kitchen. Evening meals are available too, by prior arrangement, and these can be served in the kitchen or in the formal dining room. The opening of a small, exclusive restaurant is anticipated for the summer of 2007.

Recommended in the area

Donington Grand Prix Collection; Calke Abbey; Whatton Gardens.

Medieval stone bridge and 13th-century Church of St Giles.

Medbourne Grange

★★★★ FARMHOUSE

Address: MEDBOURNE, Market Harborough LE16 8EF
Tel: 01858 565249
Fax: 01858 565257
Website: www.medbournegrange.co.uk
Map ref: 3, SP89
Directions: 2m NE of Medbourne. Between Market Harborough & Uppingham off B664
Rooms: 3 en suite, S £30 D £50 **Parking:** 6
Notes: ⊗ on premises ⊗ on premises

This charming farmhouse is situated in one of the most beautiful, unspoilt areas of central England. It lies on the outskirts of the hamlet of Nevill Holt with its magnificent Hall, dating back 700 years. The Grange is also close to the village of Medbourne, complete with a stream and ducks, church, pub, restaurant and village store. The en suite bedrooms have colour TV, hair dryer, radio/alarms and tea and coffee tray. All rooms are decorated with country house style furnishings. A traditional farmhouse breakfast with home-made preserves is served and there is a heated swimming pool in the summer.
Recommended in the area
Rutland Water; Burghley House; Barnsdale Gardens

LINCOLNSHIRE

The Grantham Canal at Denton.

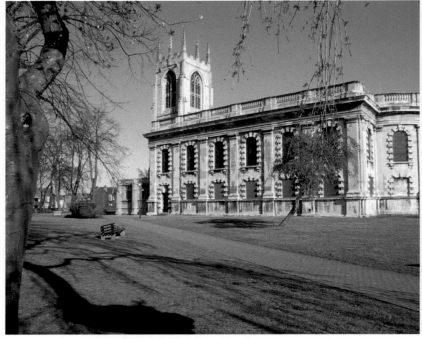

All Saints church, Gainsborough.

Wesley Guest House

★★★★ GUEST ACCOMMODATION

Address:	16 Queen Street, EPWORTH DN9 1HG
Tel:	01427 874512
Fax:	01427 874592
Email:	enquiries@wesleyguesthouse.com
Website:	www.wesleyguesthouse.com
Map ref:	8, SE70

Directions: In town centre, 200yds off Market Place

Rooms: 4 en suite, S £30–50 D £60–80 Parking: 4

Notes: ⊘ on premises ⊗ on premises

A pleasurable stay is a certainty at this friendly and well-maintained detached house in the market town of Epworth. Epworth is the birthplace of John Wesley, founder of Methodism, and places associated with Wesley are all within walking distance. The good-size bedrooms, decorated in soft pastels, have mini-fridges, fresh flowers and complimentary toiletries. Cheerful tablecloths and lovely views over the large garden enhance the pristine breakfast room. Unwind with a game on the full-size snooker table or try one of the leisure options nearby, such as golf and fishing.

Recommended in the area

Normanby Hall and Park; Sandtoft Museum; John Wesley Museum; St Andrew's Church, Epworth

Church Farm B&B

★ ★ ★ ★ B&B

Address:	High Street, FILLINGHAM,
	Gainsborough DN21 5BS
Tel:	01427 668279
Email:	enquiries@churchfarm-fillingham.co.uk
Website:	www.churchfarm-fillingham.co.uk
Map ref:	8, SK98

Directions: Off B1398 into village, first house on right

Rooms: 3 (1 en suite), S £38–38 D £55–55 **Parking:** 6

Notes: ⊗ on premises ⊗ on premises No children under 5 **Closed:** 24 Dec–1 Jan

Church Farm lies on the edge of the small, peaceful stone village of Fillingham, which nestles at the base of the Lincolnshire Scarp, the limestone edge that slices through the country and extends down to the Cotswolds. Relax and unwind in this large 19th-century stone farmhouse set in secluded mature gardens overlooking farmland. The traditional bedrooms decorated in various styles offer one en suite twin, and a double and a single that share a bathroom. Plush sofas and chairs and an open fire in the lounge make for a relaxed atmosphere. The English breakfast includes cereals, porridge, yoghurts and fresh fruit to start, followed by local bacon and sausages, free-range eggs cooked to your liking and fresh mushrooms and tomatoes, plus a choice of breads and a selection of preserves. Special dietary needs can be catered for and packed lunches can be provided if advance notice is given. Host Kathleen Needham is very proud (and rightly so) of her housekeeping and warm hospitality – if you arrive before 6pm you are greeted with complimentary tea and home-made cake. For the keen angler, there is a large, privately owned lake in the village offering fishing with a daily permit (£10) open to Church Farm's guests.

Recommended in the area

Lincoln's cathedral, castle and museums; RAF Scampton (Red Arrows); antiques at Neward; Swinderby and Hemswell

Bailhouse & Mews

♦♦♦♦♦

Address:	34 Bailgate,
	LINCOLN LN1 3AP
Tel:	01522 520883
Fax:	01522 521829
Email:	info@bailhouse.co.uk
Website:	www.bailhouse.co.uk
Map ref:	8, SK97
Directions:	100yds N of catherdral

Rooms: 10 en suite, S £64.50–105.50 D £79–165
Parking: 16 **Notes:** ⊗ on premises ⊗ on premises

Bailhouse commands a prime position on the Bailgate in the historic cathedral quarter of the city of Lincoln, just 230 yards from the cathedral and castle. This outwardly Georgian house encapsulates remains of a 14th-century hall, including part of the beamed roof and exposed stone walls. The building has evolved over the years into a carefully restored guesthouse with spacious, interesting bedrooms which are comfortably furnished with antique and reproduction pieces and equipped with the most up-to-date facilities. Each room has a view of the castle, cathedral spires or the Bailgate. Colour televisions, telephones and hostess trays are provided in all rooms. For that special occasion there is a luxurious double room with a vaulted ceiling and exposed brickwork, a large plasma screen TV, and a separate bath and shower en suite, while another double room has an ornately carved four-poster bed, a feature fireplace and a comfy sofa. Guests can relax in the lounge which has a flat screen TV and DVD player, and make use of the breakfast room which doubles as a quiet reading room during the day and also has a computer with wireless Internet access. Breakfast is taken around

a large polished table, and offers a choice of full continental or traditional English, with plenty of tea, coffee, orange juice and toast. Evening meals are not available but there are many good restaurants all, within a few minutes' walking distance of the hotel, and the proprietors are happy to make a booking for you. There are extensive enclosed gardens, with a heated outdoor swimming pool (seasonal), barbeque and patio area, and to the rear is a secure car park. A number of activites can be arranged from the hotel including local walks, fishing trips, golf, shooting and horse riding. High-quality self-catering cottages are available in the grounds of Bailhouse.

Recommended in the area

Lincoln Castle; Lincoln Cathedral; Lincolnshire Wolds; Museum of Lincolnshire Life; The Usher Gallery

Black Swan Guest House

♦♦♦♦

Address: 21 High Street, MARTON,
Gainsborough DN21 5AH
Tel/Fax: 01427 718878
Email: info@blackswanguesthouse.co.uk
Website: www.blackswanguesthouse.co.uk
Map ref: 8, SK88
Directions: On A156 in village centre
Rooms: 10 en suite, S £45–50 D £68–78 Twin £68
Parking: 10 **Notes:** ⊘ on premises 🐕 allowed in bedrooms

Located in the village centre, the 18th-century Black Swan offers good hospitality and comfortable bedrooms with modern facilities. A four-poster bedroom is also available. The guesthouse caters to business travellers, tourists and local families, who return frequently for the home-from-home comforts. Generous, tasty breakfasts are served in the dining room and a comfortable lounge is available. An added bonus is transport to and from nearby pubs and restaurants. Golf packages can be arranged to take advantage of several top-class courses in the vicinity.

Recommended in the area

Lincoln Cathedral; Humber Bridge and Humber Estuary nature reserves; Sherwood Forest

La Casita

♦♦♦♦♦

Address: Frith House, Main Street, NORMANTON,
Grantham NG32 3BH
Tel: 01400 250302
Fax: 01400 250302
Email: jackiegonzalez@btinternet.com
Website: www.lacasitabandb.co.uk
Map ref: 8, SK94
Directions: From A1, Normanton on A607 Grantham
to Lincoln rd
Rooms: 1 en suite, S £95 D £125 **Parking:** 3 **Notes:** ⊘ on premises

This converted stable offers considerable luxury in the heart of Lincolnshire. Set independently in the grounds of the owners, the studio provides a rural retreat and complete privacy in spacious, open-plan accommodation with its own entrance and patio. There is a living room with a kitchen area and the large bedroom sleeps up to four people. The slate-tiled bathroom is pure "state of the art". Extras include two flat-screen TVs, DVD, CD and broadband Internet. Full english breakfast is provided.

Recommended in the area

Newark Showground; Belton House (NT); Lincoln Minster; Belvoir Castle

LONDON

The Houses of Parliament and Big Ben from across the River Thames.

MIC Hotel & Conference Centre

★★★★ 🛏 GUEST ACCOMMODATION

Address:	81–103 Euston Street,
	LONDON NW1 2EZ
Tel:	020 7380 0001
Fax:	020 7387 5300
Email:	sales@micentre.com
Website:	www.micentre.com
Map ref:	3, TQ38

Directions: Euston Rd left at lights onto Melton St, 1st left onto Euston St, MIC 100yds on left
Rooms: 28 en suite, S £85–130 D £85–130
Notes: ⊘ on premises ⊗ on premises

The top floor of the MIC building was completely overhauled in 2004 and has been designed to offer the highest standards and value for money. The hotel is staffed around the clock, thus ensuring a safe environment – it also has a concierge service until 10.30pm. The stylish, air-conditioned bedrooms are en suite and come with LCD televisions and radios, room safes, a desk space with Internet access, complimentary hospitality trays and mineral water. The spacious and airy Atrium Bar and Restaurant is perfect for an informal meeting, drink or meal. For breakfast, a traditional English buffet features eight hot items with eggs cooked to order, pancakes and waffles served with maple syprup or sauces, fruit juices, a good selection of cereals, a fruit and yoghurt bar, plus assorted teas and fresh coffee. The centre also offers a range of meeting rooms and private dining rooms for special events, which can be catered for. There are special weekend discount rates. The hotel is located in a quiet street close to Euston Station which has a mainline station, an underground and local bus connections.

Recommended in the area

West End theatres; The BA London Eye; Madame Tussauds

Waterloo bridge and the South bank.

Windermere Hotel

★★★★ GUEST ACCOMMODATION

Address:	142/144 Warwick Way, Victoria, LONDON SW1V 4JE
Tel:	020 7834 5163
Fax:	020 7630 8831
Email:	reservations@windermere-hotel.co.uk
Website:	www.windermere-hotel.co.uk
Map ref:	3, TQ38
Directions:	On B324 off Buckingham Palace Rd, at junction of Alderney St

Rooms: 20 en suite, S £89–99 D £114–139 **Notes:** ⊗ on premises

Individual care and attention is paramount at this small hotel, which retains its charm and character while successfully combining tradition with modern living. The individually styled bedrooms are well equipped and for the business executive there are ISDN 2 facilities for video conferencing. The Pimlico licensed restaurant (open to non-residents) offers a hearty cooked breakfast and delicious evening meals. It is in a central location close to the capital's many attractions and Victoria Station.

Recommended in the area

Buckingham Palace; Houses of Parliament; Tate Britain

Claverley Hotel

★★★★ GUEST HOUSE

Address: 13–14 Beaufort Gardens,
Knightsbridge,
LONDON SW3 1PS
Tel: 020 7589 8541
Fax: 020 7584 3410
Email: reservations@claverleyhotel.co.uk
Website: www.claverleyhotel.co.uk
Map ref: 3, TQ27
Directions: Off A4 Brompton Rd, 350yds SW of
Knightsbridge tube station
Rooms: 29 (26 en suite), S £84–99 D £126–149
Notes: ⊗ on premises

This stylish hotel is hidden away in a quiet, leafy
Knightsbridge cul-de-sac, only a short walk from Harrods and the Victoria & Albert Museum. Owned
by Mrs Demitra Antoniou for over two decades, the distinctive character of the Claverley reflects her
personal dedication, ensuring a reputation for excellence that encourages guests to return again and
again. Service is warm and attention to detail paramount. The bedrooms, most with a marble bathroom
and power shower, are individually designed and some have four-poster beds. All have colour TV with
satellite channels and direct dial telephones. The public areas include a comfortable lounge and
a wood-panelled reading room where you can enjoy complimentary tea, coffee, hot chocolate and
biscuits throughout the day. Impressive breakfasts include a choice of traditional full English, home-
made waffles, fresh salmon kedgeree, and a selection of mouth-watering croissants and brioche,
which are delivered daily from a local bakery. Wireless Internet is availale thorughout the hotel and
there is a laptop for hire.

Recommended in the area

Harrods; South Kensington museums; Hyde Park; Royal Albert Hall

City Hall on the south bank of the Thames.

The Mayflower Hotel

★★★★ GUEST HOUSE

Address:	26–28 Trebovir Road, LONDON SW5 9NJ
Tel:	020 7370 0991
Fax:	020 7370 0994
Email:	info@mayflower-group.co.uk
Website:	www.mayflowerhotel.co.uk
Map ref:	3, TQ38

Directions: From Earls Court tube station left onto Trebovir Rd, premises on left
Rooms: 47 (46 en suite), S £62–72 D £69–99
Parking: 4 Notes: ⊘ on premises

Hospitality and service are the keywords here at this smart hotel not far from Earls Court and Olympia. Each of the individually designed bedrooms have a marbled walk-in bath or shower room, as well as satellite TV and refreshment trays. Public areas include a stylish lounge and a bright dining room.

Recommended in the area

Kensington Palace; Harrods; Madame Tussauds; Victoria & Albert Museum

The Gallery

★★★★ GUEST ACCOMMODATION

Address:	8–10 Queensberry Place,
	South Kensington,
	LONDON SW7 2EA
Tel:	020 7915 0000
Fax:	020 7915 4400
Email:	reservations@eeh.co.uk
Website:	www.eeh.co.uk
Map ref:	3, TQ38

Directions: Off A4 Cromwell Rd opp Natural History Museum, near South Kensington tube station

Rooms: 36 en suite, S £129–153 D £164–188

The concept behind The Gallery is "the Victorian artist at home", and the hotel features original Victorian paintings and antiques throughout. The decor of the two master suites, Rosetti and Leighton, is stunning. They each have a private roof terrace, Jacuzzi, fax and CD and DVD players. The en suite bedrooms are well appointed and have bathrooms with marble tiling, brass fittings and soft white towels. Sumptuous public rooms include the mahogany-panelled reception, lobby and lounge, and the arts and crafts style Morris Room complete with an original Manxman piano and antique bar-billiards table. The highest level of service is available 24 hours a day, and business guests benefit from wired and wireless broadband in each room and the public areas, and there is a boardroom-style meeting room. All bedrooms have interactive televisions with pay movies. The Gallery is an ideal base from which to explore London's host of attractions – the Science Museum, Natural History Museum and Victoria & Albert Museum are virtually on the doorstep. The hotel offers special discounts during the week and at weekends.

Recommended in the area

Victoria & Albert Museum; Harrods; Kensington Palace and Gardens; Hyde Park;
The Queen's Gallery, Buckingham Palace

Hart House Hotel

★★★★ GUEST ACCOMMODATION

Address: 51 Gloucester Place, Portman Sq,
LONDON W1U 8JF
Tel: 020 7935 2288
Fax: 020 7935 8516
Email: reservations@harthouse.co.uk
Website: www.harthouse.co.uk
Map ref: 3, TQ38
Directions: Off Oxford St behind Selfridges, near Baker
St or Marble Arch tube stations
Rooms: 16 en suite, S £65–80 D £89–110
Notes: ⊗ on premises ⊗ on premises

This delightful, well-cared for property occupies a
Georgian terrace just off Oxford Street. Much of its
original elegance and grand ambience survive from the late 18th century, when during the French
Revolution it was home for members of the French aristocracy. The hotel has been carefully restored
so that modern comforts abound, and the en suite bedrooms have been refurbished to a high standard
with quality furnishings and smart bathrooms. The rooms are each equipped with a desk or writing
table, relaxing seating, direct-dial telephone with modem point, a multi-channel television, individually
controlled heating and a hospitality tray. There is a choice of single, double, twin and family rooms.
A tasty traditional English breakfast is served in the cottage-style dining room. Andrew Bowden, whose
family has owned and run the hotel for many years, is a charming and helpful host who is justly proud
of his reputation for providing a comfortable and hospitable atmosphere. Hart House is well placed for
both business and leisure travellers visiting London and is within easy walking distance of public
transport and London's major tourist attractions.

Recommended in the area

Madame Tussauds; Oxford Street; West End theatres

The London Eye.

The Cottage

★★★★ GUEST ACCOMMODATION

Address:	150–152 High Street,
	CRANFORD,
	Hounslow TW5 9WB
Tel:	020 8897 1815
Fax:	020 8897 3117
Email:	bermuthecottage@tinyworld.co.uk
Website:	www.cottageguesthouse-heathrow.co.uk
Map ref:	3, TQ17

Directions: M4 junct 3, A312 towards Feltham, left at lights, left after 1st pub on left Jolly Gardner

Rooms: 17 en suite, S £49.50–67 D £67–75 T £80 Family room £75–90

Parking: 18 Notes: ⊘ on premises

It is hard to believe that Heathrow Airport is just 3 miles away, so peaceful is this attractive guesthouse tucked away in a cul-de-sac behind the high street. Hospitality is particularly strong, and the willing family owners go to great lengths to ensure an enjoyable visit. The en suite bedrooms in the main building are attractively presented in keeping with the style of the house, and equipped with colour television, beverage trays, hairdryers and radio alarm clocks. The new luxury bedrooms are situated in the large landscaped garden, with its fruit trees, shrubs and flowerbeds, and are connected to the main building by a covered walkway. They offer a high level of comfort enhanced by beamed ceilings, spacious luxury bathrooms, fridges and ironing facilities.The comfortable atmosphere extends to the public areas, which include a stylish dining room, where delicious breakfasts are served at separate tables. Secure parking is a welcome feature here, and as well as being close to the airport, there is easy access to central London via the nearby M4 or the underground.

Recommended in the area

Syon House, Isleworth; Kew Gardens; Windsor Castle and Legoland; Hampton Court Palace; Thorpe Park; Twickenham Rugby Ground

MERSEYSIDE

The Royal Liver Building on the River Mersey.

Bay Tree House B&B

★★★★   🛏 GUEST ACCOMMODATION

Address:	No1 Irving Street, Marine Gate, SOUTHPORT PR9 0HD
Tel:	01704 510555
Fax:	01704 510551
Email:	baytreehouseuk@aol.com
Website:	www.baytreehousesouthport.co.uk
Map ref:	5, SD31
Directions:	Off Leicester St

Rooms: 6 en suite, S £39.50–55 D £60–99 **Parking:** 2
Notes: ⊗ on premises 🐕 allowed in bedrooms
Closed: 14 Dec–1 Feb

Bay Tree House is an immaculate and very welcoming retreat, located a short walk from the promenade and central attractions of Southport. There are 15 golf courses within half an hour's drive, six of which are of championship standard. The six individually decorated bedrooms are equipped with a wealth of thoughtful extras – towelling bathrobes, complimentary slippers, and a selection of high quality toiletries are offered as a matter of course. Mini-fridges, beverage facilities, including fruit teas and chocolate, an iron and ironing board, and wireless broadband Internet access are available in every room. One bedroom has a particularly large shower room. Delicious, imaginative breakfasts using local produce are a highlight of a stay here. Don't miss the porridge with whisky, honey and cream, or the local free-range eggs, all served in an attractive dining room overlooking the pretty front patio garden. Evening meals are available by arrangement, alternatively there are many quality restaurants within a 5-minute walk. Reiki and other complementary therapy treatments and training courses are available.

Recommended in the area

Royal Birkdale Golf Course; Knowsley Safari Park; Tate Liverpool

NORFOLK

The Norfolk Broads National Park at sunset.

Blakeney House

★★★★★ GUEST HOUSE

Address: High Street, BLAKENEY, Holt NR25 7NX
Tel: 01263 740561
Fax: 01263 741750
Email: blakeneyhouse@aol.com
Website: www.blakeneyhouse.com
Map ref: 4, TG04
Directions: In village centre
Rooms: 8 (7 en suite), S £50–85 D £60–130 **Parking:**
8 **Notes:** ⊗ on premises ⊗ on premises
No children under 12

Ideally situated for exploring the coast and countryside of north Norfolk, Blakeney House is set in
2 acres of beautiful grounds in the heart of the village. This former Victorian manor house is enhanced
by a charming Victorian-style conservatory, set off by lawns and mature trees. The bedrooms have
colour-coordinated fabrics and many thoughtful touches, such as tea- and coffee-making facilities and
televisions. Breakfast is served at separate tables in the dining room, which overlooks the garden.
Recommended in the area
Boat trips to Blakeney Point; historic halls at Felbrigg, Holkham, Houghton and Blickling

Staffordshire House

★★★★ GUEST ACCOMMODATION

Address: Station Road, Docking,
             BURNHAM MARKET PE31 8LS
Tel: 01485 518709
Email: enquiries@staffordshirehouse.com
Website: www.staffordshirehouse.com
Map ref: 4, TF84
Directions: 5.5m SW of Burnham Market. On B1153 in
Docking, 300yds N of church
Rooms: 3 (1 en suite), D £62–70 **Parking:** 4
Notes: ⊗ on premises

Staffordshire House, dating from 1760, has been variously an inn, saddlery, haberdasher's and a radio
repair shop, and during the war munitions were stored in its barns. These days the house provides
informal country style bed and breakfast in a village 4.5 miles from the coast, and is the hub of
an Internet Art Gallery. There is a drawing room and an elegant dining room leading out onto a terrace
and pretty garden. Bedrooms are individually furnished and come with tea and coffee facilities.
Recommended in the area
Sandringham; Holkham Hall; North Norfolk coast, birdwatching

Bon Vista

★★★★ GUEST HOUSE

Address: 12 Alfred Road,
CROMER NR27 9AN
Tel: 01263 511818
Email: (Jim Ramshaw) jim@bonvista.efhbb.com
Website: www.broadland.com/bonvista
Map ref: 4, TG24
Directions: From pier onto A148 Runton Rd, 400yds left onto Alfred Rd
Rooms: 5 en suite, D £52–54
Notes: ⊘ on premises

One might consider this the epitome of the traditional seaside bed-and-breakfast, a sturdy, three-storey Victorian home, peacefully set in a residential area near the town and beach, which, along with its neighbours, sums up much of the character of this charming east-coast resort. Jim and Margaret have renovated the house to a very high standard, while retaining many of its 100-year-old features and have dedicated more than a decade to endowing it with a warm and friendly atmosphere. The first-floor lounge, with its original fireplace and big bay window, makes the most of the sea views and is a cosy place to relax in the evening. The dining room is on the ground floor and it's here that the traditional English breakfasts can be enjoyed, bathed in the light of the morning sun. The five bedrooms, each with an en suite bathroom, are very prettily decorated with cottagey wallpapers and colour-coordinated fabrics. Some still have their original fireplaces, and the climb up to the front room on the top floor is rewarded with a sea view. The other top-floor bedroom can accommodate a family, with bunk beds for the children. Each room has a TV, and Sky channels are available in the lounge. Another plus point here is the off-street parking, but it is limited so early arrival is recommended.

Recommended in the area

Cromer Pier Pavilion Theatre; North Norfolk Railway; Sheringham Park (NT).

Shrublands Farm

★★★★ FARMHOUSE

Address: Church Street, Northrepps,
CROMER NR27 0AA
Tel/Fax: 01263 579297
Email: youngman@farming.co.uk
Website: www.broadland.com/shrublands
Map ref: 4, TG24
Directions: Off A149 to Northrepps, through village,
past Foundry Arms, cream house 50yds on left
Rooms: 3 (1 en suite, 2 private bathrooms), S £38–40
D £56–60 **Parking:** 5 **Notes:** ⊘ on premises ⊗ on premises No children under 12

Shrublands is a working farm set in mature gardens amid 300 acres of arable farmland, an ideal base for exploring the coast and countryside of rural north Norfolk. Traditional hospitality is a distinguishing feature at the 18th-century farmhouse, with good cooking using home-grown and fresh local produce. Breakfast is served at a large table in the dining room, and there is also a cosy lounge, with a log fire, books and a television. The bedrooms have TVs, radio alarms and tea and coffee facilities. No pets.
Recommended in the area
Blickling Hall and Felbrigg Hall (NT); Sandy beaches at Cromer and Overstrand; Blakeney Point

The White Cottage

★★★★ B&B

Address: 9 Cliff Drive, CROMER NR27 0AW
Tel: 01263 512728
Email:
jboocock@whitecottagecromer.freeserve.co.uk
Website: www.whitecottagecromer.co.uk
Map ref: 4, TG24
Directions: Off A149 Norwich Rd onto Overstrand Rd,
2nd right
Rooms: 3 en suite (2D & 1T) D £70–84 **Parking:** 3
Notes: ⊘ on premises ⊗ on premises No children **Closed:** Xmas

This immaculate detached house, situated on the cliff path at Cromer, offers a high standard of comfort and attentive service. The spacious bedrooms are individually decorated and equipped with every home comfort including tea and coffee trays, electric blankets and micro fridges. The delicious breakfast, using local produce, and home-made bread and preserves, is served in an elegant dining room, on the terrace in summer, or in the cosy breakfast room in winter. Packed lunches to order.
Recommended in the area
Felbrigg Hall (NT); Norfolk Shire Horse Centre; Cley bird reserves

Whitehouse Farm

★★★★★ GUEST ACCOMMODATION

Address: Knapton,
NORTH WALSHAM NR28 0RX
Tel: 01263 721344
Email: info@whitehousefarmnorfolk.co.uk
Website: www.whitehousefarmnorfolk.co.uk
Map ref: 4, TG23
Directions: Follow the A149 south of Cromer
Rooms: 3 en suite, S £40 D £50–60 **Parking:** 8
Notes: ⊗ on premises No children under 12

Enjoy a true taste of country living at this delightful Grade II listed 18th-century flint cottage, which is in close proximity of the miles of sandy beaches that make up Norfolk's Heritage Coastline. At Whitehouse farm caring hosts, Graham and Catherine Moorhouse, offer a very warm welcome. The property is surrounded by open farmland and has been carefully restored to ensure the modern decor blends beautifully with the historic character and period features of the farmhouse. The three large, very tastefully decorated bedrooms have luxury en suite bathrooms and are equipped with many thoughtful touches including tea- and coffee-making facilties and colour television. The tranquil Pulford Room has a four-poster bed and far-reaching views across the fields, while the Orton Room, also with a four-poster bed, looks out onto the farm – there is an additional single bedroom in this suite that can be used to provide twin accommodation if preferred. A traditional full English breakfast that features home-made and local produce is served in the smart dining room and guests have the use of a lounge which is decorated in warm peach shades and has plush sofas and a cosy log fire. Set in the peaceful mature gardens, are two charming self-catering cottages which are suitable for families. There is ample off-road parking at Whitehouse Farm. No children under 12 years in the bed and breakfast accommodation.

Recommended in the area

Sandringham; Blickling Hall and Felbrigg Hall (NT); Norfolk Broads

Old Thorn Barn

★★★★ GUEST ACCOMMODATION

Address:	Corporation Farm, Wymondham Road, Hethel, NORWICH NR14 8EU
Tel:	01953 607785
Fax:	01953 601909
Email:	enquires@oldthornbarn.co.uk
Website:	www.oldthornbarn.co.uk
Map ref:	4, TG20

Directions: 6m SW of Norwich. Follow signs for Lotus Cars from A11 or B1113, on Wymondham Rd

Rooms: 7 en suite, S £33–37 D £52–56 **Parking:** 14 **Notes:** ⊘ on premises ⊗ on premises

Reconstruction of a group of derelict buildings has resulted in this delightful conversion. The substantial 17th-century barns and stables feature a stylish open-plan dining room, where you can linger over breakfast around individual oak tables. At the other end of the room there is a cosy lounge area with a wood-burning stove. Antique pine furniture and smart en suites are a feature of the spacious bedrooms which have tea and coffee trays, trouser presses and hairdryers.

Recommended in the area

Fairhaven Woodland and Water Garden; Pettitts Animal Adventure Park; Wolterton Park

At Knollside

★★★★ B&B

Address:	43 Cliff Road, SHERINGHAM NR26 8BJ
Tel/Fax:	01263 823320
Email:	millar@knollside.free-online.co.uk
Website:	www.broadland.com/knollsidelodge.html
Map ref:	4, TG14

Directions: 250yds E of town centre. A1082 to High St, onto Wyndham St & Cliff Rd

Rooms: 3 en suite, D £60–70 **Parking:** 3 **Notes:** ⊘ on premises ⊗ on premises No children under 2

You're welcomed with a glass of sherry and fresh fruit in your room at this guest house a short walk along the promenade from the centre of Sheringham. The bedrooms offer twin, king size and super king beds, or a carved four-poster bed, enhanced with crisp white linen. Easy chairs and tea and coffee facilities, trouser press, hair dryer and television are provided for extra comfort. Each bathroom is crammed with thoughtful toiletries such as hair spray, mousse, hand cream, shower gel, shampoo and cotton wool. Some rooms have sea views. Start the day with the impressive full English breakfast.

Recommended in the area

Felbrigg Hall (NT); North Norfolk Heritage Coast – Blakeney; Holkam Hall

Pheasant Cottage

★★★★★ B&B

Address:	Long Common Lane,
	SWANTON ABBOT NR10 5BH
Tel/Fax:	01692 538169
Email:	melanie@pheasantcottage.freeserve.co.uk
Website:	www.pheasantcottage.com
Map ref:	4, TG22

Directions: Off B1150 at x-rds signed Swanton Abbott, turn right over bridge at x-rds. Straight across onto Long Common Ln, 1.5m on left

Rooms: 2 en suite, S £45 D £79–89 **Parking:** 4 **Notes:** ⊘ on premises ⊗ on premises

Tea and home-made scones are offered on arrival at 17th-century Pheasant Cottage which has a cosy lounge with a log-burning stove, a dining room with original oak beams and spacious bedrooms with many thoughtful touches. The gardens are delightful and there are stunning views across fields to the church. Delicious English and continental breakfasts, prepared using local produce, are a highlight. Afternoon teas, with tasty home-made preserves, are served in the Swedish log cabin in the orchard.

Recommended in the area

Blickling Hall (NT); Felbrigg Hall (NT); Norfolk Broads

Holly Lodge

★★★★★ ⇔ B&B

Address:	The Street, THURSFORD NR21 0AS
Tel/Fax:	01328 878465
Email:	info@hollylodgeguesthouse.co.uk
Website:	www.hollylodgeguesthouse.co.uk
Map ref:	4, TF93

Directions: Off A148 into Thursford village

Rooms: 3 en suite S £60–90 D £80–110

Parking: 6 **Notes:** ⊘ on premises ⊗ on premises

No children under 14 **Closed:** Jan

This 18th-century property is situated in a picturesque location surrounded by open farmland. The lovely landscaped gardens include a large sundeck, which overlooks the lake and water gardens, providing a great place to relax. The lodge and its guest cottages have been transformed into a splendid guesthouse, with stylish ground-floor bedrooms that are individually decorated and beautifully furnished. En suite bathrooms, televisions and lots of thoughtful extras make for a pleasant stay. The attractive public areas are full of character, with flagstone floors, oak beams and open fireplaces.

Recommended in the area

North Norfolk Coast; Thursford Museum; Walsingham

Thursford Hall.

Bramble House

★★★★ GUEST ACCOMMODATION

Address:	Cats Common, Norwich Road, Smallburgh, WROXHAM NR12 9NS
Tel/Fax:	01692 535069
Email:	bramblehouse@tesco.net
Website:	www.bramblehouse.com
Map ref:	4, TG31

Directions: 3m NE of Wroxham on A1151 Norwich Rd, off lay-by on left

Rooms: 3 en suite, S £38–40 D £54–60 **Parking:** 6

Notes: ⊘ on premises ⊗ on premises No children under 12 **Closed:** Xmas & New Year

This modern detached house is just a short drive from the centre of Wroxham and not far from the coast. The luxury bedrooms are individually furnished and have hairdryers and hospitality trays; one room has a sauna. Breakfast is a farmhouse feast, served at individual tables in the dining room. Sausages come from a local pork specialist and eggs straight from the establishment's own free-range hens. Sue and James Ross are happy to cater for vegetarians and any other dietary requirements.

Recommended in the area

Cruises on the Broads; Blickling Hall (NT); East Ruston Old Vicarage Garden

NORTHAMPTONSHIRE

Holdenby House.

Hunt House Quarters

◆◆◆◆

Address: Main Road, KILSBY,
Rugby CV23 8XR
Tel: 01788 823282
Email: luluharris@hunthouse.fsbusiness.co.uk
Website: www.hunthousekilsby.com
Map ref: 3, SP57
Directions: On B3048 in village
Rooms: 4 en suite, S £59.95–85 D £75–85
Parking: 8 **Notes:** ⊗ on premises

Hunt House Quarters in Kilsby is set in a beautiful peaceful courtyard and forms one part of a magnificently restored 1656 thatched hunting lodge and covered stables. Steeped in history, the lodge was originally used for deer hunting. The property is ideally placed as a touring base for visiting Stratford-upon-Avon, the Cotswolds and Warwick. Nearby there are stately homes, castles and gardens to visit as well as opportunities for some excellent walking. The spacious en
suite bedrooms have their own character and are named the Manger, the Smithy, the Saddlery and the Tack Room. Set around a large courtyard, they retain features such as oak beams and old glass but are furnished in a modern, contemporary style. All rooms are equipped to a high standard and have Internet broadband connection, colour TV, tea- and coffee-making facilities and hairdryer. Breakfast is served in the restaurant where guests are offered the choice of full English, continental or vegetarian breakfast. All breakfasts are freshly cooked and prepared to order at times convenient to the guests. For other meals, there are two village pubs serving food seven days per week, and a selection of Indian, Chinese, Italian, Mexican, English, Thai restaurants only 5-10 minutes away. The gardens surrounding Hunt House Quarters are a peaceful haven in which to relax and take a stroll.

Recommended in the area

Rugby School; Crick Boat Show; National Exhibition Centre

Spanhoe Lodge

◆◆◆◆ 🛏

Address:	Harringworth Road, LAXTON, Near Corby NN17 3AT
Tel:	01780 450328
Fax:	01780 450328
Email:	jennie.spanhoe@virgin.net
Website:	www.spanhoelodge.co.uk
Map ref:	3, SP99
Directions:	Off A43 to Laxton, through village, Spanhoe Lodge 0.5m on right

Rooms: 4 en suite, S £40–60 D £65–90 **Parking:** 50 **Notes:** ⊗ on premises 🐕 allowed in bedrooms

Standing in extensive gardens, this modern lodge offers luxury, peace and tranquillity. The large bedrooms, all on the ground floor, come equipped with fridges, hospitality tray, toiletries, magazines, modern technology access and a full media entertainment system. Using locally sourced ingredients, breakfast is tailor-made to personal choice. Located in the grounds are outside dining facilities and a hot tub. Spanhoe Lodge is pet friendly, has plenty of parking and is able to accommodate horseboxes.

Recommended in the area

Rutland Water; Rockingham Motor Speedway; Burghley House; Uppingham, Oundle, Stamford

The Courtyard

◆◆◆◆◆

Address:	Rutland Lodge, West Street, STANWICK NN9 6QY
Tel:	01933 622233
Fax:	01933 622276
Email:	bookings@thecourtyard.me.uk
Website:	www.thecourtyard.me.uk
Map ref:	3, SP97
Directions:	A45 rdbt to Stanwick, 0.3m right onto drive

Rooms: 6 en suite, S £45–50 D £60–75 **Parking:** 12
Notes: ⊗ on premises ⊗ on premises No children

Comfort and luxury abound at this attractive house, where the hospitality is unforgettable. The house stands in delightful large gardens on the edge of Stanwick village. The bedrooms have either garden or country views, and are well equipped and stamped with quality. They are stylish and modern, and all rooms come with Internet access, satellite televisions, and tea and coffee facilities. A business meeting room is available. Breakfasts are in keeping with the high standards. Secure parking is available.

Recommended in the area

Rockingham Castle; Oundle; Santa Pod

NORTHUMBERLAND

Heather clad hills at Yeavering Bell.

Bamburgh Castle.

Market Cross Guest House

◆◆◆◆

Address: 1 Church Street, BELFORD NE70 7LS
Tel: 01668 213013
Email: details@marketcross.net
Website: www.marketcross.net
Map ref: 10, NU13
Directions: Off A1 into village, opp church
Rooms: 3 en suite, S £45–65 D £65–80 **Parking:** 3
Notes: ⊘ on premises ⊀ allowed in bedrooms

Set in the heart of the charming village of Belford, just off the Great North Road, this Grade II listed building is well placed for visiting the Northumbrian coast. The traditional northern hospitality here is matched by the high quality of the accommodation, with bedrooms that are large enough to include easy chairs and sofas. Each has a flat screen TV and a wealth of extras including a fridge with fresh milk for the complimentary beverages, fruit, and fresh flowers. The breakfasts, which may include kedgeree, smoked salmon scrambled eggs, pancakes and griddle scones, have an AA Award for their quality and range. Many ingredients are sourced locally and there are also vegetarian options.

Recommended in the area

Lindisfarne (Holy Island); Alnwick Castle and gardens; the Farne Islands; Northumberland National Park

Ivy Cottage

★★★★★ 🛏 GUEST ACCOMMODATION

Address: 1 Croft Gardens, Crookham,
CORNHILL-ON-TWEED TD12 4ST
Tel: 01890 820667
Fax: 01890 820667
Email: ajoh540455@aol.com
Website: www.ivycottagecrookham.co.uk
Map ref: 10, NT83
Directions: 4m E of Cornhill. Off A697 onto B6353
into Crookham village

Rooms: 2, S £42 D £62–70 **Parking:** 2 **Notes:** ⊘ on premises ⇥ by arrangement
No children under 5

This lovely stone-built modern cottage is the culmination of the many years spent in the hospitality industry by the owners Alan and Doreen Johnson, a kind of retirement project that demonstrates the depth of their experience and their dedication to guests' well being. In the heart of the village of Crookham, it is perfectly located for exploring the Northumberland coast and the Cheviot Hills. The house is set in neat gardens, and there's a summerhouse where guests can enjoy tea on a nice afternoon. Inside the house everything is bright and spotless, and the two bedrooms – one on the ground floor and one upstairs – are spacious and beautifully furnished. With fresh flowers, crisp embroidered bed linen, TV and tea-making facilities they are immediately welcoming and relaxing. Each has its own private bathroom with a deep tub and Crabtree & Evelyn toiletries, and huge terry towels and bathrobes are provided. Wonderful breakfasts are served, either in the formal dining room or in the farmhouse-style kitchen, with its Aga cooking range. Whichever room is used, the feast will be the same, including local free-range eggs and other produce, home made preserves, freshly squeezed orange juice and bread that's home baked using stone-ground flour from nearby Heatherslaw Mill.

Recommended in the area

Holy Island; Alnwick Castle and Gardens; Flodden Battlefield.

Pheasant Inn

★★★★ INN

Address: Stannersburn, FALSTONE NE48 1DD
Tel/Fax: 01434 240382
Email: enquiries@thepheasantinn.com
Website: www.thepheasantinn.com
Map ref: 6, NY78
Directions: A68 onto B6320, signs for Kielder Water
Rooms: 8 en suite, S £50 D £85 Parking: 40
Notes: ⊗ on premises Closed: Xmas

Set close by the magnificent Kielder Water, this classic country inn, built in 1624, has exposed stone walls, original beams, low ceilings, open fires and a display of old farm implements in the bar. Run by the welcoming Kershaw family since 1985, the inn has been refurbished to a very high standard. Bright modern bedrooms, some with their own entrances, are all contained in stone buildings adjoining the inn. All the rooms are spotless, well equipped, and have tea and coffee facilities and country views. Delicious home-cooked breakfasts and evening meals are served in the bar or in the attractive dining room. Irene and her son Robin are responsible for the traditional home cooking using local produce.
Recommended in the area
Hadrian's Wall; Keilder Water Reservoir (sports facilities); Cragside House (NT)

Vallum Lodge

★★★★ GUEST HOUSE

Address: Military Road, Twice Brewed,
HALTWHISTLE NE47 7AN
Tel/Fax: 01434 344488
Email: stay@vallum-lodge.co.uk
Website: www.vallum-lodge.co.uk
Map ref: 6, NY76
Directions: On B6318, 400yds W of Once Brewed
National Park visitors centre
Rooms: 6 en suite, S £46–56 D £60–66 Parking: 15
Notes: ⊘ on premises ⊗ on premises No children under 3 Closed: Nov–Feb

This licensed roadside guesthouse provides a home from home in the heart of the Northumberland National Park. It is perfectly placed for walking and cycling in this unspoiled part of England. The bedrooms are all on the ground floor. They have all been refurbished and feature hospitality trays and complimentary toiletries. Laundry and drying facilities are also available. Breakfast is served in the smart dining room and there is a cosy lounge with a television and a selection of books and games.
Recommended in the area
Hadrian's Wall; Vindolanda; Housesteads; Roman Army Museum; the Pennine Way

Peth Head Cottage

★ ★ ★ ★ B&B

Address:	Juniper,
	HEXHAM NE47 0LA
Tel:	01434 673286
Fax:	01434 673038
Email:	peth_head@btopenworld.com
Website:	www.peth-head-cottage.co.uk
Map ref:	7, NY96

Directions: B6306 S from Hexham, 200yds fork right, next left. Continue 3.5m, house 400yds on right after Juniper sign

Rooms: 2 en suite, S £27 D £54 **Parking:** 2

Notes: ⊘ on premises ⊗ on premises

This lovingly maintained rose-covered cottage dates back to 1825 and is popular for its warm welcome, idyllic setting, and home comforts. Tea and hand-made biscuits are offered on arrival, and the delicious home baking is enjoyed at breakfast too, along with freshly made bread and tasty preserves. The inviting sandstone cottage is set in peaceful, well-kept gardens. There are two bright, south-facing bedrooms, both overlooking the garden, with shower rooms en suite, a hairdryer, colour TV, radio alarm and hospitality trays. The cosy lounge is heavily beamed and furnished with comfy chairs; there is plenty of tourist information and maps are on hand for visitors to browse through and plan your day. Peth Head Cottage is ideallly situated for visiting Durham and Newcastle, as well as nearby Roman sites and there are plenty of opportunites for walking and cycling in the area. Owner Joan Liddle is an excellent host. There is private off-road parking. Sorry, no pets.

Recommended in the area

Beamish Open Air Museum; Hadrian's Wall; the Northumberland coast; Durham Cathedral; Finchale Priory; Lanercost Priory

The Orchard House

★★★★★ 🏛 GUEST ACCOMMODATION

Address: High Street,
ROTHBURY NE65 7TL
Tel: 01669 620684
Email: graham@orchardhouserothbury.com
Website: www.orchardhouserothbury.com
Map ref: 10, NU00
Directions: In village centre
Rooms: 4 en suite, D £80–150
Notes: ⊘ on premises ⊗ on premises
Closed: Xmas & New Year

The Orchard House stands in an elevated location within easy walking distance of Rothbury village. This peaceful Georgian stone house has lots of character and offers excellent comfort. Bedrooms are sumptuous with crisp white linen and duck-down duvets, and well equipped with complimentary bathrobes, daily newspapers and fresh flowers, while the super bathrooms have luxury toiletries. Guests can unwind in the elegant antique-furnished drawing room, which has a bar service in the evenings. Breakfast is a lavish affair with the emphasis on fresh local ingredients, organic and Fairtrade produce. The free-range eggs come from a local farm, the orange juice is freshly squeezed, and the croissants are freshly baked. Traditional English breakfasts and more modern interpretations are available alongside a range of lighter choices including a generous selection of local cheeses, fresh fruits and home-baked pastries. Vegetarian, wheat-free and special diets are available on request. The Orchard House is well-situated for those who enjoy outdoor pursuits: walking, hiking, cycling, fishing, horse riding and golf are some of the many activities available the area. The Rothbury Golf Club, bordering the River Coquet and with splendid views of the Cheviot Hills, welcomes guests from The Orchard House with discounted Green fees.

Recommended in the area

North Northumberland Heritage Coast; Bamburgh Castle; Alnwick Castle and Gardens

The Cheviot mountains from Yeavering Bell.

The Old Manse

♦♦♦♦♦

Address:	New Road, Chatton, WOOLER NE66 5PU
Tel:	01668 215343
Email:	chattonbb@aol.com
Website:	www.oldmansechatton.co.uk
Map ref:	10, NT92
Directions:	4m E of Wooler. On B6348 in Chatton

Rooms: 3 en suite, S £30–55 D £60–80 **Parking:** 4

Notes: ⊘ on premises No children under 13

Built in 1875 and commanding excellent views over the open countryside, this imposing former manse stands on the edge of the pretty village of Chatton between the Cheviot Hills and the scenic North Northumberland Heritage Coast. You approach the house by a sweeping gravel drive bordered with lawns and conifers. You can explore the extensive gardens, which include a wildlife pond. The Rosedale Suite is an elegant four-poster room with a Victorian-style bathroom en suite; Buccleuch has a sitting room and private patio. All rooms are well appointed, spacious and luxurious. Enjoy home-made cakes and biscuits and hearty breakfasts in the elegant conservatory-dining room.

Recommended in the area

Alnwick Garden; Chillingham Castle and wild cattle; Bamburgh Castle

Roses in the former Kitchen Gardens of Newstead Abbey.

Autumn in Sherwood Forest

Compton House

★★★★ GUEST HOUSE

Address:	117 Baldertongate, NEWARK-ON-TRENT NG24 1RY
Tel:	01636 708670
Email:	info@comptonhousenewark.com
Website:	www.comptonhousenewark.com
Map ref:	8, SK75

Directions: 500yds SE of town centre. Off B6326 onto Sherwood Av, 1st right onto Baldertongate

Rooms: 7 (6 en suite), S £45–55.50 D £75.50–105

Parking: 2 **Notes:** ⊘ on premises ⊗ on premises

An elegant Grade II listed town house just a few minutes' walk from central Newark with its restaurants, pubs and cafés. The charming bedrooms come with courtesy tray, large soft towels and superior toiletries. There is a relaxing drawing room and a pretty courtyard garden. The comprehensive breakfast, and dinner by arrangement, is served in the dining room.

Recommended in the area

Nottingham; Newark Air Museum; Lincoln Cathedral

OXFORDSHIRE

Pleasure boats on the Thames at Henley.

The Boar's Head

◆◆◆◆   ◉◉

Address:	Church Street, ARDINGTON, Wantage OX12 8QA
Tel/Fax:	01235 833254
Email:	info@boarsheadardington.co.uk
Website:	www.boarsheadardington.co.uk
Map ref:	3, SU48
Directions:	In village next to church

Rooms: 3 en suite, S £75–105 D £85–130 Parking: 20
Notes: ⊗ on premises

Located in the downland village of Ardington, this inn combines a village pub, a first-class restaurant and stylish accommodation. The village is part of the Lockinge Estate, a great base for walking and cycling, and only a half-hour drive from Oxford. Great care has gone into creating a stylish bedrooms, while retaining many original features. One room has a luxurious bathroom, another has an adjoining sitting room. Food is a passion, with ingredients fresh, local and seasonal whenever possible. Fish is a particular speciality. Excellent wines and good local ales.

Recommended in the area

Oxford colleges; Vale of the White Horse; Blenheim Palace

The Mill House Country Guest House

★ ★ ★ ★   GUEST ACCOMMODATION

Address:	North Newington Rd, BANBURY OX15 6AA
Tel:	01295 730212
Fax:	01295 730363
Email:	lamadonett@aol.com
Website:	www.themillhousebanbury.com
Map ref:	3, SP44
Directions:	M40 junct 11, signs to Banbury Cross, onto B4035, 2m right for Newington

Rooms: 7 en suite, S £54–79 D £79–112 Parking: 20 Notes: ⊘ on premises

The former miller's house, surrounded by rolling countryside, offers comfortable accommodation and four refurbished self-contained cottages in the courtyard. The en suite rooms have telephones and tea and coffee equipment. The cottages are available on a self-catering or bed and breakfast basis, and have a separate lounge-kitchen. There is a charming lounge bar in the main house.

Recommended in the area

Blenheim Palace; Strafford-upon-Avon; The Cotswolds

Burford House

◆◆◆◆◆

Address:	99 High Street,
	BURFORD OX18 4QA
Tel:	01993 823151
Fax:	01993 823240
Email:	stay@burfordhouse.co.uk
Website:	www.burfordhouse.co.uk
Map ref:	3, SP21
Directions:	Off A40 into town centre

Rooms: 8 en suite, D £125–160
Notes: ⊗ on premises

In the heart of this famous Cotswold town, Burford House, with its leaded windows and half-timbered and stone exterior, is an individual hotel with many welcoming touches. The charming bedrooms, all individually furnished, have fresh flowers and are equipped with colour TV, hairdryers, magazines, toiletries and complimentary mineral water. Some have queen- or king-size beds and one has a four-poster bed. There is wireless broadband Internet access in all the bedrooms. Many of the attractive bathrooms have free-standing Victorian tubs and separate shower stalls. Antique furniture, pictures and porcelain adorn the rooms which overlook either the historic hight street or the garden. Downstairs are two intimate sitting rooms both with comfortable sofas; one has a log fire and an honesty bar, while the bright garden room has doors leading out onto the courtyard where there is more seating. Both are the perfect venue for relaxing with a book or a drink. Superb breakfasts are served in the dining room and later, morning coffee, light lunches and the most delicious afternoon teas, featuring home-made scones, pastries and cakes. Your hosts, Jane and Simon Henty, make a point of supporting local suppliers and much of what you'll enjoy – granary bread, honey, smoked salmon, clotted cream – is top local produce.

Recommended in the area

Historic Burford; Cotswold Wildlife Park; River Windrush

Oxfordshire

The Bliss Tweed Mill, Chipping Norton.

The Forge

★ ★ ★ ★   GUEST ACCOMMODATION

Address: Churchill, CHIPPING NORTON OX7 6NJ
Tel: 01608 658173
Email: enquiries@cotswolds-accommodation.com
Website: www.cotswolds-accommodation.com
Map ref: 3, SP32
Directions: B4450 from Chipping Norton to Churchill 2.5m
Rooms: 5 en suite, S £50–70 D £65–85 **Parking:** 6
Notes: ⊗ on premises ⊗ on premises
No children under 11

Debby and Martin Rushbrooke offer a warm welcome and stylish accommodation at this 200-year-old honey-stone house in the village of Churchill just a short drive from Chipping Norton. The stylish bedrooms – one with a Jacuzzi bath – are individually designed. Three rooms have four-poster beds, and all are filled with thoughtful extras. The cottage-style breakfast room leads into a pleasant lounge. Breakfast is a feast of sausages and bacon from the local butcher. The village pub is almost opposite.
Recommended in the area
Blenheim Palace; Warwick Castle; Stratford-upon-Avon

The Cherry Tree Inn

★★★★ ◎ 🍽 RESTAURANT WITH ROOMS

Address: Stoke Row,
HENLEY-ON-THAMES RG9 5QA
Tel: 01491 680430
Website: www.thecherrytreeinn.com
Map ref: 3, SU78
Directions: 6m W of Henley. Off B841 into Stoke Row
Rooms: 4 en suite, D £75–95 **Parking:** 30
Notes: ⊘ on premises ⊗ on premises
Closed: 25–26 Dec

The Cherry Tree is in an Area of Outstanding Natural Beauty within the Chilterns, yet only 20 minutes from Reading and motorway connections. New owners Paul Gilchrist and Richard Coates have over 25 years' experience in the hospitality industry, which includes working in several prestigious restaurants. The contemporary furnishings and strong colours complement the original flagstone floors, beamed ceilings and fireplaces. The bedrooms, situated in an old converted barn to the side of the inn, have a modern design, and spacious bathrooms with luxurious toiletries. Added touches include mineral water, fresh fruit, and a tea and fresh coffee maker. The philosophy in the contemporary restaurant is quality, fresh ingredients with uncomplicated presentation, and value for money. Classic and modern European dishes and daily specials are offered, and the home-made Sunday roast is a favourite. The pub is a popular resting point for both walkers and cyclists, tempted by the first-class beers and delicious meals. There is a non-smoking policy through-out the restaurant, bar and letting rooms.

Recommended in the area

Rowing and River Museum, Henley-on-Thames; Oxford; Mahajarah's Well, Stoke Row; The Savill Garden, Windsor Great Park

The Gate Hangs High

♦♦♦♦

Address:	HOOK NORTON, Banbury OX15 5DF
Tel:	01608 737387
Fax:	01608 737870
Email:	gatehangshigh@aol.com
Map ref:	3, SP33

Directions: 0.6m N of village on x-rds
Rooms: 4 en suite, S £40–45 D £50–60 Parking: 40
Notes: 🐕 allowed in bedrooms Closed: Xmas night

A delightful country inn located between the historic towns of Banbury and Chipping Norton, ideally placed for touring the Cotswolds and visiting Oxford. The surrounding countryside is perfect for walking and there are good views from the inn. The attractively decorated spacious en suite bedrooms exude a warm cosy ambience with their deep red walls and soft lighting. All rooms come with TV and tea and coffee trays. The excellent restaurant is warm and inviting and the menu served is of a high quality, the dishes all carefully prepared and well presented. There is a good international wine list and a selection of beers from the local Hook Norton Brewery.

Recommended in the area

Blenheim Palace; Broughton Castle; Water Fowl Sanctuary and Children's Farm

The Tollgate Inn & Restaurant

♦♦♦♦

Address:	Church Street,
	KINGHAM OX7 6YA
Tel:	01608 658389
Email:	info@thetollgate.com
Website:	www.thetollgate.com
Map ref:	3, SP22

Directions: Turn off B4450 (towards Chipping Norton)
Rooms: 9 en suite, S £60 D £80–100 Parking: 12

Nestling in an idyllic village of stone cotswold cottages, this 17th-century farmhouse blends in perfectly with its surroundings, and makes a good base from which to explore the beautiful countryside. The building is fronted by neat lawns and outside seating. Step inside and The Tollgate Inn and Restaurant creates an informal yet stylish, atmosphere with flagstone floors, beamed ceilings, huge inglenook fireplaces and friendly faces. The inn has been lovingly restored to provide nine en suite bedrooms each with an individual identity. Some of the finest food in the area, well-kept beers and good wines await you at The Tollgate Inn's restaurant.

Recommended in the area

Blenheim Palace; Batsford Park Arboretum; Oxford city

Blenheim Palace and gardens, Woodstock.

Duke of Marlborough Country Inn

★★★★ INN

Address:	A44, Woodleys,
	WOODSTOCK OX20 1HT
Tel:	01993 811460
Fax:	01993 810165
Email:	sales@dukeofmarlborough.co.uk
Website:	www.dukeofmarlborough.co.uk
Map ref:	3, SP41
Directions:	1m N of Woodstock on A44 x-rds

Rooms: 13 en suite, S £65–85 D £80–120 **Parking:** 42 **Notes:** ⊘ on premises

This attractive stone inn has en suite bedrooms, in an adjacent lodge-style building, offering high standards of quality and comfort for both the business and holiday traveller. There is a cosy traditional bar restaurant, with log fire and Cotswold stone walls, and a modern function room and restaurant. Dishes are home cooked and beautifully prepared using local produce, steaks and fish.

Recommended in the area

Blenheim Palace; Oxford; Broughton Castle

SHROPSHIRE

The Iron Bridge over the Severn.

The Laurels

★ ★ ★ ★   GUEST HOUSE

Address:	Broadoak, Six Ashes,
	BRIDGNORTH WV15 6EQ
Tel:	01384 221546
Email:	george@broadoak75.fsnet.co.uk
Website:	www.thelaurelsbandb.co.uk
Map ref:	2, SO79

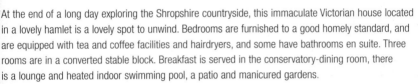

Directions: On right 5m from Bridgnorth travelling towards Stourbridge on the A458

Rooms: 6 (5 en suite), S £25–30 D £50 **Parking:** 6

Notes: ⊘ on premises ⊗ on premises **Closed:** Xmas & New Year

At the end of a long day exploring the Shropshire countryside, this immaculate Victorian house located in a lovely hamlet is a lovely spot to unwind. Bedrooms are furnished to a good homely standard, and are equipped with tea and coffee facilities and hairdryers, and some have bathrooms en suite. Three rooms are in a converted stable block. Breakfast is served in the conservatory-dining room, there is a lounge and heated indoor swimming pool, a patio and manicured gardens.

Recommended in the area

Ironbridge; Black Country Museum; Redhouse Cone

The Orchards

★ ★ ★ ★ ★   B&B

Address:	Eaton Road, Ticklerton,
	CHURCH STRETTON SY6 7DQ
Tel:	01694 722268
Email:	lnutting@btinternet.com
Website:	www.theorchardsticklerton.com
Map ref:	2, SO49

Directions: From A49 take B4371, after 3m turn right to Ticklerton. Turn left in village, last house on left.

Rooms: 3 (2 en suite), S £25–30 D £50–60 **Parking:** 6

Notes: ⊘ on premises No children under 3

This modern house, set in more than 4 acres of grounds, gardens and, of course, an orchard, offers high standards of comfort throughout. The bedrooms are thoughtfully equipped with hairdryers, tea- and coffee-making facilities, TV, armchairs and radio alarms, an iron and ironing board available on request, and each has a private bathroom, all but one of them en suite. Ann and Lloyd Nutting, the owners, not only maintain the quality but also provide the exceptionally warm and welcoming atmosphere.

Recommended in the area

Long Mynd and the Carding Mill Valley; Shropshire Hills Discovery Centre; Ironbridge Gorge museums

The Crown Inn

Address: Hopton Wafers,
CLEOBURY MORTIMER DY14 0NB
Tel: 01299 270372
Fax: 01299 271127
Email: desk@crownathopton.co.uk
Website: www.crownathopton.co.uk
Map ref: 2, SO67
Directions: Ludlow on A4117 from Kiddermister.
Nearest motorway is M5 junct 6
Rooms: 18 en suite, S £59.50–69.50 D £95–115
Parking: 50 **Notes:** 🐕 allowed in bedrooms

Surrounded by farmland, wooded valleys and tumbling streams, this 16th-century coaching inn offers fine hospitality. The bedrooms vary: you can choose between the original, oak-beamed rooms of the inn, self-contained cottage-style rooms, and luxurious new rooms. Each is decorated in cottage style, with quality fabrics. Cosy sofas in the public areas are inviting, and there is a choice of dining rooms. The menus feature modern cuisine, which is imaginatively prepared using fresh local produce.

Recommended in the area

Ludlow; Severn Valley Railway; Bridgnorth; Wyre Forest

The Library House

★★★★★ 🏠 B&B

Address: 11 Severn Bank, IRONBRIDGE,
Telford TF8 7AN
Tel: 01952 432299
Fax: 01952 433967
Email: info@libraryhouse.com
Website: www.libraryhouse.com
Map ref: 2, SJ60
Directions: 50yds from Iron Bridge
Rooms: 4 en suite, S £55–60 D £70–80
Notes: No children under 10

Located just 60 yards from the famous Iron Bridge, this Grade II listed Georgian building is tucked away in a peaceful thoroughfare yet close to good pubs and restaurants. Hanging baskets and window boxes enhance the creeper-covered walls of the former library, and in the spring and summer the gardens are immaculate. All of the bedrooms have a television with DVD, a small DVD library, and a hospitality tray. Excellent breakfasts are served in the pine-furnished dining room.

Recommended in the area

Ironbridge World Heritage Site; Telford International Exhibition Centre; Blists Hill Victorian Town

Top Farm House

★★★★ 🏛 GUEST HOUSE

Address:	KNOCKIN SY10 8HN
Tel:	01691 682582
Fax:	01691 682070
Email:	p.a.m@knockin.freeserve.co.uk
Website:	www.topfarmknockin.co.uk
Map ref:	5, SJ32
Directions:	In Knockin, past Bradford Arms & shop, past turning for Kinnerley

Rooms: 3 en suite, S £35–55 D £60–70 Parking: 6

Notes: 🐕 allowed in bedrooms

Set in pretty gardens and retaining many original features, including exposed beams and open log fires, Top Farm House combines traditional hospitality with elegant surroundings. The bedrooms are equipped with many thoughtful extras. There is a relaxing beamed drawing room with a grand piano, and imaginative and comprehensive breakfasts are served in the spacious period dining room which overlooks the garden. The village of Knockin is one of the prettiest in this part of Shropshire.

Recommended in the area

Shrewsbury; Powis Castle (NT); Llanthaedr Waterfall

Angel House

★★★★ B&B

Address:	Bitterley, LUDLOW SY8 3HT
Tel:	01584 891377
Email:	stay@angelhousecleehill.co.uk
Website:	www.angelhousecleehill.co.uk
Map ref:	2, SO57
Directions:	On A4117 towards Kidderminster

Rooms: 2 en suite, S £40–65 D £65 Parking: 10

Notes: ⊘ on premises 🐕 allowed in bedrooms

No children under 5

With views over four counties, 17th-century Angel House is a great place to take a break, whether visiting nearby Ludlow, exploring the historic sights, or walking the Shropshire Way. The views continue from the spacious modern bedrooms, which are thoughtfully equipped. There is a cosy dining room, a lounge, and conservatory that looks out towards Ludlow. Breakfast is a highlight and evening meals and packed lunches, also of a very high standard, can be ordered in advance. You will be greeted on arrival by the resident dog, Spencer, who welcomes other friendly and well-behaved canines.

Recommended in the area

Ludlow Castle; Stokesay Castle; Shropshire Way footpath

The 12th century Ludlow Castle.

Bromley Court B&B

★★★★★ B&B

Address: Lower Broad Street, LUDLOW SY8 1PQ
Tel: 01584 876996/07809 699 665
Email: phil@ludlowhotels.com
Website: www.ludlowhotels.com
Map ref: 2, SO57
Directions: Off B4361 at bridge into town centre
Rooms: 3 en suite, S £75–115 D £95–120
Notes: ⊘ on premises

Located close to the river and attractions of the historic town, these three tiny Tudor cottages have each been converted into a private suite, complete with exposed oak beams, inglenook fireplaces (in two cottages) and a stylish decorative theme. Each suite has a sitting room and bathroom en suite, antique bed with quality furnishings, many thoughtful extras and access to a lovely courtyard garden. A continental breakfast is offered in the comfort of the suites (or the garden in warm weather), or a full English breakfast is available at the nearby Bull Hotel. All of Ludlow's AA Rosetted restaurants are within walking distance.

Recommended in the area

Ludlow town, castle and church; woodland and riverside walks; Shropshire Hills Discovery Centre

The Clive Bar and Restaurant with Rooms

Address:	Bromfield,
	LUDLOW SY8 2JR
Tel:	01584 856565
Fax:	01584 856661
Email:	info@theclive.co.uk
Website:	www.theclive.co.uk
Map ref:	2, SO57

Directions: 2m N of Ludlow on A49 in village of Bromfield
Rooms: 15 en suite, S £50–75 D £75–97.50 **Parking:** 100
Notes: ⊘ on premises ⊗ on premises **Closed:** 25–26 Dec

A stylish makeover of a former farmhouse has given The Clive a smart contemporary look. Food is the heart of the operation here with the well-known restaurant where you can enjoy superb British cooking. There is an emphasis on the use of fresh produce ranging from local meats, smoked products and vegetables to Cornish fish. Vegetarian options are on the menu and special dietary requirements can be catered for on request. Service is friendly but not fussy. There is a traditional 18th-century bar with a log fire and a more modern bar with an adjoining courtyard, with tables and parasols, where you can enjoy traditional Hobsons ale from nearby Cleobury Mortimer, wines by the glass and light snacks. Spacious en suite bedrooms have been refurbished to provide well-equipped modern accommodation. All rooms have colour TV, radio and alarm, telephone and Internet access point as well as facilities for making tea and coffee; some rooms have easy access for guests with mobility problems. Paul and Barbara Brooks and their young team offer a sincere welcome and a warm atmosphere throughout.

Recommended in the area

Stokesay Castle, Craven Arms; Ludlow Food Hall; Ludlow Race Course and Golf Club; Offa's Dyke

Number Twenty Eight

★ ★ ★ ★ 🛎 B&B

Address:	28 Lower Broad Street,
	LUDLOW SY8 1PQ
Tel:	01584 875466
Fax:	01584 875466
Email:	enquiries@no28ludlow.co.uk
Website:	www.no28ludlow.co.uk
Map ref:	2, SO57

Directions: In town centre. Over Ludford Bridge onto
Lower Broad St, 3rd house on right
Rooms: 2 en suite, S £60–80 D £80–90
Notes: ⊗ on premises ⊗ on premises
No children under 16 Closed: Nov–Mar

Run by Eileen and Albie Fermor-Harris, who aim to offer
the highest possible standards of accommodation and levels of comfort, this early Georgian half-
timbered house, built about 1770, lies near Ludlow's historic centre, and is close to Ludford Bridge
and Horseshoe Weir. Ludlow market, the castle, pottery, craft and antique shops, and excellent
restaurants are all ust a short walk away. Number Twenty Eight has charming, well-equipped
bedrooms that come with home-made biscuits and hospitality trays. There is a cosy sitting room, or in
fine weather you can relax in the pretty courtyard garden. For breakfast, freshly squeezed orange juice,
fruit salad, local bacon, sausages, eggs and breads will set you up for a day of exploring. Options
includes Ludlow, beautiful Whitcliffe Common, longer excursions around south Shropshire or a trip to
Ironbridge. Evening meals are not provided at Number Twenty Eight, but you are close to many first-
class restaurants, some of which are among the finest in the country.

Recommended in the area

Ludlow Castle; Berrington Hall (NT); Croft Castle (NT); Stokesay Castle; Shropshire Hills Discovery
Centre; Offa's Dyke footpath

Haywood Farm B&B

★★★★ B&B

Address:	Haywood Lane, Cheswardine, MARKET DRAYTON TF9 2LW
Tel:	01630 661788
Email:	haywoodfarm@hotmail.com
Map ref:	6, SJ63
Directions:	3m S of Market Drayton. Off A529 for Cheswardine, over canal bridge, 1st left
Rooms:	5 (1 en suite), S £30–45 D £60 Parking: 6
Notes:	⊘ on premises ⊗ on premises

Enjoy a traditional country break at this welcoming farmhouse, set in rolling countryside close to Goldstone Common. The 19th-century building provides comfortable accommodation with many pleasurable extras. The spacious bedrooms have superb views of the garden and surroundings, and are attractively decorated and furnished. Breakfast is cooked to order on the kitchen Aga, and served in the smart dining room, while the stylish sitting room with its open fire and comfy seating is perfect for unwinding after a busy day sightseeing or walking by the nearby Shropshire canal.

Recommended in the area

Ironbridge World Heritage Site; Alton Towers; Chester

Pool Cottage

★★★★ B&B

Address:	Gravels, MINSTERLEY, Shrewsbury SY5 0JD
Tel:	01743 891621
Email:	reservations@poolcottage.com
Website:	www.poolcottage.com
Map ref:	2, SJ30
Directions:	Off A488, signed Pool Cottage
Rooms:	3 en suite, S £27–30 D £55 Parking: 51
Notes:	No pets ⊘ on premises Closed: Christmas

This engaging cottage-style guesthouse of great charm is in an ideal spot for walking, birdwatching, or just relaxing. You can bring your own horse and make use of the stables and grazing – there is direct access to Stapeley Common. Well appointed in every detail, the modern accommodation has quite spacious bedrooms and includes a double aspect family room with stunning views. Full English or continental breakfasts are served around one table in the breakfast room.

Recommended in the area

The Long Mynd; Ludlow; Shrewsbury

Crown Country Inn

★★★★ ◉◉ 🍽 INN

Address:	MUNSLOW, Craven Arms SY7 9ET
Tel:	01584 841205
Fax:	01584 841255
Email:	info@crowncountryinn.co.uk
Website:	www.crowncountryinn.co.uk
Map ref:	2, SO58
Directions:	Off B4368 into village

Rooms: 3 en suite, D £70–75 **Parking:** 20 **Notes:** ⊗ on premises ⊗ on premises **Closed:** 25 Dec

The historic character of impressive Tudor inn is retained in the massive oak beams, flagstone floors and a large inglenook fireplace in the main bar area. The bedrooms, in a converted stable block at the rear, have sitting areas, hospitality trays, fresh fruit and mineral water. Traditional ales and food prepared from local produce are served in the bar and restaurant, and the day begins with a substantial English breakfast.

Recommended in the area

Ironbridge World Heritage Site; Discovery Centre, Craven Arms; Ludlow Castle

Abbey Court Guest House

★★★★ GUEST HOUSE

Address:	134 Abbey Foregate,
	SHREWSBURY SY2 6AU
Tel:	01743 364416
Fax:	01743 358559
Email:	info@abbeycourt.biz
Website:	www.abbeycourt.biz
Map ref:	2, SJ41
Directions:	N of river off A5112

Rooms: 10 en suite, S £35–40 D £55–60 **Parking:** 10

Located within easy walking distance from the town centre, this Grade II listed former coaching inn provides a range of homely bedrooms, some of which are in an attractive extension. All rooms have a hospitality tray, a shower room en suite and some also have a bath. Freshly cooked breakfasts are served in the cosy dining room, and continental and vegetarian options are available. Val and Andy MacLeod always give a warm welcome at Abbey Court, and are happy to recommend restaurants nearby for an evening meal. This is an excellent base for visiting the attractions of Shropshire.

Recommended in the area

Shrewsbury Castle and Abbey; Attingham Park (NT); Ironbridge Gorge and museums

Fieldside Guest House

★ ★ ★ ★ GUEST HOUSE

Address: 38 London Road,
SHREWSBURY SY2 6NX
Tel: 01743 353143
Fax: 01743 354687
Email: robrookes@btinternet.com
Website: www.fieldsideguesthouse.co.uk
Map ref: 2, SJ41
Directions: A5 onto A5064, premises 1m on left
Rooms: 4 en suite, S £40 D £60 **Parking:** 8
Notes: ⊘ on premises ⊗ on premises

Fieldside, which dates back to 1835, is just 1 mile from the centre of Shewsbury and a 5-minute walk from Shrewsbury Abbey. This delightful house is attractively furnished and decorated and offers both single and double/twin rooms, all en suite. The bedrooms feature period-style furniture and are equipped with tea and coffee facilities. Breakfast is served at individual tables in the spacious dining room. Traditional English or vegetarian or lighter options are available. There is ample private parking.
Recommended in the area
Shrewsbury Castle and Abbey; Attingham Park (NT); Ironbridge Gorge and museums

Avenue Farm Bed & Breakfast

◆ ◆ ◆ ◆

Address: Uppington, TELFORD TF6 5HW
Tel: 01952 740253
Fax: 01952 740401
Email: jones@avenuefarm.fsnet.co.uk
Website: www.virtual-shropshire.co.uk/avenuefarm
Map ref: 2, SJ60
Directions: M54 junct 7, B5061 for Atcham, 2nd left signed Uppington. Right after sawmill, farm 400yds on right
Rooms: 3 en suite, S £30–35 D £50–55 **Parking:** 4

The Jones family have farmed here since 1916, and are happy to share their 18th-century farmhouse with their guests. Magnificent views of the Wrekin can be enjoyed from the spacious en suite bedrooms, which are filled with thoughtful extras. There is a cosy sitting room and a comfortable dining room where hearty farmhouse breakfasts are served.
Recommended in the area
Ironbridge Gorge and museums; Weston Park; Shrewsbury

Soulton Hall

◆◆◆◆ 🍴

Address: Soulton, WEM SY4 5RS
Tel: 01939 232786
Fax: 01939 234097
Email: enquiries@soultonhall.co.uk
Website: www.soultonhall.co.uk
Map ref: 6, SJ52
Directions: 2m NE of Wem off B5065
Rooms: 7 en suite, S £39–60 D £78–120 **Parking:** 52
Notes: ⊘ on premises 🐕 allowed in bedrooms

The Ashton family can trace their tenure of this impressive hall back to the 16th century, and much evidence of the building's age remains. The family and their staff offer excellent levels of personal service where the care of guests is of the utmost importance. The welcoming entrance lounge leads into the well-stocked bar on one side and an elegant dining room on the other. Here a good range of freshly prepared dishes, using fresh local produce wherever possible, are served in a friendly and relaxed formal setting. After the meal, coffee and liqueurs are served in the lounge hall in front of a blazing log fire in season. The house has central heating as well as log fires. The bedrooms in the hall reflect the character of the house with mullioned windows and exposed timbers; one room also has wood panelling. The converted carriage house across the garden offers ground-floor accommodation in two spaciouse double rooms each with spa baths, one room has an adjoining sitting room and there is a small south-facing courtyard with woodland views. Standing in its own grounds beyond the walled garden, Cedar Lodge provides a choice of a peaceful four-poster suite or more modest family accommodation. Three self-catering cottages are also available on the estate. Soulton Hall stands in 500 acres of open farmland, parkland and anciet oak woodland and you are welcome to explore the grounds. These include stretches of the River Roden and Soulton Brook where guests can fish.

Recommended in the area

Chester; Ironbridge; Shrewsbury

Bridge over the River Severn, Shrewsbury.

Barley Mow House

★★★★ B&B

Address: Aston Rogers, WESTBURY,
ShrewsburySY5 9HQ
Tel: 01743 891234
Email: colinrigby@astonrogers.fsnet.co.uk
Website: www.stmem.com/barleymowhouse
Map ref: 2, SJ30
Directions: 2m S of Westbury. Off B4386 into Aston
Rogers, house 400yds opp Aston Hall
Rooms: 3 en suite, S £28–34 D £48–60 **Parking:** 4
Notes: ⊗ on premises ⊗ on premises

Dating from the 17th century, this property provides modern facilities with a cosy farmhouse style.
It is surrounded by beautiful gardens, where you can enjoy tea and biscuits on the pretty patio. The Old
Farmhouse bedroom is large and sunny with a king-size bed and a bathroom en suite; the split-level
studio bedroom, in the converted malt house, has a single and double bed, an adjoining room with
a single bed, and a large bathroom. An Aga-cooked English breakfast is served in the dining room.
Recommended in the area
Powis Castle (NT); Stiperstones Hills; Shrewsbury Castle and Abbey

SOMERSET

Pulteney Bridge at dusk.

Apsley House

★★★★★ B&B

Address:	Newbridge Hill,
	BATH BA1 3PT
Tel:	01225 336966
Fax:	01225 425462
Email:	info@apsley-house.co.uk
Website:	www.apsley-house.co.uk
Map ref:	2, ST76
Directions:	1.2m W of city centre on A431

Rooms: 11 en suite, S £55–140 D £70–170
Parking: 11 **Notes:** ⊘ on premises ⊗ on premises
Closed: 1 wk Xmas

Built by the Duke of Wellington in 1830, this country house in the city, owned and run by Nick and Claire Potts, offers a gracious taste of Georgian Bath at its finest. Here guests can really soak up the atmosphere of Britain's only World Heritage City. The location of Apsley House, in a peaceful residential area about a mile from the city centre, ensures a truly relaxing stay, and this is enhanced by the presence of a charming and secluded rear garden, to which two of the bedrooms have direct access. The on-site parking and walking distance into the heart of the Bath are also great benefits in a city that can at times seem besieged by traffic. Public rooms include a large drawing room with bar and a light and elegant dining room, where the outstanding, freshly cooked breakfasts are served. All of the bedrooms have en suite bathrooms, complete with Molton Brown toiletries, and each is individually decorated and furnished. The beds are either super-king size or four-posters, and other in-room facilities include flatscreen TVs, Freeview, hospitality trays, direct-dial telephones and wireless Internet access. Apsley House is an aristocrat among bed and breakfast establishments and, maintained to the highest standards, is, in fact, fit for a duke.

Recommended in the area

Roman Baths and Pump Room and the many museums in Bath; Longleat; Cheddar Gorge

Trim Street, Bath.

Aquae Sulis

★★★★ GUEST HOUSE

Address:	174/176 Newbridge Road, BATH BA1 3LE
Tel:	01225 420061
Fax:	01225 446077
Email:	enquiries@aquaesulishotel.co.uk
Website:	www.aquaesulishotel.co.uk
Map ref:	2, ST76
Directions:	On A4 1.8m W of city centre

Rooms: 13 (11 en suite), S £55–99 D £65–99

Parking: 12 (also free on-road parking) Notes: ⊘ ⊀ allowed in some bedrooms Closed: 25–26 Dec

Situated within easy reach of the city sights, yet away from the crowds, this non-smoking Edwardian house offers a warm and genuine welcome. The good size en suite rooms are equipped with beverage trays, hairdryers, Sky TV, radio alarms and Wi-fi access. There is a lounge with a small but well-stocked bar and a separate TV lounge and patio garden for those warm summer evenings. Traditional English or Continental breakfast is served in the dining room and snacks are available in the evening. It's just a 25 minute walk to Bath centre and local shuttle and doorstep bus services give fast, easy access.

Recommended in the area

Roman Baths; Longleat; Cheddar Gorge and Caves

The Ayrlington

★★★★★ GUEST ACCOMMODATION

Address: 24/25 Pulteney Road, BATH BA2 4EZ
Tel: 01225 425495
Fax: 01225 469029
Email: mail@ayrlington.com
Website: www.ayrlington.com
Map ref: 2, ST76
Directions: A4 onto A36, pass Holburne Museum, premises 200yds on right
Rooms: 14 en suite, S £75–175 D £100–175
Parking: 14 Notes: ⊘ on premises ⊗ on premises No children under 14
Closed: 22 Dec–5 Jan

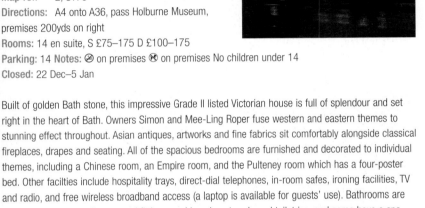

Built of golden Bath stone, this impressive Grade II listed Victorian house is full of splendour and set right in the heart of Bath. Owners Simon and Mee-Ling Roper fuse western and eastern themes to stunning effect throughout. Asian antiques, artworks and fine fabrics sit comfortably alongside classical fireplaces, drapes and seating. All of the spacious bedrooms are furnished and decorated to individual themes, including a Chinese room, an Empire room, and the Pulteney room which has a four-poster bed. Other facilties include hospitality trays, direct-dial telephones, in-room safes, ironing facilities, TV and radio, and free wireless broadband access (a laptop is available for guests' use). Bathrooms are equipped with quality fixtures and fittings, and luxurious towels and toiletries, and some have a spa bath. While you enjoy your freshly cooked breakfast you can also enjoy superb views over the Oriental style walled gardens to Bath and the medieval abbey. There is also a bar and a welcoming lounge. This hotel offers a tranquil atmosphere and has ample secure parking. Simon and Mee-Ling also own the Lopburi Art & Antiques gallery, which is within walking distance. Bath's magnificent historic sites and many excellent restaurants are also close by.

Recommended in the area

Bath Abbey; Thermal Bath Spa; Museum of East Asian Art

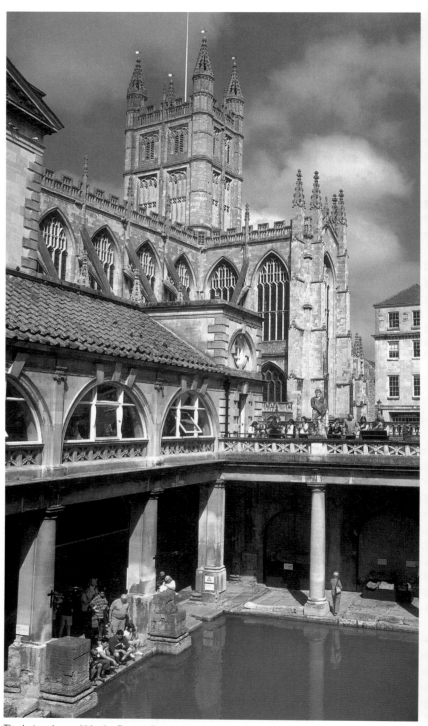

The hot springs within the Roman Baths.

Bailbrook Lodge Hotel

★ ★ ★ ★   GUEST HOUSE

Address: 35/37 London Road West, BATH BA1 7HZ
Tel: 01225 859090
Fax: 01225 852299
Email: hotel@bailbrooklodge.co.uk
Website: www.bailbrooklodge.co.uk
Map ref: 2, ST76
Directions: M4 junct 18, A46 S to A4 junct, left signed Batheaston, Lodge on left
Rooms: 15 (14 en suite), S £55–65 D £70–135
Parking: 15 **Notes:** ⊘ on premises ⊗ on premises

Lovely manicured lawns and gardens surround this stately Georgian country house just 1.5 miles from the city centre. The rooms retain their period charm and are well equipped. Five of the rooms have four-poster beds and additional facilities, including dressing gowns and cotton slippers. A bar and lounge overlook the patio and garden, and in the dining room the breakfast menu has an English flavour. Dinners are available in the nearby Waterwheel Restaurant, which is under the same ownership.

Recommended in the area

Roman Baths; Bath Abbey; Thermae Spa

Beckfords B&B

★ ★ ★ ★   B&B

Address: 59 Upper Oldfield Park, BATH BA2 3LB
Tel: 01225 334959
Email: post@beckford-house.com
Website: www.beckford-house.com
Map ref: 2, ST76
Directions: Off A36 Lower Bristol Rd onto Lower Oldfield Park at Green Park Tavern opp Renault, 3rd left
Rooms: 2 en suite, S £48–65 D £68–90 **Parking:** 2
Notes: ⊘ on premises ⊗ on premises No children under 11 **Closed:** Xmas

Anthony O'Flaherty maintains high standards of service at this spacious Victorian residence, which is in a quiet location close to the attractions. The bedrooms are well equipped, with unusual extras such as a binoculars to appreciate the views. The beds are king size and the showers are twice the usual size. The breakfast room has French windows overlooking a small, walled garden. Local organic produce features wherever possible in the traditional English breakfast menu.

Recommended in the area

Georgian Bath; Wells; Dyrham Park (NT)

Pulteney Bridge, Bath.

Brocks Guest House

★★★★ GUEST ACCOMMODATION

Address: 32 Brock Street, BATH BA1 2LN
Tel: 01225 338374
Email: brocks@brocksguesthouse.co.uk
Website: www.brocksguesthouse.co.uk
Map ref: 2, ST76
Directions: on N side of Bath btwn Royal Crescent and Circus
Rooms: 6 en suite, S £65–75 D £79–99 Family room £115
Parking: 1 **Notes:** ⊘ on premises ⊗ on premises **Closed:** 24 Dec–2 Jan

For an authentic taste of Georgian Bath, there are few places to surpass Brocks, which enjoys a superb location, between the Royal Crescent and The Circus. The accommodation, in rooms that retain all the elegance of that bygone age, is supremely comfortable and all the expected conveniences are there. The service and atmosphere is pleasantly informal and the hosts will help guests plan their sightseeing trips to make the most of their time here.
Recommended in the area
Royal Crescent; Prior Park; Thermae Bath Spa

Cheriton House

★★★★★ GUEST ACCOMMODATION

Address: 9 Upper Oldfield Park, BATH BA2 3JX
Tel: 01225 429862
Fax: 01225 428403
Email: info@cheritonhouse.co.uk
Website: www.cheritonhouse.co.uk
Map ref: ST76
Directions: A36 onto A367 Wells Rd, 1st right
Rooms: 11 en suite, S £55–80 D £80–120
Parking: 11 **Notes:** ⊘ on premises ⊗ on premises
No children under 12

This grand Victorian house has panoramic views over Bath and is only a short walk from the city centre. Expect a friendly welcome from proprietors Iris and John who work hard to achieve a relaxed atmosphere at Cheriton House. The carefully restored en suite bedrooms are all charmingly individual and are furnished with a mix of antiques and modern furniture, and include a two-bedroom suite in a converted coach house. All rooms have colour TV and a well-stocked hospitality tray. Wireless Internet access is also available for guests' use. A substantial breakfast is served in the large conservatory-breakfast room overlooking beautifully manicured and secluded gardens which are ablaze with colour during the summer months. The morning gets off to a good start with an excellent buffet of cereals, fruits and juices with a traditional full English breakfast to follow. Special dietary requirements can be catered for. Plan your day in the comfortable lounge, where you can browse the ample supply of brochures and guide books and discover all that the city and the surrounding area has to offer. Dinner is not available but Bath has many excellent restaurants and Iris and John are happy to make recommendations to help you with your choice. Cheriton House is a non-smoking establishment.

Recommended in the area

The Abbey and the many museum in Bath; Cheddar Gorge; Wells; Longleat

Cranleigh

★★★★ B&B

Address:	159 Newbridge Hill, BATH BA1 3PX
Tel:	01225 310197
Fax:	01225 423143
Email:	cranleigh@btinternet.com
Website:	www.cranleighguesthouse.com
Map ref:	2, ST76
Directions:	1.2m W of city centre on A431

Rooms: 9 en suite, S £45–65 D £60–95 **Parking:** 5
Notes: ⊘ on premises ⊗ on premises
No children under 5 **Closed:** 25–26 Dec

Denise and Colin Potter offer the very best traditional hospitality and are happy to share their well-kept Victorian semi with their guests. Cranleigh is located in a quiet suburban area of Bath and within easy reach of the centre of the city. As you are shown to your room you get your first real impression of how a Victorian middle-class family lived – from the sweeping staircase, original fireplaces, large sash windows to chandeliers and cornices. But the house has not stayed in the past completely – there is every modern comfort including TV (some with LCD screens) DVD players, broadband Internet access, luxurious en suite bathrooms and a garden hot tub (small extra charge). The spacious individually decorated bedrooms glow with colour. Two have stylish four-poster beds, another a distinctive canopied bed, and several can accommodate families. Five rooms have magnificent views over the rear of the house and the Avon Valley. All rooms are equipped with thought and care to include most modern extras. Enjoy a choice of breakfast from the extensive and imaginative menu including not only a traditional English grill, but also scrambled eggs with salmon and a delicious fruit salad before embarking on your day. There is private parking.

Recommended in the area

Roman Baths; Royal Crescent; Cheddar Gorge; Longleat

Devonshire House

◆◆◆

Address: 143 Wellsway, BATH BA2 4RZ
Tel: 01225 312495
Email: enquiries@devonshire-house.uk.com
Website: www.devonshire-house.uk.com
Map ref: 2, ST76
Directions: 1m S of city centre. A36 onto A367 Wells Rd & Wellsway
Rooms: 3 en suite, S £49–69 D £69–89 **Parking:** 6
Notes: ⊘ on premises ⊗ on premises

Under new ownership, this charming house, built in 1880 has kept its Victorian character. The friendly proprietors make every effort to ensure your stay is pleasant and memorable. The attractive en suite bedrooms have been refurbished to a high quality, and considerate extras include tea and coffee trays. An excellent cooked breakfast is served in the attractive dining room. There is secure parking.

Recommended in the area

Roman Baths; Longleat; Wells Cathdral

Dorian House

★★★★ 🛏 GUEST ACCOMMODATION

Address: 1 Upper Oldfield Park, BATH BA2 3JX
Tel: 01225 426336
Fax: 01225 444699
Email: info@dorianhouse.co.uk
Website: www.dorianhouse.co.uk
Map ref: 2, ST76
Directions: A36 onto A367 Wells Rd, right onto Upper Oldfield Park, 3rd building on left
Rooms: 11 en suite ,S £55–95 D £65–180 **Parking:** 11
Notes: ⊘ on premises

Tim Hugh is Principal Cellist with the LSO (hear him play on the house CD), and with his wife Kathryn they have filled their elegant Victorian house with artworks acquired on their travels. Inside the mood is instantly welcoming, with the cosy lounge offering plenty of reading material and an honesty bar. The period charm of the en suite bedrooms is enhanced by luxurious fabrics and furnishings. Two rooms have oak four posters. There are lovely views across the city, and the centre is just a walk away.

Recommended in the area

Roman Baths and rhe abbey; Royal Crescent and The Circus; Stourhead (NT)

Grove Lodge

★★★★ GUEST ACCOMMODATION

Address: 11 Lambridge, BATH BA1 6BJ
Tel: 01225 310860
Email: stay@grovelodgebath.co.uk
Website: www.grovelodgebath.co.uk
Map ref: 2, ST76
Directions: 0.6m NE of city centre. Off A4, 400yds W from junct A46
Rooms: 5 (4 en suite), S £40–45 D £60–75
Notes: ⊘ on premises ⊗ on premises No children under 6 **Closed:** Xmas & New Year

Owners Isobel Miles and her husband Peter Richards have refurbished their Grade II listed Georgian home to highlight the period features. Bedrooms are spacious with original marble or stone fireplaces. Furnishings blend modern and antique styles, and all rooms have large bathrooms. Each room has a radio-alarm clock, hair dryer, king-size bed and a courtesy tray. Healthy breakfasts are served in the sunny dining room; vegetarian and gluten-free diets are catered for with prior notice.

Recommended in the area

Georgian Bath; Roman Baths; Bath Abbey

Number 30

★★★★ GUEST ACCOMMODATION

Address: 30 Crescent Gardens, BATH BA1 2NB
Tel/Fax: 01225 337393
Email: david.greenwood12@btinternet.com
Website: www.numberthirty.com
Map ref: 2, ST76
Directions: 0.5m from Queens Sq towards Bristol
Rooms: 3 (2 en suite), S £59–79 D £82–109
Parking: 3 **Notes:** ⊘ on premises No children under 12

Number 30 is a friendly Victorian guesthouse, with parking, just a stroll from the city centre. The refurbished accommodation represents housekeeping at its best. The light and airy bedrooms have a contemporary feel and all come with tea and coffee facilities. Each room is named after a famous person who contributed to the building and character of Bath. Detail is paid to the cleanliness of the rooms, which have been designed with allergy sufferers in mind. Freshly prepared breakfasts, featuring home-made preserves, are served in the light, pleasant dining room, which has an original fireplace. The hosts are always happy to provide local information to help you make the most of your stay.

Recommended in the area

Roman Baths; Royal Crescent; Jane Austen Centre

Oakleigh House

★★★★ GUEST HOUSE

Address:	19 Upper Oldfield Park, BATH BA2 3JX
Tel:	01225 315698
Email:	oakleighhouse@tiscali.co.uk
Website:	www.oakleigh-house.co.uk
Map ref:	2, ST76
Directions:	A36 onto A367 Wells Rd, 1st right
Rooms:	3 en suite, S £50–70 D £70–95 **Parking:** 4
Notes:	⊘ on premises ⊗ on premises No children
Closed:	phone for details

This large Victorian house offers spacious accommodation in a quiet location just a 10-minute walk from the city centre. Jenny King is an enthusiastic host who soon makes her guests feel like old friends. The bedrooms are equipped with a clock radio, tea and coffee facilities and a hairdryer. There is a pleasant, cosy lounge offering the chance to relax with the daily papers and plenty of books, games and local information. The attractive dining room is the venue for freshly cooked breakfasts.

Recommended in the area

Roman Baths; Royal Crescent and The Circus

St Leonards

★★★★ GUEST ACCOMMODATION

Address:	Warminster Road, BATH BA2 6SQ
Tel:	01225 465838
Fax:	01225 442800
Email:	stay@stleonardsbath.co.uk
Website:	www.stleonardsbath.co.uk
Map ref:	2, ST76
Directions:	1m E of city centre. A4 onto A36 Warminster Rd, up hill 200yds on left
Rooms:	6 en suite, S £45–85 D £69–95 **Parking:** 8
Notes:	⊘ on premises No children under 6 **Closed:** Xmas

From its vantage point high above Bath this well-maintained house has superb views over the city and the Avon Valley. Despite a modern makeover the Victorian residence retains its original character. The bedrooms are spacious and thoughtfully equipped, and have gleaming bathrooms. Wonderful country views can be savoured over a full English breakfast in the dining room, and there are lovely walks along the Kennet and Avon Canal near to the house, either into Bath or to a delightful canalside pub.

Recommended in the area

Thermae Bath Spa; Roman Baths; Bath Abbey

Charmouth and Lyme Regis from Golden Cap.

Whittles Farm

◆◆◆◆◆

Address:	BEERCROCOMBE TA3 6AH
Tel:	01823 480301
Fax:	01823 480301
Email:	dj.cm.mitchem@themail.co.uk
Website:	www.whittlesfarm.co.uk
Map ref:	2, ST32

Directions: Off A358 through Hatch Beauchamp to Beercrocombe, 0.75m S of village

Rooms: 2 en suite, S £38–40 D £60–64 **Parking:** 4

Notes: ⊘ on premises ⊗ on premises No children under 16 **Closed:** Dec & Jan

The 200-year-old farmhouse, with lots of original character and luxurious furnishings, is ideally set on a no-through road, with lovely walks nearby. The en suite bedrooms, with zip-link beds, are light and spacious, and guests have their own cosy lounge with an inglenook fireplace, and a dining room with a large dining table where excellent breakfasts are served. Owners John and Claire Mitchem have been receiving guests here for more than 20 years, and their friendly hospitality is a highlight of any stay.

Recommended in the area

Montacute House; Forde Abbey; Barrington Court (NT)

Clanville Manor

★★★★ 🏠 FARMHOUSE

Address:	CASTLE CARY BA7 7PJ
Tel:	01963 350124
Fax:	01963 350719
Email:	info@clanvillemanor.co.uk
Website:	www.clanvillemanor.co.uk
Map ref:	2, ST63

Directions: A371 onto B3153, 0.75m entrance to Clanville Manor via white gate & cattle grid under bridge
Rooms: 4 en suite, S £27.50–35 D £55–70 **Parking:** 6
Notes: ⊗ on premises No children under 10
Closed: 21 Dec–2 Jan

Clanville Manor is a beef-rearing farm, and has been owned by the Snook family since 1898. Built in 1743 from local honey-coloured Cary stone, its flagstone entrance hall and polished oak staircase lead up to individually decorated bedrooms, which retain much original character. The single, twin and double rooms each have en suite bath or shower, central heating, colour TV, radio alarm clock, hairdryer and tea- and coffee-making facilities. Hearty breakfasts are served in the elegant dining room overlooking the pond and the driveway of the farmhouse. Fresh golden-yolked eggs come from the farm's own hens, and the full English breakfast is cooked on the Aga – lighter alternatives are available from the breakfast menu. For the evening there are several excellent restaurants and pubs in the locality, or just unwind in the spacious drawing room. In summer you can make a splash in the outdoor heated swimming pool, and there are walks along the banks of the River Brue. The farm has a pond and an old orchard, and in summer there are often new born calves and chicks. Only assistance dogs are allowed. Two self-catering cottages available for rent.

Recommended in the area

Glastonbury; Stourhead (NT); Wells Cathedral; Cheddar Gorge and the Wookey Hole Caves; Glastonbury Tor and abbey

Batts Farm

★★★★★ FARMHOUSE

Address:	Nyland,
	CHEDDAR BS27 3UD
Tel:	01934 741469
Email:	clare@batts-farm.co.uk
Website:	www.batts-farm.co.uk
Map ref:	2, ST45

Directions: A371 from Cheddar towards Wells, 2m right towards Nyland, Batts Farm 1m on left

Rooms: 3 en suite, S £55 D £70–85 **Parking:** 6

Notes: ⊗ on premises No children under 12

Batts Farm overlooks open farmland and moors at the foot of the Mendip Hills. The 200 year-old property, built of local Draycott stone, is full of character and owners Clare and John Pike make you feel at home. Clare's home-made biscuits and cakes are just part of the warm welcome here. The large bedrooms, all located on the first floor, are decorated and furnished to a high standard and include especially comfortable beds. One splendid room, with views to the Mendips, has a king-size antique four-poster bed with light drapes, a large bath and a double shower cubicle. Original sash windows, tiled floors and Victorian fireplaces have been retained throughout the farmhouse. Guests can relax in the lounge or retreat to the walled garden with its summerhouse which is furnished with comfy sofas, for a drink or a cream tea or just relax and read a book. Otherwise sit in the romantic formal garden and watch the birds in the water feature. Breakfast in the bright dining room, where guests sit around one large table, is a wide choice with home-made bread and local preserves. There are excellent walks in the area to help you work off all the delicious food and there are flat, quiet lanes for cycling – storage is available if you want to bring your own bike. There is plenty of parking on the gravel drive.

Recommended in the area

Cheddar Caves and Gorge; Wookey Hole Caves; Wells

Manor Farm

★★★★ GUEST ACCOMMODATION

Address:	Wayford, CREWKERNE TA18 8QL
Tel/Fax:	01460 78865
Website:	www.manorfarm.biz
Map ref:	2, ST40
Directions:	B3165 from Crewkerne to Lyme Regis, 3m in Clapton right onto Dunsham Ln, Manor Farm 0.5m up hill on right

Rooms: 5 en suite, S £30–45 D £60–70 **Parking:** 14
Notes: ⊗ on premises ⊗ on premises

Built of local Ham stone and brick, this imposing farmhouse is on a working farm of 20 acres, including three stocked ponds where guests can fish. The views are wonderful, across open country to the Axe Valley, and you can bring your own horses. The farm is on the Liberty Trail, an ancient footpath, and close to several National Trust properties. Bedrooms are comfortably furnished and have showers en suite, hospitality trays and ironing facilities. A self-catering apartment is also available. Breakfast is served in the cosy dining room, and there is a spacious lounge.

Recommended in the area

Cricket St Thomas Wildlife Park; Forde Abbey; Lyme Regis coast; Montacute Houose (NT)

Tarr Farm Inn

★★★★★ ◉ ⊜ ≌ INN

Address:	Tarr Steps, Exmoor National Park, DULVERTON TA22 9PY
Tel:	01643 851507
Fax:	01643 851111
Email:	enquiries@tarrfarm.co.uk
Website:	www.tarrfarm.co.uk
Map ref:	2, SS92
Directions:	4m NW of Dulverton. Off B3223 signed Tarr Steps, signs to Tarr Farm Inn

Rooms: 9 en suite, S £90 D £150 **Parking:** 10 **Notes:** 🐕 allowed No children under 14

Tarr Farm dates from the 16th century and nestles just above Tarr Steps and the River Barle. The new bedrooms with en suite bathrooms display careful attention to detail with thick fluffy bathrobes, fridges, organic toiletries and much more. When it comes to food you will not be disappointed with wonderful cream teas, scrumptious breakfasts and delicious dinners with ingredients sourced from Devon and Somerset farms and suppliers. The farm is set in beautiful countryside ideal for walkers.

Recommended in the area

Exmoor National Park; South West Coast Path; Dunster Castle (NT)

Dollons House

♦♦♦♦♦

Address:	10–12 Church Street, DUNSTER TA24 6SH
Tel:	01643 821880
Email:	dollonshouse@btconnect.com
Website:	www.visitdunster.co.uk
Map ref:	2, SS94
Directions:	In village centre

Rooms: 3 en suite, S £38.50 D £58 **Notes:** ⊗ on
premises No pets on premises No children under 16

Situated in the heart of one Exmoor's prettiest villages, Dollons House is a Grade II listed property, older than its 19th-century front suggests. The surrounding national park is ideal for walking, riding, fishing or golf. The house was originally two cottages and was at one time the village pharmacy. These days it provides a ground-floor gift shop, first-floor bed and breakfast accommodation, and an attractive garden at the rear. Bedrooms are full of character, two of them have views of the castle. Walkers are especially welcome and drying facilities are available. There is private parking nearby.

Recommended in the area

Dunster Castle (NT); Exmoor National Park; Exmoor Heritage Coast

Grasmere Court Hotel

★★★★ GUEST HOUSE

Address:	22–24 Bath Road, KEYNSHAM BS31 1SN
Tel:	0117 986 2662
Fax:	0117 986 2762
Email:	grasmerecourt@aol.com
Website:	www.grasmerecourthotel.co.uk
Map ref:	2, ST66
Directions:	On B3116 just off A4

Rooms: 16 en suite, S £52–65 D £70–90 **Parking:** 18
Notes: ⊗ on premises ⊗ on premises

Located between Bath and Bristol, this is a grand family-run Victorian guest house. The bedrooms have everything you need to ensure a comfortable stay, they vary in size and one has a four-poster bed. Two lounges, one with a bar, are available for socialising and enjoying your favourite tipple. At the start of the day, a freshly cooked full English breakfast is served, plus a choice of cereal, fruit and yoghurt. Evening meals are available from Monday to Thursday and a traditional Sunday roast can be booked in advance. Mid-week, the hotel is popular with a business clientele.

Recommended in the area

Bath Royal Crescent and Roman Baths; Cheddar Gorge; Longleat; Bristol

Glendower House

★★★★ GUEST HOUSE

Address:	30-32 Tregonwell Road,
	MINEHEAD TA24 5DU
Tel:	01643 707144
Fax:	01643 708719
Email:	info@glendower-house.co.uk
Website:	www.glendower-house.co.uk
Map ref:	2, SS94

Directions: A39 into Minehead, last exit at minirdbt, 200yds right by school onto Ponsford Rd & Tregonwell Rd

Rooms: 12 en suite, S £40–50 D £65–80 **Parking:** 14 **Notes:** ⊘ on premises
Closed: mid-Dec to Feb

A friendly atmosphere fills this family-run establishment in an Edwardian terrace not far from the seafront, harbour and town centre. The enthusiastic proprietors have redecorated to provide elegantly furnished bedrooms with modern shower rooms, tea and coffee facilities, radio alarms and hairdryers. There is a comfortable lounge or you can relax on the garden patio on a sunny day.

Recommended in the area

West Somerset Railway; Exmoor National Park; Dunster Castle (NT)

Freedom Cottage

★★★★ B&B

Address:	Cumhill, PILTON BA4 4BG
Tel/Fax:	01749 890188
Email:	freedomcottage@aol.com
Website:	www.freedomcottage.com
Map ref:	2, ST54
Directions:	On A361 SW of Shepton Mallet

Rooms: 2 en suite, S £45 D £56–70 **Parking:** 9
Notes: ⊘ on premises No children under 12
Closed: Mid Dec–13 Jan

Bob and Dee will welcome you to this ideal base for exploring the Somerset countryside. This recently developed accommodation is smart, light and airy and the individually styled bedrooms are spacious. There are two lounges, one an open plan mezzanine area, the other is a cosy TV room. Breakfasts use local produce and are served around a family-style table, where the hosts can be seen preparing dishes in the adjoining kitchen.

Recommended in the area

Wells; Glastonbury Tor; Bath and West Showground

Collett Park, Shepton Mallet.

Cannards Grave Farmhouse

★★★★ GUEST ACCOMMODATION

Address: Cannards Grave,
SHEPTON MALLET BA4 4LY
Tel/Fax: 01749 347091
Email: sue@cannardsgravefarmhouse.co.uk
Website: www.cannardsgravefarmhouse.co.uk
Map ref: 2, ST64
Directions: On A37 between Shepton Mallet & The Bath
& West Showground, 100yds from Highwayman pub
towards showground on left

Rooms: 4 en suite, S £40–50 D £55–65 Family room £75–80 **Parking:** 6 **Notes:** ⊗ on premises ⊗ on premises No children under 5

Charming host Sue Crockett offers quality accommodation at this welcoming 17th-century farmhouse. The bedrooms are delightful and have thoughtful touches such as hospitality trays, mineral water, biscuits and mints. One room has a four-poster bed and a fridge with fresh milk. Delicious breakfasts are served in the garden conservatory and there is a comfortable lounge to relax in.

Recommended in the area

Bath and West Showground; Historic Wells; Glastonbury Tor; City of Bath

Barkham

★★★★ B&B

Address:	Sandyway,
	SIMONSBATH EX36 3LU
Tel:	01643 831370
Fax:	01643 831370
Email:	adie.exmoor@btinternet.com
Website:	www.holidays-exmoor.com
Map ref:	2, SS73

Directions: 4m S of Simonsbath. Off A361 through North Molton, onto moor signed Sandyway, left at x-rds signed Simonsbath, 400yds right

Rooms: 3 (2 en suite), S £38 D £71–80 **Parking:** 6

Notes: ⊘ on premises ⊗ on premises No children under 12

Barkham, a traditional building with an attractive courtyard and today the home of John and Penny Adie, was one of the first farmhouses built in the Old Royal Park on Exmoor. The extensive grounds include a steep wooded valley, pasture with a stream, and a large treehouse. Walks, riding, trout and salmon fishing in season, are all close at hand. The drawing room, with its wide range of CDs and many books collected over the years, has an inglenook fireplace and french windows opening onto the patio and garden with a croquet lawn. Bedrooms are satisfyingly simple, one has a bathroom en suite and a king-size double bed – the other rooms are en suite or have private facilities. One bedroom has views of the valley, the others overlook the courtyard. Breakfast is served in the oak-panelled dining room. One of the barns has been converted into an art gallery where concerts take place; other cottages in the grounds provide self-catering accommodation. A number of courses are run at Barkham and it is the home of the Two Moors Festival.

Recommended in the area

Arlington Court (NT); Dunkery Beacon; Quince Honey Farm

Maunsell Lock, on the Bridgewater and Taunton Canal.

Lower Farm

★★★★ FARMHOUSE

Address: Thornfalcon, TAUNTON TA3 5NR
Tel/Fax: 01823 443549
Email: doreen@titman.eclipse.co.uk
Website: www.somersite.co.uk
Map ref: 2, ST22
Directions: M5 junct 25, 2m SE on A358, left opp Nags
Head pub, farm signed 1m on left
Rooms: 11 (8 en suite), S £40–45 D £60–65
Notes: ⊘ on premises ⊗ on premises No children under 5

This charming thatched 15th-century longhouse is full of character. Lovely gardens and open farmland surround this pretty property, where beamed ceilings and inglenook fireplaces testify to its age. The bedrooms include some in a converted granary, and all are either en suite or have private facilities. All rooms have high standards of furnishings – some are ideal for families. A hearty breakfast is cooked on the Aga and served in the farmhouse kitchen, using quality local bacon and sausages, and free-range eggs from proprietor Doreen Titman's own hens.

Recommended in the area

Hestercombe Gardens; Willow and Wetlands Visitors Centre; Quantock Hills

Crown & Victoria

★ ★ ★ ★ ⬭ INN

Address:	The Ale House Ltd,
	Farm Street,
	TINTINHULL, Yeovil BA22 8PZ
Tel:	01935 823341
Fax:	01935 825786
Email:	info@crownandvictoriainn.co.uk
Website:	www.crownandvictoriainn.co.uk
Map ref:	2, ST41
Directions:	Off A303, signs for Tintinhull Gardens

Rooms: 5 en suite, S £65 D £85 **Parking:** 60
Notes: ⊗ on premises ⊘ on premises No children under 5

The Crown and Victoria country inn stands in the heart of the pretty village of Tintinhull. In days gone by, as well as being the village pub the inn was also a private school – lessons took place where the existing bar is situated. Today, above the new restaurant, the unfussy bedrooms are light and airy and very well equipped with hairdryers, TVs with DVD players, tea and coffee facilities, and wireless broadband Internet access. The staff ensure you are well cared for. The contemporary bar and restaurant offers a successful combination of traditional pub atmosphere and quality dining. Carefully presented dishes are available for lunch and dinner under the direction of head chef, London-trained Stephen Yates. The menu ranges from traditional English dishes such as steak and ale pie to the more elaborate pan-roasted breast of duck on a bed of spinach with a potato rösti, plum and port jus. The extensive wine list includes ten fine house wines and there is a choice of local real ales. When the weather is kind, guests can relax in the garden with a drink or a light meal or enjoy a candlelit dinner in the conservatory with lovely garden views.

Recommended in the area

Tintinhull House Garden (NT); Montacute House (NT); Barrington Court (NT); Yeovil;
Fleet Air Arm Museum, Yeovilton

Double-Gate Farm

★★★★ FARMHOUSE

Address:	Godney,
	WELLS BA5 1RX
Tel:	01458 832217
Fax:	01458 835612
Email:	doublegatefarm@aol.com
Website:	www.doublegatefarm.com
Map ref:	2, ST54

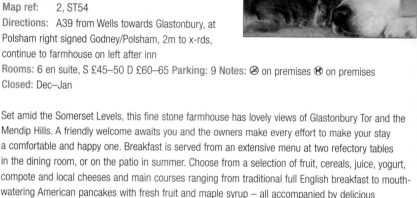

Directions: A39 from Wells towards Glastonbury, at Polsham right signed Godney/Polsham, 2m to x-rds, continue to farmhouse on left after inn

Rooms: 6 en suite, S £45–50 D £60–65 Parking: 9 Notes: ⊘ on premises ⊗ on premises
Closed: Dec–Jan

Set amid the Somerset Levels, this fine stone farmhouse has lovely views of Glastonbury Tor and the Mendip Hills. A friendly welcome awaits you and the owners make every effort to make your stay a comfortable and happy one. Breakfast is served from an extensive menu at two refectory tables in the dining room, or on the patio in summer. Choose from a selection of fruit, cereals, juice, yogurt, compote and local cheeses and main courses ranging from traditional full English breakfast to mouth-watering American pancakes with fresh fruit and maple syrup – all accompanied by delicious home-made bread. In summer, weather permitting, breakfasts are served in the garden. Other meals can be taken at local inns, including the pub next door. A wide range of facilities includes a lounge, laundry, and a games room with a full-size snooker table, table tennis and darts. Well-equipped en suite bedrooms feature hairdryers and complimentary tea and coffee. Guests can also expect a warm welcome from the family cats and dogs – Jasper-Pilchards, Paddy4paws, Laid-Back-Jack and Miss Jessops.

Recommended in the area

Wells (England's smallest city); Glastonbury; Cheddar Gorge

Camellia Lodge

★★★★ B&B

Address:	76 Walliscote Road,
	WESTON-SUPER-MARE BS23 1ED
Tel/Fax:	01934 613534
Email:	dachefscamellia@aol.com
Website:	www.camellialodge.net
Map ref:	2, ST36
Directions:	200yds from seafront

Rooms: 5 en suite, S £27.50–30 D £55–60

Notes: ⊗ on premises 🐾 allowed in bedrooms

With the mile-long promenade and pier right on the doorstep, Camellia Lodge is a great choice for a seaside break. The proprietors create a warm atmosphere that makes you want to return again and again – they are so pleased to have you stay they will even collect you from the train or bus stations. Inside their three-storey Victorian home you will find immaculate bedrooms well equipped for a long or short stay. Most are a good size and have all bathrooms en suite. Breakfast is a wide choice using local produce and evening meals are available. Both are served the dining room.

Recommended in the area

Weston Golf Club; Sea Life Centre; Cheddar Gorge

Beverley Guest House

★★★ GUEST HOUSE

Address:	11 Whitecross Road,
	WESTON-SUPER-MARE BS23 1EP
Tel/Fax:	01934 622956
Email:	beverley11@hushmail.com
Website:	www.beverleyguesthouse.co.uk
Map ref:	2, ST36
Directions:	Off A370 Beach Rd onto Ellenborough Park

Rd South & 2nd right

Rooms: 5 en suite, D £55 Parking: 1 Notes: ⊗ on premises ⊗ on premises Closed: Xmas

Friendly hosts Mary and Peter Morgan offer holiday breaks at their charming Victorian guesthouse in a quiet residential area close to the beach. Children are warmly welcomed. Bedrooms are individually decorated and furnished, and each has a beverage tray, shoe-cleaning kit and a torch. One double room is on the ground floor, and there is a family suite. Breakfast ingredients are sourced locally whenever possible, and there is plenty of choice. The conservatory lounge is an appealing retreat.

Recommended in the area

Weston-Super-Mare beach; Clevedon Court (NT); Wookey Hole caves

The Tarr Steps, Exmoor National Park.

Karslake House

♦♦♦♦ ◎

Address:	Halse Lane, WINSFORD,
	Exmoor National Park TA24 7JE
Tel:	01643 851242
Fax:	01643 851242
Email:	enquiries@karslakehouse.co.uk
Website:	www.karslakehouse.co.uk
Map ref:	2, SJ66
Directions:	In village centre

Rooms: 6 (5 en suite), S £55–70 D £76–111
Parking: 15 **Notes:** ⊘ on premises 🐕 allowed in bedrooms No children under 12 **Closed:** Feb & Mar

This small country hotel is very much a family home where guests are made to feel like old friends. Original beams and fireplaces feature and quality is evident in the furnishings throughout the house. The bedrooms are attractively decorated and thoughtfully equipped – one has a four-poster bed. Food is a highlight, and interesting menus, home-baked bread, and home-made preserves are offered in the spacious restaurant. Riding, fishing and shooting can be arranged. Dogs are welcome.

Recommended in the area

Tarr Steps (medieval clapper bridge); Holnicote Estate (NT); Minehead

Peak District National Park.

Prospect House

★★★★ 🍽 GUEST HOUSE

Address:	334 Cheadle Road, CHEDDLETON, Leek ST13 7BW
Tel:	01782 550639
Fax:	0870 756 4155
Email:	prospect@talk21.com
Website:	www.prospecthouseleek.co.uk
Map ref:	7, SJ95
Directions:	4m S of Leek on A520

Rooms: 5 en suite, S £23–25 D £46–50 **Parking:** 5

Built in 1838, this comfy guest house nestles in the stunning North Staffordshire moorlands close to the Peak District National Park. Glorious walks and drives, sprinkled with pubs and tearooms, are plentiful and cycling and pony-trekking can be arranged nearby. Bedrooms are housed in a beamed coach house in a courtyard setting, and offer single, twin, double or family rooms. Guests can chill out in the cosy sitting room or in the conservatory overlooking the garden, where there is a separate play area for children. Mealtimes are flexible and served in a traditionally furnished dining room.

Recommended in the area

Alton Towers; spa town of Buxton; Chatsworth House

Coppers End

★★★★ GUEST HOUSE

Address:	Walsall Road, Muckley Corner, LICHFIELD WS14 0BG
Tel:	01543 372910
Fax:	01543 360423
Email:	info@coppersendguesthouse.co.uk
Website:	www.coppersendguesthouse.com
Map ref:	3, SK10
Directions:	A5 onto A461 N for 100yds

Rooms: 6 (4 en suite), S £34–42 D £50–62 **Parking:** 9
Closed: Xmas & New Year

This family-run establishment provides well-appointed modern bedrooms: two are on the ground floor for easy access. All rooms have vanity units, tea- and coffee-making facilities, TV, Wi-fi, hairdryers, a safe and cooling fans. The spacious lounge with a TV is just the place to unwind before bedtime. A full English breakfast, accompanied by a selection of fruit and cereals, is served in the modern conservatory dining room which overlooks a patio and pretty walled garden. Special diets can be catered for.

Recommended in the area

Lichfield Cathedral; Cannock Chase Country Park; Shugborough Estate

The Crewe and Harpur Arms

★★★★ 🍴 RESTAURANT WITH ROOMS

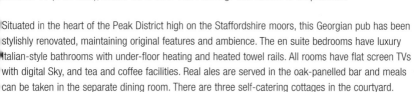

Address: Market Square, LONGNOR,
BuxtonSK17 0NS
Tel: 01298 83205
Fax: 01298 83689
Email: enquiries@creweandharpur.co.uk
Website: www.creweandharpur.co.uk
Map ref: 7, SK06
Directions: S from Buxton on A515, after 3m, right onto
B5053. Establishment in Market Square
Rooms: 11 (8 en suite), S £35–65 D £70–130 **Parking:** 100 **Notes:** ⊗ on premises

Situated in the heart of the Peak District high on the Staffordshire moors, this Georgian pub has been stylishly renovated, maintaining original features and ambience. The en suite bedrooms have luxury Italian-style bathrooms with under-floor heating and heated towel rails. All rooms have flat screen TVs with digital Sky, and tea and coffee facilities. Real ales are served in the oak-panelled bar and meals can be taken in the separate dining room. There are three self-catering cottages in the courtyard.

Recommended in the area

Buxton; Haddon Hall; Peak Rail

Colton House

★★★★ GUEST HOUSE

Address: Colton, RUGELEY WS15 3LL
Tel: 01889 578580
Fax: 01889 578580
Email: mail@colton-house.com
Website: www.colton-house.com
Map ref: 3, SK01
Directions: 1.5m N of Rugeley Off B5013 into Colton,
B&B 0.25m on right
Rooms: 3 en suite, S £39–65 D £54–85 **Parking:** 15
Notes: ⊘ on premises ⊗ on premises No children under 12

Colton House, an elegant Grade II residence dating from the 1730s, stands in lovely grounds on the edge of Cannock Chase. The grand interior features a carved stone fireplace in the hall, original oak panelling, and a stunning oak staircase. The bedrooms have their own distinctive style, from the Four Poster Room and the bright Summer Room, to beamed rooms at the top of the house. Owners Ron and Gay Lawrence are dedicated to ensuring you have an enjoyable stay.

Recommended in the area

The Potteries; Cannock Chase; Shugborough Estate (NT)

Haywood Park Farm

★★★★ FARMHOUSE

Address: Shugborough, STAFFORD ST17 0XA
Tel/Fax: 01889 882736
Email: haywood.parkfarm@btopenworld.com
Website: www.haywoodparkfarm.co.uk
Map ref: 7, SJ92
Directions: 4m SE of Stafford off A513. Brown signs to Shugborough, B&B on right 400yds past Hall
Rooms: 2 en suite, D £65–70 **Parking:** 4
Notes: ⊘ on premises ⊗ on premises

The attractive farmhouse stands on a 120-acre arable and sheep farm on Cannock Chase, part of the Shugborough Estate. The large, attractively furnished bedrooms have a host of extras such as fresh flowers, fruit, tea facilities and shortbread. Large fluffy towels are provided in the luxury bathrooms, one room has a roll-top bath. After a hectic day you can relax in the pretty sitting room. Breakfast, using local produce, is served in the lounge-dining room. The area is a paradise for walkers and cyclists. Fishing is offered in the lake, which is well stocked with carp and other coarse fish.

Recommended in the area

Shugborough Estate (NT); Wedgewood Museum; Alton Towers; Trentham Gardens

Harlaston Post Office

★★★★ GUEST HOUSE

Address: Main Road, Harlaston, TAMWORTH B79 9JU
Tel: 01827 383324
Fax: 01827 383746
Email: info@harlastonpostoffice.co.uk
Website: www.harlastonpostoffice.co.uk
Map ref: 3, SK20
Directions: 4.5m N, off A513 into Harlaston village
Rooms: 4 en suite, S £27.50–30 D £48–50 **Parking:** 5
Notes: ⊘ on premises ⊗ on premises

The Post Office is a row of traditional cottages that has been renovated to create a desirable guesthouse. Still incorporating a Post Office and stores, it stands opposite the church in an idyllic village, with pretty gardens behind. The bedrooms have been individually decorated and furnished, and have comfy beds, bathrooms and hospitality trays, and plenty of thoughtful extras. Other considerate touches are the guest kitchen, laundry and lounge, ideal for families with young children. Joyce Rowe is a delightful host, and her hearty cooked breakfasts have to be experienced.

Recommended in the area

Drayton Manor Theme Park; Lichfield Cathedral; National Memorial Arboretum, Alrewas

Gas Street Basin, Birmingham.

Oak Tree Farm

★★★★★ 🛏 GUEST HOUSE

Address:	Hints Road, Hopwas, TAMWORTH B78 3AA
Tel:	01827 56807
Fax:	01827 56807
Email:	oaktreefarm1@aol.com
Map ref:	3, SK20

Directions: 2m NW of Tamworth. Off A51 in Hopwas
Rooms: 7 en suite, S £57–100 D £75–100 **Parking:** 20
Notes: ⊗ on premises

This beautifully renovated farmhouse is on the edge of the village of Hopwas, northwest of Tamworth. It is surrounded by spacious gardens and overlooks the River Thame. Two rooms are in the main house and the others are on the first and ground floors of a converted former grain store and farm building. All rooms are en suite. There is an attractive breakfast room, where separate tables are provided. Other facilities include an indoor swimming pool and steam room. Mrs Lovett creates a friendly and relaxing atmosphere and really enjoys welcoming guests. Despite the tranquil rural location, the house is a convenient base for visitors to Tamworth, Lichfield, Birmingham and the National Exhibition Centre.

Recommended in the area

Tamworth Snow Dome; Drayton Manor Pleasure Park; Lichfield Cathedral

Row of colour washed terrace houses viewed over the beach at Aldeburgh, Suffolk

The Toll House

★★★★ GUEST HOUSE

Address: 50 Victoria Road, ALDEBURGH IP15 5EJ
Tel: 01728 453239
Email: tollhouse@fsmail.net
Website: www.tollhouse.travelbugged.com
Map ref: 4, TM45
Directions: B1094 into town until rdbt, B&B on right
Rooms: 6 en suite, S £60 D £70–75 **Parking:** 5
Notes: ⊘ on premises ⊗ on premises

Expect a warm welcome at this delightful Victorian brick house, situated just a short walk from the seafront and half a mile from the centre of Aldeburgh, with its associations with composer Benjamin Britten. This coastal area is a paradise for birdwatchers and walkers. Snape Maltings, 5 miles away, is a collection of traditional buildings nestling beside the River Alde with shops, galleries, restaurants and the world-class concert hall. The bedrooms at The Toll House – twins and doubles – all have bathrooms en suite, attractive co-ordinated fabrics and tea and coffee facilities. Breakfast is served at individual tables in the smart dining room that overlooks the pretty, secluded garden.

Recommended in the area

Minsmere Bird Sanctuary (RSPB); Concert Hall, Snape; Suffolk Heritage Coast

Earsham Park Farm

◆◆◆◆

Address: Old Railway Road, Earsham,
BUNGAY NR35 2AQ
Tel: 01986 892180
Fax: 01986 894796
Email: aa@earsham-parkfarm.co.uk
Website: www.earsham-parkfarm.co.uk
Map ref: 4, TM38
Directions: 3m SW of Bungay on A143
Rooms: 3 en suite, S £42–62 D £62–82 **Parking:** 11
Notes: ⊘ on premises 🐾 allowed in bedrooms

The farmhouse, part of a working farm, has been refurbished by Bobbie and Simon Watchorn to retain its Victorian charm while providing modern comforts. The spacious bedrooms all feature antique furniture and are beautifully decorated and fully equipped. One room has a four-poster bed. Delicious breakfasts feature sausages and bacon from the farm's free-range pigs, accompanied by home-made breads and preserves. You can buy the pork produce and relive the farmhouse experience at home.

Recommended in the area

Bungay market town; Earsham Otter Trust; Suffolk Heritage Coast

The Chantry

★★★★ 🛏 GUEST ACCOMMODATION

Address:	8 Sparhawk Street,
	BURY ST EDMUNDS IP33 1RY
Tel:	01284 767427
Fax:	01284 760946
Email:	chantryhotel1@aol.com
Website:	www.chantryhotel.com
Map ref:	4, TL86

Directions: From cathedral S onto Crown St, left
onto Sparhawk St

Rooms: 15 en suite, S £69–79 D £79–99 **Parking:** 16

A delightful Grade II buidling where parking for each
room is provided via a 19th-century carriage access.
Bedrooms are decorated in period style, and the spacious
superior double rooms (all non-smoking) have antique beds. There is a cosy lounge bar, and breakfast
and dinner are served in the restaurant. Dishes are home cooked and prepared from fresh ingredients.

Recommended in the area

Abbey Gardens and ruins; Theatre Royal (NT); Ickworth (NT)

Clarice House

★★★★★ 🛏 GUEST ACCOMMODATION

Address:	Horringer Court, Horringer Road,
	BURY ST EDMUNDS IP29 5PH
Tel:	01284 705550
Fax:	01284 716120
Email:	bury@claricehouse.co.uk
Website:	www.claricehouse.co.uk
Map ref:	4, TL86

Directions: 1m SW from town centre on A143 towards
Horringer

Rooms: 13 en suite, S £55–60 D £85–100 **Parking:** 85

Notes: ⊘ on premises ⊗ on premises

This large mansion is set in 20 acres of landscaped
grounds just a short drive from Bury St Edmunds. The
family-run residential spa, with superb leisure facilites, has spacious, well-equipped bedrooms. Public
rooms include a smart lounge bar, an intimate restaurant, a further lounge and a conservatory.

Recommended in the area

Bury St Edmunds; Abbey Gardens; Ickworth House and Garden (NT)

The Three Kings

★ ★ ★ ★   INN

Address:	Hengrave Road, Fornham All Saints, BURY ST EDMUNDS IP28 6LA
Tel:	01284 766979
Email:	thethreekings@keme.co.uk
Website:	www.the-three-kings.com
Map ref:	4, TL86
Directions:	A14 junct 42, B1106 to Fornham, left onto B1101, establishment on left

Rooms: 9 en suite, S £57.50 D £75 **Parking:** 28

The Kings Lodge is an attractive new building to the rear of the Three Kings, a 17th-century coaching inn situated in the pleasant village of Fornham All Saints. The Lodge contains the immaculate en suite bedrooms, which have an excellent range of facilities including minibars, bath or shower, radios, hairdryers, tea and coffee facilities, trouser presses, telephones and Internet access. You can unwind with a drink in the friendly atmosphere of the lounge bar or conservatory in the Three Kings, where wholesome traditional English food is available. A Sunday carvery is served in the main restaurant.

Recommended in the area

Bury St Edmunds Abbey and Gardens; Ickworth House; West Stow Anglo-Saxon Village

Edge Hall

★ ★ ★ ★ ★   GUEST ACCOMMODATION

Address:	2 High Street, HADLEIGH IP7 5AP
Tel:	01473 822458
Fax:	01473 827751
Email:	r.rolfe@edgehall-hotel.co.uk
Website:	www.edgehall-hotel.co.uk
Map ref:	4, TM04
Directions:	B1070 into Hadleigh. 1st property in High St on right

Rooms: 10 en suite, S £55–65 D £80–99 **Parking:** 20

Notes: ⊗ on premises 🐾 allowed in bedrooms in Lodge House

This imposing 16th-century house is at the quiet end of High Street in the heart of Constable Country. Run by the same family for over 25 years, the proprietors have a good eye for detail. The flagstone hall and fine staircase give a superb first impression, and the rest of the house is just as pleasing. Spacious bedrooms are furnished in period style and the bathrooms have efficient showers – one room has a four-poster bed. Traditional breakfasts are served in the stately dining room.

Recommended in the area

Sutton Hoo (NT); Flatford Mill; Beth Chatto Gardens

Lavenham Priory

★★★★★ 🏛 GUEST ACCOMMODATION

Address:	Water Street,
	LAVENHAM,
	Sudbury CO10 9RW
Tel:	01787 247404
Fax:	01787 248472
Email:	mail@lavenhampriory.co.uk
Website:	www.lavenhampriory.co.uk
Map ref:	4, TL94

Directions: A1141 to Lavenham, turn by side of Swan onto Water St & right after 50yds onto private drive

Rooms: 6 en suite, S £75–85 D £98–160 **Parking:** 11 **Notes:** ⊘ on premises ⊗ on premises No children under 10 **Closed:** 21 Dec–2 Jan

Gilli and Tim Pitt have created a sumptuous haven in the midst of historic Lavenham, one of England's prettiest medieval villages. The building dates back to the 15th century and retains many fine early features, including an oak Jacobean staircase, leading to beautiful bedrooms with crown posts, Elizabethan wall paintings and oak floors. Each room has a spectacular bed: a four poster, lit bateau (sleigh) bed, or domed canopy polonaise bed – some were made for the rooms by a Lavenham cabinetmaker. All are en suite, some with a slipper bath, and all have TV and tea and coffee facilities. The house stands in 3 acres of private grounds, all attractively landscaped and stocked with period herbs, plants and shrubs. Breakfast, taken in the Merchant's Room at an imposing polished table, is a choice of fruit compotes, yoghurts, orange juice, cereals, a traditional English breakfast, kippers, haddock, smoked salmon and scrambled eggs, and various breads, croissants, jams and preserves. The great hall with its Tudor inglenook fireplace and an adjoining lounge are lovely places to relax and are well stocked with books and board games.

Recommended in the area

Lavenham Guildhall (NT); Sutton Hoo (NT); Kentwell Hall

Wood Hall

★★★★ B&B

Address: Little Waldingfield, LAVENHAM CO10 0SY
Tel: 01787 247362
Fax: 01787 248326
Email: susan@woodhallbnb.fsnet.co.uk
Website: www.thewoodhall.co.uk
Map ref: 4, TL94
Directions: A1141 onto B1115 into Little Waldingfield,
Wood Hall 200yds on left past Swan pub
Rooms: 2 en suite, S £40 D £70–75 **Parking:** 4 **Notes:**
⊛ on premises No children under 10 **Closed:** 21 Dec–2 Jan

The Georgian façade of this delightful Grade II listed 15th-century hall hides a heavily beamed Tudor house. With pleasant views over the rolling Suffolk countryside, Wood Hall has just two bright and airy bedrooms. The house has a sweeping staircase and large dining room with an inglenook fireplace and a wood-burning stove; the furnishings are quintessentially English country house in style. Breakfast is sourced from local organic produce and in summer can be taken on the terrace.
Recommended in the area
Lavenham Guild Hall; Flatford Mill; Gainsborough's House, Sudbury

Abbe Guest House

★★★★ GUEST ACCOMMODATION

Address: 322 London Road South,
LOWESTOFT NR33 0BG
Tel: 01502 581083
Email: info@abbehousehotel.com
Website: www.abbehousehotel.com
Map ref: 4, TM59
Directions: On A12, 1.5m from the Pakefield Water
Tower rdbt, 50yds past Rectory Rd
Rooms: 4 (3 en suite), S £20–25 D £50–60 **Parking:** 1
Notes: ⊗ on premises **Closed:** 21 Dec–6 Jan

After a change of management, superb facilities await you at this small, seaside hotel a short walk from the beach and town centre. Bedrooms are well decorated are equipped with TV, hospitality tray, hairdryer, iron and complimentary toiletries. Served in an elegant dining room, the breakfasts use only locally sourced ingredients. The smoked fish is from the oldest smoke house in the area and the 'sunrise coast' eggs are a speciality. Guests can also make use of the cosy licensed lounge bar.
Recommended in the area
Great Yarmouth; The Broads; Suffolk Heritage Coast

Exercising racehorses near Newmarket,

The Garden Lodge

★ ★ ★ ★ B&B

Address:	11 Vicarage Lane, Woodditton, NEWMARKET CB8 9SG
Tel:	01638 731116
Email:	swedishgardenlodge@hotmail.com
Website:	www.gardenlodge.net
Map ref:	4, TL66
Directions:	3m S of Newmarket in Woodditton village

Rooms: 3 en suite, S £30–35 D £50–60 **Parking:** 6

Notes: ⊘ on premises ⊗ on premises

There's a true home-from-home feel to this cabin annexe, due in no small part to the natural warmth and hospitality of Anna Tyler and Charles Smith. The Swedish-style building is in their lovely garden, and consists of three en suite bedrooms each equipped with a minibar-fridge and a hospitality tray. The rooms are comfortably furnished, and all are adaptable to doubles, twins or singles. Freshly cooked evening meals including wine are available in the main house, where the delicious full English or continental breakfasts are also served. Guests are given their own keys, and there is ample parking

Recommended in the area

Newmarket Races; Cambridge University; Ely Cathedral

Gables Farm

★★★★ B&B

Address: Earsham Street,
               WINGFIELD, Diss IP21 5RH
Tel: 01379 586355
Email: enquiries@gablesfarm.co.uk
Website: www.gablesfarm.co.uk
Map ref: 4, TM27
Directions: B1118 left to Wingfield Green, turn right
after 1m, B&B 1.7m on right
Rooms: 3 en suite, S £38–50 D £55–60 **Parking:** 5
Notes: ⊖ on premises 🐕 allowed in bedrooms
Closed: 20–25 Dec

This delightful 16th-century Grade II listed farmhouse is set amid 2 acres of moated gardens on the outskirts of the village of Wingfield. As one of the original Tudor wool villages, Wingfield was wealthy and this can be seen from the privately owned castle, 16th-century Wingfield College and the impressive St Andrew's Church. Gables Farm is well placed for visiting the major East Anglian towns, the pretty coastal attractions of Southwold and Dunwich and the more lively resort of Lowestoft. There are plenty of excellent restaurants and pubs in the vicinity, renowned for first class food and some with fine locally brewed beers. The area is excellent for both walkers and cyclists. The farmhouse has spacious bedrooms, all of which are en suite and well equipped with hospitality tray, room heaters, TV and hairdryer, and thoughtful extras including fresh fruit and flowers, magazines and a fan for summer months. The rooms feature original beams and are sympathetically furnished. Breakfast is served in the lovely beamed dining room and local produce is used where possible. Home-made preserves and eggs from Gables Farm free-range chickens are a special treat. Bicycles are available for the not too serious cyclists – enquire when booking.

Recommended in the area

Minsmere Nature Reserve (RSPB); Framlingham Castle; Norwich

SURREY

Hampton Court.

Pembroke House

◆◆◆◆

Address:	Valley End Road, CHOBHAM GU24 8TB
Tel:	01276 857654
Fax:	01276 858445
Email:	pembroke_house@btinternet.com
Map ref:	3, SU96

Directions: A30 onto B383 signed Chobham, 3m right onto Valley End Rd, B&B 1m on left
Rooms: 5 (2 en suite), S £40–50 D £80–130
Parking: 10 **Notes:** ⊗ on premises 🐾 allowed in bedrooms No children under 6

Julia Holland takes great pleasure in treating guests as friends at spacious neo-Georgian home set amid rolling fields. The elegant public areas include an imposing entrance hall and a dining room with views over the surrounding countryside. The bedrooms are filled with thoughtful extras. Two single rooms share a bathroom, while the other rooms are en suite. There are many top-class golf clubs in the vicinity, as well as polo, horseracing and shooting. There is a tennis court in the attractive grounds.
Recommended in the area
Windsor Castle; Wisley RHS Gardens; shooting at Bisley

Bentley Mill

★★★★★ 🏠 B&B

Address:	Bentley, FARNHAM GU10 5JD
Tel:	01420 23301
Fax:	01420 22538
Email:	ann.bentleymill@supanet.com
Website:	www.bentleymill.com
Map ref:	3, SU84

Directions: Off A31 Farnham-Alton road, opp Bull Inn, turn left onto Gravel Hill Rd
Rooms: 4 (2 en suite), S £80-110 D £95–130 **Parking:** 6 **Notes:** ⊗ on premises ⊗ on premises No children under 8

Ann and David do everything to ensure you enjoy your stay at their country home, a former corn mill beside a river and set in 5 acres of beautifully tended grounds. The two main suites are in the former mill rooms where all the original beams survive. The rooms are of superior quality featuring antiques, luxurious beds and deep sofas. A full breakfast is cooked on the Aga or choose seasonal fruit, croissants or bagels. The room service menu is available 7pm–9pm providing hot and cold snacks.
Recommended in the area
Jane Austen's House, Chawton; The Watercress Line, Alresford; Portsmouth Historic Dockyard

EAST SUSSEX

Michelham Priory.

Brighton House

★★★★ GUEST ACCOMMODATION

Address:	52 Regency Square, BRIGHTON BN1 2FF
Tel:	01273 323282
Email:	info@brighton-house.co.uk
Website:	www.brighton-house.co.uk
Map ref:	3, TQ30
Directions:	Opp West Pier

Rooms: 14 en suite, S £35–55 D £50–140 Notes: ⊘ on premises ⊗ on premises No children under 12

This charming Regency town house is perfectly placed for shopping in the Lanes, all the town's attractions and the beach. Every smartly furnished bedroom has beds and linens of a high standard, TV, tea- and coffee-making facilities, hairdryers and fans for summer. The continental buffet-style breakfast provides a broad choice with produce locally sourced. Many ingredients are organic and the selection is impressive. There is a parking arrangement with the nearby car park.

Recommended in the area

Brighton Pavilion; Brighton seafront; South Downs

Nineteen

★★★★ GUEST ACCOMMODATION

Address:	19 Broad Street, BRIGHTON BN2 1TJ
Tel:	01273 675529
Fax:	01273 675531
Email:	info@hotelnineteen.co.uk
Website:	www.hotelnineteen.co.uk
Map ref:	3, TQ30
Directions:	A23 to Brighton Pier, left onto Marine Parade, Broad St 3rd on left

Rooms: 8 en suite, S £56–90 D £80–275

Notes: ⊘ on premises ⊗ on premises No children under 10

Only a stone's throw from Brighton Pier, this trendy establishment is in a quiet street. Bedrooms have wooden floors, contemporary artwork and glass beds illuminated by subtle blue lighting (king size rooms only). All rooms have flat-screen TVs, DVD and CD players. The Courtyard Room has a hot tub in its own secluded garden. A continental breakfast (with complimentary Bloody Marys or Champagne at weekends) is served in your bedroom. Beauty treatments offered in the privacy of your own room.

Recommended in the area

Brighton seafront; Royal Pavilion; South Downs; The Lanes

Judins

◆◆◆◆

Address: Heathfield Road, BURWASH TN19 7LA
Tel: 01435 882455
Email: sjudins@aol.co.uk
Map ref: 4, TQ62
Directions: A265 to Burwash, through village, past BP station on right, house 0.5m on left
Rooms: 3 en suite, D £75–90 **Parking:** 8
Notes: ⊘ on premises

Nestled in 40 acres of countryside and with 2 acres of formal gardens, 300-year-old Judins is perfect for a relaxing break. The attractive bedrooms are carefully furnished and thoughtfully equipped; the main bedroom has a king-size bed and lovely views. Public rooms include a sunny conservatory, a lounge and an elegant dining room. Breakfast is an excellent feast and your welcoming host Sandra Jolly uses the finest home-grown produce and free-range eggs and pork. Evening meals are available by arrangement. The heated outdoor swimming pool is available from May to September. No pets are allowed on the premises.

Recommended in the area

Bateman's (NT); Royal Tunbridge Wells; Battle Abbey

Yew House Bed & Breakfast

★★★★ B&B

Address: Crowborough Hill,
CROWBOROUGH TN6 2EA
Tel: 01892 610522
Fax: 07789 993982
Email: yewhouse@yewhouse.com
Website: www.yewhouse.com
Map ref: 4, TQ53
Directions: From High St over mini-rdbt, pass police station on left, Yew House on left

Rooms: 4 (2 en suite), S £35–60 D £55–60 **Parking:** 3 **Notes:** ⊘ on premises **Closed:** 25 Dec

A warm welcome is guaranteed at this new eco-friendly house offering pristine accommodation just minutes from local transport links and within easy reach of many Sussex attractions. The bright spacious bedrooms have been finished to a high standard with lovely accessories. One room has a four-poster bed and a double shower. A delicious breakfast and home-cooked evening meals, by arrangement, are enjoyed in the pleasant dining room overlooking the garden.

Recommended in the area

Crowborough; Ashdown Forest; Royal Tunbridge Wells

stbourne seafront

The Manse B&B

★★★★ B&B

dress:	7 Dittons Road, EASTBOURNE BN21 1DW
:	01323 737851
ail:	anne@themansebandb.co.uk
ebsite:	www.themansebandb.co.uk
ap ref:	4, TV69
rections:	A22 to town centre railway station, onto Old chard Rd, right onto Arlington Rd
ooms:	3 en suite, S £40–48 D £64–80 **Parking:** 2
tes:	⊘ on premises

is character home is in a quiet residential area only a 5-minute walk from the town centre. It was
ilt as a Presbyterian manse in 1906 in the arts and crafts style and retains many original features
ch as oak panelling and stained-glass windows. The beautifully decorated en suite bedrooms are
acious and comfortable, and come with armchairs, radios, tea and coffee trays and hairdryers.
nne Walker's breakfasts are very good, using a range of quality produce. If the traditional English
too much then try the continental (smoked ham, cheese, tomato and olives) or vegetarian options.
ecommended in the area
uth Downs and Beachy Head; Charleston Farmhouse (Bloomsbury group); Michelham Priory

Ocklynge Manor

★★★★★ GUEST ACCOMMODATION

Address:	Mill Road,
	EASTBOURNE BN21 2PG
Tel:	01323 734121
Email:	ocklyngemanor@hotmail.com
Website:	www.ocklyngemanor.co.uk
Map ref:	4, TV69

Directions: From Eastbourne Hospital follow town centre/seafront sign, 1st right onto Kings Av, Ocklynge Manor at top of road

Rooms: 3 (2 en suite), D £60–70 Parking: 3 Notes: ⊗ on premises ⊗ on premises

Instantly inviting, this 300-year-old house is set in extensive grounds and it's hard to imagine that you are just 10 minutes' walk from the centre of Eastbourne. The manor is on land that was previously occupied by a monastery, and this was also site of a 12th-century Commandery of the Knights of St John of Jerusalem. More recently, according to a blue plaque on the roadside wall, the house was once the home of the renowned children's book illustrator Mabel Lucie Atwell. Today, David and Wendy Dugdill welcome guests to the manor, providing a charming personal touch to every aspect of the place. The bedrooms, all accessed via the main staircase, are spacious and sunny, with views across the garden from the large windows. The decor and furnishings are comfortable and elegant, and top quality Egyptian cotton bed linen and towels are provided. Fresh flowers, a TV, DVD, radio, hairdryers and plenty of lamps are among the extra touches that so enhance a stay here. The bathrooms are modern and luxurious, and two adjoining rooms can be used as a suite. The public rooms include a gracious drawing room with grand piano and the beautiful garden is a lovely place to stroll on a summer evening. A full English breakfast is served in the dining room and light evening suppers are available by arrangement

Recommended in the area

South Downs Way; Beachy Head; Great Dixter; Bodiam Castle; Bateman's

Parkside House

◆◆◆◆◆

Address:	59 Lower Park Road, HASTINGS & ST LEONARDS TN34 2LD
Tel:	01424 433096
Fax:	01424 421431
Email:	bkentparksidehse@aol.com
Map ref:	4, TQ80
Directions:	A2101 to town centre, right at rdbt, 1st right

Rooms: 5 (4 en suite), S £30–45 D £60–65

Notes: ⊘ on premises ⊗ on premises

Parkside House is in a quiet conservation area opposite Alexandra Park, with its lakes, tennis courts and bowling green, yet is only a 15-minute walk from the seafront. The rooms are stylishly furnished, with many antique pieces, and generously equipped with video recorders, hairdryers, tongs, toiletries, bathrobes, and beverage trays. A good choice of breakfast – English or continental – is served at individual tables in the elegant dining room, and there is also an inviting lounge.

Recommended in the area

Battle Abbey; Bodiam Castle (NT); Michelham Priory

Stream House

★★★★★ GUEST ACCOMMODATION

Address:	Pett Level Road, Fairlight, HASTINGS & ST LEONARDS TN35 4ED
Tel:	01424 814916
Email:	info@stream-house.co.uk
Website:	www.stream-house.co.uk
Map ref:	4, TQ80
Directions:	4m NE of Hastings. Off A259 on unclassified road between Fairlight & Cliff End

Rooms: 2 (1 en suite), D £65–80 Parking: 4

Notes: ⊘ in house No pets No children under 10 Closed: Dec–Feb

Lovingly renovated from three cottages, Stream House is situated in 3 acres of grounds within attractive countryside, and is only a mile from the beach at Pett Level and cliff walks at Fairlight. The pretty bedrooms, with quality furnishings, are well equipped with complimentary toiletries, hospitality tray, TV and good-sized baths and power showers. Breakfast is served in the lounge dining room, which has an original inglenook fireplace; there are plenty of books and magazines to read.

Recommended in the area

Hastings Country Park; Rye; Great Dixter House and Gardens

Tower House

★★★★ GUEST ACCOMMODATION

Address:	26–28 Tower Road West,
	HASTINGS & ST LEONARDS,
	TN38 0RG
Tel:	01424 427217
Fax:	01424 430165
Email:	reservations@towerhousehotel.com
Website:	www.towerhousehotel.com
Map ref:	4, TQ80

Directions: 1m NW of Hastings centre. Off A21 London Rd onto A2102 London Rd, 250yds right onto Tower Rd West

Rooms: 10 en suite, S £49.50–55 D £65–75

Notes: ⊗ on premises

In an elevated position in the peaceful heart of St-Leonards-on-Sea, this elegant, double-fronted Victorian brick and tile house has enormous character and charm. Privately-owned, Tower House is less than a mile from the sea front at Hastings, with all its amenities and family attractions, and a just short drive from some pretty, unspoilt Sussex villages and countryside. Nevertheless, it is as suited to business guests as it is to holidaymakers. The house has a sumptuous lounge, with a huge window overlooking the beautiful garden, and a grand old fireplace where log fires add to the warm glow in the cooler months, while a well-stocked bar is an inviting place to enjoy an aperitif or digestif in the evenings. The formal dining room is the setting for the varied and interesting menu of freshly prepared dishes, which always includes vegetarian choices, and in summer breakfast is taken in the spacious

conservatory which has views over the gardens. The decor is completely in keeping with the period of the house and this extends to the bedrooms, each of which has been individually designed. Co-ordinating colour schemes create a relaxing atmosphere and some of the rooms have four-poster or half-tester beds. They all have en suite bathrooms, televisions, direct-dial telephones, hairdryers and tea- and coffee-making facilities. On a warm summer evening, the beautiful gardens, which capture the sun until late, are a lovely place to stroll and unwind. Pamper and themed weekends a speciality.

Recommended in the area

Fishermen's Museum, Hastings; Shipwreck Heritage Centre, Hastings; Hastings Country Park; 1066 Battle of Hastings Abbey and Battlefield; Buckleys Yesterday World, Battle; Kent and East Sussex Railway

Wartling Place

★ ★ ★ ★ ★   GUEST ACCOMMODATION

Address:	Wartling Place, Wartling,
	HERSTMONCEUX,
	Hailsham BN27 1RY
Tel:	01323 832590
Fax:	01323 831558
Email:	accom@wartlingplace.prestel.co.uk
Website:	www.countryhouseaccommodation.co.uk
Map ref:	4, TQ61

Directions: Off A271 signed Wartling, Wartling Place on right opp St Mary Magdelan Church

Rooms: 4 en suite, S £70–90 D £95–145 **Parking:** 10 **Notes:** ⊘ on premises ⊗ on premises

Formerly a rectory, this Grade II listed Georgian country house has grand reception rooms furnished with antiques. The standard of the decor and furnishings throughout Wartling Place is matched by equally high levels of service and hospitality provided by your hosts Barry and Rowena Gittoes. Each bedroom has a bath and shower en suite and features a superb king-size bed made up with quality linen; two rooms have four-poster beds, and all are comprehensively equipped with TV, DVD, hairdryer, trouser-press, tea- and coffee-making facilities, mineral water, luxury toiletries and large fluffy towels. Guests can relax in the stylish comfort of the drawing room, and a fine choice of breakfast is served in the elegant dining area overlooking the 2 acres of gardens with lawns and majestic trees. There are views across the Pevensey Levels to Eastbourne and the South Downs, and the house is ideally situated for visiting the many historic towns, castles, country houses and gardens in Sussex. A self-catering cottage with its own garden is situated within the grounds of Wartling Place. For dining out, the village inn and restaurant are within walking distance, and there are a number of fine restaurants just a short drive away.

Recommended in the area

Bodiam Castle (NT); Great Dixter; Bateman's, Burwash (NT)

The Blacksmiths Arms

★★★★ 🛏 INN

Address: London Road, Offham, LEWES BN7 3QD
Tel: 01273 472971
Email: blacksmithsarms@tiscali.co.uk
Website: www.theblacksmithsarms-offham.co.uk
Map ref: 3, TQ41
Directions: A27 onto A277, left at Lewes Prison. A275
N to Chailey, 2m on left
Rooms: 4 en suite, S £30–45 D £60–75 **Parking:** 22
Notes: ⊘ on premises ⊗ on premises
No children under 5

Nestling in beautiful countryside beneath the Sussex
Downs, this 18th-century roadside village inn is cosy and
full of character. It is ideally placed for keen walkers
wishing to explore the South Downs Way and opera lovers with tickets for Glyndebourne, and it's within
easy reach of the south coast. Bernard and Sylvia Booker have recently refurbished the bedrooms with
restful pale colours, crisp linens and good quality furniture, and they all have en suite bathrooms, flat-
screen television and tea- and coffee-making facilities. Downstairs, there's a traditional bar, warmed
by open log fires on cool winter days, where you can try the local Harveys Sussex Bitter or order from
a brasserie-style blackboard menu of creative seasonal dishes. The food is a cut above the usual pub
fare, with the best and freshest local ingredients used, including fresh fish landed at ports along the
nearby south coast. The menu might include roast loin of free-range pork, or perhaps fresh salmon
fillet on a lobster sauce, and a couple of interesting vegetarian options, and all meals are cooked
to order. There's a good wine list to complement the menu. To complete the experience, convivial
evenings can be spent here in the company of the friendly hosts and their local clientele.
Recommended in the area
Brighton; South Downs Way; Bentley Wildfowl and Motor Museum

Nightingales

◆◆◆◆

Address:	The Avenue, Kingston,
	LEWES, BN7 3LL
Tel:	01273 475673
Fax:	01273 475673
Email:	jean.hudson@xln.co.uk
Website:	www.users.totalise.co.uk/~nightingales/
Map ref:	3, TQ41
Directions:	2m SW of Lewes. A23 onto A27 to Lewes,

rdbt exit for Kingston, right at 30mph sign, house is second from the far end of 'The Avenue' on the righthand side

Rooms: 2 en suite, S from £45 D £65–70 Parking: 3 Notes: ⊘ on premises ⊗ on premises

Nightingales is a modern bungalow on a quiet country road, surrounded by beautifully-kept gardens featuring large lawns, mature trees and herbacious borders. Guests are welcome to sit anywhere in the gardens and are free to explore the grounds. Both bedrooms are very comfortably furnished with Vi-Spring beds, and have en suite facilities. They also include a TV, armchairs and Jean Hudson thoughtfully provides a range of extras in the rooms, including tea, coffee, chocolate and sherry. Home-made refreshments are always offered on arrival, and you can relax in the conservatory. Car parking is also available. With advance notice Jean is happy to provide a supper tray for single travellers. Local restaurants can also be recommended and a 15th-century pub is nearby. A footpath leads from a back gate to the South Downs Way and the historic town of Lewes provides a fascinating day excursion. In addition, Nightingales also offers a very well appointed self-catering garden flat, which faces south and overlooks the front garden. It comprises a large, sunny, well-fitted kitchen/living room with a large, comfortable bedroom with twin beds. The bedroom has a fully refurbished en suite facility, with a walk-in shower. The flat is open all year round.

Recommended in the area

Anne of Cleeves House Museum & Lewes Castle; South Downs Way; Battle Abbey

Kent and East Sussex Railway.

Wellington House

★★★★ 🛏 B&B

Address:	Dixter Road, NORTHIAM, Rye TN31 6LB
Tel:	01797 253449
Email:	fanny@frances14.freeserve.co.uk
Map ref:	4, TQ82

Directions: Into Northiam from S, turn left after Post Office signed Great Dixter Gardens. B&B 50yds up Dixter Rd on left

Rooms: 2 en suite, S £40 D £65 **Parking:** 1

Notes: ⊗ on premises ⊘ in bedrooms No children under 7 Credits Cards are not accepted **Closed:** Xmas & New Year

Set in the quiet village of Northiam, this charming Victorian house is perfect for a tranquil break. The spacious double bedrooms offer a high level of comfort with added extras such as home-made biscuits and hot water bottles cleverly disguised as teddy bears. The bathrooms have lots of pampering goodies. Enjoy afternoon tea by the open fire in the lounge. The hearty breakfast features home-made bread, local sausages and fish, and the freshest of free range eggs all served around one elegant table.

Recommended in the area

Battle Abbey; Rye; Great Dixter House and Gardens; Bodiam Castle; Camber Castle; Hastings Castles

Jeake's House

★★★★★ GUEST ACCOMMODATION

Address:	Mermaid Street,
	RYE TN31 7ET
Tel:	01797 222828
Fax:	01797 222623
Email:	stay@jeakeshouse.com
Website:	www.jeakeshouse.com
Map ref:	4, TQ92
Directions:	Approach from High St or The Strand

Rooms: 11 (10 en suite), S £50–75 D £90–122
Parking: 21 **Notes:** 🐾 allowed in bedrooms No children under 8

A fine building in one of the most beautiful parts of Rye, Jeake's House dates from 1689 and during its colourful history it has been both a wool store and a Baptist school. In the early 20th century it was the home of American poet and author Conrad Potter Aiken, and was the setting for many literary get-togethers. The house is owned and run by Jenny Hadfield who offers relaxed hospitality and excellent accommodation of a high standard. The public rooms include an oak-beamed lounge and a book-lined bar where you can relax over a drink. The original galleried chapel has been converted into a dining room where a breakfast of fruit juices, fresh fruit, prunes, figs and cereals are followed by traditional cooked dishes, prepared from fresh local produce, and served with toast of your choice and home-made preserves. A vegetarian option is available. The bedrooms are individually styled with sumptuous furnishings including brass or mahogany bedsteads dressed with linen sheets. Ten rooms are en suite, and all offer TV, telephones, hospitality trays and luxuriously fluffy towels. There is a private car park nearby. Jenny is always happy to advise her guests places to visit in the area including historic castles, beautiful gardens and picturesque villages; and can recommend the local restaurants and friendly inns

Recommended in the area

Bodiam Castle (NT); Battle; Sissinghurst Castle Garden (NT)

Little Orchard House

★★★★★ GUEST ACCOMMODATION

Address:	West Street, RYE TN31 7ES
Tel:	01797 223831
Fax:	01797 223831
Email:	info@littleorchardhouse.com
Website:	www.littleorchardhouse.com
Map ref:	4, TQ92

Directions: A259 into town via Landgate Arch & High St, 3rd left

Rooms: 2 en suite, S £50–70 D £80–110 **Parking:** 2

Notes: ⊛ on premises ⊗ on premises No children under 12

In a central position in Rye, the house dates from around 1720 and has been renovated and meticulously maintained. The proprietors create an informal atmosphere and guests are made to feel like old friends. There are views over the cobbled street or walled garden from beautifully appointed rooms which have four-poster beds and many thoughtful extras.There is a panelled book room and a cosy sitting room. The traditional breakfast features local organic and free-range produce.

Recommended in the area

Sissinghurst Castle; Great Dixter Gardens; Saxon Shore Way; Lamb House, Rye (NT)

Manor Farm Oast

★★★★★ ➔ GUEST ACCOMMODATION

Address:	Windmill Lane, RYE TN36 4WL
Tel/Fax:	01424 813787
Email:	manor.farm.oast@lineone.net
Website:	www.manorfarmoast.co.uk
Map ref:	4, TQ92

Directions: 4m SW of Rye. A259 W past Icklesham church, left at x-rds onto Windmill Ln, after sharp left bend left into orchards

Rooms: 3 (2 en suite), S £54–64 D £84–94 **Parking:** 8

Notes: ⊛ on premises No children under 11 **Closed:** 28 Dec–15 Jan

Built in 1860 and surrounded by a working orchard on the edge of the Icklesham, Manor Farm Oast is ideal for a quiet break. The oast house has been converted to keep the unusual original features both inside and out – the double bedroom in one tower is completely round. Your host Kate Mylrea provides a very friendly welcome. Kate is passionate about food: as well as a traditional English breakfast or a healthier alternative, she can prepare a top quality five-course dinner by arrangement.

Recommended in the area

Battle Abbey; historic Rye; Ellen Terry's House (NT)

Old Borough Arms

★★★★ GUEST HOUSE

Address:	The Strand, RYE TN31 7DB
Tel/Fax:	01797 222128
Email:	info@oldborougharms.co.uk
Website:	www.oldborougharms.co.uk
Map ref:	4, TQ92
Directions:	A259 onto The Strand. Hotel at foot of Mermaid St overlooking Strand Quay
Rooms:	9 en suite, S £40–55 D £70–110
Notes:	⊘ on premises ⊗ on premises

There has been a hotel or inn on this site since the 15th century, and today the Arms is run by Lynn, Lynne and their family. The inn has an elevated position at the foot of cobbled Mermaid Street, which winds up to Rye's parish church. The bedrooms come in a variety of sizes and styles and each one is well equipped. Breakfast is served in the charming dining room – Sussex bacon and sausages made to an exclusive recipe distinguish the full English, but there are continental or vegetarian selections too. There is a cosy lounge bar, and a coffee shop downstairs open during the day.

Recommended in the area

Tenterden Vineyard; Saxon Shore Way; Lamb House, Rye (NT)

The Strand House

★★★★ GUEST ACCOMMODATION

Address:	Tanyards Lane, Winchelsea, RYE TN36 4JT
Tel:	01797 226276
Fax:	01797 224806
Email:	info@thestrandhouse.co.uk
Website:	www.thestrandhouse.co.uk
Map ref:	4, TQ92
Directions:	2m SW of Rye on A259, 1st on left after Winchelsea town sign
Rooms:	10 en suite, S £50 D £60–85 **Parking:** 12
Notes:	⊘ on premises ⊗ on premises No children under 5

The Strand House is an attractive, traditional Sussex building with tile-hanging on the exterior and old beams, sloping floors and inglenook fireplaces inside. It has masses of character, with its antique furniture and cosy charm, but each of the bedrooms has the modern facilities you would expect. Run with style and enthusiasm by owners Jan and Peter Clarke, the house includes a residents' bar and dining room, where guests can breakfast on fresh local produce before setting out for the day.

Recommended in the area

Kent and East Sussex Railway; Smallhythe Place (NT); Tenterden Vineyard Park

The Avondale

★★★ GUEST ACCOMMODATION

Address: Avondale Road,
SEAFORD BN25 1RJ
Tel: 01323 890008
Fax: 01323 490598
Email: avondalehotel@btconnect.com
Website: www.theavondale.co.uk
Map ref: 3, TV49
Directions: In town centre, off A259 behind war memorial

Rooms: 14 (8 en suite), S £30–50 D £50–75 Notes: ⊘ on premises ⊗ on premises

Guests frequently comment on how well they sleep in the centrally heated, spotlessly clean bedrooms at The Avondale. The beds are certainly comfortable, but the friendly service, relaxed atmosphere and fresh flowers also play their part in the home-from-home experience. Jane and Martin Home and their experienced staff will spare no effort to make your stay relaxing and enjoyable with a perfect blend of modern comforts with traditional courtesy and service. First-floor bedrooms are accessible by stair lift and 8 of the 14 rooms are en suite. All rooms have free wireless broadband Internet access, a hospitality tray, complimentary toiletries, radio and TV, with a DVD player available on request. An inviting lounge is available during the day for guests. The dining room is light and spacious with individual tables and the quality and choice of the breakfasts often receive admiring comments. Dinners and hot/cold buffets can be catered for, wherever possible, with home cooked local produce. The Avondale is convenient for both the town centre and the sea front, and Seaford Leisure Centre can be found close by. There are plenty of pubs and restaurants within walking distance of The Avondale all serving good quality food.

Recommended in the area

South Downs walks and views, including the Seven Sisters; Beachy Head Countryside Centre; Firle Place; Clergy House, Alfriston (NT) Brighton; Eastbourne

The Gallery

★★★★ GUEST ACCOMMODATION

Address: Cliff Road,
SEAFORD BN25 1BB
Tel: 01323 491755
Email: jackie@wrightplace.info
Website: www.wrightplace.info
Map ref: 3, TV49
Directions: Off A259 onto Marine Parade, E along Esplanade to tower, left & 1st right
Rooms: 3 en suite, D £55–80 **Parking:** 3
Notes: ⊘ on premises ⊗ on premises

The Gallery is only a stroll from the beach and a short walk from Seaford town centre with its inns, restaurants and antique shops. A warm welcome is guaranteed at this refurbished house with wonderful sea views and in a prime position for coastal walks, the South Downs and a golf course. Within a couple of miles is the South Downs Way long-distance path, which can take energetic walkers to Eastbourne. The bedrooms, named after the French impressionists, are large and well appointed with tea and coffee facilities and DVD televisions. The king-size four-poster Monet room has beautiful sea views from all windows. It is furnished to a high standard with a sofa, fridge and a table and chairs. The luxury en suite has a modern corner bath, a seperate double shower and a trendy glass basin and vanity unit. Renoir is a beautiful double room with a stunning canopied bed, those wonderful sea views and a large double shower. The spacious twin bedded room Sisley is tastefully decorated and also has a large double shower. Artwork by local artists adorns the walls of the breakfast room where an excellent meal is served. For a beautiful place to stay in a wonderful location The Gallery offers the ideal break. Off-road parking is available.

Recommended in the area

Seven Sisters Country Park, Seaford; Clergy House (NT), Alfriston; Brighton

Crossways

★★★★ ◉◉ RESTAURANT WITH ROOMS

Address:	Lewes Road, WILMINGTON, Polegate BN26 5SG
Tel:	01323 482455
Fax:	01323 487811
Email:	stay@crosswayshotel.co.uk
Website:	www.crosswayshotel.co.uk
Map ref:	4, TQ50
Directions:	On A27 between Lewes and Polegate, 2m E of Alfriston rdbt

Rooms: 7 en suite, S £62 D £85–110 Parking: 30
Notes: No children under 12 Closed: 24 Dec–23 Jan

Under the watchful gaze of the famous Long Man of Wilmington, an impressive figure cut in the chalk hillside, this small country house is in a good location for all kinds of activities – walking on the downs, visiting the coast or touring the stately homes and gardens in the area. The building, surrounded by lovely grounds, has a chequered history. It was built for a London merchant as a home for his sisters, but they were later evicted for running it as a house of ill repute. Later it is thought to have been the home of Colonel and Mrs Gwynn, the parents of renowned cookery writer Elizabeth David. Appropriately, fine food is once again the main attraction, and the regularly changing menu might include seafood pancake, Stilton banana bake or hot savoury cheese peaches. Each evening is something of an occasion, with guests, local diners and the owners often chatting animatedly, in true country-house fashion. The bedrooms each have an individual decor, smart furnishings and an en suite bathroom, and guests can choose between the standard and superior rooms. The whole place exudes a delightfully warm atmosphere and it is little wonder that many guests return here time and time again.

Recommended in the area

Eastbourne; Beachy Head Countryside Centre; Michelham Priory

WEST SUSSEX

rundel, West Sussex.

Arundel House Restaurant and Rooms

★★★★★ GUEST ACCOMMODATION

Address: 11 High Street, ARUNDEL BN18 9AD
Tel: 01903 882136
Email: mail@arundelhouseonline.co.uk
Website: www.arundelhouseonline.co.uk
Map ref: 3, TQ00
Directions: In town centre opp Post Office
Rooms: 5 en suite, D £100–160 **Notes:** ⊘ on premises
No children under 16 in rooms **Closed:** 2 wks end-Feb

The extremely high standard of accommodation is apparent from the moment you enter what is one of Arundel's newest and most exciting places to stay. Its location, in the heart of this historic town, is another advantage because you can just stroll out to enjoy the attractions right on the doorstep. The building has been the subject of a major refurbishment and there is an atmosphere of luxury and indulgence you would expect to find in a top-class hotel. In the bedrooms the restful beds made up with Egyptian cotton bedlinen and original artwork enhances the stylish contemporary interior design. There are full-size writing desks, wireless Internet access, direct-dial telephones, flat-screen TVs, and CD/clock/radios, and the bathrooms are equipped with 8-inch shower roses and Gilchrist and Soames toiletries. The food is a highlight of a stay here, with modern British cuisine (with an occasional French or Mediterranean influence) served in the intimate restaurant. Wild, local and seasonal ingredients are brought together here at the height of their flavour and cooked with considerable skill, and there's an extensive wine list. Billy Lewis-Bowker and Luke Hackman are to be congratulated on their achievement in creating this exceptional establishment.

Recommended in the area

Arundel Castle; Wildfowl and Wetlands Trust, Arundel; Amberley Working Museum

Chichester Cathedral.

Royal Oak Inn

★★★★★   INN

Address:	Pook Lane, CHICHESTER PO18 0AX
Tel:	01243 527434
Fax:	01243 775062
Email:	enquiries@royaloaklavant.co.uk
Website:	www.thesussexpub.co.uk
Map ref:	3, SU80
Directions:	Off A286 just N of Chichester
Rooms:	5 en suite and 3 cottages, S £75–85

£80–115 Cottages from £125 per night **Parking:** 25

Located close to the Goodwood Estate only 2 miles from Chichester, this stylish inn is full of character, with beamed ceilings, timber floors and open fires in the public areas. The bedrooms, all finished to a very high standard, are in the inn, a converted barn and three adjacent cottages – each room has a flat-screen TV and CD player, a library of DVDs, and Sky television. The luxurious bathrooms are fitted with power showers. Home-made museli and local produce feature on the interesting breakfast menu. The popular restaurant serves a combination of French, Mediterranean and modern English cuisine.

Recommended in the area

Chichester; South Downs; Goodwood; Local beaches

The Chilgrove White Horse

Address:	CHILGROVE,
	Chichester PO18 9HX
Tel:	01243 535219
Fax:	01243 535301
Email:	info@whitehorsechilgrove.co.uk
Website:	www.whitehorsechilgrove.co.uk
Map ref:	3, SU81
Directions:	Off A286 onto B2141 to village

Rooms: 9 en suite, S £65–120 D £95–150 **Parking:** 60
Notes: ⊘ on premises 🐾 allowed in bedrooms
Closed: Sun evening & all day Mon

Nestling at the foot of the South Downs, this restaurant with rooms was originally built as a coaching inn in 1765 and combines excellent cuisine award-winning wine lists (over 600 labels) and nine rooms (seven of which are named after wines and two after champagnes). All rooms have firm super-king beds, large bathrobes, five channel TV, CD facilities, wooden floors with rugs, and the use of a private flint-walled garden. Some have power showers, others have baths. The two 'champagne' rooms also have a wide flat-screen TV, DVD, video, sofa, fridge and power showers. One also has a small courtyard and a bath. Dining is available in the smart restaurant which features a pianist on Saturday night, and also in the casual bar where local, seasonal and organic specialities such as partridge, grouse, lobster and sea bass can be enjoyed. Guests can then relax in front of open fires, have a massage (when available) or walk and cycle the beautiful countryside in any direction straight from the front door. The whole venue is non-smoking and was awarded the Gold Green Business Tourism Award for environmental managemen, in 2004. Dogs are very welcome here.

Recommended in the area

Weald and Downland Open Air Museum; Uppark (NT); Fishbourne Roman Palace; Chichester; Bosham

Racing Greens

★ ★ ★ ★   B&B

Address:	70 South Terrace,
	LITTLEHAMPTON BN17 5LQ
Tel:	01903 732972
Fax:	01903 719389
Email:	racingreens@aol.com
Website:	www.littlehampton-racing-greens.co.uk
Map ref:	3, TQ00

Directions: A259 onto B2187 for Littlehampton seafront, brown signs to seafront, B&B faces the Greens and sea near Harbour Park Entertainment Centre
Rooms: 2 (1 en suite), S £35–55 D £60–80 **Notes:** ⊘ on premises ⊗ on premises No children

Littlehampton Greens and the seafront form the main outlook from this Victorian terraced property. The Blue Flag sandy beach and riverside walks are only minutes away, and a marina, shops and many other attractions are also close at hand. Proprietors Alan and Eileen Thomas have combined Victorian and modern features giving a character home with a relaxing atmosphere where they provide individual care and attention. The two spacious bedrooms, one is on the ground floor but accessed by steps, have either en suite or private facilities, and are fitted with large beds and quality mattresses. Refreshment trays, alarm clocks, hairdryers and TVs are also supplied along with wireless Internet access. A satisfying breakfast is served in the sunny dining room while you enjoy fine views over the seafront Greens. Your selection is made from a wide-ranging menu of dishes personally prepared by Alan to suit individual tastes and preferences. A variety of superior Sussex produce always features in the cooking, with the speciality breads and sausages from Bairds (the nearby award-winning farm shop) firm favourites.

Recommended in the area

Sussex coast; South Downs; Chichester; Arundel

The Lawn Guest House

★★★★ GUEST HOUSE

Address:	30 Massetts Road,
	GATWICK AIRPORT RH6 7DF
Tel:	01293 775751
Fax:	01293 821803
Email:	info@lawnguesthouse.co.uk
Website:	www.lawnguesthouse.co.uk
Map ref:	3, TQ24

Directions: M23 junct 9, signs to A23 (Redhill), 3rd exit at rdbt by Esso station, 300yds right at lights

Rooms: 12 en suite, S £40–45 D £58–60 **Parking:** 15 **Notes:** ⊗ on premises ⋔ allowed in bedrooms

Handy for Gatwick, this is an efficient well-run airport guesthouse. Thoughtful extras include scales to weigh luggage, airport parking, free airport transfers and an on-line computer. Bedrooms and bathrooms are fresh and bright, and include hairdryers, tea and coffee facilities, direct-dial phones, early call system, fans and Internet access. A choice of hot and cold breakfast dishes is served in the attractive dining room, and there is a pretty garden. A good choice for the international traveller.

Recommended in the area

Hever Castle; Chessington World of Adventure; Leonardslee Gardens

Vulcan Lodge Guest House

★★★★ B&B

Address:	27 Massetts Road,
	GATWICK AIRPORT RH6 7DQ
Tel:	01293 771522
Fax:	01293 775376
Email:	reservations@vulcan-lodge.com
Website:	www.vulcan-lodge.com
Map ref:	3, TQ24

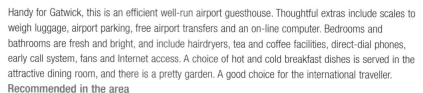

Directions: M23 junct 9, A23 into Horley, off A23 Brighton Rd

Rooms: 4 (3 en suite,) S £36–40 D £55 **Parking:** 13 **Notes:** ⊗ on premises ⋔ allowed in bedrooms

This late 17th-century house is convenient for Gatwick Airport. Set back from the main road in neat gardens, it gives the impression of being in beautiful countryside. Established as a bed and breakfast for more than a decade, the rooms are well equipped and have nice finishing touches – most are en suite. The lounge-dining room comes with a cosy coal-effect fire. A choice of breakfast, including vegetarian, is provided, and a continental breakfast can be brought to your room outside normal hours.

Recommended in the area

Hever Castle; Wakehurst Place (NT); Box Hill (NT)

Rivermead House

★★★★★ B&B

Address: Hollist Lane, MIDHURST GU29 9RS
Tel: 01730 810907
Email: mail@bridgetadler.com
Website: www.bridgetadler.com
Map ref: 3,SU82
Directions: 0.5 m from A286. 1m from centre of Midhurst
Rooms: 1 en suite, D £60–80 **Parking:** 2
Notes: ⊗ on premises ⊗ in bedrooms
Closed: 24–26 Dec

This gracious Sussex home is set in a semi-rural location on the edge of Midhurst, and the bedroom has glorious country views, with the South Downs in the distance. It is light and spacious, with room for a put-up bed or cot for children, and is equipped with TV, tea- and coffee-making facilities, hairdryer and radio alarm. A full English breakfast is served informally in the farmhouse-style kitchen, and evening meals are available if booked in advance. Pets are welcome, though not in the bedroom.

Recommended in the area

Weald and Downland Open-Air Museum; Goodwood; Chichester

Orchard Mead

★★★★ ⊜ 🛏 B&B

Address: Toat Lane, PULBOROUGH RH20 1BZ
Tel: 01798 872640
Email: siggy.rutherford@ukonline.co.uk
Map ref: 3, TQ01
Directions: Off A29 1m N of Pulborough onto Blackgate Ln, left onto Pickhurst Ln & right onto Toat Ln, Orchard Mead at end
Rooms: 2 en suite S £45–55 D £35–45 **Parking:** 2
Notes: ⊗ on premises ⊗ on premises
No children under 12 **Closed:** Xmas & Etr

Orchard Mead is a comfortable home set in the heart of the Sussex Weald, within easy reach of the local train station and 30 minutes from Chichester. John and Siggy Rutherford aim to make your stay a memorable one. Both bedrooms are well furnished with thoughtful touches, and attention to detail is evident with afternoon tea on arrival, and beds turned down each evening. There is a lovely drawing room to relax in, an excellent breakfast, and a delicious evening meal can be provided on request.

Recommended in the area

Petworth House (NT); South Downs Way; Holly Gate Cactus Garden, Ashington

The Penfold Gallery Guest House

★★★★ GUEST HOUSE

Address:	30 High Street, STEYNING BN44 3GG
Tel:	01903 815595
Email:	johnturner57@aol.com
Website:	www.artyguesthouse.co.uk
Map ref:	3, TQ11

Directions: Leave A27 between Brighton and Worthing and follow signs to Steyning on A283.

Rooms: 2 en suite, S £76 D £98 Notes: ⊘ on premises No children under 12

Parts of this listed building date back to the 15th century, and restoration has exposed many original beams. The bedrooms are spacious and comfortable, and one has a king-size bed. In the heart of a historic town nestling beneath the South Downs, thia guest house owes much of its charm to owners John and Joy Turner, who do so much to make guests feel at home. Joy is also an accomplished artis and her artistic flair is as much in evidence in the decor and cuisine as in her fine paintings.

Recommended in the area

Brighton; Arundel; South Downs Way.

The Beacons

★★★★ GUEST ACCOMMODATION

Address:	18 Shelley Road, WORTHING BN11 1TU
Tel:	01903 230948
Email:	thebeacons@btconnect.com
Map ref:	3, TQ10

Directions: From A27/A24 follow signs to town centre, continue W and follow brown signs to The Beacons

Rooms: 8 en suite, S £36–40 D £62–76 Parking: 8

Notes: ⊘ on premises

The Beacons is conveniently situated for all local amenities, including the shopping centre, marine garden, theatres, nightclubs, pier and promenade. The bowling greens at Beach House Park and Marine Gardens are only a short walk from the house. It is also well placed for touring the south coa and the towns of Brighton, Chichester and Arundel are within easy reach. The bedrooms all have colour TV, tea- and coffee-making facilities, hairdryer and clock. Breakfast, served at individual table is taken in the dining room and there is a comfortable lounge to relax in after a busy day sightseeing There is ample car parking on the premises. Dogs are allowed in rooms with prior arrangement.

Recommended in the area

Brighton Pavilion; The Lanes, Brighton; South Downs

Worthing beach.

The Moorings

★ ★ ★ ★   GUEST ACCOMMODATION

Address:	4 Selden Road, WORTHING BN11 2LL
Tel:	01903 208882
Fax:	01903 236878
Email:	themooringsworthing@hotmail.co.uk
Website:	www.mooringsworthing.co.uk
Map ref:	3, TQ10
Directions:	Off A259
Rooms:	6 en suite, S £30–40 D £60–70
Notes:	⊘ on premises ⊗ on premises

Colourful container plants and window boxes greet guests to this fine Victorian house, in a quiet residential area yet handy for the sea front and town centre. Inside, the spacious rooms are beautifully decorated, in keeping with the age of the house, and the good-sized bedrooms have coordinated colour schemes, original fireplaces, teddy bears on the beds and light flooding in from the big windows. Each has a TV and tea- and coffee-making facilities, and two are large enough to accommodate a family. In addition to the stylish dining room, there's a cosy lounge, with books, magazines and games.

Recommended in the area

Pier and sea front; Aquarena; Bowling Greens.

Warwick Castle.

Fulready Manor

◆◆◆◆◆

Address:	Fulready, ETTINGTON,
	Stratford-upon-Avon CV37 7PE
Tel:	01789 740152
Fax:	01789 740247
Email:	stay@fulreadymanor.co.uk
Website:	www.fulreadymanor.co.uk
Map ref:	3, SP24
Directions:	2.5m SE of Ettington. 0.5m S off A422 at

Pillerton Priors

Rooms: 3 en suite, D £105–135 **Parking:** 6 **Notes:** ⊗ on premises ⊗ on premises
No children under 15

Set in 125 acres, this brand new luxury home appears from afar to be a 16th-century castle. Full of character, the entrance hall has a stone fireplace and a floor-to-ceiling front window while one of the bedrooms has a four-poster bed with gold-embroidered muslin. The Manor offers old-fashioned comfort and the breakfasts are a feast. It was awarded AA Guest Accommodation of the Year 2006.

Recommended in the area

Warwick Castle; Warwick; Royal Shakespeare Theatre, Stratford-upon-Avon; The Cotswolds

The Old Coach House

◆◆◆◆

Address:	GREAT WOLFORD,
	Shipston on Stour CV36 5NQ
Tel:	01608 674152
Email:	theoldcoachhouse@thewolfords.net
Website:	www.theoldcoachhouseatthewolfords.co.uk
Map ref:	3, SP23
Directions:	Off A44 signed Great Wolford,

B&B 2m, 1st on right

Rooms: 2 en suite, S £50 D £80 **Parking:** 2
Notes: ⊗ on premises No children under 8

Only minutes from the thriving market town of Moreton-in-Marsh, this converted coach house is perfect for touring or walking in the north Cotswolds. Bedrooms have a wealth of thoughtful extras, and quality decor and furnishings enhance the intrinsic charm of the property. Exposed beams, a flagstone floor and wood-burning stove are features in the relaxing sitting room, which overlooks the delightful garden. All food is prepared using local produce and the pub next door serves excellent meals.

Recommended in the area

Chastleton House (NT); Hidcote Manor (NT); Royal Shakespeare Theatre, Stratford-upon-Avon

The Town Hall, Royal Leamington Spa.

Bubbenhall House

★★★★ GUEST ACCOMMODATION

Address:	Paget's Lane,
	ROYAL LEAMINGTON SPA CV8 3BJ
Tel/Fax:	024 7630 2409
Email:	wharrison@bubbenhallhouse.freeserve.co.uk
Website:	www.bubbenhallhouse.com
Map ref:	3, SP36

Directions: 5m NE of Leamington. Off A445 at Bubbenhall S onto Pagets Ln, 1m on single-track lane (over 4 speed humps)

Rooms: 3 en suite, S £50–55 D £65–75 Parking: 12

Located between Leamington Spa and Coventry, this large Edwardian house stands in 5 acres of woodland and grounds. This award-winning guest house features oak beams, a fine Jacobean-style staircase, an elegant dining room serving first-class breakfasts and a choice of sumptuous lounges. Thoughtful extras are provided in the large bedrooms, each with its own individual character and splendid views. The owners are pet friendly and there is also a championship surface hard tennis court

Recommended in the area

Stoneleigh Abbey; Ryton Organic Gardens; Warwick Castle

Holly End Bed & Breakfast

★ ★ ★ ★   GUEST ACCOMMODATION

Address: London Road,
SHIPSTON-ON-STOUR CV36 4EP

Tel: 01608 664064

Email: hollyend.hunt@btinternet.com

Website: www.holly-end.co.uk

Map ref: 3, SP24

Directions: 0.5m S of Shipston-on-Stour on A3400

Rooms: 3 (2 en suite, 1 private bathroom), S £45–65
D £65–90 **Parking:** 6 **Notes:** ⊘ on premises ⊗ on
premises No children under 9

Holly End provides top-drawer accommodation on the edge of the Cotswolds, midway between Moreton-on-Marsh and Stratford-upon-Avon. Whether your preferences lie with long country hikes and exploring quaint Cotswold villages or discovering the history and culture of Shakespeare country, this bed and breakfast is suitably placed for both. The modern detached family house, immaculately maintained and spotlessly clean, is just a short walk from the centre of Shipston-on-Stour. Shipston, once an important sheep market town, was also an important stop for coaches, and many of the inns in the High Street date from that era. The spacious, comfortable bedrooms – king-size, twin and double – with subtle soft furnishings and decor have shower-baths, while dormer windows add to the character. You can pamper yourself with the Sanctuary spa products provided in each room. Colour televisions and tea- and coffee making facilities are also provided. A comprehensive freshly cooked English breakfast uses the best of local produce (organic wherever possible). Afternoon tea or sherry and snacks are offered on arrival. There is a beautiful sunny garden with a lawn and patio dotted with many container plants.

Recommended in the area

Stratford-upon-Avon; Hidcote Manor (NT); Warwick Castle; Kiftsgate Court Garden, Mickleton; Cotswold Falconry Centre

Ambleside Guest House

♦♦♦♦

Address: 41 Grove Road,
STRATFORD-UPON-AVON CV37 6PB
Tel: 01789 297239
Fax: 01789 295670
Email: ruth@amblesideguesthouse.com
Website: www.amblesideguesthouse.com
Map ref: 3, SP25
Directions: On A4390 opp Firs Park
Rooms: 7 (5 en suite) S, £25–35 D £50–80 **Parking:** 7
Notes: ⊗ on premises ⊗ on premises
No children under 4

Ambleside is a comfortable guesthouse in the heart of Stratford-upon-Avon, where owners Ruth Rogers and Peter Halford provide a warm welcome. A recent refurbishment has left the house in sparkling condition, and the accommodation can suit every need. Choose from a family room which is situated on the ground floor, a double or twin. One room has a four-poster bed – ideal for that special occasion. Many rooms have shower rooms en suite, and each one is equipped with a colour TV, hairdryer and a hospitality tray. Ironing facilities are also available. The choice at breakfast ensures that no one will go hungry, the traditional full English and vegetarian options are freshly cooked. Breakfast is served in the bright and spacious dining room, which looks over the charming front patio garden. Ambleside stands opposite pleasant Firs Park and is just a short stroll into the town centre where there is a good choice of restaurants, cafés and inns and a wealth of shops, ancient buildings, town trails and the Shakespeare attractions. There is a private car park at the rear of the house.

Recommended in the area

Shakespeare's birthplace; Royal Shakespeare Theatre; Anne Hathaway's Cottage; Warwick Castle; Warwick; Charlecote Park (NT)

Cross o'th' Hill Farm

◆◆◆◆

Address:	Broadway Road, STRATFORD-UPON-AVON CV37 8HP
Tel:	01789 204738
Email:	decimanoble@hotmail.com
Website:	www.crossothhillfarm.com
Map ref:	3, SP25
Directions:	0.5m S of Stratford. A3400 S from Stratford for Shipston, 0.75m onto B4632, farm signed 0.25m on right, farmhouse 200yds

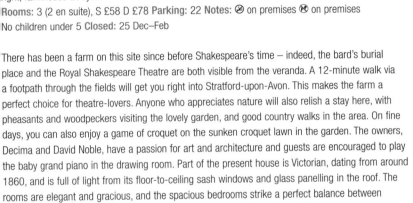

Rooms: 3 (2 en suite), S £58 D £78 **Parking:** 22 **Notes:** ⊘ on premises ⊗ on premises No children under 5 **Closed:** 25 Dec–Feb

There has been a farm on this site since before Shakespeare's time – indeed, the bard's burial place and the Royal Shakespeare Theatre are both visible from the veranda. A 12-minute walk via a footpath through the fields will get you right into Stratford-upon-Avon. This makes the farm a perfect choice for theatre-lovers. Anyone who appreciates nature will also relish a stay here, with pheasants and woodpeckers visiting the lovely garden, and good country walks in the area. On fine days, you can also enjoy a game of croquet on the sunken croquet lawn in the garden. The owners, Decima and David Noble, have a passion for art and architecture and guests are encouraged to play the baby grand piano in the drawing room. Part of the present house is Victorian, dating from around 1860, and is full of light from its floor-to-ceiling sash windows and glass panelling in the roof. The rooms are elegant and gracious, and the spacious bedrooms strike a perfect balance between practicality and homeliness. Fairtrade and organic local products, including home-made preserves using home-grown fruits from the garden and orchard, are used in the delicious low-fat breakfasts served each morning.

Recommended in the area

Royal Shakespeare Company Theatres; Hidcote Gardens; Charlecote Park; Upton House; the Cotswolds

Loxley Farm

★★★★ B&B

Address:	Loxley, STRATFORD-UPON-AVON CV35 9JN
Tel:	01789 840265
Fax:	01789 840645
Email:	loxleyfarm@hotmail.com
Website:	www.loxleyfarm.co.uk
Map ref:	3, SP25
Directions:	4m SE off A422 to village T-junct, left, 3rd house on right

Rooms: 2 en suite, S £50 D £75 **Parking:** 10

Notes: ⊘ on premises 🐕 allowed in bedrooms **Closed:** Xmas & New Year

Easily reached via the M40 and a short drive from Stratford, this thatched former farmhouse stands in attractive cottage gardens in the peaceful village of Loxley. The thoughtfully equipped bedrooms are in a converted 17th-century shieling or cart barn, and each room has an adjacent sitting area. The friendly hostess ensures a warm and genuine welcome for her guests. Tasty breakfasts are served around a family table in the main house dining room.

Recommended in the area

Warwick Castle; Shakespeare sites in Stratford; The Cotswolds

Victoria Spa Lodge

★★★★ GUEST ACCOMMODATION

Address:	Bishopton Lane, Bishopton, STRATFORD-UPON-AVON CV37 9QY
Tel:	01789 267985
Fax:	01789 204728
Email:	ptozer@victoriaspalodge.demon.co.uk
Website:	www.victoriaspa.co.uk
Map ref:	3, SP25
Directions:	A3400 1.5m N to junct A46, 1st left onto Bishopton Ln, 1st house on right

Rooms: 7 en suite, S £50 **Parking:** Park and ride 4 minutes away **Notes:** ⊘ on premises ⊗ on premises **Closed:** Xmas & New Year

Opened in 1837 by Princess Victoria, whose coat-of-arms is built into the gables, this attractive house is in a peaceful country setting on the edge of town. The beautifully appointed bedrooms offer spacious comfort with quality furniture, stylish fabrics and thoughtful touches. Expect a warm welcome and high standards of service. Stratford is a gentle 20-minute walk away.

Recommended in the area

Warwick Castle; Shakespeare theatres & properties; The Cotswolds

WEST MIDLANDS

Canon Hill Park.

Black Firs

★★★★ GUEST HOUSE

Address:	113 Coleshill Road,
	Marston Green,
	BIRMINGHAM B37 7HT
Tel:	0121 779 2727
Fax:	0121 779 2727
Email:	julie@b-firs.co.uk
Website:	www.b-firs.co.uk
Map ref:	3, SP08

Directions: M42 junct 6, A45 W, onto B4438, signs for Marston Green

Rooms: 6 en suite, S £59–89 D £69–89 **Parking:** 6

Notes: ⊘ on premises ⊗ on premises

The location in a mainly residential area on the edge of the National Exhibition Centre (a major venue for concerts, exhibitions, conferences and sporting events throughout the year) makes this majestic house a popular choice all year round. Being close to Birmingham International Airport and the city centre are also bonuses. Julie and Clive Matthews take pride in porviding the best in both service and comfort for their guests. Black Firs is beautifully maintained and spotlessly clean, and has a range of well-decorated and individually furnished bedrooms – there are double, single and family rooms – all with pretty co-ordinated fabrics and smart shower rooms. Each room also has a TV and tea- and coffee-making facilities. Memorable breakfasts, offering a good choice of dishes, are served in a dining room that overlooks immaculate gardens. The comfortable guest lounge is a restful area ideal for a chat or a quiet read, and from here there are french doors opening onto a patio which leads onto the mainly lawned garden.

Recommended in the area

Belfry golf course; Warwick; Stratford-upon-Avon; West Midlands Safari Park; Drayton Manor Park; Alton Towers

WILTSHIRE

Hackpen Hill, Wiltshire.

The Close

◆◆◆◆

Address:	Tidworth Road, BOSCOMBE, Salisbury SP4 0AB
Tel:	01980 611989
Email:	theclose@moocowco.com
Website:	www.moocowco.com/theclose
Map ref:	3, SU23

Directions: Off A338 towards Boscombe Church. The Close is next to church
Rooms: 2 en suite, S £40 D £60 Parking: 2
Notes: ⊘ on premises Closed: 24–26 Dec

Suited to both business and leisure visitors, the spacious bedrooms at this Grade II listed former farmhouse are carefully furnished and come with fresh fruit and flowers, beverages and a range of toiletries. There is a relaxing drawing room, where a log fire burns in the inglenook fireplace creating an inviting atmosphere on cooler evenings. Breakfast, prepared from fresh local produce, is served round a communal table in the dining room. No evening meals but there is a pub a brisk walk away.

Recommended in the area

Salisbury Cathedral; Old Sarum; Stonehenge

White Smocks

★★★★ B&B

Address:	Ashley, BOX SN13 8AJ
Tel:	01225 742154
Fax:	01225 742212
Email:	whitesmocksashley@hotmail.com
Website:	www.whitesmocks.com
Map ref:	2, ST86

Directions: A4 1m W of Box turn opp The Northy, at T-junct White Smocks right of thatched cottage
Rooms: 2 en suite, S £45–50 D £65–70 Parking: 3
Notes: ⊘ on premises

Located in the pleasant village of Ashley, White Smocks offers a relaxing escape. Angela and Paul Berry make you feel at home, and they can advise on visits to surrounding attractions. You are encouraged to enjoy the pleasant garden in the summer, real fires in the winter, and the Jacuzzi all year round. The bedrooms and bathrooms are immaculately presented and comfortably furnished, and there is a welcoming lounge. Tasty, well-cooked meals are enhanced by fresh ingredients.

Recommended in the area

Bath; Lacock; Castle Combe

Home Farm

★★★★ B&B

Address: Farleigh Road, Wingfield,
BRADFORD-ON-AVON BA14 9LG
Tel/Fax: 01225 764492
Email: info@homefarm-guesthouse.co.uk
Website: www.homefarm-guesthouse.co.uk
Map ref: 2, ST86
Directions: 2m S in Wingfield village on A366
Rooms: 3 en suite, D £60 **Parking:** 30
Notes: ⊘ on premises ⊗ on premises

Home Farm is an imaginative conversion of what were originally cattle stalls, feeding rooms and a hay loft belonging to Wingfield House. It fronts onto the original farmyard, which provides ample private parking. There is a 2-acre garden and a large, comfortably furnished lounge to relax in. Breakfasts, cooked on an Aga, offer a wide selection including fish dishes, and home-made bread is a feature. Spacious bedrooms comprise a family room, a double, and a ground-floor twin. All rooms have dual-aspect windows, televisions, radios, hairdryers, trouser presses, bathrobes and hospitality trays.

Recommended in the area
Roman Baths, Bath; Longleat; Stonehenge.

Junipers

★★★★ B&B

Address: 3 Juniper Road, FIRSDOWN,
Salisbury SP5 1SS
Tel: 01980 862330
Email: junipersbedandbreakfast@btinternet.com
Website: www.junipersbedandbreakfast.co.uk
Map ref: 3, SU23
Directions: 5m from Salisbury on A30, A343 to London
follow Junipers brown signs into Firsdown
Rooms: 3 en suite, D £55–60 **Parking:** 6
Notes: ⊘ on premises No children

Set in a peaceful little hamlet, convenient for visiting the many local attractions, this bungalow reflects the dedication and enthusiasm of its owner, Laurence Slater, who has lavished his attention on the place for more than 20 years – and this includes hand-crafting much of the furniture. The bedrooms each have hand-made maple beds, and the one at the back has patio doors opening onto the garden, where the steel spider-web gazebo is also one of Mr Slater's creations. Breakfast is a real treat.

Recommended in the area
Salisbury; Stonehenge; Wilton House

At the Sign of the Angel

Address:	6 Church Street, LACOCK,
	Chippenham SN15 2LB
Tel:	01249 730230
Fax:	01249 730527
Email:	angel@lacock.co.uk
Website:	www.lacock.co.uk
Map ref:	2, ST96
Directions:	Off A350 into Lacock, follow Local

Traffic sign

Rooms: 10 en suite, S £72–85 D £105–155 **Parking:** 7 **Notes:** 🐕 allowed in bedrooms

Log fires, oak panelling and low beams create a wonderful atmosphere in this 15th-century house. The same family has owned this inn for over half a century and the restaurant is internationally renowned for its traditional cooking. Four bedrooms are in the cottage across the footbridge over a stream. Furnished with antiques, one has an enormous bed that was owned by the Victorian engineer Isambard Kingdom Brunel, another has a four-poster, and a third room has a French tented bed.

Recommended in the area

Lacock Abbey (NT); Fox Talbot Museum; Bowood House and Gardens

Chetcombe House

★ ★ ★ ★ GUEST ACCOMMODATION

Address:	Chetcombe Road, MERE,
	Warminster BA12 6AZ
Tel:	01747 860219
Fax:	01747 860111
Email:	mary.butchers@lineone.net
Map ref:	2, ST83
Directions:	Off A303

Rooms: 5 en suite, S £45 D £60 **Parking:** 10
Notes: ⊘ on premises

Looking across an acre of well-tended gardens towards Gillingham and the Blackmore Vale, Chetcombe House, built in 1937, oozes elegance and charm. The property, just a few minutes from the centre of Mere, is a good base from which to explore the many local attractions. Chetcombe is pleasantly spacious and extremely comfortable. The bedrooms, one of which is a family room, have tea and coffee facilities, and the attractive dining room, with garden and countryside views, is the venue for a substantial breakfast. Pubs and restaurants nearby provide plenty of options for evening meals.

Recommended in the area

Stourhead (NT); Stourton House; Longleat

The Old Farmhouse

♦♦♦♦♦

Address:	Bagbury Lane, Restrop, PURTON, Swindon SN5 4LX
Tel:	01793 770130
Email:	stay@theoldfarmhouse.net
Website:	www.theoldfarmhouse.net
Map ref:	3, SU08
Directions:	M4 junct 16, signs for Wootton Bassett then Purton, right at 1st x-rds, Bagbury Ln 1st left

Rooms: 6 en suite, D £75–160 **Parking:** 20
Notes: ⊘ on premises ⊗ on premises No children

18th-century Old Farmhouse is a wonderful place, set in tranquil countryside only a short distance from Swindon and the M4. Style and quality abound here, and the hospitality and housekeeping are also great strengths. Each bedroom is individually styled and very comfortable, and all are provided with a host of thoughtful knick-knacks. Four of the rooms are situated in lovingly converted cow stalls. One of these rooms, The Manger, has a large living area with a cottage-style three-piece suite and dining table, a kitchen area with an Aga and a separate bedroom. There are two suites in the main farmhouse. The Apple Rooms, which take up the first floor of the east wing, consist of a private drawing room, bedroom with a king-size four-poster and a bathroom, while the Cheese Room has a comfortable old French carved bed, and a living area with a sofa and dining room table and chairs. Soft furnishings and bed linen are sumptuous throughout and the bathing facilities verge on the sensual. An impressive continental breakfast is served in each room – ingredients are local, home-made or organic. There is a private, 9-hole golf course here for guests, and its free. Hot tubs and spa treatments are also available.

Recommended in the area

Cotswold Water Park, Ashton Keynes; Wiltshire chalk horses; Avebury; Lydiard Park; Swindon; Cirencester; Bowood House and Gardens

Salisbury Cathedral

The Old House

★ ★ ★ ★ GUEST ACCOMMODATION

Address:	161 Wilton Road,
	SALISBURY SP2 7JQ
Tel:	01722 333433
Fax:	01722 335551
Map ref:	3, SU12

Directions: On A36 1m W from city centre
Rooms: 7 en suite, S £40–55 D £50–55 **Parking:** 10
Notes: ⊘ on premises ⊗ on premises No children under 7

Charming accommodation is offered at this 17th-century house, located on the Wilton road within walking distance of Salisbury city centre. Ground-floor areas are beautifully furnished in keeping with the building's period character. The mature gardens are a lovely surprise, with three distinct areas providing privacy on summer evenings. Bedrooms have been tastefully decorated and equipped with modern facilities, including bath or shower rooms en suite. There are two rooms at ground-floor level and one room with a splendid four-poster bed, all the bedrooms are equipped with hairdryers and hospitality trays.

Recommended in the area

Stourhead (NT); Heale Garden; Wilton House

Ardecca

★★★★   GUEST HOUSE

Address:	Fieldrise Farm, Kingsdown Lane, Blunsdon, SWINDON SN25 5DL
Tel:	01793 721238
Email:	chris-graham.ardecca@fsmail.net
Website:	www.ardecca-bedandbreakfast.co.uk
Map ref:	3, SU18
Directions:	Off A419 at Turnpike rdbt, left onto Turnpike Rd, 1st right

Rooms: 4 en suite, S £35 D £55 **Parking:** 5 **Notes:** ⊘ on premises ⊗ on premises No children under 6

Ardecca (the name is an amalgamation of the names Rebecca and Richard, the owners' children) has been the family home of Chris and Graham Horne for over 25 years. The large modern bungalow is immaculate inside and out and sits in 16 acres of pastureland on the edge of Blunsdon village, in a quiet rural setting in north Wiltshire within easy reach of Swindon and Cirencester, the Cotswolds and the Marlborough downs. A great find and an asset to the area, the house offers spacious first-class accommodation in a friendly and relaxed atmosphere created by Chris and Graham. All the rooms are on the ground floor, larger than average and are equipped with modern amenities including TV, video, radio alarm and tea-and coffee-making facilities. A full English breakfast is provided and freshly cooked evening meals are available by arrangement, alternatively there are many good pubs and restaurants in the area. There is an outdoor patio area with seating and you can explore the immediate area on public footpaths leading through meadows. Ample parking is available. Please note that credit cards are not accepted.

Recommended in the area

Cotswold Water Park; Avebury stone circle; Marlborough, the Savernake Forest; Lydiard Park; Thames Path; Buscot Park (NT); Stonehenge

Stonehenge.

The Woodfalls Inn

★★★ INN

Address:	The Ridge, WOODFALLS SP5 2LN
Tel:	01725 513222
Fax:	01725 513220
Email:	woodfallsi@aol.com
Website:	www.woodfallsinn.co.uk
Map ref:	3, SU12

Directions: M27 junct 1, onto B3079, then B3078 towards Fordingbridge, onto B3080
Rooms: 10 en suite, S £49.95–55 D £77.90–85
Parking: 30 **Notes:** ⌖ allowed in bedrooms

Woodfalls Inn has been providing hospitality to travellers since 1870. Its position on the northern edge of the New Forest National Park makes it perfect for outdoor pursuits and there is a championship golf course just 2 miles away. Refurbished, the inn also has additional new accommodation. The rooms are decorated in English country style and some rooms have four-posters. Eating is a pleasure here, whether it is the full English breakfast, or a meal in the bar, conservatory or restaurant.

Recommended in the area

New Forest National Park; Salisbury Cathedral; Broadlands, Romsey

Iron Age hill fort in the Malvern Hills.

The Dell House

★★★★ B&B

Address:	Green Lane, Malvern Wells, MALVERN WR14 4HU
Tel:	01684 564448
Fax:	01684 893974
Email:	burrage@dellhouse.co.uk
Website:	www.dellhouse.co.uk
Map ref:	2, S074
Directions:	2m S of Great Malvern on A449. Turn left

off A449 onto Green Ln. House at top of road on right

Rooms: 3 en suite, S £33–42 D £56–64 **Parking:** 6 **Notes:** ⊘ on premises ⊗ on premises No children under 10

The Dell House was built around 1820 when one of Malvern's famous healing springs was diverted to its grounds. Ian and Helen Burrage offer spacious, individually styled bedrooms where period elegance is combined with homely comforts; two rooms have wonderful views to the Cotswolds. Breakfast is served in the impressive Morning Room with superb views over the Severn valley.

Recommended in the area

Three Counties Showground; Malvern Hills; Malvern Theatre

Garden Cottages

★★★★ B&B

Address:	Stoney Lane, Crossway Green, STOURPORT-ON-SEVERN DY13 9SL
Tel/Fax:	01299 250626
Email:	gardencottages@btinternet.com
Website:	www.gardencottages.co.uk
Map ref:	2, S087
Directions:	3m SE of Stourport off A449 rdbt

Rooms: 4 (3 en suite), S £40 D £70 **Parking:** 5 **Notes:** ⊘ on premises 🐕 allowed in bedrooms **Closed:** Xmas

A pretty cottage set in beautiful countryside within easy reach of the city of Worcester. The traditional oak-beamed property has been modernised to a high standard without spoiling the original character. Bedrooms have en suites or private bathrooms, refreshment trays, clock radios and good toiletries. Breakfast is served in the dining room, using freshly laid eggs and local farm produce. Gardens, a sun lounge and sun terrace add to the facilities. There is a self-catering cottage in the grounds.

Recommended in the area

Severn Valley Railway; Elgar Birthplace Museum; Worcester Cathedral

Fangdale beck, Bilsdale

Shallowdale House

★★★★★ ⇔ 🏠 GUEST ACCOMMODATION

Address:	West End, AMPLEFORTH YO62 4DY
Tel:	01439 788325
Fax:	01439 788885
Email:	stay@shallowdalehouse.co.uk
Website:	www.shallowdalehouse.co.uk
Map ref:	8, SE58
Directions:	Off A170 at W end of village

Rooms: 3 (2 en suite), S £67.50–77.50 D £85–105
Parking: 3 **Notes:** ⊗ on premises ⊗ on premises
No children under 12 **Closed:** Xmas & New Year

Owned by Anton van der Horst and Phillip Gill, Shallowdale House is in a stunning location overlooking an Area of Outstanding Natural Beauty. The spacious south-facing bedrooms have huge picture windows and lovely views, and the atmosphere is relaxed and friendly. The four-course dinners are a highlight, featuring local and seasonal produce, and equal care is taken with breakfast, which can feature Whitby kippers and local sausages, as well as home-made preserves.

Recommended in the area

Castle Howard; Rievaulx Abbey; Nunnington Hall (NT)

Elmfield House

★★★★ GUEST HOUSE

Address:	Arrathorne, BEDALE DL8 1NE
Tel:	01677 450558
Email:	stay@elmfieldhouse.co.uk
Website:	www.elmfieldhouse.co.uk
Map ref:	7, SE28

Directions: 4m NW of Bedale. A684 from Bedale for Leyburn, right after Patrick Brompton towards Richmond, B&B 1.5m on right
Rooms: 7 en suite, S £47–52 D £70–78 **Parking:** 7
Notes: ⊗ on premises ⊗ on premises

The former gamekeeper's cottage has been extended to provide spacious, well-equipped bedrooms with tea and coffee facilities. Two rooms have four-poster beds and two have easier access. There is a pleasant lounge area with an honesty bar, a conservatory-lounge and a games room. Relax in the gardens or stroll to the 14-acre wood and fishing lake for sightings of deer and kingfishers. The full English breakfast using local produce is a highlight; evening meals can be ordered by arrangement.

Recommended in the area

Bedale; Richmond; Yorkshire Dales and Moors

The Downe Arms Inn

★★★★ INN

Address:	3 High Street, CASTLETON, WhitbyY O21 2EE
Tel/Fax:	01287 660223
Email:	info@thedowneams.co.uk
Website:	www.thedownearms.co.uk
Map ref:	8, NZ60
Directions:	4m S off A171 in village centre

Rooms: 5 en suite, S £35–40 D £60–70 **Parking:** 6
Notes: ⊗ on premises

Phil and Susie offer a warm welcome to their country inn, set in the beautiful upper Esk Valley in *Heartbeat* country. The North York Moors National Park Centre at Danby is just a short walk away, and there are plenty of opportunities for walking, horse riding and cycling. The refurbished bedrooms are of a high standard and come with complimentary toiletries, crisp white linen and hospitality trays. Relax in the lounge bar with its open log fire, original beamed ceiling and exposed stone walls. The resident chef uses local and organic produce to create English classics and exotic meals.

Recommended in the area

Danby; Whitby; York

Ashfield House Hotel

♦♦♦♦♦ ⇔

Address:	Summers Fold, GRASSINGTON, Skipton BD23 5AE
Tel:	01756 752584
Fax:	07092 376562
Email:	info@ashfieldhouse.co.uk
Website:	www.ashfieldhouse.co.uk
Map ref:	7, SE06
Directions:	B6265 to village centre Main St, left onto Summers Fold

Rooms: 8 (7 en suite), S £61–115 D £85–120 **Parking:** 8 **Notes:** ⊘ on premises ⊗ on premises
No children under 5

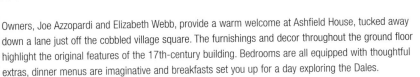

Owners, Joe Azzopardi and Elizabeth Webb, provide a warm welcome at Ashfield House, tucked away down a lane just off the cobbled village square. The furnishings and decor throughout the ground floor highlight the original features of the 17th-century building. Bedrooms are all equipped with thoughtful extras, dinner menus are imaginative and breakfasts set you up for a day exploring the Dales.

Recommended in the area

Bolton Abbey; Stump Cross Caverns; Aysgarth Falls

The Kings Head Hotel & Restaurant

★★★★ GUEST ACCOMMODATION

Address:	The Green, GUISBOROUGH,
	Nr Great Ayton TS9 6QR
Tel:	01642 722318
Fax:	01642 724750
Email:	info@kingsheadhotel.co.uk
Website:	www.kingsheadhotel.co.uk
Map ref:	8, NZ61

Directions: A173 to Newton under Roseberry, under Roseberry Topping landmark

Rooms: 8 en suite, S £55–95 D £69.50–99.50 Parking: 96 Notes: ⊘ on premises ⊗ on premises

Closed: 25–26 Dec, 1 Jan

This family-owned establishment offers stylish, thoughtfully equipped bedrooms. The restaurant, next door, offers quality food with produce sourced from the local area. A full English or continental breakfast is served in the glass-roofed breakfast area with unspoiled views of Roseberry Topping.

Recommended in the area

Cleveland Way; North York Moors National Park; Whitby

Fountains B&B

★★★★ GUEST HOUSE

Address:	27 Kings Road, HARROGATE HG1 5JY
Tel:	01423 530483
Fax:	01423 705312
Email:	dave@fountains.fsworld.co.uk
Website:	www.thefountainshotel.co.uk
Map ref:	7, SE35

Directions: 500yds N of town centre. Off A59 Skipton Rd onto Kings Rd, 0.75m on right

Rooms: 10 en suite, S £38–55 D £65 Parking: 8

Notes: ⊘ on premises No children under 6 Closed: 24 Dec–2 Jan

Fountains is just a short walk from the Harrogate International Centre and the town centre with its fine restaurants and exclusive shops. Welcoming owners Dave and Nell Giles have combined original Victorian splendour with modern day facilities. The bedrooms are stylish, individually decorated, and have extensive hospitality trays. Two bedrooms are on the ground floor for easier access. Home cooking is a speciality and breakfast is prepared from produce sourced from local suppliers.

Recommended in the area

Betty's Café Tea Rooms, Harrogate; Yorkshire Dales; Fountains Abbey (NT)

asterside Hill, Hawnby

Laskill Grange

★★★★ 🏠 GUEST ACCOMMODATION

Address:	Hawnby, HAWNBY YO62 5NB
Tel:	01439 798268
Fax:	01439 798498
Email:	suesmith@laskillfarm.fsnet.co.uk
Website:	www.laskillgrange.co.uk
Map ref:	SE59
Directions:	6m N of Helmsley on B1257

Rooms: 4 en suite, D £60–70 **Parking:** 20 **Notes:** ⊗ on premises 🐾 allowed in bedrooms **Closed:** 25 Dec

Laskill is a charming 19th-century house in the North York Moors National Park. There are splendid walks in the surrounding countryside and fishing in the River Seph, which runs through the grounds. The elegant house has exposed beams and open fireplaces, and the immaculate bedrooms are decorated to a very high standard and come with hot-drink trays and flowers. Generous breakfasts are prepared using home-grown produce wherever possible. Across the courtyard from the farmhouse are converted barns for self catering. There is an activity centre for children too.

Recommended in the area

Rievaulx Abbey; Castle Howard; Nunnington Hall (NT)

Brickfields Farm

★★★★ GUEST ACCOMMODATION

Address: Kirby Mills,
KIRKBYMOORSIDE YO62 6NS
Tel: 01751 433074
Email: janet@brickfieldsfarm.co.uk
Website: www.brickfieldsfarm.co.uk
Map ref: 8, SE68
Directions: A170 E from Kirbymoorside, 0.5m right
into Kirby Mills (signed), farm 1st right
Rooms: 6 en suite, D £70–85 Parking: 8
Notes: ⊗ on premises No children

Janet Trousdale inherited the family farm and has since turned it into a highly successful guesthouse. The refurbished bedrooms have been individually styled and filled with plenty of homely and luxury extras. All rooms at Brickfields are on the ground floor. In the farmhouse you'll find the comfortable double Green Room with an antique French bed and there is also a spacious twin room with a large window which lets in the morning sunshine. This room has been converted from the former stables. A new barn conversion of the same high standard of comfort and quality will be available in 2007, consisting of two doubles featuring king-size beds and two twins. One of the twin rooms will be specially designed with wheelchair-accessible facilities. Modern showers, fluffy bath sheets and bathrobes, flatscreen TV, DVD, Freeview, fresh flowers, a selection of teas, coffees, herbal infusions and biscuits add to the comfort. There's also a mini-fridge with fresh milk and mineral water in each room. A short morning stroll across the former farmyard brings you back to the conservatory for a generous and appetizing Yorkshire breakfast. There are plenty of restaurants and pubs in the area and Janet is happy to advise. Brickfields Farm is an ideal base for exploring the North York Moors, the Yorkshire Dales, Whitby and the east coast, as well as the area's stately homes, abbeys and castles.

Recommended in the area

Rievaulx Abbey; Castle Howard; North Yorkshire Moors Railway

Gallon House

Address: 47 Kirkgate, KNARESBOROUGH HG5 8BZ
Tel: 01423 862102
Email: gallon-house@ntlworld.com
Website: www.gallon-house.co.uk
Map ref: 8, SE35
Directions: Next to railway station
Rooms: 3 en suite, S £75 D £99
Notes: ⊗ on premises

Situated overlooking Nidd Gorge, Gallon House offers first-class accommodation and welcoming atmosphere. The stylish bedrooms are individually furnished with many extras, including CD players, bathrobes and superb refreshment trays. Rick Hodgson's culinary delights are not to be missed and he places strong emphasis on local ingredients. Dinner, by arrangement, features quality local bread, pâtés and chutneys and the beef casserole is prepared using local Yorkshire ale.

Recommended in the area

Leeds; York; Fountains Abbey (NT)

Newton House

★★★★ GUEST ACCOMMODATION

Address: 5–7 York Place, KNARESBOROUGH HG5 0AD
Tel: 01423 863539
Fax: 01423 869748
Email: newtonhouse@btinternet.com
Website: www.newtonhouseyorkshire.com
Map ref: 8, SE35
Directions: On A59 in Knaresborough, 500yds from town centre
Rooms: 11 (10 en suite), S £50 D £85–95 **Parking:** 10 **Notes:** 🐾 allowed in bedrooms
Closed: 1 wk Xmas

Proprietors Kevin and Sara Earl work hard to ensure you have an enjoyable stay at Newton House, a former 18th-century coaching inn. Modern, individually decorated bedrooms are well equipped and some have four-posters and king-size doubles. Children are welcome and family rooms are available. There is an inviting lounge, and individually cooked breakfasts are served in an attractive dining room.

Recommended in the area

Harewood House; Fountains Abbey; Knaresborough Castle

The Old Town Hall Guest House

★★★★ GUEST ACCOMMODATION

Address: The Old Town Hall, Redmire,
LEYBURN DL8 4ED
Tel: 01969 625641
Fax: 01969 624982
Email: enquiries@theoldtownhall.co.uk
Website: www.theoldtownhall.co.uk
Map ref: 7, SE19
Directions: In village centre, signs for tea room & guest house
Rooms: 3 (1 en suite), S £40–60 D £65–90 **Parking:** 3 **Notes:** ⊗ on premises

The Old Town Hall, dating from 1862, is ideally placed in Wensleydale and is perfect for touring or walking in the Yorkshire Dales. There are three delightful rooms known as Penhill, Scarth Nick and Scar View; these vary in style and come with a host of extras and luxury touches. A hearty Yorkshire breakfast is served in the bright airy dining room, which transforms into a tearoom throughout the day.
Recommended in the area
Yorkshire Dales National Park; Bolton Castle; Richmond

River House Hotel

★★★ GUEST HOUSE

Address: MALHAM,
Skipton BD23 4DA
Tel: 01729 830315
Email: info@riverhousehotel.co.uk
Website: www.riverhousehotel.co.uk
Map ref: 7, SD96
Directions: Off A65, 7m N to Malham
Rooms: 8 en suite, S £45–65 D £60–65 **Parking:** 5
Notes: ⊗ on premises No children under 8

A warm welcome awaits you at this attractive Victorian house close to the Pennine Way. The superb countryside is excellent for walking, mountain biking and horse riding. The bedrooms are bright and well equipped and some have original fireplaces – one room on the ground floor has easier access. The public areas include a cosy lounge with a wood burning stove, and a large, well-appointed dining room. The owners provide exceptional breakfasts, including scrumptious sausages and black pudding from the local butcher. Delicious dinners also feature local produce.
Recommended in the area
Settle to Carlisle Railway; Skipton; Pennine Way

Bank Villa Guest House

★★★★ 🛏 ⚜ GUEST HOUSE

Address: MASHAM,
Ripon HG4 4DB
Tel: 01765 689605
Email: bankvilla@btopenworld.com
Website: www.bankvilla.com
Map ref: 7, SE28
Directions: Enter on A6108 from Ripon, property on right
Rooms: 6 (4 en suite), S £45–65 D £50–95 Triple £75–105 **Parking:** 6 **Notes:** ⊘ on premises ⊗ on premises No children under 5

Graham and Liz Howard-Barker have created a welcoming atmosphere in their charming Georgian home, a great base for exploring the Dales. Relax in the lovely terraced gardens, in one of two comfortable lounges, or the conservatory, all of which have plenty of character. Individually decorated bedrooms feature beams, stripped pine period furniture and crisp white linens. Liz's cooking uses home-grown and local produce whenever possible, served in the relaxed licensed restaurant.
Recommended in the area
Black Sheep and Theakstons breweries; Rievaulx Abbey; Fountains Abbey; Yorkshire Dales

The Moorlands Country House Hotel

★★★★★ 🛏 ⚜ GUEST ACCOMMODATION

Address: Levisham, PICKERING YO18 7NL
Tel: 01751 460229
Fax: 01751 460470
Email: ronaldoleonardo@aol.com
Website: www.moorlandslevisham.co.uk
Map ref: 8, SE78
Directions: A169 N from Pickering 6m, left to Lockton & Levisham
Rooms: 7 en suite, S £50–75 D £100–140 **Parking:** 10 **Notes:** ⊘ on premises ⊗ on premises No children under 15 **Closed:** Dec–Feb

The Leonards maintain the highest standards of comfort and hospitality at Moorlands. Set in extensive grounds with stunning views, the North York Moors National Park starts just outside the gate, and after you have walked up an appetite, you can return to a delicious evening meal – a highlight of any stay.
Recommended in the area
Castle Howards; Rievaulx Abbey; North Yorkshire Moors Railway

The New Inn

◆◆◆◆

Address: Maltongate, Thornton le Dale,
PICKERING YO18 7LF
Tel: 01751 474226
Email: terryandjo1@btconnect.com
Website: www.the-new-inn.com
Map ref: 8, SE78
Directions: on A177 in centre of Thornton le Dale
Rooms: 6 en suite, S £43–48 D £66–76 **Parking:** 15
Notes: ⊗ on premises

Originally a Georgian coaching inn, The New Inn sits in an idyllic spot at the centre of Thornton le Dale overlooking the village green. Picturesque Thornton le Dale has a beck running alongside the main street and the village stocks and market cross are still in existence. The New Inn itself has undergone extensive alterations but still retains lots of charm. The bedrooms have either en suite bath or shower, hand-made pine furniture and many extras to ensure every comfort. There is a friendly atmosphere in the locals' bar and the restaurant prides itself on serving interesting local dishes.

Recommended in the area

City of York; North Yorkshire Moors; Castle Howard

Whashton Springs Farm

★★★★ FARMHOUSE

Address: RICHMOND, North Yorkshire DL11 7JS
Tel: 01748 822884
Fax: 01748 826285
Email: whashtonsprings@btconnect.com
Website: www.whashtonsprings.co.uk
Map ref: 7, NZ10
Directions: In Richmond N at lights towards
Ravensworth, 3m down steep hill, farm at bottom on left
Rooms: 8 en suite, S £35 D £56–60 **Parking:** 10
Notes: ⊗ on premises ⊗ on premises No children under 5 **Closed:** late Dec–Jan

This family-run, working farm in the heart of the countryside makes a perfect base for exploring the Yorkshire Dales. The lambing season is a particularly good time to visit when the farm's new arrivals are on show. Accommodation is either in the large farmhouse or within the delightful courtyard rooms. Jane Turnbull serves a hearty breakfast in the dining room overlooking the garden, and is on hand to chat and answer questions. The stylish lounge provides somewhere to contemplate the day ahead.

Recommended in the area

Richmond; Swaledale; York; Yorkshire Dales; the Lake District; North Yorkshire Moors

Mallard Grange

★★★★★ 🏠 FARMHOUSE

Address:	Aldfield, RIPON HG4 3BE
Tel:	01765 620242
Fax:	01765 620242
Email:	maggie@mallardgrange.co.uk
Website:	www.mallardgrange.co.uk
Map ref:	7, SE37
Directions:	B6265 W fom Ripon, Mallard Grange

2.5m on right

Rooms: 4 en suite, D/Twin £70–90 **Parking:** 6

Notes: ⊘ on premises No children under 12

Closed: Xmas & New Year

This fine Yorkshire farmhouse retains many original features dating back to the 16th century and in fact there has been a house on this site since 1355. The Johnson family have farmed the land and lived in the historic house since 1933. Located in glorious countryside near Ripon, Mallard Grange is ideally placed for touring the Yorkshire Dales and Moors and for visiting the many fine country houses and gardens in the area. Each room has a distinct character with quality furnishings including antique pine or mahogany furniture and pretty quilts and curtains. Extra touches include sofas, refreshment trays, hairdryers, TVs and radio alarm clocks. All rooms have en suite bathrooms, complete with toiletries, big soft towels and bathrobes. Two of the bedrooms are in a converted smithy on the ground floor, just a short distance from the main house. Breakfast is a real farmhouse treat and as an AA Breakfast Award winner the standard is very high. The choice is comprehensive and the produce locally sourced with ingredients such as Thirsk black pudding, Whitby kippers and Wensleydale cheese – quintessential Yorkshire fare.

Recommended in the area

Fountains Abbey (NT); Harrogate; Newby Hall

St George's Court

★★★★ 🔔 FARMHOUSE

Address:	Old Home Farm, Grantley, RIPON HG4 3PJ
Tel/Fax:	01765 620618
Email:	stgeorgescourt@bronco.co.uk
Website:	www.stgeorges-court.co.uk
Map ref:	7, SE37

Directions: B6265 W from Ripon, right signed Grantley
& Winksley, up hill 1m past Risplith sign & next right
Rooms: 5 en suite, S £40–50 D £60–75 Parking: 12
Notes: ⊘ on premises

Warm hospitality is the hallmark of this renovated farmhouse complex on the edge of Wensleydale and close to Fountains Abbey World Heritage Site. The elegant house is set in 20 acres that includes a small lake, home to numerous waterfowl. The ground floor rooms, each with their own front door, are located around a pretty central courtyard, and have quality beds, refreshment trays and spacious bathrooms. One unit with two bedrooms is ideal for families. Imaginative breakfasts, using fine local ingredients, are served in the conservatory-dining room.

Recommended in the area

Fountains Abbey (NT); Brimham Rocks; Newby Hall

Low Skibeden Farmhouse

★★★ GUEST ACCOMMODATION

Address:	Harrogate Road, SKIPTON BD23 6AB
Tel:	01756 793849
Website:	www.yorkshirenet.co.uk/accgde/lowskibeden
Map ref:	7, SD95

Directions: At E end of Skipton bypass off
A65/A59, 1m on right
Rooms: 5 (4 en suite), S £36–52 D £52–60
Parking: 6 Notes: ⊘ on premises ⊗ on premises

Yorkshire hospitality at its best is just part of the appeal of this lovely stone farmhouse. You are greeted with tea and cakes on arrival, and there are plenty of other home comforts. The traditionally decorated and furnished bedrooms are equipped with lots of thoughtful extras, and the bathrooms are modern. There is a comfy lounge, while in the evening Heather Simpson serves suppertime drinks. Breakfast is an occasion, when hearty full English dishes are served in the dining room. Outside there are lovingly tended gardens to enjoy and the beautiful Yorkshire Dales National Park to be explored. No children or pets.

Recommended in the area

Harrogate; Ingleton waterfalls; Bronte Parsonage, Haworth

The Blackwell Ox Inn

◆◆◆◆ ◎ ⌣

Address:	Huby Road,
	SUTTON-ON-THE-FOREST YO61 1DT
Tel:	01347 810328
Fax:	01904 691529
Email:	enquiries@blackwelloxinns
Website:	www.blackwelloxinn.co.uk
Map ref:	8, SE56
Directions:	Off A1237, onto B1363 to Sutton-on-the-

Forest. Left at T-junct, 50yds on right

Rooms: 5 en suite, S £90 D £90 **Parking:** 18 **Notes:** ⊘ on premises ⊗ on premises

Picturesque Sutton-on-the-Forest is only 7 miles from York, making it a good base for exploring the city and the surrounding countryside. This refurbished inn offers attractive, individually designed bedrooms and pleasing public rooms. Chef Steven Holding prepares excellent dishes in the restaurant using local produce to create French-inspired dishes and the bold flavours of Spain's Catalan region. Tasty puddings round off the experience. Children welcome but only guide dogs please.

Recommended in the area

Castle Howard; Jorvic Centre, York; Railway Museum, York

Spital Hill

★★★★★ ⌣ ⌂ GUEST ACCOMMODATION

Address:	York Road, THIRSK YO7 3AE
Tel:	01845 522273
Fax:	01845 524970
Email:	spitalhill@spitalhill.entadsl.com
Website:	www.spitalhill.co.uk
Map ref:	8, SE48
Directions:	1.5m SE of town, set back 200yds from

A19, driveway marked by 2 white posts

Rooms: 5 (4 en suite), S £56–61 D £84–95 **Parking:** 6
Notes: ⊘ on premises ⊗ on premises No children under 12

Robin and Ann Clough warmly welcome guests to their beautiful home, a fine country house set in its gardens and parkland surrounded by open countryside. Ann produces an excellent set dinner each evening as an optional extra, using good fresh produce, much of which comes from the garden. Breakfast is also a highlight. Bedrooms are furnished with quality and style, and thoughtfully equipped with many extras; there is no tea making equipment as Ann prefers to offer tea as a service.

Recommended in the area

Herriott Centre, Thirsk; Byland Abbey; York Minster

Woodhouse Farm

★ ★ ★ ★ 🏠 FARMHOUSE

Address:	WESTOW, York YO60 7LL
Tel:	01653 618378
Fax:	01653 618378
Email:	stay@wood-house-farm.co.uk
Website:	www.wood-house-farm.co.uk
Map ref:	8, SE76

Directions: Off A64 to Kirkham Priory & Westow. Right at T-junct, farm drive 0.5m out of village on right
Rooms: 3 en suite, S £30–40 D £55–70 **Parking:** 12
Notes: ⊘ on premises ⊗ on premises **Closed:** Xmas, New Year & Mar to mid-Apr

This 500-acre family-run working farm is set in rolling countryside nestled between the Vale of York, the Yorkshire Wolds and the Howardian Hills. The 18th-century farmhouse has been sympathetically restored retaining original beams and open log fires to provide a homely feel. All rooms are well equipped and consist of king-size and family rooms. Start the day with a delicious country breakfast sourced from locally produced sausages and bacon, plus home-made preserves, cakes and scones.

Recommended in the area

Castle Howard; York Minster; North Yorkshire Moors

Corra Lynn

★ ★ ★ ★ GUEST ACCOMMODATION

Address:	28 Crescent Avenue, WHITBY YO21 3EW
Tel:	01947 602214
Fax:	01947 602214
Map ref:	8, NZ81

Directions: Corner A174 & Crescent Av
Rooms: 5 en suite, S £24 D £52 **Parking:** 5
Closed: 21 Dec–5 Jan

Bruce and Christine Marot have a passion for what they

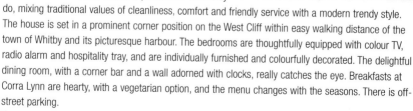

do, mixing traditional values of cleanliness, comfort and friendly service with a modern trendy style. The house is set in a prominent corner position on the West Cliff within easy walking distance of the town of Whitby and its picturesque harbour. The bedrooms are thoughtfully equipped with colour TV, radio alarm and hospitality tray, and are individually furnished and colourfully decorated. The delightful dining room, with a corner bar and a wall adorned with clocks, really catches the eye. Breakfasts at Corra Lynn are hearty, with a vegetarian option, and the menu changes with the seasons. There is off-street parking.

Recommended in the area

Whitby Abbey; Captain Cook Memorial Museum; Robin Hood's Bay

The River Esks at Whitby.

Netherby House Hotel

◆◆◆◆ ⊜

Address:	90 Coach Road, Sleights,
	WHITBY YO22 5EQ
Tel/Fax:	01947 810211
Email:	info@netherby-house.co.uk
Website:	www.netherby-house.co.uk
Map ref:	8, NZ81
Directions:	In village of Sleights, off A169

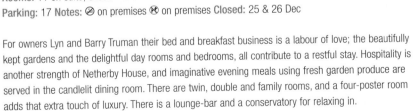

Whitby-Pickering road

Rooms: 11 en suite, S £35–42.50 D £70–85

Parking: 17 **Notes:** ⊘ on premises ⊗ on premises **Closed:** 25 & 26 Dec

For owners Lyn and Barry Truman their bed and breakfast business is a labour of love; the beautifully kept gardens and the delightful day rooms and bedrooms, all contribute to a restful stay. Hospitality is another strength of Netherby House, and imaginative evening meals using fresh garden produce are served in the candlelit dining room. There are twin, double and family rooms, and a four-poster room adds that extra touch of luxury. There is a lounge-bar and a conservatory for relaxing in.

Recommended in the area

Historic Whitby; North Yorkshire Moors National Park; North Yorkshire Moors Railway

Ascot House

★★★★ GUEST HOUSE

Address: 80 East Parade,
YORK YO31 7YH
Tel: 01904 426826
Fax: 01904 431077
Email: admin@ascothouseyork.com
Website: www.ascothouseyork.com
Map ref: 8, SE65
Directions: 0.5m NE of city centre. Off A1036 Heworth
Green onto Mill Ln, 2nd left
Rooms: 15 (12 en suite), S £30–65 D £60–75
Parking: 14 **Notes:** 🐾 allowed in bedrooms **Closed:** 21–28 Dec

This Victorian villa was built for a prominent family in 1869 close to the city centre. The owners have retained many original features, yet they have improved the building to provide modern standards of comfort. Bedrooms are equipped with period furniture, and most of the spacious rooms on the first floor have four-poster or canopy beds. Two rooms are on the ground floor, and most have en suites along with hospitality trays and colour TV. The curved stained-glass window on the landing is a particularly attractive feature. There is a spacious and comfortable lounge where you can relax, watch television or enjoy a drink from the Butlers Pantry. Tea and coffee are also served in the lounge throughout the day. Delicious traditional, vegetarian and continental breakfasts are served in the dining room; the generous portions are sure to set you up for the day. Ascot House is a welcoming property that can be reached from the city by bus in just a few minutes, or by a short brisk walk. It has an enclosed car park, and the public park next door has two tennis courts and two bowling greens. A nearby pub serves good food, and there are also many restaurants, wine bars and theatres within walking distance.

Recommended in the area

Jorvik Viking Centre; National Railway Museum; York Minster

The 'Needle's Eye', a folly in the grounds of the Wentworth Woodhouse.

Sheffield Park Gardens.

Padley Farm B&B

◆◆◆◆

Address:	Dungworth Green, SHEFFIELD S6 6HE
Tel/Fax:	0114 285 1427
Email:	aandlmbestall@btinternet.com
Website:	www.padleyfarm.co.uk
Map ref:	8, SK38

Directions: M1 onto A61 to Loxley, B6077 to Bradfield & B6076 to Dungworth

Rooms: 7 en suite, S £27–37 D £54–60 **Parking:** 8

Notes: ⊘ on premises ⊗ on premises

Padley Farm is just 10 minutes from Sheffield by car, while enjoying a peaceful village setting with panoramic views over the Loxley Valley. This lovely barn conversion has retained much character, including its great oak beams, while providing high quality accommodation. Bedrooms, which benefit from under-floor heating, have shower rooms, televisions with DVD players, tea- and coffee-making facilities and an information folder. Two rooms are on the ground floor and accessible to wheelchair-users. There are seats in the lovely garden, and inside there's a full-size snooker table.

Recommended in the area

Country walks; Sheffield museums and entertainment venues; Abbeydale Industrial Hamlet

altaire Mill was purpose built in the 1850s by Sir Titus Salt.

The Huddersfield Central Lodge

★★★★ GUEST ACCOMMODATION

Address:	11–15 Beast Market,
	HUDDERSFIELD HD1 1QF
Tel:	01484 515551
Fax:	01484 432349
Email:	enquiries@centrallodge.com
Website:	www.centrallodge.com
Map ref:	7, SE11

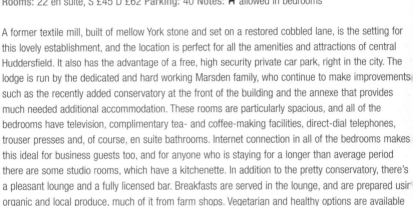

Directions: In town centre off Lord St. Signs for Beast Market from ring road
Rooms: 22 en suite, S £45 D £62 Parking: 40 Notes: ⌖ allowed in bedrooms

A former textile mill, built of mellow York stone and set on a restored cobbled lane, is the setting for this lovely establishment, and the location is perfect for all the amenities and attractions of central Huddersfield. It also has the advantage of a free, high security private car park, right in the city. The lodge is run by the dedicated and hard working Marsden family, who continue to make improvements such as the recently added conservatory at the front of the building and the annexe that provides much needed additional accommodation. These rooms are particularly spacious, and all of the bedrooms have television, complimentary tea- and coffee-making facilities, direct-dial telephones, trouser presses and, of course, en suite bathrooms. Internet connection in all of the bedrooms makes this ideal for business guests too, and for anyone who is staying for a longer than average period there are some studio rooms, which have a kitchenette. In addition to the pretty conservatory, there's a pleasant lounge and a fully licensed bar. Breakfasts are served in the lounge, and are prepared usin organic and local produce, much of it from farm shops. Vegetarian and healthy options are available in addition to the traditional English breakfast.

Recommended in the area

Huddersfield University; Lawrence Batley Theatre; Kingsgate Shopping Centre

The Weavers Shed Restaurant with Rooms

★★★★ ◎◎ 🍴 🏠 RESTAURANT WITH ROOMS

Address: 86 Knowl Road, Golcar,
HUDDERSFIELD HD7 4AN
Tel: 01484 654284
Fax: 01484 650980
Email: info@weaversshed.co.uk
Website: www.weaversshed.co.uk
Map ref: 7, SE11
Directions: 3m W of Huddersfield. A62 onto B6111 to Milnsbridge & Scar Ln to Golcar, right onto Knowl Rd, signed Colne Valley Museum
Rooms: 5 en suite, S £75 D £100 **Parking:** 20 **Closed:** Xmas/New Year

Converted from a cloth-finishing mill in the 1970s, with original features making an interesting talking point, the Weavers Shed continues to impress. Chef-patron Stephen Jackson and his wife Tracy have achieved their ideal of providing a near self-sufficient restaurant, where guests can retire after a superb meal for a luxurious night's sleep. The superior bedrooms are a blend of traditional and classic styles with modern comforts. All rooms are named after local textile mills, are en suite and have colour TVs, telephones, hairdryer and bathrobes. The restaurant, where the delicious breakfasts, including home-made preserves are served, specialises in modern British cooking and simply presented dishes. Situated on the ground floor of the mill, the restaurant retains many original features including wooden beams and stone arches. Tables are laid with white linen tablecloths and in summer bouquets of herbs and wild flowers decorate the tables. The kitchen garden – over an acre of land consisting of a large vegetable plot, greenhouses, an orchard and a soft fruit garden – lies about 15 minutes away in

the village of Holywell Green. It supplies virtually all of the fruit, herb and vegetable requirements for the restaurant, and allows the chef to offer excellent seasonal menus. Much of what is served has been picked the same day. Hens and ducks roam around the kitchen garden and provide fresh eggs every day. South West France dominates the wine list, with less well-known vineyards that produce small-yield quality wines.

Recommended in the area

Royal Armouries Museum; National Museum of Film and Television; National Coal Mining Museum; Peak District National Park; Yorkshire Sculpture Park; Pennine Way

CHANNEL ISLANDS

St Peter Port. Guernsey

The Panorama

★★★★★ 🏛 GUEST ACCOMMODATION

Address:	La Rue du Crocquet,
	ST AUBIN, JERSEY JE3 8BZ
Tel:	01534 742429
Fax:	01534 745940
Email:	info@panoramajersey.com
Website:	www.panoramajersey.com
Map ref:	13

Directions: In village centre
Rooms: 14 en suite, S £36–61 D £72–122
Notes: ⊘ on premises ⊗ on premises No children
Closed: mid-Oct to mid-Apr

A genuine warm welcome and spectacular views across St Aubin's Bay can be expected at this aptly named hotel in a pretty seafront street. Savour the glorious outlook from the sunny terrace or relax in the public areas with their seaward vistas. Antiques feature here, in particular the elegant fireplaces and the hotel is notable for its collection of teapots – there were over 500 at the last count. A hallmark of the bedrooms is the luxury pocket-sprung beds, most of which are well over six feet long. The breakfast is excellent, with each meal individually cooked to order. Dishes such as Grand Slam and Elegant Rarebit are long-time favourites on the extended menu. For lunch or your evening meal the area is well served with restaurants using the best Jersey produce from both land and sea. Many are within walking distance, and the owners are happy to make recommendations. The Panorama is a good base for walking, cycling (there is a cycle track along the promenade to St Helier) or travelling around the island by bus. Day trips by boat are available to the neighbouring islands of Guensey, Herm and Sark and also to St Malo in Brittany. The accommodation is unsuitable for children. This is a no-smoking establishment.

Recommended in the area

Picturesque village of St Aubin; Railway Walk to Corbière; Beauport and Les Creux Country Park

a Hougue Bie, Jersey.

Millbrook House

★★★★ GUEST ACCOMMODATION

Address:	Rue De Trachy,
	Millbrook, ST HELIER,
	JERSEY JE2 3JN
Tel:	01534 733036
Fax:	01534 724317
Email:	millbrook.house@jerseymail.co.uk
Website:	www.millbrookhousehotel.com
Map ref:	13

Directions: 1.5m W of town off A1
Rooms: 27 en suite, S £40–44 D £80–86
Parking: 20 Notes: ⊗ on premises ⊘ on premises
Closed: Oct–early May

The gracious Georgian mansion stands in 10 acres of mature gardens and parkland overlooking the sea and there are many secluded spots to sit and enjoy the peace and quiet and those views. George and Philippa Pirouet's warm hospitality reflects the friendly Jersey atmosphere and with good food too. They have been doing this successfully for well over 20 years, and Millbrook House is ideal for the independent traveller seeking an establishment of character at an acceptable price. It has been in the same island family since 1848, with extensions providing modern accommodation on three floors to the rear. The grounds have a 5-hole pitch and putt golf course, as well as ample parking. The lounges, dining room and public areas are furnished with antiques. Each of the bedrooms has a private bathroom, and most of them have sea and garden views. Direct-dial telephones and hospitality trays are provided, and there is a lift to all floors. In the dining room, an imaginative menu is supported by an extensive wine list. There are also three self-catering studio apartments.

Recommended in the area

Coastal walks; Elizabeth Castle; WWII German Underground Hospital

la Coupee, the road across a ridge to Little Sark.

Hotel Petit Champ

ddress:	SARK, Channel Islands, GY9 0SF
el:	01481 832046
ax:	01481 832469
mail:	info@hotelpetitchamp.co.uk
Vebsite:	www.hotelpetitchamp.co.uk
lap ref:	13, TQ38
irections:	Signs from the Methodist Chapel
ooms:	10 en suite, S £61.75–71.25

£119.50–138.50 **Notes:** ⊗ on premises
o children under 7 **Closed:** Nov–Etr

he sea views and sunsets from this small hotel are magnificent and its splendid position overlooking
ie neighbouring Channel Islands is matched by very high standards of hospitality and service. Chris
nd Caroline guarantee to send you home refreshed and happy. The bedrooms have no televisions
here is a television lounge) and morning tea or coffee is brought to your room. Breakfasts and the
ve-course dinners make excellent use of fresh local produce, and there is a well-stocked wine cellar.

ecommended in the area

a Seigneurie Gardens; Horse and carriage tours; boat trips

ISLE OF MAN

The world's largest working water wheel, the Lady Isabella.

Dreem Ard

◆◆◆◆ 🛏

Address:	Ballanard Road, DOUGLAS, ISLE OF MAN IM2 5PR
Tel:	01624 621491
Fax:	01624 621491
Map ref:	5, SC37

Directions: From St Ninians Church along Ballanard Rd for 1m, over Johnny Watterson Ln x-rds, past farm on left, Dreem Ard on left

Rooms: 3 en suite, D £50–65 Parking: 6

Notes: ⊘ on premises ⊗ on premises No children under 8

Cliff and Rosemary Walters are semi-retired teachers whose philosophy is 'to make people happy and feel at home'. Their elegant house stands above the wooded slopes of the Glass River Valley, just a few minutes from Douglas. Splendid breakfasts and evening meals (by arrangement) served around a circular table are a feature here, and the en suite bedrooms are comfortable and stylish. Some rooms also have seating areas (the family room has a separate lounge), and hospitality trays are provided.

Recommended in the area

Manx Museum; Gaiety Theatre; superb countryside

Aaron House

◆◆◆◆◆ 🛎

Address:	The Promenade, PORT ST MARY , ISLE OF MAN IM9 5DE
Tel:	01624 835702
Website:	www.aaronhouse.co.uk
Map ref:	5, SC26

Directions: Signs for South & Port St Mary, left at Post Office, house in centre of Promenade overlooking harbour

Rooms: 4 en suite, D £70–118

Notes: ⊘ on premises ⊗ on premises

No children under 16 Closed: 21 Dec–3 Jan

This family-run establishment lovingly recreates the property's original Victorian style, with exquisite interior design, cast-iron fireplaces in the public rooms and sparklingly polished period furniture. Delicious home-made cakes served on arrival and the luxurious bedrooms have a hot water bottle placed in your bed at night. Breakfast is a treat and evening meals are offered in the winter only (Monday–Friday). Smoking and alcohol are not permitted. There is free parking 70 yards away.

Recommended in the area

Cregneash Folk Village; Victorian Steam Railway; Sound and Calf of Man (bird sanctuary)

Sunset over Ramsey and St David's Head

The River House

♦♦♦♦

Address:	RAMSEY,
	ISLE OF MAN IM8 3DA
Tel:	01624 816412
Fax:	01624 816412
Map ref:	5, SC49
Directions:	From town ctr follow signs to Morragh Pk,

turn L just bfr Northshore Rd, River Hse is at lane end.
Rooms: 3 en suite, D £75–95 **Parking:** 12
Notes: ⊗ on premises **Closed:** Feb–Mar

Nicely situated in over 3 acres of mature gardens beside the River Sulby, this Georgian house is a perfect place to unwind. From here you can explore this fascinating island with its own parliament and currency. There are wonderful walks, superb stretches of unspoiled coast and many attractions. The spacious accommodation has luxurious facilities: all rooms have bathrooms en suite and overlook the river. The breakfast room, also with good river views, is a lovely place to savour the delicious food. The hospitality here is spontaneous and friendly, which explains why guests return again and again.

Recommended in the area

Manx Electric Railway; Millennium Way long-distance path; Ramsey Bay

SCOTLAND

The Lake of Menteith

Callater Lodge Guest House

★★★★ GUEST HOUSE

Address: 9 Glenshee Road,
                  BRAEMAR ,
                  ABERDEENSHIRE AB35 5YQ
Tel: 013397 41275
Email: hampsons@hotel-braemar.co.uk
Website: www.hotel-braemar.co.uk
Map ref: 12, NO19
Directions: Next to A93, 300yds S of Braemar centre
Rooms: 6 en suite, S £30–32 D £56–60
Parking: 6 **Notes:** ⊘ on premises ⊗ on premises
Closed: Xmas & New Year

Callater Lodge, built of local granite in 1861, stands in spacious and attractive grounds at the south end of this pretty village with its royal connections. A warm welcome is assured at any time, but especially in the winter when this beautifully kept house is heated round the clock. Sink into deep leather chairs in the lounge after a day walking, climbing, golfing, cycling, fishing or skiing. The library with its inglenook fireplace and licensed bar is another peaceful option. The individually styled en suite bedrooms have lovely soft furnishings, colour TV, tea- and coffee-making facilities, thermostatically controlled heating, hairdryer and bathrobes and the bathrooms contain a good selection of toiletries. Breakfast is served in the bright dining room and offers a wide choice. Later, soup of the day, snacks and a variety of tasty sandwiches are served between 5–8pm. Surrounded by fine hills, magnificent Braemar Castle can be reached by one of many pretty walks. For guests returning from a day out on the hills or ski slopes there is a drying room available to hang up wet clothing and boots; there is also secure storage for bicycles, golf clubs and skis.

Recommended in the area

Balmoral Castle; Cairngorms National Park; Glenshee Ski Centre, Cairnwell

Kirkton House

◆◆◆◆

Address:	Darleith Road, CARDROSS , ARGYLL & BUTE G82 5EZ
Tel:	01389 841951
Fax:	01389 841868
Email:	aa@kirktonhouse.co.uk
Website:	www.kirktonhouse.co.uk
Map ref:	9, NS37
Directions:	0.5m N of village. N off A814 onto Darleith Rd at W end of village. Kirkton House 0.5m on right

Rooms: 6 en suite, S £38–41 D £54–60 **Parking:** 12 **Notes:** ⊘ on premises 🐾 allowed in bedrooms **Closed:** Dec–Jan

Guests feel at ease here thanks to Gillian and Stewart Macdonald's warm hospitality and their comfortable home. The converted 18th-century farmhouse stands in a peaceful countryside with panoramic views of the River Clyde. Stone walls and large fireplaces give a cosy, rustic atmosphere, while the mainly spacious bedrooms are individually styled. The full Scottish breakfast is a high point.

Recommended in the area

Loch Lomond; The Hill House, Helensburgh (NTS); Burrell Collection, Glasgow

Ards House

★★★★ 🏠 GUEST HOUSE

Address:	CONNEL, Oban, ARGYLL & BUTE PA37 1PT
Tel:	01631 710255
Fax:	01631 710857
Email:	info@ardshouse.com
Website:	www.ardshouse.com
Map ref:	NM93
Directions:	On A85, 4m N of Oban

Rooms: 4 en suite, S £45–65 D £70–90 **Parking:** 12 **Notes:** ⊘ on premises No children under 10 **Closed:** Dec–Jan

This Victorian house is in a truly stunning setting with the Firth of Lorn and the Morven Hills spread out before it, and the scenic Loch Etive just a few miles away. The house itself is warm and welcoming, and owner Margaret Kennedy has added plenty of stylish touches since taking over. An open fire and plenty of games and books feature in the spacious drawing room, and the bedrooms are well equipped. Delicious breakfasts made from fresh local produce are worth setting the alarm for.

Recommended in the area

Dunstaffnage Castle, Oban; Bonawe Iron Furnace; Arduaine Garden

Coylet Inn

★★★★ INN

Address:	Loch Eck, DUNOON ,
	ARGYLL & BUTE PA23 8SG
Tel:	01369 840426
Fax:	01369 840426
Email:	coylet@btinternet.com
Website:	www.coylet-locheck.co.uk
Map ref:	9, NS17
Directions:	N from Dunoon on A815

Rooms: 4 en suite, S £37.50–40 D £65–75
Parking: 35 Notes: ⊗ on premises ⊗ on premises Closed: 25 Dec

This charming 17th-century coaching inn on the shore of Loch Eck is an ideal base for hill walking, golf, water sports and pony trekking, and boats are available for fishing on the loch. The bedrooms offer a high standard of comfort – one room has an enormous bath in the window, perfect for watching the world go by. Delicious and imaginative food using fine local produce is served in the dining room and there is a well-stocked bar with a fine selection of malt whiskies and real ale.

Recommended in the area

Dunoon; Benmore Botanical Gardens; Quadmania Outdoor Adventure Centre

Lethamhill

♦♦♦♦♦

Address:	West Dhuhill Drive, HELENSBURGH,
	ARGYLL & BUTE G84 9AW
Tel:	01436 676016
Fax:	01436 676016
Email:	Lethamhill@talk21.com
Website:	www.lethamhill.co.uk
Map ref:	9, NS28
Directions:	1m N of pier/town centre.

Off A818 onto West Dhuhill Dr

Rooms: 3 en suite, S £55 D from £37.50 Parking: 6 Notes: ⊗ on premises ⊗ on premises

This large spacious property with lovely well-tended gardens offers superb hospitality and impressive bedrooms that ensure guests return time and again; Jane's delicious breakfasts made from fresh Scottish produce are another lure. The rooms come with superb bathrooms, great beds and flat-scree televisions, along with many thoughtful extras. Public areas are equally comfortable, with a spacious lounge and a delightful dining room that looks out to the garden. Minimum stay two nights.

Recommended in the area

The Hill House, Helensburgh (NTS); Loch Lomond; Glasgow Airport

Alltavona House

★★★★ 🏛 GUEST HOUSE

Address: Corran Esplanade,
OBAN,
ARGYLL & BUTE PA34 5AQ
Tel: 01631 565067
Fax: 01631 565067
Email: carol@alltavona.co.uk
Website: www.alltavona.co.uk
Map ref: 9, NM82
Directions: From Oban centre along seafront past cathedral, 5th house from the end of Esplanade
Rooms: 6 en suite, S £35–70 D £60–80 **Parking:** 6 **Notes:** ⊘ on premises ⊗ on premises
No children under 12 **Closed:** 12–30 Dec

An elegant Victorian villa within a 10-minute walk of central Oban, Alltavona House has the added benefit of stunning views over Oban Bay to the islands of Lismore and Kererra. The town boasts good shops and many fine restaurants offering local produce. The surrounding area has much to offer with superb walking and the possibility of boat trips to the Islands of Mull, Staffa and Iona. Bird watching, fishing, sailing and horse riding are also available, and skiing is a winter option approximately one hour away. Alltavona offers a warm and friendly family atmosphere, and your hosts Allan and Carol take every care to cater to their guests' individual requirements. The attractive en suite bedrooms are individually styled and feature quality furnishings all in harmony with the age and style of the property. The rooms come equipped with colour TV and tea- and coffee-making facilities. The public areas, some with tartan carpets, include an elegant dining room and a small, cosy reading room. You will

be unable to resist the delicious breakfasts that feature the best of local produce. Choose from traditional porridge, cereals or fruit and then treat yourself to a full Scottish breakfast complete with Stornoway black pudding, sausages direct from the local butcher and haggis. If a lighter option is preferred there are free-range eggs, Mull smoked salmon or fresh poached local smoked haddock. A continental-style breakfast of cold baked ham, a selection of cheeses served with warm, freshly baked croissants or rolls and bread is another tasty alternative.

Recommended in the area

Oban Rare Breeds Farm Park; Scottish Sea Life Sanctuary; Dunstaffnage Castle; Barcaldine Castle; Caithness Glass; Ardanaiseig Garden; Glasdrum Wood; Arduaine Gardens (NTS); Kilmartin House

Glenburnie House

★★★★ 🏠 GUEST HOUSE

Address:	The Esplanade, OBAN,
	ARGYLL & BUTE PA34 5AQ
Tel:	01631 562089
Fax:	01631 562089
Email:	graeme.strachan@btinternet.com
Website:	www.glenburnie.co.uk
Map ref:	9, NM82

Directions: On Oban seafront. Follow signs for Ganavan

Rooms: 12 en suite, S £40–50 D £80–100 **Parking:** 12

Notes: ⊘ on premises ⊗ on premises No children under 12 **Closed:** Nov–Mar

From its prime position on the Esplanade, this handsome establishment has dazzling views across the Firth of Lorne to the Isle of Mull. The bedrooms, including a superior four-poster and a mini-suite, are beautifully decorated and equipped with modern facilities. Delicious breakfasts feature the best of local produce and home-made preserves. The Strachans are happy to advise you on the restaurants in the town centre, which is just a stroll away. AA Landlady of the Year finalist 2004–2005. Private parking.

Recommended in the area

Crarae and Arduaine gardens; fishing and golf; boat hire and cruises

Wallamhill House

★★★★ B&B

Address:	Kirkton, DUMFRIES,
	DUMFRIES & GALLOWAY DG1 1SL
Tel:	01387 248249
Email:	wallamhill@aol.com
Website:	www.wallamhill.co.uk
Map ref:	5, NX97

Directions: Off A701 signed Kirkton, 1.5m on right

Rooms: 3 en suite, S £35 D £56 **Parking:** 6

Notes: ⊘ on premises ⊗ on premises

Hospitality is a real strength at Wallamhill House, a very nice house set in well-tended gardens and peaceful countryside 3 miles from Dumfries. The large bedrooms are extremely well equipped, plus there is a drawing room, and a mini health club with sauna, steam shower and gym equipment. Evening meals (by arrangement) are served in the dining room around one large table, and you can bring your own wine. The area offers great walking (follow the footsteps of Rabbie Burns along the nearby River Nith), cycling, or mountain biking in the Ae and Mabie forests.

Recommended in the area

Nithdale; Sweetheart Abbey, New Abbey; Caerlaverock Castle

Baytree House

Address: 110 High Street, KIRKCUDBRIGHT,
DUMFRIES & GALLOWAY DG6 4JQ
Tel: 01557 330824
Email: ruary@baytreekirkcudbright.co.uk
Website: www.baytreekirkcudbright.co.uk
Map ref: 5, NX65
Directions: Off main St onto Saint Cuthbert's St and
Baytree House at top of Castle St
Rooms: 3 en suite, S £40–54 D £30–32
Notes: ⊗ on premises ⇥ allowed in bedrooms
No children under 12

Bay Tree House is a beautifully restored Georgian House just off the town centre. The attractive bedrooms are thoughtfully equipped and furnished in keeping with the style of the house, and the bright airy ground-floor dining room overlooks the secluded garden. Aileen and Ruary Muirhead will warmly welcome you and ensure you have an enjoyable visit. Breakfasts are a splendid way to start the day at this bed and breakfast.

Recommended in the area

Threave Gardens; Broughton House; Tolbooth Art Centre

Limetree House

★ ★ ★ ★   GUEST ACCOMMODATION

Address: Eastgate, MOFFAT,
DUMFRIES & GALLOWAY DG10 9AE
Tel: 01683 220001
Email: info@limetreehouse.co.uk
Website: www.limetreehouse.co.uk
Map ref: 10, NT00
Directions: Off High St onto Well St, left onto Eastgate,
house 100yds
Rooms: 6 en suite, S £35 D £28.50–33.50 **Parking:** 3
Notes: ⊗ on premises ⇥ allowed in bedrooms

This quiet property near Moffat's High Street has high standards of accommodation with many original features, where Katherine and Derek make you feel as comfortable as possible. The rooms, smartly furnished, include refreshment trays and hairdryers. Derek's legendary pancakes and a wide choice of buffet and cooked dishes are offered at breakfast time.

Recommended in the area

Craigieburn Gardens; Grey Mare's Tail waterfall; St Mary's Loch

Gillbank House

◆◆◆◆◆

Address:	8 East Morton Street,
	THORNHILL,
	DUMFRIES & GALLOWAY DG3 5LZ
Tel:	01848 330597
Fax:	01848 331713
Email:	hanne@gillbank.co.uk
Website:	www.gillbank.co.uk
Map ref:	5, NX89

Directions: In town centre off A76

Rooms: 6 en suite (two rooms on the ground floor), S £40 D £60 **Parking:** 8

Notes: ⊘ on premises No children under 8

Once the home of a wealthy Edinburgh merchant, Gillbank is a charming late Victorian house located in a quiet street in the picturesque town of Thornhill. Surrounded by beautiful countryside, this is an ideal base for outdoor sports and activities, including golf, cycling and walking. Salmon fishing is another popular pastime with the local river providing some excellent sport and the area is popular for fishing holidays. Gillbank House is easily accessible from the A76 Dumfries bypass or off the M74 at Elvanfoot and through the scenic Dalveen Pass. All the town's facilities, with shops, pubs and restaurants, are just a couple of minutes' walk away. Look out for the natural sculptures by Andy Goldsworthy in the surrounding countryside. The homely accommodation at Gillbank House includes spacious bedrooms all with smart en suite shower rooms. One room has an impressive four-poster bed; all have Victorian features and have been recently refurbished. Each room has a TV and tea- and coffee-making facilities. Breakfast is served at individual tables in the bright, airy dining room, which is next to the comfortable lounge. Cyclists are especially welcome and bicycle storage is available. The house has a private car park.

Recommended in the area

Drumlanrig Castle; River Nith (salmon fishing); Thornhill Golf Course

Bonnington Guest House

◆◆◆◆

Address:	202 Ferry Rd, CITY OF EDINBURGH EH6 4NW
Tel/Fax:	0131 554 7610
Email:	booking@thebonningtonguesthouse.com
Website:	www.thebonningtonguesthouse.com
Map ref:	10, NT27
Directions:	On A902

Rooms: 7 (5 en suite), S £45 D £60–90 **Parking:** 9

Notes: ⊘ on premises ⊗ on premises

Just 10 minutes from Edinburgh city centre, this elegant listed building dates from 1840 and retains many of its original features. There is private off-road parking and good public transport links to the city centre. The bedrooms are spacious, comfortable and well equipped with extras including TV, Freeview, a complimentary decanter of sherry and bottled water. Guests are treated to a substantial, freshly-prepared breakfast to set them up for a day's sightseeing.

Recommended in the area

Royal Yacht *Britannia*; Edinburgh Castle; Palace of Holyroodhouse

Dunstane House Hotel

◆◆◆◆◆

Address:	4 West Coates, Haymarket, CITY OF EDINBURGH EH12 5JQ
Tel:	0131 337 6169
Fax:	0131 337 6060
Email:	reservations@dunstanehousehotel.co.uk
Website:	www.dunstane-hotel-edinburgh.co.uk
Map ref:	10, NT27
Directions:	On A8 between Murrayfield Stadium and

Haymarket railway station. 15 mins from airport

Rooms: 16 en suite, S £59–95 D £98–190 **Parking:** 12 **Notes:** ⊘ on premises ⊗ on premises

Enjoy a country house atmosphere within walking distance of the city centre. The smart bedrooms have plenty of quality extras – business guests will appreciate the direct-dial telephones with fax and modem points. Delicious meals are served the stylish Skerries Seafood Restaurant, where many of the ingredients are from Orkney and Shetland. The bar stocks malt whiskies and serves light meals.

Recommended in the area

Edinburgh Castle; Edinburgh International Conference Centre; Murrayfield Stadium

Ellesmere House

★★★★ GUEST HOUSE

Address: 11 Glengyle Terrace,
CITY OF EDINBURGH EH3 9LN
Tel: 0131 229 4823
Email: celia@edinburghbandb.co.uk
Website: www.edinburghbandb.co.uk
Map ref: 10, NT27
Directions: S of city centre off A702
Rooms: 4 en suite, S £35–48 D £70–96 **Notes:** ⊘ on
premises ⊗ on premises No children under 14

Ellesmere House is part of a handsome Victorian terrace overlooking Bruntsfield Links. The latter was once an 18-hole golf course – reputedly the oldest in the world. The location is convenient for the city centre and all the major tourist attractions, including the castle, Princes Street, the Royal Mile, the universities and museums. The bedrooms are individually designed and vary in size; there is a single, twin, double and a family room, and one room features a four-poster bed. All come with tea and coffee facilities. Breakfast is prepared from the best of local produce and is served in the lounge-dining room.

Recommended in the area

Edinburgh Castle and Royal Mile; Princes Street; Palace of Holyroodhouse

Elmview

★★★★★ ≜ GUEST ACCOMMODATION

Address: 15 Glengyle Terrace,
CITY OF EDINBURGH EH3 9LN
Tel: 0131 228 1973
Email: nici@elmview.co.uk
Website: www.elmview.co.uk
Map ref: 10, NT27
Directions: 0.5m S of city centre. Off A702 Leven St
onto Valleyfield St, one-way to Glengyle Ter
Rooms: 3 en suite, D £80–110 **Parking:** 2 **Notes:** ⊘ on
premises ⊗ on premises No children under 15 **Closed:** Dec–Feb

This substantial Victorian property, a mile from the Old Town, offers superior accommodation which appeals to tourist and business travellers. The bedrooms have stylish bathrooms and a good level of comfort, which compensates for the absence of a lounge. The rooms are exceptionaly well equipped, with extras such as wine glasses and a fridge with fresh milk. Nicki and Robin Hill are always on hand when needed. The highlight of your stay will be the excellent breakfasts taken at one large table.

Recommended in the area

Edinburgh Castle; Edinburgh Old Town; Museum of Scotland

Edinburgh Castle.

The International Guest House

★★★★ GUEST HOUSE

Address:	37 Mayfield Gardens,
	CITY OF EDINBURGH EH9 2BX
Tel:	0131 667 2511
Fax:	0131 667 1112
Email:	intergh1@yahoo.co.uk
Website:	www.accomodation-edinburgh.com
Map ref:	10, NT27
Directions:	On A701 1.5m S of Princes St

Rooms: 9 en suite, S £30–65 D £50–120 **Parking:** 3
Notes: ⊗ on premises ⊗ on premises

This attractive Victorian terrace house, on the south side of the city 1.5 miles from Edinburgh Castle, is on a main bus route to the city centre. All the bedrooms, decorated and fitted in matching period floral prints, have fresh flowers and modern en suites. Some rooms have magnificent views across to the extinct volcano known as Arthur's Seat. A hearty Scottish breakfast is served on fine bone china at separate tables in the dining room which features a lovely marble fireplace.

Recommended in the area

Edinburgh Castle; Palace of Holyroodhouse; University of Edinburgh

Kew House

★★★★★ GUEST ACCOMMODATION

Address:	1 Kew Terrace, Murrayfield,
	CITY OF EDINBURGH EH12 5JE
Tel:	0131 313 0700
Fax:	0131 313 0747
Email:	info@kewhouse.com
Website:	www.kewhouse.com
Map ref:	10, NT27

Directions: On A8 Glasgow road, 1m W of city centre, close to Murrayfield Rugby Stadium

Rooms: 6 en suite S £70–75 D £85–150 **Parking:** 6

Notes: ⊘ on premises ⊨ allowed in bedrooms

Kew House forms part of a listed Victorian terrace dating from around 1869, located a mile west of the city centre, convenient for Murrayfield Rugby Stadium, and just a 15-minute walk from Princes Street. Regular bus services from Princes Street pass the door. The house is ideal for both business travellers and holidaymakers, with secure private parking. While many period features have been retained, the interior design is contemporary, and the standards of housekeeping are superb. Expect complimentary sherry and chocolates on arrival, and you can order supper in the lounge and bar. Full Scottish breakfast with an alternative vegetarian choice is included in the room tariff, and light snacks, with room service, are available all day. Bedrooms, including some on the ground floor, are en suite and well equipped with remote control television with digital channels, direct-dial telephones, modem points, hairdryers, trouser presses, fresh flowers and tea and coffee facilities. The superior rooms also have thier own fridge. Kew House also offers two very comfortable serviced apartments accommodating up to five people.

Recommended in the area

Edinburgh Castle; Edinburgh International Conference Centre; Murrayfield Rugby Stadium; National Gallery of Scotland; National Museum of Scotland; Princes Street and its spacious gardens

Southside Guest House

★ ★ ★ ★ GUEST HOUSE

Address: 8 Newington Road,
CITY OF EDINBURGH
EH9 1QS
Tel: 0131 668 4422
Fax: 0131 667 7771
Email: info@southsideguesthouse.co.uk
Website: www.southsideguesthouse.co.uk
Map ref: 10, NT27
Directions: E end of Princes St take North Bridge to
the Royal Mile, continue S 0.5m, house on right
Rooms: 8 en suite, S £42–70 D £64–140
Notes: ⊘ on premises ⊗ on premises

Southside Guest House is an elegant Victorian sandstone
terraced house in the centre of Edinburgh, only a few minutes from Holyrood Park. The owners Lynne
and Franco have been involved in the hotel trade for many years and have happily made their home in
the capital. Lynne is from the Highlands, and Franco hails from Florence. They offer individually
designed, stylish, well-equipped bedrooms, with direct-dial telephones, DVD players, free wireless
Internet access, and many other comforts including quality mattresses and crisp fine linen to ensure a
good night's sleep. Two of the rooms have four-poster beds and comfortable sofas, and the remaining
rooms come in a variety of colour schemes and bed sizes. Breakfast at Southside is guaranteed to
satisfy with its great choice of traditional freshly cooked Scottish dishes, cheeses, oatcakes, fresh fruit
and real coffee. Guests sit at separate tables in the attractive dining room.

Recommended in the area

Edinburgh Castle; Edinburgh Festival Theatre; The Palace of Holyroodhouse; Old Town; Holyrood Park;
Princes Street shops and gardens

Edinburgh Castle, from Calton Hill.

Violet Bank House

♦♦♦♦♦

Address:	167 Lanark Road West, Currie,
,	CITY OF EDINBURGH EH14 5NZ
Tel:	0131 451 5103
Email:	reta@violetbankhouse.co.uk
Website:	www.violetbankhouse.co.uk
Map ref:	10, NT27

Directions: On A70 in village centre, corner Lanark Rd West & Kirkgate

Rooms: 3 (2 en suite), S from £45 D from £90

Parking: 3 **Notes:** ⊗ on premises No children under 14

Lying to the south of Edinburgh within easy reach of the airport and Herriot Watt University, Violet Bank is a lovely stone house with smart, very well-equipped bedrooms, stylish bathrooms and the very best in hospitality. Thoughtful little extras include fresh flowers, Crabtree and Evelyn toiletries, and tea and coffee facilities. The inviting lounge overlooks the attractive rear garden, and delicious, perfectly presented breakfasts using excellent Scottish produce are served in the charming dining room.

Recommended in the area

Edinburgh Castle; Rosslyn Chapel; Malleny Gardens (NTS)

The Witchery by the Castle

★★★★★ ◉ RESTAURANT WITH ROOMS

Address:	352 Castlehill, The Royal Mile,
	CITY OF EDINBURGH EH1 2NF
Tel:	0131 225 5613
Fax:	0131 220 4392
Email:	mail@thewitchery.com
Website:	www.thewitchery.com
Map ref:	10, NT27

Directions: At the top of the Royal Mile at the gates of Edinburgh Castle

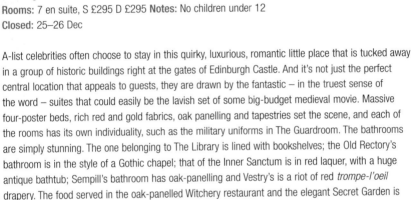

Rooms: 7 en suite, S £295 D £295 Notes: No children under 12
Closed: 25–26 Dec

A-list celebrities often choose to stay in this quirky, luxurious, romantic little place that is tucked away in a group of historic buildings right at the gates of Edinburgh Castle. And it's not just the perfect central location that appeals to guests, they are drawn by the fantastic – in the truest sense of the word – suites that could easily be the lavish set of some big-budget medieval movie. Massive four-poster beds, rich red and gold fabrics, oak panelling and tapestries set the scene, and each of the rooms has its own individuality, such as the military uniforms in The Guardroom. The bathrooms are simply stunning. The one belonging to The Library is lined with bookshelves; the Old Rectory's bathroom is in the style of a Gothic chapel; that of the Inner Sanctum is in red laquer, with a huge antique bathtub; Sempill's bathroom has oak-panelling and Vestry's is a riot of red *trompe-l'oeil* drapery. The food served in the oak-panelled Witchery restaurant and the elegant Secret Garden is equally renowned – hardly surprising since the establishment was the brainchild of Scotland's most famous restaurateur, James Thomson. The room rates include a continental breakfast and a bottle of champagne; absolutely free is the chance of being neighbour to some member of the Hollywood elite.

Recommended in the area

Edinburgh Castle; the Royal Mile; Museum of Scotland; National Gallery of Scotland

The Spindrift

★★★★ 🏛 GUEST ACCOMMODATION

Address:	Pittenweem Road, ANSTRUTHER,
	FIFE KY10 3DT
Tel/Fax:	01333 310573
Email:	info@thespindrift.co.uk
Website:	www.thespindrift.co.uk
Map ref:	10, NO50

Directions: Entering town from W on A917,
1st building on left

Rooms: 8 (7 en suite), S £38.50–48 D £55–76
Parking: 12 **Notes:** ⊗ on premises 🐾 allowed in bedrooms No children under 10
Closed: Xmas–late Jan

A unique feature of this house is the top-floor Captain's Room, made to resemble a shipmaster's cabin by the original owner – the east-facing window looks towards Anstruther harbour. All the individually furnished, spacious bedrooms are brightly decorated and have a wide range of extras. The lounge has an honesty bar for a pre-dinner drink, and enjoyable, home-cooked fare is served in the dining room.
Recommended in the area
Scottish Fisheries Museum; St Andrews; East Neuk coastal villages

The Roods

◆◆◆◆

Address:	16 Bannerman Avenue, INVERKEITHING,
	FIFE KY11 1NG
Tel:	01383 415049
Fax:	01383 415049
Email:	isobelmarley@hotmail.com
Website:	www.theroods.com
Map ref:	10, NT18

Directions: N of town centre off B981 Church St then
Chapel Pl, turn left into Bannerman Ave

Rooms: 2 en suite, S £26–30 D £50–60 **Parking:** 4 **Notes:** ⊖ on premises ⊗ on premises

In a secluded setting, this delightful house is within easy reach of both the railway station and the town centre. The individually furnished bedrooms are on the ground floor and have smart new bathrooms. Thoughtful touches bring a personal feel to the rooms, which have direct-dial telephones, central heating and tea and coffee facilities. The lounge has an inviting open fire and breakfast is served at individual tables in the pretty conservatory. Evening meals by arrangement. No dogs please.
Recommended in the area
Culross Palace, Town House and The Study; Pittencrieff House Museum; Aberdour Castle

Hillpark House

★★★★ GUEST HOUSE

Address:	96 Main Street, LEUCHARS, FIFE KY16 0HF
Tel:	01334 839280
Fax:	01334 839051
Email:	enquiries@hillparkhouse.com
Website:	www.hillparkhouse.com
Map ref:	10, NO42
Directions:	Leaving Leuchars for St Michaels, house 1st on right

Rooms: 5 (3 en suite) Family room £70–90 **Parking:** 6
Notes: ⊘ on premises ⊗ on premises

Six miles from St Andrews, Hillpark House appeals to golfers and it's also a good base for glorious walks and visiting the towns and unspoilt coastline of eastern Scotland. Bedrooms are larger than average, with en suite shower rooms or an adjoining private bathrooms. All have TV and VCR, electric blankets, hairdryers and hospitality trays. Breakfast features yoghurt, cheeses, a Scottish breakfast, smoked haddock, kippers and pancakes with maple syrup. Special diets are catered for.

Recommended in the area

Falkland Palace and Gardens; St Andrews; Discovery Point, Dundee

Dunclutha Guest House

★★★ GUEST HOUSE

Address:	16 Victoria Road, LEVEN, FIFE KY8 4EX
Tel:	01333 425515
Fax:	01333 422311
Email:	pam.leven@blueyonder.co.uk
Website:	www.dunclutha.myby.co.uk
Map ref:	10, NO30
Directions:	A915, B933 Glenlyon Rd into Leven, rdbt left onto Commercial Rd & Victoria Rd, Dunclutha opp church on right

Rooms: 4 (3 en suite), S £28–35 D £54–60 **Parking:** 3 **Notes:** ⊘ on premises ⊗ on premises

The original splendour of this former Victorian rectory sits well with modern trappings, making this an impressive place to stay. Three spacious bedrooms and a cosy fourth room make up the excellent accommodation. All of the rooms are smartly decorated. The lounge is filled with interesting items as well as a piano, and is a sociable place in the evenings. The adjoining dining room is the setting for hearty breakfasts, which include delicious home-made preserves and bread.

Recommended in the area

St Andrews; Levens Links golf course; Fife Coastal Path

The Inn at Lathones

★★★★ ◉◉ INN

Address: Largoward, ST ANDREWS, FIFE KY9 1JE
Tel: 01334 840494
Fax: 01334 840694
Email: lathones@theinn.co.uk
Website: www.theinn.co.uk
Map ref: 10, NO51
Directions: 5m S of St Andrews on A915, 0.5m before village of Largoward on left just after hidden dip
Rooms: 13 en suite, S £95–110 D £130–160
Parking: 35 **Notes:** ⊘ on premises ⊁ allowed in bedrooms **Closed:** 26 Dec & 3–23 Jan

The Inn dates back to c1603 and over the last 10 years it has been sympathetically restored to provide comfortable light, cosy bedrooms. Facilities include a hospitality tray, satellite TV, radio, direct-dial telephone and computer access. The restaurant is widely acclaimed and the Inn welcomes the return of the former chef Marc Guilbert after a short break over which time he has further honed his special skills. Marc's style of cooking is clean and modern European with slight Asian influences.

Recommended in the area

St Andrews Old Course, British Golf Museum; Castle and Visitor Centre; St Andrews

Mellondale

◆◆◆◆ 🏛

Address: 47 Mellon Charles, AULTBEA,
HIGHLAND IV22 2JL
Tel/Fax: 01445 731326
Email: mellondale@lineone.net
Website: www.mellondale.co.uk
Map ref: 11, NG88
Directions: A832 to Aultbea & Mellon Charles
Rooms: 4 en suite, D £54–60 **Parking:** 6 **Notes:** ⊘ on premises ⊗ on premises **Closed:** Nov–Mar

This is a modern house set in landscaped grounds with panoramic views over Loch Ewe. You can relax in the attractive lounge throughout the day and watch television, play games, or just soak up the scenery. The pretty bedrooms, including two on the ground floor, are well equipped, with thoughtful touches like fruit and biscuits, complimentary toiletries and magazines. All of the rooms are en suite, with their own sitting areas, and those overlooking the loch enjoy stunning sunsets. The bright dining room is just the place to linger over delicious home-cooked breakfasts, and feast on the views.

Recommended in the area

Inverewe Gardens; Gairloch Heritage Museum; Beinn Eighe Nature Reserve

Aviemore

The Old Minister's House

★★★★★ GUEST HOUSE

Address:	Rothiemurchus, AVIEMORE, HIGHLAND PH22 1QH
Tel:	01479 812181
Fax:	0871 6619324
Email:	kate@theoldministershouse.co.uk
Website:	www.theoldministershouse.co.uk
Map ref:	12, NH81
Directions:	B970 from Aviemore signed Glenmore & Coylumbridge, establishment 0.75m at Inverdruie

Rooms: 4 en suite, S from £42 D £75–80 **Parking:** 4 **Notes:** ⊗ on premises ⊗ on premises No children under 12

Built in 1906, this former Church of Scotland manse is situated in the Cairngorm National Park. An exceptional eye for detail can be seen in the beautifully furnished rooms. After a day out in the countryside, the sitting room provides a haven of relaxation with plenty of books and a selection of board games. Breakfast includes local sausages, big farm eggs, smoked fish and freshly baked bread.

Recommended in the area

The Cairngorms; Strathspey Steam Railway; RSPB Nature Reserve

Craiglinnhe House

Address: Lettermore, SOUTH BALLACHULISH,
HIGHLAND PH49 4JD
Tel: 01855 811270
Email: info@craiglinnhe.co.uk
Website: www.craiglinnhe.co.uk
Map ref: 9,NN05
Directions: On the A628 Oban Rd, 1m from the
Ballachulish Bridge on the left
Rooms: 5 en suite, S £40–65 D £56–80 **Parking:** 5
Notes: ⊘ on premises ⊗ on premises
No children under 13 **Closed:** 24–26 Dec, 3–31 Jan

Stunning views across Loch Linnhe to the village of Onich present guests here with Highland scenery at its very best, and even local residents who see it every day never tire of gazing up to the Ballchulish Bridge and the Pap of Glencoe. Craiglinnhe House was built in 1885 by the owner of the local slate quarry, and though it retains all of its Victorian style and character, it has been modernised to provide the utmost comfort. Everything is in superb decorative order, and the public areas are particularly impressive. The elegant lounge has wonderful views of the loch, and is a lovely place to relax and enjoy the variety of music that is played there. The dining room provides a fine setting for the set, three-course evening meals cooked by owner David Hughes, whose wife, Beverly is on hand to greet guests and serve them drinks. The stylish bedrooms, with en suite shower rooms, are very attractive and are equipped with hairdryers, hospitality trays, televisions with video players and CD players. The house has a library of videos and CDs which guests are welcome to borrow during their stay. Outside, the house has a neat garden and its own car park. There are plenty of opportunities in the area for walking or climbing, also skiing in the winter.

Recommended in the area

Glencoe; Fort William; Whisky distillery.

Lyn-Leven Guest House

◆◆◆

Address:	West Laroch, SOUTH BALLACHULISH, HIGHLAND PH49 4JP
Tel:	01855 811392
Fax:	01855 811600
Email:	macleodcilla@aol.com
Website:	www.lynleven.co.uk
Map ref:	9, NN06
Directions:	Off A82 signed on left West Laroch
Rooms:	12 en suite, D&T £30–39 (w/ dinner)

Parking: 12 **Notes:** ⊘ on premises ⊀ allowed in bedrooms **Closed:** Xmas

Beautifully situated, this guest house maintains high standards in all areas. Highland hospitality puts guests at their ease, and the spectacular views of Loch Leven guarantee plenty to talk about. Bedrooms vary in size, are prettily decorated, and have showers and some thoughtful extras. The spacious lounge and smart dining room make the most of the scenic outlook, and delicious home-cooked evening meals and breakfasts are served at separate tables. There is ample parking.

Recommended in the area

Dragon's Tooth Golf Course, Ballachulish; Glencoe Visitor Centre; Fort William

Shorefield House

★★★ ≙ GUEST HOUSE

Address:	Edinbane, EDINBANE, Isle of Skye, HIGHLAND IV51 9PW
Tel:	01470 582444
Fax:	01470 582414
Email:	shorefieldhouse@aol.com
Website:	www.shorefield.com
Map ref:	11, NG35
Directions:	12m from Portree & 8m from Dunvegan, off B850 into Edinbane, 1st on right

Rooms: 4 en suite, S £47–60 D £70–90 **Parking:** 10 **Notes:** ⊘ on premises ⊗ on premises **Closed:** Oct–Easter

The Prall family settled on Skye 11 years ago to provide modern accommodation in family, double, twin and single bedrooms and ground floor rooms with ramped access. Traditional Highland breakfasts or a lighter buffet alternative are served in the dining room (special diets are catered for). The adjoining conservatory has books, games and a TV. There are excellent local restaurants for evening meals.

Recommended in the area

Dunvegan Castle and seal colony; The Three Chimneys Restaurant; Talisker Whisky Distillery

Ashburn House

♦♦♦♦♦ 🏠

Address:	8 Achintore Road, FORT WILLIAM,
	HIGHLAND PH33 6RQ
Tel:	01397 706000
Fax:	01397 702024
Email:	christine@no-1.fsworld.co.uk
Website:	www.scotland2000.com/ashburn
Map ref:	12, NN17
Directions:	500yds S of town centre on A82

Rooms: 7 en suite, S £40–50 D £80–100 **Parking:** 8
Notes: ⊘ on premises ⊗ on premises No children under 12 **Closed:** Xmas

Wonderful views of Loch Linnhe and the Ardgour Hills can be enjoyed from many of the bedrooms at this imposing Victorian property just a 5-minute walk from the centre of Fort William. A loving restoration has brought the house back to its former glory. Bedrooms are individually designed and spacious, with little luxuries, hairdryers and hospitality trays. Wake up to the aroma of Christine MacDonald's freshly baked scones and plan your day out consulting the knowledgeable Willie.
Recommended in the area
Nevis Range Gondola; Ben Nevis; Jacobite Steam Train

Distillery House

★★★★ 🏠 GUEST HOUSE

Address:	Nevis Bridge, North Road, FORT WILLIAM,
	HIGHLAND PH33 6LR
Tel:	01397 700103
Fax:	01397 702980
Email:	disthouse@aol.com
Website:	www.stayinfortwilliam.co.uk
Map ref:	12, NN17
Directions:	A82 from Fort William towards Inverness,

on left after Glen Nevis rdbt
Rooms: 10 en suite, S £28–40 D £56–90 **Parking:** 21 **Notes:** ⊘ on premises

Distillery House is a conversion of three houses in the grounds of the former Glenlochy Distillery. It stands on the banks of the River Nevis at the end of the West Highland Way, just a 5-minute walk from the centre of Fort William. The well-equipped bedrooms have hospitality trays and hairdryers. You are greeted with a complimentary whisky and home-made shortbread. Breakfast, including kippers, haggis, home baking, fresh fruits, preserves and cereals, is served in the dining room.
Recommended in the area
Ben Nevis and Distillery Visitor Centre; skiing and walking in Nevis range; West Highland Way

The Grange

◆◆◆◆

Address:	Grange Road, FORT WILLIAM, HIGHLAND PH33 6JF
Tel:	01397 705516
Fax:	01397 701595
Email:	info@thegrange-scotland.co.uk
Website:	www.thegrange-scotland.co.uk
Map ref:	12, NN17
Directions:	A82 S from Fort William, 300yds from rdbt left onto Ashburn Ln, at top on left

Rooms: 4 en suite, D £95–110 **Parking:** 4 **Notes:** ⊘ on premises ⊗ on premises No children under 13 **Closed:** Nov–Mar

Years of careful planning and hard work have gone into the restoration of this lovely property, to provide only the highest standards. Meticulous attention to detail is evident throughout the house, and warm Highland hospitality is assured. Attractive decor and pretty fabrics are used to stunning effect in the charming bedrooms, all of which have beautiful views over Loch Linnhe.

Recommended in the area

Ben Nevis; Jacobite steam train; Loch Ness

Mansefield Guest House

★★★★ GUEST HOUSE

Address:	Corpach, FORT WILLIAM, HIGHLAND PH33 7LT
Tel:	01397 772262
Email:	mansefield@btinternet.com
Website:	www.fortwilliamaccommodation.com
Map ref:	12, NN17
Directions:	2m N of Fort William A82 onto A830, house 2m on A830 in Corpach

Rooms: 6 en suite, S £24–32 D £48–58 **Parking:** 7
Notes: ⊘ on premises ⊗ on premises No children under 12

Mansefield Guest House is a former manse set in mature gardens overlooking Loch Linnhe with great mountain views. The friendly, family-run guest house provides bedrooms with country-style decor and Laura Ashley furnishings, plus complimentary toiletries and hospitality trays. You can even request blankets if you prefer them to duvets. The cosy sitting room overlooks the garden, and a roaring coal fire burns on cold evenings as you browse the many books, magazines and tourist literature.

Recommended in the area

Treasures of the Earth Exhibition, Corpach; Ben Nevis; boat trips to Seal Island, Loch Linnhe

Foyers Bay House

◆◆◆◆ 🍴

Address:	Lochness, FOYERS, HIGHLAND IV2 6YB
Tel:	01456 486624
Fax:	01456 486337
Email:	carol@foyersbay.co.uk
Website:	www.foyersbay.co.uk
Map ref:	12, NH42
Directions:	Off B852 into Lower Foyers

Rooms: 6 en suite, S £33–48 D £56–66 **Parking:** 6
Notes: ⊘ on premises ⊗ on premises

Set on the quiet, undeveloped side of Loch Ness among hillside woodlands with a colourful abundance of rhododendrons, this delightful house has stunning views with forest walks and nature trails. There is a comfortable lounge adjacent to a plant-filled conservatory café-restaurant, where traditional breakfasts are served or where you can enjoy a cappuccino or a delicious evening meal. The attractive bedrooms, which vary in size, all have bath or shower rooms en suite, direct-dial telephones, tea and coffee facilities and fresh fruit. Self-catering lodges are also available.

Recommended in the area

Inverness; Loch Ness; Glen Affric

An Cala Guest House

★★★★★ GUEST ACCOMMODATION

Address:	Woodlands Terrace, GRANTOWN-ON-SPEY, Morayshire, HIGHLAND PH26 3JU
Tel/Fax:	01479 873293
Email:	ancala@globalnet.co.uk
Website:	www.ancala.info
Map ref:	12, NJ02

Directions: From Aviemore on the A95 bear left on the B9102 at the rdbt outside Grantown. After 400yds, 1st left & An Cala opp

Rooms: 4 en suite, S £50–55 D £60–70 **Parking:** 6 **Notes:** ⊘ on premises No children under 3
Closed: Xmas

The large Victorian house is set above the town and surrounded by well-tended gardens. Val and Keith Dickinson provide an attractive setting where you can relax. They offer beautifully decorated bedrooms with king-size or four-poster beds and antique furniture, and smart en suites. The house is in the Cairngorms National Park, and Grantown centre is an easy walk away.

Recommended in the area

The Malt Whiske Trail; Ballindalloch Castle; Osprey Centre, Boat of Garten

Acorn House

★★ GUEST HOUSE

Address:	2A Bruce Gardens, INVERNESS, HIGHLAND IV3 5EN
Tel:	01463 717021
Fax:	01463 714236
Email:	enquiries@acorn-house.freeserve.co.uk
Website:	www.acorn-house.freeserve.co.uk
Map ref:	NH64
Directions:	From town centre onto A82, on W side of river, right onto Bruce Gardens

Rooms: 6 en suite, S £40–49.95 D £59–65 **Parking:** 7 **Notes:** ⊗ on premises ⊁ allowed in bedrooms

A strong Scottish theme, with much memorabilia and bold use of tartan in the decoration and fabrics, distinguishes this Highland guest house set in a quiet residential area, just a 5-minute walk from the city centre. The rooms are well equipped, some have the extra luxury of four-poster beds, and there is a sauna and a Jacuzzi, which are very popular after a busy day touring.

Recommended in the area

Eden Court Theatre; Fort George; Loch Ness

The Lodge-Daviot Mains

◆◆◆◆

Address:	Daviot Mains, DAVIOT, Inverness, HIGHLAND IV2 5ER
Tel:	01463 772215
Fax:	01463 772099
Email:	info@thelodge-daviotmains.co.uk
Website:	www.thelodge-daviotmains.co.uk
Map ref:	12, NH64
Directions:	Off A9, 5m S of Inverness onto B851 signed Croy. B&B 1m on left

Rooms: 7 en suite, S £40–45 D £75–95 **Parking:** 10 **Notes:** ⊗ on premises ⊁ allowed in bedrooms no children under 5 **Closed:** telephone for dates

This lovely small country house offers luxury accommodation just south of Inverness amid 80 acres of pastureland. The Hutcheson family have been welcoming guests for 20 years and won the AA Guest Accommodation of the Year for Scotland 2005. The attractive bedrooms have co-ordinated furnishings and the master bedroom has a four-poster bed. One room is on the ground floor for easy access.

Recommended in the area

Loch Ness; Culloden Battlefield (NTS); Cawdor Castle

The Kessock Bridge across the Ness Estuary.

Moyness House

♦♦♦♦♦

Address:	6 Bruce Gardens, INVERNESS, HIGHLAND IV3 5EN
Tel/Fax:	01463 233836
Email:	stay@moyness.co.uk
Website:	www.moyness.co.uk
Map ref:	12, NH64
Directions:	Off A82 Fort William road, almost opp

Highland Regional Council headquarters

Rooms: 7 en suite, S £32.50–40 D £65–80

Parking: 10 **Notes:** ⊘ on premises 🐕 allowed in bedrooms

Restoring this gracious Victorian villa to its former glory is a labour of love for Jenny and Richard Jones. They still have plenty of time to care for their guests, who find this quiet residential area ideal for touring the Highlands. Inviting public rooms overlook the garden to the front, and the pretty walled garden to the rear is a favourite spot in warm weather. Bedrooms are attractively decorated, have bath or shower rooms en suite and hospitality trays to make your stay comfortable.

Recommended in the area

Culloden Battlefield; Loch Ness; Urquhart Castle

Trafford Bank

★★★★★ GUEST ACCOMMODATION

Address:	96 Fairfield Road,
	INVERNESS,
	HIGHLAND IV3 5LL
Tel:	01463 241414
Email:	enquiries@
	invernesshotelaccommodation.co.uk
Website:	www.traffordbankhotel.co.uk
Map ref:	12, NH64
Directions:	Off A82 at Kenneth St, Fairfield Rd 2nd left,
	300yds on right

Rooms: 5 en suite, S £60–75 D £80–98 **Parking:** 8
Notes: ⊘ on premises ⊗ on premises

Luxurious accommodation and Highland hospitality go hand in hand at this guest house run by Lorraine Freel and Koshal Pun. This multilingual pair can welcome you in Italian, French, Hindi and Swahili. Located within walking distance of the city centre and the Caledonian Canal, Trafford Bank was built in 1873 and was once the local bishop's home. Lorraine's flair for interior design has produced a pleasing mix of antique and contemporary furniture, some of which she has designed herself; the dining-room chairs are a special feature, and there is unusual lighting and original art throughout the house. The bright bedrooms are individually themed; all are en suite and have enticing extras like Arran aromatic products and Skye soap. The Floral Suite, with a lovely modern half-tester bed, is ideal for that special occasion. Breakfast is prepared using the best Highland produce and served on Anta pottery in the stunning conservatory. There are two spacious lounges and the house is surrounded by mature gardens that you are welcome to enjoy. Wi-fi is available throughout the house.

Recommended in the area

Cawdor Castle; Culloden Battlefield (NTS); Loch Ness; Moniack Castle (Highland Winery)

Westbourne Guest House

♦♦♦♦

Address:	50 Huntly Street, INVERNESS, HIGHLAND IV3 5HS
Tel:	01463 220700
Fax:	01463 220700
Email:	richard@westbourne.org.uk
Website:	www.westbourne.org.uk
Map ref:	12, NH64

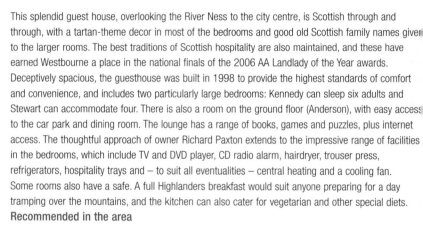

Directions: A9 onto A82 at football stadium, over 3 rdbts & Friars Bridge, 1st left onto Wells St & Huntly St
Rooms: 10 en suite, S £42 D £60–70 **Parking:** 6 **Notes:** ⊘ on premises 🐕 allowed in bedrooms
Closed: Xmas & New Year

This splendid guest house, overlooking the River Ness to the city centre, is Scottish through and through, with a tartan-theme decor in most of the bedrooms and good old Scottish family names given to the larger rooms. The best traditions of Scottish hospitality are also maintained, and these have earned Westbourne a place in the national finals of the 2006 AA Landlady of the Year awards. Deceptively spacious, the guesthouse was built in 1998 to provide the highest standards of comfort and convenience, and includes two particularly large bedrooms: Kennedy can sleep six adults and Stewart can accommodate four. There is also a room on the ground floor (Anderson), with easy access to the car park and dining room. The lounge has a range of books, games and puzzles, plus internet access. The thoughtful approach of owner Richard Paxton extends to the impressive range of facilities in the bedrooms, which include TV and DVD player, CD radio alarm, hairdryer, trouser press, refrigerators, hospitality trays and – to suit all eventualities – central heating and a cooling fan. Some rooms also have a safe. A full Highlanders breakfast would suit anyone preparing for a day tramping over the mountains, and the kitchen can also cater for vegetarian and other special diets.

Recommended in the area

Loch Ness; Inverness Castle; Culloden Battlefield

The Osprey

★★★★★  GUEST ACCOMMODATION

Address:	Ruthven Road, KINGUSSIE, HIGHLAND PH21 1EN
Tel/Fax:	01540 661510
Email:	jmbseil@aol.com
Website:	www.ospreyhotel.co.uk
Map ref:	12, NH70
Directions:	At S end of the main street
Rooms:	8 en suite, S £25–32.50 D £55–65
Notes:	⊘ on premises 🐾 allowed in bedrooms

Expect warm hospitality, comfortable accommodation and fine food at this informal guest house in the Spey Valley. Surrounded by the Grampian Mountains, it stands next to the memorial gardens in the village centre. Its reputation for good food is well deserved, with lavish dinners based on fresh local ingredients served in the dining room, and hearty breakfasts including home-made breads and preserves. Relax with a drink after dinner in one of two lounges, before retiring to the well-equipped bedrooms. All rooms are fitted with refreshment trays, hairdryers and electric blankets.

Recommended in the area

Ruthven Barracks; Highland Wildlife Park; Cairngorm Mountain and Funicular Railway

Crubenbeg House

◆◆◆◆

Address:	Falls of Truim, NEWTONMORE, HIGHLAND PH20 1BE
Tel:	01540 673300
Email:	enquiries@crubenbeghouse.com
Website:	www.crubenbeghouse.com
Map ref:	12, NN79
Directions:	4m S of Newtonmore. Off A9 for

Crubenmore, over railway bridge & right, signed

Rooms: 4 (3 en suite), S £30–36 D £50–75 (1 room with disabled facilities) **Parking:** 10 **Notes:** ⊘ on premises 🐾 allowed in bedrooms No children

Crubenbeg House occupies a stunning location and is very well located for the Cairngorm Highlands' many attractions. John and Irene England, top twenty finalists for AA Landlady of the Year 2006, offer a warm welcome and ensure a relaxing stay with spacious bedrooms, splendid lounge, crackling fire, and wines, beers and malts. Breakfasts include home-made and local produce, and vegetarian choices.

Recommended in the area

Cairngorms Mountain Railway; Highland Wildlife Park; Highland Folk Museum

Corriechoille Lodge

★★★★ 🛏 GUEST HOUSE

Address: SPEAN BRIDGE, HIGHLAND PH34 4EY
Tel: 01397 712002
Website: www.corriechoille.com
Map ref: 12, NN28
Directions: Off A82 signed Corriechoille, continue 2.5m
keeping left at road fork (10mph sign). At end of tarmac,
turn right up hill & left
Rooms: 4 en suite, S £38–45 D £56–70 **Parking:** 7
Notes: ⊘ on premises ⊗ on premises
No children under 7 **Closed:** Nov–Mar and Mon & Tues nights

Dating in parts from the 18th century, the constantly improving Corriechoille has been in its time
a farmhouse and fishing lodge for the Inverlochy Estate. Now it provides stylish accommodation and
informal hospitality in a rural location. The first-floor lounge and some of the bedrooms enjoy mountain
views. All rooms are spacious and are thoughtfully equipped. In addition to the hearty breakfast,
home-cooked candlelit dinners are offered along with a varied wine list and a range of single malts.
Recommended in the area
Ben Nevis; Loch Ness; Glencoe

Smiddy House

★★★★ ◎◎ 🛏 🔖 GUEST HOUSE

Address: Roy Bridge Road, SPEAN BRIDGE,
   HIGHLAND PH34 4EU
Tel: 01397 712335
Fax: 01397 712043
Email: enquiry@smiddyhouse.co.uk
Website: www.smiddyhouse.co.uk
Map ref: 12, NN28
Directions: In village centre, A82 onto A86
Rooms: 4 en suite, S £45–70 D £60–75 **Parking:** 15

Notes: ⊘ on premises 🐾 allowed in bedrooms (with advance notification) **Closed:** Nov

Located in the village of Spean Bridge within The Great Glen, 60 miles of splendour from Fort
William to Inverness, Smiddy House offers genuine Scottish hospitality in luxurious surroundings. The
well-appointed guest rooms are attractive with fresh flowers and bottled water. Delicious dinners
are served in Russell's 2 AA rosette restaurant located on the ground floor. A residents lounge, offering
a place to unwind and relax, is scheduled for 2007.
Recommended in the area
Ben Nevis; Loch Ness; Glencoe

The Haughs Farm

◆◆◆◆

Address: KEITH, MORAY AB55 6QN
Tel/Fax: 01542 882238
Email: jiwjackson@aol.com
Website: www.haughsfarmbedandbreakfast.net
Map ref: 10, NJ45
Directions: 0.5m NW of Keith off A96, signed Inverness
Rooms: 3 en suite, S £30–33 D £44–48 **Parking:** 11
Notes: ⊘ on premises ⊗ on premises
Closed: October–Easter

You are assured of a warm welcome at this comfortable farmhouse on the outskirts of town. The friendly owners have been providing bed and breakfast for over 40 years in this lovely part of Scotland. The large en suite bedrooms, offer a comprehensive range of accessories including tea-making facilities. The large lounge has scenic views of the surrounding countryside, and meals are served in the sunroom overlooking the garden. The land of this mixed farm is now rented to a neighbouring farmer, but you will always receive a traditional farmhouse stay here.

Recommended in the area

Whisky Trail, Keith; Baxters Visitor Centre, Fochabers; Moray coast

Whin Park

★★★★ GUEST HOUSE

Address: 16 Douglas Street, LARGS,
NORTH AYRSHIRE KA30 8PS
Tel: 01475 673437
Fax: 01475 687291
Email: enquiries@whinpark.co.uk
Website: www.whinpark.co.uk
Map ref: 9, NS25
Directions: N of Largs off A78 signed Brisbane Glen
Rooms: 4 en suite, S £34–36 D £60–64 **Parking:** 4
Notes: ⊘ on premises ⊗ on premises **Closed:** Feb

This comfortable guest house is situated close to the seafront in a quiet residential area of Largs. It is within easy reach of the promenade and the town centre with its excellent choice of restaurants. The bedrooms come well equipped with toiletries, quality towels, hospitality tray, TV, hairdryer and ironing facilities. The bright spacious breakfast room, with individual tables, is a fine setting for the hearty and delicious breakfast featuring the best of local produce.

Recommended in the area

Islands of the Firth of Clyde; Loch Lomond; Culzean Castle

Tigh Na Leigh Guesthouse

Address: 22–24 Airlie Street, ALYTH,
PERTH & KINROSS PH11 8AJ
Tel: 01828 632372
Fax: 01828 632279
Email: bandcblack@yahoo.co.uk
Website: www.tighnaleigh.co.uk
Map ref: 10, NO24
Directions: In town centre on B952
Rooms: 5 en suite, S £37.50 D £80–100 **Parking:** 5
Notes: ⊗ on premises ✈ allowed in bedrooms No children under 12 **Closed:** Nov–Feb

AA Guest Accommodation of the Year for Scotland 2006/2007, this guest house in the heart of Alyth is an absolute delight. Daunting from the outside, inside the property is superbly modernised and furnished with an eclectic mix of modern and antique furniture. The large, luxurious and individually decorated bedrooms are very well equipped, some rooms have spa baths. Delicious home-cooked meals and breakfasts are served in the huge conservatory overlooking the lovely garden.

Recommended in the area

Scone Palace; Glamis Castle; Dunkeld Cathedral

Merlindale

Address: Perth Road, CRIEFF,
PERTH & KINROSS PH7 3EQ
Tel: 01764 655205
Fax: 01764 655205
Email: merlin.dale@virgin.net
Website: www.merlindale.co.uk
Map ref: 10, NN82
Directions: On A85 350yds from E end of High St
Rooms: 3 en suite, S £45–65 D £60–75 **Parking:** 3
Notes: ⊗ on premises ⊗ on premises **Closed:** 9 Dec–10 Feb

First impressions of this stylish detached house and its neat garden are pleasing indeed, and once through the door this is reinforced at every turn. There is a spacious lounge and an impressive library, and an elegant dining room where delicious evening meals are available (with 24 hours' notice) in addition to the traditional Scottish breakfasts. Bedrooms are pretty and comfortable. In a quiet residential area, Merlindale is within walking distance of the town centre.

Recommended in the area

Drummond Castle; Perth; Scone

Adam Guest House

★ ★ ★   GUEST HOUSE

Address: 6 Pitcullen Crescent, PERTH,
PERTH & KINROSS PH2 7HT
Tel/Fax: 01738 627179
Email: enquiriesadam@aol.com
Map ref: 10, NO12
Directions: From town centre over bridge onto A94
Coupar road, house on left
Rooms: 4 en suite, S £30–40 D £50–60 **Parking:** 6
Notes: ⊘ on premises ⌁ allowed in bedrooms

The friendly Wilson family have run this stylish guesthouse for over 16 years, and Jane is ably assisted by daughter Josie and her son Stewart. All three enjoy meeting their visitors who come to stay from all over the world. The attractive bedrooms are well equipped and carefully maintained, and have smart bathrooms and plenty of home comforts. Downstairs, there is a pleasant lounge and a cosy dining room. Breakfast is served at individual tables in the dining room, a traditional Scottish choice guaranteed to set you up for the day. The Adam Guest House is located beside the Coupar Angus road.
Recommended in the area
Scone Palace; Cherrybank Gardens; Glamis Castle

Cherrybank Bed & Breakfast

★ ★ ★ ★   GUEST ACCOMMODATION

Address: 217–219 Glasgow Road, PERTH,
PERTH & KINROSS PH2 0NB
Tel: 01738 451982
Fax: 01738 561336
Email: m.r.cherrybank@blueyonder.co.uk
Map ref: 10, NO12
Directions: 1m SW of town centre on A93
Rooms: 4 (3 en suite), S £35–40 D £50 **Parking:** 4
Notes: ⊘ on premises ⊗ on premises

Suited to business travellers and holidaymakers, Cherrybank is located in central Perth, convenient for the motorway network and close to the many attractions the area and the town itself has to offer. Maggie and Robert extend a warm welcome at their home, which offers bedrooms with TV, video, radio alarm, hairdryer and a welcome tray. All are beautifully presented with an emphasis on good linen and home comforts. Enjoy a quieter moment in the tastefully furnished lounge, and satisfy your appetite with a delicious traditional Scottish breakfast served at individual tables in the bright dining room.
Recommended in the area
Scone Palace; Glamis Castle; Pitlochry

Torrdarach House

★★★★　GUEST HOUSE

Address:　Golf Course Road, PITLOCHRY,
　　　　　　PERTH & KINROSS PH16 5AU
Tel/Fax:　01796 472136
Email:　torrdarach@msn.com
Map ref:　10, NN95
Directions:　In town centre. Off A924 Atholl Rd onto
Larchwood Rd to top of hill, turn left, Torrdarach Hse is on
right
Rooms: 7 (6 en suite), S £24–32 D £48–64 **Parking:** 7
Notes: ⊘ on premises ⊗ on premises

From an elevated position overlooking the Tummel Valley, this impressive detached Edwardian house is the home of June and Douglas McDougall. Standing in delightful secluded gardens – home to a family of red squirrels – and with a highland burn running through its own wooded glen, it's hard to believe this peaceful haven is a few minutes' walk from the town centre and golf course. The bedrooms have been refurbished in a contemporary style with quality linen and individual touches.

Recommended in the area

Salmon Ladder; Blair Castle; Edradour Distillery

The Glenholm Centre

★★★　GUEST ACCOMMODATION

Address:　BROUGHTON, Biggar,
　　　　　　SCOTTISH BORDERS ML12 6JF
Tel/Fax:　01899 830408
Email:　info@glenholm.co.uk
Website:　www.glenholm.dircon.co.uk
Map ref:　10, NT13
Directions:　2m S of Broughton. Off A701 to Glenholm,
on right before cattle grid
Rooms: 4 en suite, S £27–29.50 D £48–53

Parking: 14 **Notes:** ⊘ on premises ✈ allowed in bedrooms **Closed:** Jan

Over 1,000 acres of farmland surround this welcoming guest house run by Neil Robinson and Fiona Burnett. Wholesome cooking is a special feature here, and home-baked breakfasts are the highlight of any stay; all tastes can be catered for. The bedrooms are bright and airy, and a family suite is available in an adjacent cottage, with room for up to four people. Fridges, direct-dial telephones and videos add to the comfort. The Glenholm Centre is licensed.

Recommended in the area

Dawyck Botanic Gardens; Broughton Gallery; John Buchan Museum

Ruins of Jedburgh Abbey.

Crailing Old School B&B

◆◆◆◆

Address:	CRAILING, Nr Jedburgh, BORDERS TD8 6TL
Tel:	01835 850382
Email:	jean.player@virgin.net
Website:	www.crailingoldschool.co.uk
Map ref:	10, NT62

Directions: A698 onto B6400 signed Nisbet, Crailing Old School also signed

Rooms: 4 (2 en suite, ground floor Lodge annexe suite has disabled access), S £27.50–30 D £53–64 **Parking:** 7

Notes: No children under 9 Evening meals by arrangement **Closed:** 24–27 Dec & 2 wks Feb and Nov

This delightful Victorian village school has been imaginatively renovated to combine original features with modern comforts. The sizeable bedrooms are beautifully maintained with homely extras. The best of local ingredients go into the tasty breakfasts. Jean Leach-Player was a runner-up AA Landlady of the Year in 2002, 2003 and for 2005. This is a good area for outdoor pursuits including fishing, walking and, in particular, golf. Ray Leach is a golf professional and can advise on the 22 courses in the vicinity.

Recommended in the area

St Cuthbert's Way; Teviot and Tweed rivers; Roxburghe Championship Golf Course

The Black Bull

★★★★ INN

Address:	Market Place,
	LAUDER,
	SCOTTISH BORDERS TD2 6SR
Tel:	01578 722208
Fax:	01578 722419
Email:	enquiries@blackbull-lauder.com
Website:	www.blackbull-lauder.com
Map ref:	10, NT54
Directions:	On A68 in village centre

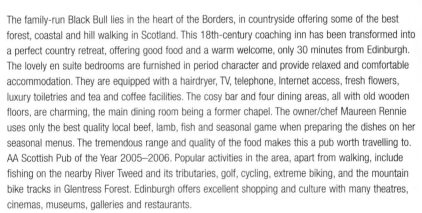

Rooms: 8 en suite, S £50–72.50 D £80–90 **Parking:** 8 **Notes:** ⊘ on premises 🐕 allowed in bedrooms **Closed:** 1st 2wks of Feb

The family-run Black Bull lies in the heart of the Borders, in countryside offering some of the best forest, coastal and hill walking in Scotland. This 18th-century coaching inn has been transformed into a perfect country retreat, offering good food and a warm welcome, only 30 minutes from Edinburgh. The lovely en suite bedrooms are furnished in period character and provide relaxed and comfortable accommodation. They are equipped with a hairdryer, TV, telephone, Internet access, fresh flowers, luxury toiletries and tea and coffee facilities. The cosy bar and four dining areas, all with old wooden floors, are charming, the main dining room being a former chapel. The owner/chef Maureen Rennie uses only the best quality local beef, lamb, fish and seasonal game when preparing the dishes on her seasonal menus. The tremendous range and quality of the food makes this a pub worth travelling to. AA Scottish Pub of the Year 2005–2006. Popular activities in the area, apart from walking, include fishing on the nearby River Tweed and its tributaries, golf, cycling, extreme biking, and the mountain bike tracks in Glentress Forest. Edinburgh offers excellent shopping and culture with many theatres, cinemas, museums, galleries and restaurants.

Recommended in the area

Edinburgh Castle; Thirlestane Castle; Rosslyn Chapel, Roslin

Fauhope House

◆◆◆◆◆

Address: Gattonside, MELROSE,
SCOTTISH BORDERS TD6 9LU
Tel: 01896 823184
Fax: 01896 823184
Email: fauhope@bordernet.co.uk
Map ref: 10, NT53
Directions: 0.7m N of Melrose over River Tweed. N off
B6360 at Gattonside 30mph sign (E) up long driveway
Rooms: 3 en suite, S £55–65 D £80–90 **Parking:** 10
Notes: ⊗ on premises ⊗ on premises

Fauhope House is a fine example of the arts and crafts style of architecture of the 1890s. Inside, stunning floral displays enhance the designs, and lavish drapes and fine furniture grace the drawing room and the magnificent dining room where full Scottish or a continental breakfast is served. The bedrooms are luxurious and generously sized with individual furnishings and thoughtful extras. Sheila Robson is an experienced host who continually pleases her discerning guests.

Recommended in the area

Abbotsford House; Melrose Abbey; Roxburghe Golf Course

Glen Orchy House

★★★★ GUEST HOUSE

Address: 20 Knab Road,
LERWICK, SHETLAND
ZE1 0AX
Tel/Fax: 01595 692031
Email: glenorchy.house@virgin.net
Website: www.guesthouselerwick.com
Map ref: 13, HU44
Directions: Next to coastguard station
Rooms: 24 en suite, S £50 D £80 **Parking:** 10
Notes: ⊗ on premises ⚓ allowed in bedrooms

Once an Episcopalian convent, this smart guest house has swapped an austere past for the modern comforts expected by discerning guests. All rooms are non-smoking and have Free View and air conditioning. One of the lounges has an honesty bar, and there are plenty of books and games for wet days. Authentic Thai cuisine is served 6.30-9pm and substantial breakfasts are also provided in the dining room. Fax and VCR facilities are available on request.

Recommended in the area

Shetland scenery; Pictish broch on the Island of Mousa; St Ninian's Isle

The Crescent

★★★★★ GUEST HOUSE

Address:	26 Bellevue Crescent, AYR,
	SOUTH AYRSHIRE KA7 2DR
Tel:	01292 287329
Fax:	01292 286779
Email:	carrie@26crescent.freeserve.co.uk
Website:	www.26crescent.freeserve.co.uk
Map ref:	9, NS32

Directions: From A70, continue to double rdbt, take exit signed town centre, 1st set of lights turn left then 1st right Bellevue St, 1st left Bellevue Crescent

Rooms: 5 en suite, S £40–45 D £60–70 **Notes:** ⊘ on premises ⊗ on premises

Right in the heart of Ayr, within an easy walk of the town centre and the beach, this is a Victorian town house run according to the principles of good Scottish hospitality. The bedrooms have been tastefully designed, and their recently refurbished en suite bathrooms are exceptionally good. Top quality toiletries are provided. Breakfasts to set you up for the day feature a mouth-watering menu.

Recommended in the area

Burns Cottage; Culzean Castle and Country Park (NTS); Royal Troon and Turnberry golf courses

---

Daviot House

Address:	12 Queens Terrace, AYR,
	SOUTH AYRSHIRE KA7 1DU
Tel:	01292 269678
Email:	daviothouse@hotmail.com
Website:	www.daviothouse.com
Map ref:	9, NS32

Directions: Off A719 onto Wellington Square & Bath Place, turn right

Rooms: 5 (4 en suite), S £30–33 D £56–60

Notes: ⊘ on premises No pets

In a quiet residential area, a short distance from the beach and town centre, Daviot House is a comfortable Victorian terraced home that retains many original features. Bedrooms are bright and prettily decorated, and equipped with thoughtful extras. In the dining room, guests congregate around one big table to start the day with a cooked Scottish breakfast.

Recommended in the area

Burns Cottage; Royal Troon and Turnberry golf courses; Culzean Castle and Country Park (NTS)

Dunduff Farm

★★★★ FARMHOUSE

Address:	DUNURE,
	SOUTH AYRSHIRE KA7 4LH
Tel:	01292 500225
Fax:	01292 500222
Email:	gemmelldunduff@aol.com
Website:	www.gemmelldunduff.co.uk
Map ref:	9, NS21
Directions:	On A719 400yds past village school

Rooms: 3 (2 en suite) S £35 D £65 **Parking:** 10 **Notes:**
⊗ on premises ⊗ on premises **Closed:** Nov–Feb

There are panoramic sea views from all rooms at this working farm, parts of which date back to the 15th and 17th centuries. From its position above the Firth of Clyde, the sheep and beef farm looks out towards Arran and the Mull of Kintyre, and over to Ailsa Craig. Thoughtful touches are evident throughout the house, and the modern bedrooms are well equipped. Specialities such as locally smoked kippers are served at breakfast, and there is a choice of places to eat in nearby Ayr.

Recommended in the area

Dunure Castle; Burns Cottage; Culzean Castle and Country Park (NTS)

Arden House

★★★★ 🏠 GUEST ACCOMMODATION

Address:	Bracklinn Road, CALLANDER,
	STIRLING FK17 8EQ
Tel:	01877 330235
Email:	ardenhouse@onetel.com
Website:	www.ardenhouse.org.uk
Map ref:	9, NN60
Directions:	Off A84 Main St onto Bracklinn Rd, house

200yds on left

Rooms: 6 en suite, S £35 D £65–75 **Parking:** 10

Notes: ⊗ on premises ⊗ on premises No children under 14 **Closed:** Nov–Mar

The fictional home of Doctors Finlay and Cameron, in a peaceful area of the town, is now owned by Ian and William, who offer a genuine welcome with tea and home-made cake on arrival. The comfortable en suite bedrooms have been refurbished and provided with thoughtful extras. A stylish lounge and bright dining room are inviting, and traditional Scottish breakfasts are a definite high spot of any visit.

Recommended in the area

Loch Lomond and Trossachs National Park; Stirling Castle; Loch Katrine; Falkirk Wheel

Creagan House

★★★★★ 🏵🏵 RESTAURANT WITH ROOMS

Address:	STRATHYRE, Callander, STIRLING FK18 8ND
Tel:	01877 384638
Fax:	01877 384319
Email:	eatandstay@creaganhouse.co.uk
Website:	www.creaganhouse.co.uk
Map ref:	9, NN51
Directions:	0.25m N of Strathyre on A84

Rooms: 5 en suite, S £65 D £110
Parking: 26 **Notes:** 🐾 allowed in bedrooms
Closed: 21 Jan–9 Mar & 4–23 Nov

This former 17th-century farmhouse has been lovingly restored to retain its original period charm. Bedrooms feature traditional furnishings and one room has a four-poster bed. Facilities in the rooms include a hospitality tray, TV, CD/radio alarm clock and gorgeous Molton Brown toiletries. The meals, taken in the superb vaulted baronial-style dining room, are based on French classic dishes with strong Scottish overtones. Fresh produce is sourced from local smallholdings.

Recommended in the area

Loch Lomond and the Trossachs National Park; West Highland Way; Breadalbane Folklore Centre

Belsyde House

★★★★ GUEST ACCOMMODATION

Address:	Lanark Road, LINLITHGOW, WEST LOTHIAN EH49 6QE
Tel/Fax:	01506 842098
Email:	hay@belsydehouse.co.uk
Website:	www.belsydehouse.co.uk
Map ref:	10, NS97
Directions:	1.5m SW on A706, 1st left over Union Canal

Rooms: 3 (1 en suite), S £25 D £50 **Parking:** 10
Notes: ⊘ on premises ⊗ on premises **Closed:** Xmas

Secluded in landscaped gardens and rolling countryside, this delightful, 18th-century farmhouse commands outstanding views over the Forth Estuary to the Ochil Hills and beyond. Inside, a country house atmosphere prevails. The Palace room, in soft and subtle shades of peach, has a double bed and is graced by limed oak furniture, while the crisp and sunny Hamilton room is suitable for families. Breakfast is taken in a bright, elegant dining room. An ideal base for exploring Central Scotland.

Recommended in the area

Linlithgow Palace; Hopetoun House; Falkirk Wheel

Linlithgow Palace.

Bomains Farm Guest House

★★★★ GUEST HOUSE

Address:	nr. Bo'Ness, LINLITHGOW, WEST LOTHIAN EH49 7RQ
Tel:	01506 822188
Fax:	01506 824433 & 822188
Email:	bunty.kirk@onetel.net
Website:	www.bomains.co.uk
Map ref:	10, NS97
Directions:	From Linlithgow, A706 1.5m N towards Bo'Ness, left at golf course x-rds, 1st farm on right

Rooms: 5 (4 en suite), from S £30 D £60 **Parking:** 8 **Notes:** ⊘ on premises 🐾 allowed in bedrooms

This friendly farmhouse has stunning views of the Firth of Forth, Linlithgow and the hills beyond. The warmth of the Kirk's welcome is apparent from the moment you step into the hallway with its impressive galleried staircase. The beautifully decorated bedrooms are enhanced by quality fabrics and modern hand-painted furniture. The traditional Scottish breakfast is served at a mahogany table. The working farm is next to a golf course with fishing nearby, yet is convenient for visiting Edinburgh.

Recommended in the area

Falkirk Wheel; Linlithgow Palace; Edinburgh Airport

WALES

Fishguard Old Harbour

Dan y Coed

★★★★ B&B

Address:	Nant y Ffin, BRECHFA, Carmarthen, CARMARTHENSHIRE SA32 7RE
Tel:	01267 202795
Fax:	01267 202794
Email:	stella@danycoed.co.uk
Website:	www.danycoed.co.uk
Map ref:	2, SN53
Directions:	2m NE of Brechfa on B4310 on left

Rooms: 2 (1 en suite), S £35 D £70 **Parking:** 4 **Notes:** ⊘ on premises ⊗ on premises No children under 12

Forget about the car when you visit this modern bungalow, as there are great opportunities to explore the beautiful Cothi Valley on foot, mountain bike or horseback. Two cosy bedrooms, one double with shower room en suite and a twin with a private luxury bathroom, are furnished with co-ordinated soft furnishings and stocked with fleecy dressing gowns and toiletries. Unforgettable Welsh breakfasts are served in the dining room, or on fine days on the veranda with panoramic views across the valley.

Recommended in the area

National Botanic Garden of Wales; Aberglasney; Dolaucothi Goldmines (NT)

Capel Dewi Uchaf Country House

★★★★ GUEST ACCOMMODATION

Address:	Capel Dewi, CARMARTHEN, CARMARTHENSHIRE SA32 8AY
Tel:	01267 290799
Fax:	01267 290003
Email:	uchaffarm@aol.com
Website:	www.walescottageholidays.uk.com
Map ref:	1, SN42
Directions:	On B4300 between Capel Dewi & junct B4310

Rooms: 3 en suite, S £47 D £70 **Parking:** 10 **Notes:** ⊘ on premises ⊗ on premises

Featuring a relaxed and easy-going atmosphere, this beautiful Grade II listed farmhouse stands in 34 acres of lush grazing meadow by the River Towy. A welcoming fire and period decor enhance the property's original features and the lovely garden includes a terrace. Fresh local produce, including home-grown vegetables, is a feature of the memorable dinners and generous Welsh breakfasts.

Recommended in the area

National Botanic Garden of Wales; Aberglasney; Newton House (NT)

Carmarthen Park.

Sarnau Mansion

★★★★ GUEST ACCOMMODATION

Address:	Llysonnen Road, CARMARTHEN, CARMARTHENSHIRE SA33 5DZ
Tel:	01267 211404
Fax:	01267 211404
Email:	fernihough@so1405.force9.co.uk
Website:	www.sarnaumansion.co.uk
Map ref:	1, SN42

Directions: 3m W of Carmarthen off A40, right to Bancyfelin. After 0.5m right into drive on brow of hill

Rooms: 3 en suite, S £40–45 D £55–65 **Parking:** 10 **Notes:** ⊘ on premises No children under 5

This fine Grade II listed Georgian mansion is set in the heart of the Carmarthen countryside, in 16 acres of grounds, which include a tennis court. It's not far from here to the many attractions and beaches of south and west Wales, and it is a delightful place to return to each evening. Many original features have been retained and the public areas are both comfortable and elegant. Bedrooms are large and nicely decorated, and all of the rooms have stunning rural views.

Recommended in the area

National Botanic Garden of Wales; Aberglasney Gardens; Dylan Thomas Boathouse, Laugharne

Coedllys Country House

★★★★★ B&B

Address:	Llangynin, ST CLEARS, CARMARTHENSHIRE SA33 4JY
Tel:	01994 231455
Fax:	01994 231441
Email:	keith@harber.fsworld.co.uk
Website:	www.coedllyscountryhouse.co.uk
Map ref:	1, SN21

Directions: A40 to St Clears rndbt. Take 3rd exit down to lights & left. 100 yards on, turn right where road forks (sign Llangynin). 3m to Llangynin, after 30mph signs turn left. After 300 yards left, signed Coedllys Uchaf

Rooms: 3 en suite, S £47.50–52.50 D £75–80 Parking: 6 Notes: ⊗ on premises ⌅ allowed in bedrooms No children under 10 Closed: Xmas

Coedllys, dating from around 1810, is the ultimate country hideaway. It is surrounded by its own farmland with a pretty woodland dell and lovely open views, known locally as Paradise Valley. Valerie and Keith Harber are mad about nature and conservation, and their sanctuary has provided a refuge for countless animals, including sheep, goats and donkeys, over the years. The large country house has been beautifully restored to provide elegant cottage-style rooms with antique furniture, luxurious fabrics and lavish thoughtful extras. Chocolates, fresh fruit, flowers and magazines join soft bathrobes and slippers, and comfy sofas to make a stay here truly special. In addition, all rooms have flat-screen TV with DVD players, free wireless internet access and a fireproof safe. Those spectacular views across the valley can be soaked up from the charming lounge, where a large wood-burning stove keeps the chill away. Breakfasts spoil you for choice, from a light breakfast with a range of cereals, yoghurts, fruit juices, to a full Welsh breakfast, and delicious evening meals three nights a week are served around one large table.

Recommended in the area

Dylan Thomas Boathouse; Millennium Coastal Path; National Botanic Garden of Wales; Stackpole Beach

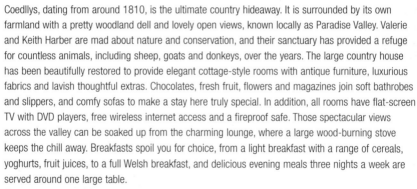

Arosfa Harbourside Guesthouse

★★★ 🏠 GUEST HOUSE

Address:	ABERAERON, CEREDIGION SA46 0BU
Tel:	01545 570120
Email:	arosfabandb@btinternet.com
Website:	www.arosfaguesthouse.co.uk
Map ref:	1, SN46
Directions:	A487 in town centre onto Market St towards sea, 150yds to Arosfa car park

Rooms: 4 en suite, S £35–45 D £56–70 **Notes:** ⊘ on premises ⊗ on premises

This Georgian house is surrounded by similar fine properties overlooking the inner harbour. Most of the bedrooms have views over the water and are comfortably furnished with a sofa or fireside chair. The dining room is the setting for memorable breakfasts, which include traditional farmhouse-cured bacon, laver bread, Aberaeron mackerel, mushrooms, local cheeses, fresh fruit salad and home-made bread.

Recommended in the area

Llanerchaeron (NT) ; Cors Caron National Nature Reserve; Devil's Bridge

Bodalwyn Guest House

★★★★ GUEST HOUSE

Address:	Queen's Avenue, ABERYSTWYTH, CEREDIGION SY23 2EG
Tel:	01970 612578
Fax:	01970 639261
Email:	enquiries@bodalwyn.co.uk
Website:	www.bodalwyn.co.uk
Map ref:	2, SN58
Directions:	N along prom towards Cliff railway. 1st right after Marine Hotel & over x-rds. Opp North Rd Clinic

Rooms: 8 en suite, S £35–45 D £55–65 **Notes:** ⊘ on premises ⊗ on premises **Closed:** 24 Dec–1 Jan

This restored Edwardian house is ideal for a relaxing break by Cardigan Bay or as a base for exploring the countryside. The spacious bedrooms have stylish modern bathrooms and plenty of homely features, such as bottled water and a hospitality tray. Breakfast is a hearty Welsh spread.

Recommended in the area

National Library of Wales; Llanerchaeron (NT); Vale of Rheidol Railway

Aberconwy House

★★★★ GUEST HOUSE

Address:	Lon Muriau, Wanrwst Road,
	BETWS-Y-COED, CONWY LL24 0HD
Tel:	01690 710202
Email:	welcome@aberconwy-house.co.uk
Website:	www.aberconwy-house.co.uk
Map ref:	5, SH75
Directions:	On A470, 0.5m N from A5 junct

Rooms: 8 en suite, S £55–61 D £60–80 **Parking:** 10
Notes: ⊘ on premises ⊗ on premises

This lovely Victorian guesthouse overlooks the charming village of Betws-y-Coed, with superb views extending across the Llugwy Valley, and it makes a perfect base for exploring the Snowdonia National Park. Owners Stuart and Emma Charlton are relative newcomers to the guest house business, but have a natural talent for it and are genuinely friendly and enthusiastic. They have made a number of improvements to the building and have great plans for the future. Most of the rooms are of a good size, one can accommodate a family, and the four-poster room is particularly impressive.

Recommended in the area

Swallow Falls; Snowdon; Portmeirion

Afon View Non Smokers Guest House

★★★★ GUEST HOUSE

Address:	Holyhead Road, BETWS-Y-COED,
	CONWY LL24 0AN
Tel/Fax:	01690 710726
Email:	welcome@afon-view.co.uk
Website:	www.afon-view.co.uk
Map ref:	5, SH75
Directions:	On A5, 150yds E of HSBC bank

Rooms: 7 en suite, S £35 D £60–70 **Parking:** 7 **Notes:** ⊘ on premises ⊗ on premises No children under 4 **Closed:** 23–26 Dec

Expect a warm Welsh welcome at this impressive 1880s stone house. Keith Roobottom takes pride in looking after guests in his comfortable home with spacious, attractive bedrooms and dramatic views of the surrounding hills. Some rooms have original slate and marble-effect fireplaces, and there is a four-poster among the bed options. A pretty dining room is the setting for wholesome Welsh breakfasts.

Recommended in the area

Snowdon Mountain Railway; Bodnant Garden (NT); Conwy

Betws-y-Coed.

Bryn Bella Guest House

★★★★ GUEST HOUSE

Address: Lon Muriau, Llanrwst Road,
BETWS-Y-COED, CONWY LL24 0HD
Tel: 01690 710627
Email: welcome@bryn-bella.co.uk
Website: www.bryn-bella.co.uk
Map ref: 5, SH75
Directions: A5 onto A470, 0.5m right onto driveway
signed Bryn Bella
Rooms: 5 en suite, D £55–80 **Parking:** 7 **Notes:** ⊗ on
premises ⊗ on premises

There are stunning views of Betws-y-Coed and
Snowdonia National Park from this elegant Victorian
house. Joan and Mark Edwards work hard to make a stay
here homely and special. Bedrooms have been renovated to a good standard since they took over
recently, and are well equipped. Comprehensive breakfasts are served in the attractive dining room.

Recommended in the area

Mount Snowdon; Caernarfon Castle; Bodnant Garden (NT)

Penmachno Hall

★★★★★ GUEST ACCOMMODATION

Address:	BETWS-Y-COED,
	CONWY LL24 0PU
Tel:	01690 760410
Fax:	01690 760410
Email:	stay@penmachnohall.co.uk
Website:	www.penmachnohall.co.uk
Map ref:	5, SH75

Directions: 5m S of Betws-y-Coed. A5 onto B4406 to Penmachno, over bridge, right at Eagles pub signed Ty Mawr

Rooms: 3 en suite, D £70–90 **Parking:** 3 **Notes:** ⊗ on premises ⊗ on premises **Closed:** Xmas & New Year

Penmachno Hall is set in over 2 acres of mature grounds within the Glasgwm Valley in Snowdonia National Park. With its breathtaking views, and quiet forest tracks leading to secret waterfalls, the valley is a haven of tranquillity within easy reach of bustling Betws-y-Coed. This impressive Victorian rectory has been lovingly restored to provide high standards of comfort. It offers country-house style quality furnishings while retaining original features. The en suite bedrooms come with a range of enticing extras, including complimentary toiletries, luxury towels and bathrobes, and all rooms benefit from garden and country views. Spacious reception rooms, with comfortable sofas and fires in winter, welcome the weary on their return from a day out exploring the surrounding countryside. Breakfast is served in the Morning Room where the bay window looks out onto the garden. The evening meals at Penmachno – taken dinner-party style around a central dining table – are a highlight and prepared using first-class local produce. The 5-course set menu is complemented by an extensive wine list.

Recommended in the area

Snowdon; Bodnant Garden (NT); Portmeirion

Tan-y-Foel Country House

★★★★★ ◎◎◎ GUEST HOUSE

Address:	Capel Garmon, BETWS-Y-COED, CONWY LL26 0RE
Tel:	01690 710507
Fax:	01690 710681
Email:	enquiries@tyfhotel.co.uk
Website:	www.tyfhotel.co.uk
Map ref:	5, SH75

Directions: 1.5m E of Betws-y-Coed. Off A5 onto A470 N, 2m right for Capel Garmon, hotel 1.5m on left
Rooms: 6 en suite, S £110–155 D £140–170
Parking: 16 **Notes:** ⊘ on premises No children under 7
Closed: Dec

The 17th-century Welsh stone exterior of this country house gives no hint of the interior, where a series of intimate and immaculately designed rooms unfold. Bold ideas fuse the traditional character of the building with contemporary style, giving it an elegant simplicity that goes hand-in-hand with luxurious facilities. Tan-y-Foel is aimed at the discerning traveller looking for a gourmet hideaway in a peaceful, location in the heart of Snowdonia National Park. The surrounding countryside is delightful, with the opportunity for some lovely walks. Independent and family run, this place offers a highly original country house experience, with the owners' influence clearly in evidence throughout. There is a range of options when it comes to the bedrooms, not only in size but in the style of decor too, and many of the regular guests have their own favourites. Naturally, each bedroom has its own bathroom, and each is well decorated and furnished, with a selection of welcoming extras. A major highlight of a stay here is the food, and dinner is a memorable occasion, consisting of carefully chosen fresh ingredients,skilfully prepared.

Recommended in the area

Bodnant Garden (NT); Snowdon Mountain Railway; Conwy Castle

Ty Gwyn Inn

◆ ◆ ◆ ◆

Address:	BETWS-Y-COED, CONWY LL24 0SG
Tel:	01690 710383
Fax:	01690 710383
Email:	mratcl1050@aol.com
Website:	www.tygwynhotel.co.uk
Map ref:	5, SH75
Directions:	Junct of A5 & A470, by Waterloo Bridge

Rooms: 13 (10 en suite), S £30–60 D £44–100
Parking: 14 **Notes:** 🐕 allowed in bedrooms
Closed: Mon–Wed in Jan

Ty Gywn is situated on the edge of the village of Betws-y-Coed, at the heart of Snowdonia National Park, making it an ideal place to explore North Wales, with many of the area's attractions on the doorstep. The village lies at the meeting place of four beautiful wooded valleys, a place of natural beauty and perfect for walking, climbing, cycling or sightseeing. The local Gwydyr Forest alone has 19 different trails and walks to explore. Just a mile outside the village are the spectacular Swallow Falls and Conwy Falls. More thrills including go-karting and scuba diving which are available within 20 minutes' drive. This family-run, historic coaching inn, bedecked with flowers in summer, retains many of its original features with beamed ceilings and exposed stone walls. Three of the bedrooms have four-poster beds beautifully hung with pretty drapes and there is also a honeymoon suite; all rooms are equipped with thoughtful extras. The attractive country furniture and furnishings sit well in the traditional surroundings, and antique beds and memorabilia further enhance the charm. There is comfortable lounge for guests' use. Ty Gwyn is renowned locally for its international cuisine using the freshest of local produce. Welsh lamb, beef and salmon feature on the menu and vegetarians are well catered for.

Recommended in the area

Snowdonia National Park; Gwydir Castle; Penmachno Woollen Mills

The Old Rectory Country House

★ ★ ★ ★ ★ GUEST ACCOMMODATION

Address:	Llanrwst Road, Llansanffraid Glan Conwy, CONWY LL28 5LF
Tel:	01492 580611
Fax:	01492 584555
Email:	info@oldrectorycountryhouse.co.uk
Website:	www.oldrectorycountryhouse.co.uk
Map ref:	5, SH77

Directions: 0.5m S from A470/A55 junct on left, by 30mph sign
Rooms: 6 en suite, S £79–129 D £99–159 **Parking:** 10 **Notes:** ✿ allowed in coach house only
No children under 5 **Closed:** 14 Dec–15 Jan

Situated in glorious gardens, The Old Rectory has stunning views over the wide Conwy estuary, the Conwy RSPB reserve, the historic walled town of Conwy (now a World Heritage site) across to the mountains of Snowdonia. The view alone merits a stay in this long etsbalished and highly acclaimed country house. The house, originally dating from Tudor times, was remodelled in the Georgian era and has traditional day rooms furnished with antiques and Victorian watercolours. Bedrooms are extremely comfortable and have stylish modern bath or power shower rooms, hospitality trays, bath robes and quality toiletries. The atmosphere is friendly and relaxing and help is willingly given with touring routes. The Welsh motto for the house 'Hardd Hafen Hedd' translates to 'Beautiful Haven of Peace'.
There are a wide selection of AA rated restaurants, inns and bistros within four miles and help will be given with making reservations and also transport if required. In Llandudno, some restaurants provide pre-theatre dinners for those who wish to visit the excellent theatre, cinemas or enjoy seeing Welsh Choirs in concert.

Recommended in the area
Bodnant Garden (NT); Conwy; Llandudno

Sychnant Pass House

♦♦♦♦♦

Address:	Sychnant Pass Road,
	CONWY LL32 8BJ
Tel:	01492 596868
Fax:	01492 585486
Email:	bre@sychnant-pass-house.co.uk
Website:	www.sychnant-pass-house.co.uk
Map ref:	5, SH77

Directions: 1.75m W of Conwy. Off A547 Bangor Rd in town onto Mount Pleasant & Sychnant Pass Rd, 1.75m on right near top of hill

Rooms: 12 en suite, S £75–160 D £95–180 **Parking:** 30 **Notes:** ⌐ allowed in bedrooms **Closed:** 24–26 December and January

Standing in 3 acres of gardens, with lawns, trees and a wild garden with ponds and a stream, this house is also adjacent to the Pensychnant Nature Reserve, in the foothills of Snowdonia National Park. Awarded AA Best Guest Accommodation in Wales in 2003–2004, this exceptional place recently got even better with the addition of a superb health, leisure and beauty centre. Its lovely indoor pool, with a counter current to swim against, is salt treated (no chlorine), and the surrounding area and changing rooms have underfloor heating, while on warm days the French windows open onto a terrace. There's also fitness equipment, a sauna, a hot tub and a café. The bedrooms are supremely comfortable, and guests are provided with dressing gowns and big fluffy towels in addition to the TV, radio alarm, refrigerator and other facilities. The ground floor bedrooms have french windows opening out onto private terraces, providing a lovely place to sit out on warm summer days. There are also cosy sitting rooms. The restaurant is also open to non-residents in the evenings, and is extremely popular for its good choice of well-cooked dishes which always includes a vegetarian option.

Recommended in the area

Conwy; Bodnant Garden (NT); Penrhyn Castle

Abbey Lodge

◆◆◆◆◆

Address:	14 Abbey Road, LLANDUDNO, CONWY LL30 2EA
Tel/Fax:	01492 878042
Email:	enquiries@abbeylodgeuk.com
Website:	www.abbeylodgeuk.com
Map ref:	5, SH78

Directions: A546 to N end of town, onto Clement Av, right onto Abbey Rd

Rooms: 4 en suite, S £50 D £75 **Parking:** 4

Notes: ⊘ on premises ⊗ on premises No children under 12 **Closed:** Dec-1 Feb

Abbey Lodge is an impressive white-painted property just a short walk along a leafy avenue from the promenade. Built in 1840 it has been restored to provide a country-house ambience with modern comforts. There is a sumptuous sitting room and smart dining room where enjoyable breakfasts are served at one splendid table. Bedrooms are thoughtfully equipped with free wireless Internet, and tea trays with mineral water and biscuits. All rooms have luxurious bathrooms. The gardens are a delight.

Recommended in the area

Conwy Castle; Bodnant Garden (NT); RSPB Reserve, Llandudno Junction

Brigstock House

★★★★ GUEST ACCOMMODATION

Address:	1 St David's Place, LLANDUDNO, CONWY LL30 2UG
Tel:	01492 876416
Email:	mtajmemory@brigstock58.fsnet.co.uk
Website:	www.brigstockhouse.co.uk
Map ref:	5, SH78

Directions: A470 into Llandudno, left onto The Parade promenade, left onto Lloyd St, left onto St Davids Rd & left onto St Davids Place

Rooms: 9 (8 en suite), S £27–31 D £54–62 **Parking:** 6 **Notes:** ⊘ on premises ⊗ on premises No children under 12 **Closed:** Xmas & New Year

The lovely Edwardian property stands in a peaceful area of Llandudno only a short walk from the shops and the sea. Martin and Alison Memory have completely updated Brigstock House over the past five years to provide bedrooms of a very high standard and two superb suites which are ideal for that special occasion. The candlelit restaurant offers an extensive, freshly prepared menu.

Recommended in the area

Snowdonia National Park; Welsh Mountain Zoo; Great Orme Dry Ski Slope

The Stratford House Guest Accommodation

★ ★ ★ ★ GUEST ACCOMODATION

Address: 8 Craig-y-Don Parade, Promenade, LLANDUDNO, CONWY LL30 1BG

Tel/Fax: 01492 877962

Email: stratfordhtl@aol.com

Website: www.stratfordguesthouse.com

Map ref: 5, SH78

Directions: A55 onto A470 to Llandudno, at rdbt 4th exit signed Craig Y Don, right at Promenade

Rooms: 10 en suite, S £32–37 D £46–58

Notes: ⊗ on premises

As soon as you step through the door you can't help but notice that little things matter the most at this guest house, situated on the Craig-y-Don promenade at Llandudno. The owners are very experienced in providing high quality accommodation and service, and ensure that your stay is comfortable and enjoyable. All the well-equipped bedrooms have either a bath or shower and the beds, either four-poster or Victorian style, are made up with crisp white linen and finished with scatter cushions to give a cosy feel. Fresh fluffy towels are placed in the rooms each day and there are ample personal toiletries. Some bedrooms have sea views, as does the pleasant breakfast room. Breakfast starts with either chilled fruit, grapefruit cocktail or cereals, followed by a traditional cooked breakfast using free-range eggs, hand-linked sausages and best back bacon. If you prefer not to eat meat there is fresh fruit, yoghurts, muesli or even kippers. This is finished off with hot buttered toast and preserves and marmalades.

Recommended in the area

Conwy Castle; Bodnant Garden (NT); Great Orme cable car or tramway; Snowdonia National Park

Plas Rhos

★★★★ 🔒 GUEST ACCOMMODATION

Address:	Cayley Promenade, RHOS-ON-SEA, CONWY LL28 4EP
Tel:	01492 543698
Fax:	01492 540088
Email:	info@plasrhos.co.uk
Website:	www.plasrhos.co.uk
Map ref:	5, SH88
Directions:	A55 junct 20 for Rhos-on-Sea, follow Promenade signs, at seafront 4th building on left

Rooms: 8 en suite S £40–55 D £60–90 **Parking:** 4 **Notes:** ⊘ on premises ⊗ on premises No children under 12 **Closed:** 21 Dec-Jan

A yearning to live by the sea and indulge their passion for sailing brought Susan and Colin Hazelden to the North Wales coast. Running a hotel in Derbyshire for many years was the ideal preparation for looking after guests at their renovated Victorian home. Built as a gentleman's residence in the late 19th century, Plas Rhos is situated on Cayley Promenade, where it enjoys panoramic views over the bay, beach and coast. Breakfast, a particularly memorable meal, is taken overlooking the pretty patio garden. It consists of cereals, fresh fruit, juices and yoghurt followed by free-range eggs cooked to your liking with Welsh sausage, local back bacon, tomato, mushrooms, beans and fried bread or your choice of a number of other hot options including kippers or scrambled eggs with smoked salmon. The two sumptuous lounges have spectacular sea views, comfy chairs and sofas, and interesting memorabilia, while the modest-size bedrooms are individually decorated and have plenty of thoughtful extras. One period room is furnished with a romantic half-tester and antiques, and enjoys those same stunning views. Wireless broadband Internet access is available in all rooms, just bring your laptop.

Recommended in the area

Conwy Castle; Bodnant Garden (NT); Snowdonia National Park

Snowdonia National Park.

Bron-y-Graig

★★★★★ 🛏 GUEST HOUSE

Address:	CORWEN, DENBIGHSHIRE LL21 0DR
Tel/Fax:	01490 413007
Email:	business@north-wales-hotel.co.uk
Website:	www.north-wales-hotel.co.uk
Map ref:	5, SJ04
Directions:	On A5, E edge of Corwen

Rooms: 10 en suite, S £39–49 D £59 **Parking:** 15

Notes: 🐕 allowed in some bedrooms

It took Judith Sansom, Lorna Roberts and David Cowan 10 years to restore Bron-y-Graig, which now provides stylish accommodation with period character and excellent service. Now in their sixth successful year, Lorna, the chef, is convinced that guests keep returning for her food, served in the small restaurant and drawing room. Judith, a classics scholar, thinks it's for the extensive library of books and videos for adults and children, while David knows that it's the decor, the 4 by 4 minibus, the gardens and the woods that are the main attractions. The bedrooms are all en suite, and the house is situated on the wooded slopes of the Berwyn Mountains in the beautiful Vale of Llangollen.

Recommended in the area

Snowdonia National Park; National Whitewater Rafting Centre; Llangollen Steam Railway.

Powys Country House

♦♦♦♦

Address:	Holyhead Road, Bonwm,
	CORWEN,
	DENBIGHSHIRE LL21 9EG
Tel:	01490 412367
Fax:	01490 412367
Email:	info@powyscountryhouse.co.uk
Website:	www.powyscountryhouse.co.uk
Map ref:	5, SJ04
Directions:	On A5 between Corwen & Llangollen

Rooms: 4 en suite, S £30–40 D £50–60 **Parking:** 12 **Notes:** ⊘ indoors
Closed: end Nov–end Mar

Though it's right on the A5 trunk road between Corwen and Llangollen (making it very easy to find), Powys Country House is supremely peaceful, within 3 acres of immaculately maintained mature gardens alongside the River Dee. Guests can just sit and relax here, or take a gentle stroll down to the river, perhaps enjoy a game of tennis on the grass court or climb the hill for wonderful views across to the Clwydian and Berwyn mountains. There's hardly any need to leave the premises, but, of course, the many delights of this part of mid-Wales await just a short distance away. This would make a particularly good base for anyone wishing to attend the International Eisteddfod at Llangollen. The house was formerly a private country residence, and the owners Toni and Terry Edwards maintain a pleasant informal atmosphere while providing first-rate service and quality accommodation. The bedrooms vary in size, with one equipped as a family room, but all have en suite bathrooms as well as tea- and coffee-making facilities. There is also a charming guest lounge. There are a couple of self-catering units on the property, housed in stone-built cottages in the grounds.

Recommended in the area

Llangollen Railway; Bala Lake; Valle Crucis Abbey

Tyddyn Llan

★★★★ ◎◎ RESTAURANT WITH ROOMS

Address:	LLANDRILLO,
	DENBIGHSHIRE LL21 0ST
Tel:	01490 440264
Fax:	01490 440414
Email:	tyddynllan@compuserve.com
Website:	www.tyddynllan.co.uk
Map ref:	5, SJ03

Directions: Take B4401 from Corwen to Llandrillo.
Tyddyn Llan on the right leaving the village.
Rooms: 13 en suite, S £65–95 D £110–180 Parking: 20 Notes: ⊘ on premises
🐕 allowed in bedrooms Closed: 2 wks Jan

Three acres of beautiful grounds, including flowering shrubs, colourful borders and a croquet lawn, surround this elegant Georgian house in the Vale of Edeyrnion, and in this setting owners Bryan and Susan Webb provide their guests with tranquillity and comfort of the highest order. It's a great place for people who enjoy country pursuits such as fishing, walking, horse riding, golf and water sports, all of which can be enjoyed within a short distance. Naturally in a house of this character, bedrooms come in different shapes and sizes, but all are individually decorated and stylishly furnished with period furniture to suit the age of the building. Each has a bathroom, television, CD player, direct-dial telephone and bathrobes, and everything is of the highest quality. The heart of the house, though, is the restaurant, and food remains a strong point here. Bryan Webb is the chef, and he maintains an uncompromising attitude to obtaining only the finest ingredients, many of which are delivered daily by a tried and tested group of local suppliers. All the major wine-producing countries are represented on the wine list, which contains more than 250 labels, and there is an excellent selection of brandies, Armagnacs and digestives. All in all, a stay at Tyddyn Llan represents a taste of good living.

Recommended in the area

Portmeirion; Snowdon Mountain Railway; castles at Caernarfon, Beaumaris and Harlech

Barratt's at Ty'N Rhyl

★★★★ ◎◎ 🏛 RESTAURANT WITH ROOMS

Address:	Ty'N Rhyl, 167 Vale Road,
	RHYL,
	DENBIGHSHIRE LL18 2PH
Tel:	01745 344138
Fax:	01745 344138
Email:	EBarratt5@aol.com
Website:	www.barrattsoftynrhyl.co.uk
Map ref:	5, SJ08
Directions:	A55 onto A525 to Rhyl, pass Sainsburys &

B&Q, straight on 400yds on right

Rooms: 3 en suite, S £55 D £75 **Parking:** 20 **Notes:** ⊘ on premises ⊗ on premises

Ty'N Rhyl is a fascinating and rewarding place to stay, with many unique features and, best of all, food cooked by an award-winning chef. The fine old stone house was built in the second half of the 17th century, and is set in an acre of grounds with mature trees and manicured lawns, all enclosed within weathered old walls. Inside it is an elegant retreat, with wood panelling and relaxing lounges with comfortable plump sofas – look especially for the carved fireplace that is, in fact, a remodelling of a bedstead belonging to Catherine of Aragon, first of the many wives of Henry VIII. Once the home of the bard Angharad Llwyd, the house is now owned by chef David Barratt and his wife Elvira. Dining at Barratt's is a highlight of any visit here, and David's creative cooking, based on local produce of the highest quality, has earned many accolades. Breakfasts are no less delicious, and are served in the lovely conservatory overlooking the garden. Special diets can be catered for and, unusually for bed-and-breakfast guests, mealtimes are quite flexible. The spacious bedrooms are well furnished with period pieces and equipped with hospitality trays, clock radio, hair dryer, toiletries and many other thoughtful extras.

Recommended in the area

Rhyl SeaQuarium; Rhuddlan Castle; Offa's Dyke

Firgrove Country House B&B

◆◆◆◆ 🏠

Address: Firgrove, Llanfwrog,
RUTHIN,
DENBIGHSHIRE LL15 2LL
Tel: 01824 702677
Fax: 01824 702677
Email: meadway@firgrovecountryhouse.co.uk
Website: www.firgrovecountryhouse.co.uk
Map ref: 5, SJ15
Directions: Exit Ruthin on A494 to Bala, at minirdbt take B5105 to Cerrig-y-Drudion. Pass church on right & Cross Key Inn on left. Firgrove is 0.25m on right
Rooms: 3 en suite, D £60–80 **Parking:** 4
Notes: ⊗ on premises ⊗ on premises No children
Closed: Dec–Jan

Firgrove was once an old stone house on Lord Bagot's estate. In 1800 it was dramatically altered by the addition of a Georgian brick façade, and Lord Bagot used it as a guest house separate from his stately pile. Anna and Philip Meadway proudly continue the tradition. The Grade II listed building has been brought up to date with well-equipped bedrooms and modern comforts. The well-proportioned rooms exhibit many original period features, plus smart bathrooms designed for pure pampering. One room has an attractive four-poster bed, while another is a self-contained ground-floor suite with an open fire, small kitchen and a sitting room. Home-made or local produce features in the memorable breakfasts served in the elegant dining room. Evening meals are available by prior arrangement. The immaculate garden is an ongoing labour of love, planted with beautiful trees and shrubs, and there are inspiring views of the Vale of Clwyd.

Recommended in the area

Offa's Dyke Path; Bodnant Garden (NT);Chester

Bach-Y-Graig

★★★★ FARM HOUSE

Address:	Tremeirchion, ST ASAPH,
	DENBIGHSHIRE LL17 0UH
Tel:	01745 730627
Fax:	01745 730971
Email:	anwen@bachygraig.co.uk
Website:	www.bachygraig.co.uk
Map ref:	SJ07

Directions: A55 onto A525 to Trefnant, left at lights onto A541 to x-rds with white railings, left down hill, over river bridge, right

Rooms: 3 en suite, S £40–50 D £68–74 **Parking:** 3 **Notes:** ⊗ on premises ⊗ on premises

The wealth of oak beams and panelling and Grade II listing testify to the historic character of this farmhouse set in 200 acres with private fishing rights on the River Clwyd. Bedrooms are furnished with fine period pieces and quality soft fabrics – some rooms have antique brass beds. The ground floor has a quiet lounge and a sitting-dining room where a scrumptuous breakfast is served.

Recommended in the area

Bodnant Garden (NT); The Old Gaol, Ruthin; Tweedmill Factory Outlets, St Asaph

Erw Feurig Guest House

★★★★ GUEST HOUSE

Address:	Cefnddwysarn, BALA, GWYNEDD LL23 7LL
Tel:	01678 530262
Fax:	01678 530262
Email:	erwfeurig@yahoo.com
Website:	www.erwfeurig.com
Map ref:	5, SH93

Directions: 3m NE of Bala off A494. 2nd left after telephone box and signed

Rooms: 4 (2 en suite), S £30–40 D £42–45 **Parking:** 6

Notes: ⊗ on premises ⊗ on premises No children **Closed:** 24–26 Dec

A warm welcome awaits you at this farmhouse, which is set in 200 acres of sheep and cattle grazing land. Gareth and Glenys Jones are the third generation of the family to live at Erw Feurig, where homely accommodation is offered in rooms with hospitality trays and toiletries; one room is situated on the ground floor. A cosy lounge is provided and breakfast is served in the pleasant dining room, at separate tables if preferred. Fishing is available on the farm. No dogs or smoking indoors.

Recommended in the area

National White Water Centre; Llyn Tegid Narrow Gauge Steam Railway; LLangollen Wharf

Llwyndu Farmhouse

★★★★ 🍽 GUEST ACCOMMODATION

Address:	Llanaber, BARMOUTH, GWYNEDD LL42 1RR
Tel:	01341 280144
Email:	lntouch@llwyndu-farmhouse.co.uk
Website:	www.llwyndu-farmhouse.co.uk
Map ref:	5,SH61

Directions: A496 towards Harlech where street lights end, on outskirts of Barmouth, take next right

Rooms: 7 en suite, D £76–80 **Parking:** 10

Notes: ⊘ on premises 🐕 allowed in bedrooms **Closed:** 25–26 Dec

The converted farmhouse, just north of the seaside town of Barmouth, has been known for its 'hospitality, song and good ale' since the 16th century. Among the original features are a circular stone staircase, inglenook fireplaces, exposed beams and mullioned windows. Owners Peter and Paula Thompson provide bedrooms which are modern and well equipped, and some have four-poster beds. There are more rooms in the converted granary next to the house, but all rooms are en suite and have hospitality trays and sofas. There is a cosy lounge to relax in or to chat to fellow travellers and plan your days. Dinner, a treat of imaginative food, local produce and fine wines, is served in the licensed dining room. Lit with candles and old lamps to create an intimate atmosphere and with a little music thrown in, it is a great experience. Breakfast specialities are kippers or naturally smoked haddock, Glamorgan vegetarian cutlets or local herb sausages, and smoked bacon and laver bread. This is a wonderful area for walking, either in the Rhinog Mountains or the nearby Panorama Walk with stunning views across Cardigan Bay to the Llyn Peninsula. Barmouth itself is situated on a beautiful estuary. Boat trips leave from the harbour and the beaches are so vast you can always find a quiet place to stroll.

Recommended in the area

Cader Idris; Portmeirion; Centre for Alternative Technology

Pengwern Farm

◆◆◆◆

Address: Saron, CAERNARFON, GWYNEDD LL54 5UH
Tel: 01286 831500
Fax: 01286 830741
Email: janepengwern@aol.com
Website: www.pengwern.net
Map ref: 5, SH46
Directions: A487 S from Caernarfon, pass supermarket on right, right after bridge, 2m to Saron, over x-rds, 1st driveway on right
Rooms: 3 en suite, S £45 D £60–70 **Parking:** 3 **Notes:** ☺ on premises ⊗ on premises
Closed: Nov–Mar

Pengwern is a delightful farmhouse surrounded by 130 acres of beef and sheep farmland running down to Foryd Bay, noted for its bird life. There are fine views from many bedrooms over to Anglesey, and the top of Snowdon can be seen on clear days. Bedrooms are generally spacious, and all are well equipped with modern facilities. A comfortable lounge is provided and good home cooking is served.
Recommended in the area
Plas Newydd, Anglesey (NT); Caernarfon Castle; Hydro-electric Mountain

Bron Rhiw Hotel

★★★★ ⊜ GUEST ACCOMMODATION

Address: Caernarfon Road, CRICCIETH, GWYNEDD LL52 0AP
Tel: 01766 522257
Email: clairecriccieth@yahoo.co.uk
Website: www.bronrhiwhotel.co.uk
Map ref: 5, SH43
Directions: Off High St onto B4411
Rooms: 9 en suite, S £40–70 D £66–70 **Parking:** 3
Notes: ☺ on premises No children under 5
Closed: Nov–Feb

Siân and Claire extend a warm welcome to Bron Rhiw, built in 1875 as a hotel just a short walk from the seafront. The bedrooms provide high standards of comfort and modern facilities and are thoughtfully furnished. The ground floor areas include a sumptuous lounge with wonderful sunset views, a cosy bar, and an elegant dining room. Cooked to order, using local produce including Welsh sausages, local bacon and free-range eggs, breakfast sets you up for a busy day.
Recommended in the area
Criccieth Castle and beaches; Llyn Peninsula; Snowdonia National Park

Tyddynmawr Farmhouse

★★★★★ 🏛 FARM HOUSE

Address: Cader Road, Islawrdref, DOLGELLAU,
GWYNEDD LL40 1TL
Tel: 01341 422331
Map ref: 2, SH71
Directions: From town centre left at top of square, left
at garage onto Cader Rd for 3m, 1st farm on left after
Gwernan Lake
Rooms: 3 en suite, S £50 D £64 **Parking:** 8 **Notes:** ⊗
on premises ⊗ on premises No children **Closed:** Jan

Birdwatchers, ramblers, photographers and artists see these spectacular surroundings as a paradise,
and the farmhouse accommodation appeals equally to those just happy to sit and look. Olwen Evans
prides herself on her home cooking and warm hospitality. Oak beams and log fires lend character
to the stone house, and bedrooms are spacious and furnished with Welsh oak furniture; one room has
a balcony, and a ground floor room benefits from a patio. The en suites are large and luxurious. This
breathtaking mountain setting is about 3 miles from the historic market town of Dolgellau.

Recommended in the area

Walking – Cader Idris, Precipice Walk, Torrent Walk, Maddach Estuary Walk; steam railways

Cadwgan Inn

★★★★ INN

Address: DYFFRYN ARDUDWY, GWYNEDD LL44 2HA
Tel: 01341 247240
Email: cadwgan.hotel@virgin.net
Website: www.cadwganhotel.co.uk
Map ref: 5, SH52
Directions: In Dyffryn Ardudwy onto Station Rd, over
railway crossing
Rooms: 6 en suite, S £50 D £70 **Notes:** ⊗ on premises

Within Snowdonia National Park, and just 5 minutes' walk from the sandy beaches at Dyffryn Ardudwy,
the Cadwgan Inn is an appealing place to stay, particularly for guests with children – there's a family
room with 60-inch television and an outdoor play area in the beer garden. The bedrooms are nicely
colour-co-ordinated, and there's a luxurious Honeymoon Suite with a four-poster bed and large corner
bath (and a complimentary bottle of bubbly). Everything has been upgraded over the last couple of
years, and the conservatory dining room is particularly pleasant.

Recommended in the area

Maes Arto Centre; Raedr Ddu Waterfall (NT); Portmeirion

Ty Clwb

★★★ B&B

Address:	The Square, FFESTINIOG, GWYNEDD LL41 4LS
Tel/Fax:	01766 762658
Email:	tyclwb@talk21.com
Website:	www.tyclwb.co.uk
Map ref:	5, SH74
Directions:	On B4391, Ffestiniog, opp church
Rooms:	3 en suite, D £46–52 **Notes:** ⊘ on premises allowed in bedrooms

In the heart of the Snowdonia National Park, this 18th-century stone house has wonderful views from all of the rooms and from the south-facing balcony. Ty Clwb makes a great base for walking in the surrounding mountains and wooded valleys, and there are many public footpaths close by. It has an interesting history, too, as the place where drovers would come to buy an early form of insurance for the livestock they were herding to markets in England. Today it ensures a relaxing and comfortable stay with high levels of hospitality. One of the bedrooms even has its own private lounge.

Recommended in the area

Ffestiniog Railway; Portmeirion; Snowdon

Brigand's Inn

★★★ INN

Address:	MALLWYD, Nr Machynlleth, GWYNEDD SY20 9HJ
Tel:	01650 511999
Fax:	01650 531208
Email:	info@brigandsinn.co.uk
Website:	www.brigandsinn.com
Map ref:	2, SH81
Directions:	In village at junct A458 & A470
Rooms:	10 en suite, S £50 D £80–95 **Parking:** 50
Notes:	⊗ on premises

Nestling on the edge of the Snowdonia National Park, the 15th-century Brigand's Inn offers the chance to relax and enjoy good food surrounded by spectacular scenery. It is the perfect place for pursuits such as shooting, fishing or superb walking. The elegant bedrooms are all spacious, with beautiful oak furniture and sumptuous beds and thoughtful extras. The chef produces fine dishes using local and seasonal produce, creating contemporary and classic Welsh cuisine.

Recommended in the area

Snowdonia National Park; Centre for Alternative Technology; King Arthur's Labyrinth and Craft Centre

Penylan Farm

★★★★ B&B

Address:	The Hendre, MONMOUTH, MONMOUTHSHIRE NP25 5NL
Tel:	01600 716435
Fax:	01600 719391
Email:	penylan@fsmail.net
Website:	www.penylanfarm.co.uk
Map ref:	2, SO51
Directions:	5m NW of Monmouth. Off B4233 to Newcastle, aft 1.5m take 1st left, next left, farm 0.5m rgt

Rooms: 5 (3 en suite), S £30–38 D £50–60 **Parking:** 5 **Notes:** ⊘ on premises ⊗ on premises **Closed:** Xmas & New Year

Penylan is a working farm and Dave and Cathy Bowen welcome you to their idyllic country retreat. Th converted granary, set in a courtyard, houses bedrooms furnished to a very high standard, and a private lounge with a TV. Breakfasts include meat from an award-winning local butcher. There are plenty of opportunities to explore the farm and watch the calves being fed.

Recommended in the area

Offa's Dyke Path; Wye Valley; Brecon Beacons National Park

The Bell at Skenfrith

★★★★★ ◎◎ 🍴 RESTAURANT WITH ROOMS

Address:	SKENFRITH, MONMOUTHSHIRE NP7 8UH
Tel:	01600 750235
Fax:	01600 750525
Email:	enquiries@skenfrith.co.uk
Website:	www.skenfrith.co.uk
Map ref:	2, SO42
Directions:	A40/A466 N towards Hereford 4m, turn left onto B4521 signed Abergavenny. 2m on left

Rooms: 8 en suite S £75–120 D £105–185

Parking: 36 **Notes:** 🐾 allowed in bedrooms **Closed:** last wk Jan to 1st wk Feb

Nestling in the idyllic countryside of Monmouthshire, The Bell is a 17th-century coaching inn that has been refurbished to a very high standard. It's located on the banks of the River Monnow and is a goo base for those who enjoy lovely country walks. Much of the original character of the building has bee retained, while the luxurious bedrooms feature modern facilities such as DVD players and direct-dial telephones. The restaurant is open for breakfast, lunch and dinner, and uses local seasonal produce.

Recommended in the area

Hay-on-Wye; Tintern Abbey; Hereford Cathedral

The Newbridge

★★★★ ◎◎ RESTAURANT WITH ROOMS

Address:	Tredunnock, USK,
	MONMOUTHSHIRE NP15 1LY
Tel:	01633 451000
Fax:	01633 451001
Email:	thenewbridge@tinyonline.co.uk
Website:	www.thenewbridge.co.uk
Map ref:	2, SO30
Directions:	Off A449, NE of Newport

Rooms: 6 en suite, S £90–100 D £110–120
Parking: 60 Notes: Closed: 1 wk Jan

Standing alongside the River Usk, just 4 miles south of Usk, The Newbridge is in an idyllic location. It has been converted into a spacious restaurant occupying the ground and first-floor levels. The smart, well-equipped bedrooms are located in a purpose built dwelling adjacent. They feature gorgeous oak and teak furniture, hand-made beds, limestone and marble tiles and roll top baths. The chef Iain Sampson brings his flair and consistency to the excellent menus and uses the best of Welsh produce.

Recommended in the area

Usk Rural Life Museum; Roman Caerleon; Black Mountains

Cwmbach Cottages Guest House

★★★★ GUEST ACCOMMODATION

Address:	Cwmbach Road, Cadoxton, NEATH,
	PORT TALBOT SA10 8AH
Tel:	01639 639825
Email:	l.morgan5@btinternet.com
Website:	www.cwmbachcottages.co.uk
Map ref:	2, SS79

Directions: 1.5m NE of Neath. A465 onto A474 & A4230 towards Aberdulais, left opp Cadoxton church, guest house signed

Rooms: 5 en suite, S £32–38 D £52–58 **Parking:** 7 **Notes:** ⊗ on premises ⊗ on premises

Three former miners' cottages have been converted into this welcoming guest house. A drying room for wet gear acknowledges the needs of walkers and bikers, while a bike shed and car park are useful. Inside there are thoughtfully furnished bedrooms, including one on the ground floor, a smart lounge and cosy breakfast room. No children under 12. Self-catering lodges are also available.

Recommended in the area

Aberdulais Falls (NT); Neath Abbey; Gnoll Estate

The Inn at the Elm Tree

★★★★★ ◉ ⬭ INN

Address: ST BRIDES WENTLOOGE,
NEWPORT NP10 8SQ
Tel: 01633 680225
Fax: 01633 681035
Email: inn@the-elm-tree.co.uk
Website: www.the-elm-tree.co.uk
Map ref: 2, ST28
Directions: 4m SW of Newport. On B4239 in
St Brides village
Rooms: 10 en suite, S £64.50–80 D £80–130
Notes: 🐕 allowed in bedrooms

This stylish barn conversion on the tranquil Wentlooge Levels has produced an inn that offers warm and friendly hospitality. The individually decorated bedrooms (double, twin or family rooms) combine the traditional and the contemporary. Hand-made iron and brass beds, beamed ceilings, hand-made pine furniture and sumptuous fabrics sit comfortably alongside minimalist bathrooms (some with a spa bath), ISDN lines and business services. The king-size beds are made up with crisp, cool cotton sheets. Meticulous attention to detail, lots of personal touches and little added luxuries make for a perfect stay. All rooms have complimentary biscuits and facilities for making tea and coffee and you can help yourself to fresh milk and bottled water from a refrigerator along the corridor. Room service is also available. The small and intimate restaurant rests on its long-standing reputation as one of the most distinguished in the area, and you can dine by log fires in winter or in the pretty courtyard in summer. An extensive choice of mouth-watering dishes includes Welsh Black beef, local seafood and game in season, with the emphasis on quality local organic ingredients.

Recommended in the area

Tredegar House and Park, Newport; Cardiff Millennium Centre and Stadium; Roman Baths and Roman Legionary Museum, Caerleon

Lower town harbour, Fishguard.

Erw-Lon Farm

★★★ FARMHOUSE

Address: Pontfaen, FISHGUARD ,
PEMBROKESHIRE SA65 9TS

Tel: 01348 881297

Map ref: 1, SM93

Directions: 5.5m SE of Fishguard on B4313

Rooms: 3 (2 en suite), S £40 D £60–70 **Parking:** 5

Notes: ⊘ on premises ⊗ on premises

No children under 10 **Closed:** Dec–Mar

This lovely old house is at the heart of a working sheep and cattle farm, and its landscaped gardens overlook the stunning Gwaun Valley towards Carningli, the Mountain of the Angels. Whilst it has been converted to provide first-class guest accommodation, there is still a very homely feel to the farmhouse and the lounge is a lovely place to relax. Lilwen McAllister is an exceptional hostess, who was selected as the AA Landlady of the Year in 2006. The bedrooms are comfortable and equipped with hair dryers, clock radios and tea- and coffee-making facilities. Mrs McAllister's traditional farmhouse cooking uses fresh local produce and meals are served in generous portions.

Recommended in the area

Castell Henllys; Strumble Head; St David's Cathedral; Pembrokeshire Coastal Path

The Waterings

★★★★ B&B

Address:	Anchor Drive, High Street, ST DAVID'S, PEMBROKESHIRE SA62 6QH
Tel:	01437 720876
Fax:	01437 720876
Email:	waterings@supanet.com
Website:	www.waterings.co.uk
Map ref:	1, SM72
Directions:	On A487 on E edge of St David's

Rooms: 5 en suite, S £50–80 D £70–80 **Parking:** 20 **Notes:** ⊗ on premises
No children under 5

The Waterings is set in 2 acres of beautiful landscaped grounds in a quiet location close to the Pembrokeshire Coast National Park Visitor Centre and only a short walk from St David's 800-year-old cathedral, which is the setting for an annual music festival at the end of May. The magnificent coastline with its abundance of birdlife is also within easy reach. The en suite bedrooms in this spacious accommodation are all on the ground floor and are set around an attractive courtyard. All the bedrooms are equipped with TV and have tea- and coffee-making facilities. The accommodation includes two family rooms with lounge, two double rooms with lounge and a double room with small sitting area. Breakfast, prepared from a good selection of local produce, is served in a smart dining room in the main house. Outside amenities at The Waterings include a picnic area with tables and benches, a barbecue and a croquet lawn. The nearest sandy beach is just a 15-minute walk away; other activities in the area include walking, boat trips to Ramsey Island an RSPB reserve a mile offshore, sea fishing, whale and dolphin spotting boat trips, canoeing, surfing, rock climbing and abseiling.

Recommended in the area

Ramsey Island boat trips; Pembrokeshire Coast National Park; Whitesands Beach

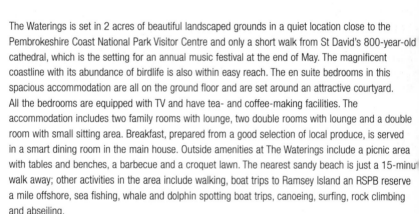

Giltar Grove Country House

★★★ GUEST ACCOMMODATION

Address: Penally, TENBY, PEMBROKESHIRE SA70 7RY
Tel: 01834 871568
Email: giltarbnb@aol.com
Website: www.giltargrove.co.uk
Map ref: 1, SN10
Directions: 2m SW of Tenby. Off A4139, 2nd right after railway bridge
Rooms: 6 en suite, S £25–35 D £50–60 **Parking:** 10
Notes: ⊘ on premises ⊗ on premises No children under 12 **Closed:** Dec–Feb

Owner Sarah Diment describes her lovely late Victorian country house as 'a warm, comfortable and friendly home run by warm, comfortable and friendly people'. It is in a beautiful setting just a stroll from the spectacular coastal path and close to several lovely beaches. The house has been beautifully restored and retains many original features. Two of the charming bedrooms have four-poster beds. A full traditional or vegetarian breakfast is served in the magnificent conservatory.

Recommended in the area

Pembrokeshire Coast National Park; Caldey Island; Manorbier Bay

Rosendale

★★★★ GUEST ACCOMMODATION

Address: Lydstep, TENBY, PEMBROKESHIRE SA70 7SQ
Tel: 01834 870040
Email: rosendalewales@yahoo.com
Website: www.rosendalepembrokeshire.co.uk
Map ref: 1, SN10
Directions: 3m SW of Tenby. A4139 W towards Pembroke, Rosendale on right after Lydstep village
Rooms: 7 en suite, S £32–45 D £50–70 **Parking:** 7
Notes: ⊘ within house ➥ welcome in one appointed room **Closed:** Dec–Jan

Set in the pretty village of Lydstep, just a 10-minute drive from Tenby, Rosendale is ideally situated for discovering the beautiful coast and countryside of Pembrokeshire. All bedrooms are well equipped, some are in an adjacent bungalow offering ground floor twin rooms. A hearty full Welsh breakfast is served in the attractive dining room and special diets are catered for, where possible, with prior notice. Group bookings for leisure pursuits are welcome, storage is available for some sporting equipment.

Recommended in the area

Tenby; National Park Coastal Walks; Manorbier Bay and historic castle

Monmouthshire and Brecon Canal.

Canal Bank

★★★★★ B&B

Address:	Ty Gardd, BRECON, POWYS LD3 7HG
Tel:	01874 623464
Email:	enquiries@accommodation-breconbeacons.co.uk
Website:	www.accommodation-breconbeacons.co.uk
Map ref:	2, SO02

Directions: Take B4601 signed for Brecon, turn left over bridge before petrol station, continue to end of rd

Rooms: 3 en suite, D £75–80 **Parking:** 5

Notes: ⊗ on premises No children

Right outside the front door there are colourful narrowboats on the canal and it's just a short walk along the towpath to Brecon's marina and town centre. There are also views of fields, hills and the River Usk. Peter and Barbara Jackson know how to choose a location, and they certainly know how to provide quality accommodation. After a day sightseeing, guests can enjoy a spa bath then sink into a big, comfy bed. In the morning, a hearty Welsh breakfast is an excellent start to the day.

Recommended in the area

Carreg Cennan Castle; the Big Pit; Brecon Beacons National Park

The Usk Inn

★★★★ ◎ INN

Address:	Station Road,
	Talybont-on-Usk,
	BRECON, POWYS LD3 7JE
Tel:	01874 676251
Fax:	01874 676392
Email:	stay@uskinn.co.uk
Website:	www.uskinn.co.uk
Map ref:	2, SO02
Directions:	Off A40, 6m E of Brecon

Rooms: 11 en suite S £65 D £90–125 **Parking:** 30 **Closed:** 25–27 Dec

Established in the 1840s as a railway inn, The Usk Inn is now well suited to those who enjoy outdoor pursuits. There are some wonderful walks nearby in the Brecon Beacons or along the Brecon to Monmouthshire Canal, as well as cycling, horse riding, fishing and golf. There are also cruises on the canal, and the many attractions of south and mid-Wales are within easy reach. The inn has also become very popular with classic car enthusiasts taking part in Brecon Motor Club events. The warm hospitality and enthusiastic management reflect the fact that the inn is family owned, and Andrew and Jillian Felix have brought with them a wealth of experience in the hospitality industry and the quality of the accommodation here earned it the AA Welsh Pub of the Year award for 2004–2005. The building has been renovated to a very high standard and improvements are constantly being made to further enhance the guest experience. The bedrooms, named after birds found along the banks of the River Usk, have an en suite bathroom and are individually decorated and furnished with locally made pine furniture. Public areas, including an open-plan bar and lounge, have a great deal of charm, and in the dining room guests can enjoy the high standard of cooking that has brought local renown and an AA Rosette award.

Recommended in the area

Brecon Beacons National Park; Brecon Mountain Railway; Brecon to Monmouthshire Canal

Llanddetty Hall Farm

★★★★ FARMHOUSE

Address:	Talybont-on-Usk,
	BRECON, POWYS LD3 7YR
Tel:	01874 676415
Fax:	01874 676415
Map ref:	2, SO02
Directions:	7m SE off B4558

Rooms: 4 (3 en suite), S £33 D £54–56 **Parking:** 6
Notes: ⊘ on premises ⊗ on premises No children under
12 **Closed:** 16 Dec–14 Jan

This listed farmhouse is part of a sheep farm in the Brecon Beacons National Park. The Brecon and Monmouth Canal flows through the farm at the rear, while the front of the house overlooks the River Usk. Bedrooms, including one on the ground floor, feature exposed beams and polished floorboards. Three rooms are en suite and one has a private bathroom – all have radio alarms and tea and coffee facilities. There is a lounge with a television, and a dining room where breakfast is served at an oak refectory table. This is a no smoking house.

Recommended in the area

Brecon Beacons National Park; Hay-on-Wye; Aberglasney

The Drawing Room

★★★★★ ⊛⊛ RESTAURANT WITH ROOMS

Address:	Cwmbach, Newbridge-on-Wye,
	BUILTH WELLS, POWYS LD2 3RT
Tel:	01982 552493
Email:	post@the-drawing-room.co.uk
Website:	www.the-drawing-room.co.uk
Map ref:	2, SO05
Directions:	A470 towards Rhayader, approx 3m on left

Rooms: 3 en suite, S £120 D £190–220 (inlcudes dinner)
Parking: 14 **Notes:** ⊘ on premises No children under 12
Closed: Sun & Mon, 2wks Jan & end of summer

Discerning good taste and quality are in evidence throughout this exceptional restaurant with rooms, which was AA Restaurant of the Year for Wales in 2006/07. The bedrooms offer the ideal solution to diners who want to enjoy the full Drawing Room experience without having to drive home. This fine Georgian house is run by chefs Colin and Melanie Dawson, who have renovated the building to a very high standard – the smart bedrooms are particularly pleasing.

Recommended in the area

Hay-on-Wye; Royal Welsh Showground; Brecon Beacons National Park

Glangrwyney Court

★★★★★   GUEST ACCOMMODATION

Address:	CRICKHOWELL, POWYS NP8 1ES
Tel:	01873 811288
Fax:	01873 810317
Email:	info@glancourt.co.uk
Website:	www.glancourt.co.uk
Map ref:	2, O21
Directions:	2m SE of Crickhowell on A40 near county boundary

Rooms: 5 (4 en suite), S £50–80 D £65–85 **Parking:** 12 **Notes:** ⊘ on premises ⊗ on premises

A Grade II listed country house, Glangrwyney Court is situated in 4 acres of beautiful gardens in the Brecon Beacons National Park, midway between Abergavenny and Crickhowell. The Georgian mansion dates back to 1825 and has typically Palladian architecture. The family has taken care to sympathetically refurbish the property resulting in an exquisite country house retreat with a relaxing and intimate atmosphere. The interior is furnished with antiques, porcelain and paintings, and blazing log fires welcome guests in winter weather. Breakfast is served in the elegant dining room and you can relax in the sumptuous lounge. There is a good choice of bedrooms, including single, twin, double and family rooms. All rooms are en suite or have private facilities, come with tea- and coffee-making equipment, and have wonderful views over the garden and surrounding countryside. The Master Suite has the additional luxury of an extra deep bath, while the twin room has its own Jacuzzi. On warm summer evenings guests can sit and enjoy a drink on one of the patios in the grounds. Croquet, boules and tennis are available in the grounds and activities such as pony trekking, golf, fishing and shooting can be arranged. There are many lovely walks in the area, with the Brecon Beacons and Black Mountains within easy reach. Children are welcome.

Recommended in the area

Brecon Beacons National Park; Dan-Yr-Ogof Caves; Big Pit National Mining Museum of Wales

Guidfa House

Address: Crossgates,
LLANDRINDOD WELLS,
POWYS LD1 6RF
Tel: 01597 851241
Fax: 01597 851875
Email: guidfa@globalnet.co.uk
Website: www.guidfa-house.co.uk
Map ref: 2, SO06
Directions: 3m N of Llandrindod Wells, at junct
of A483 & A44
Rooms: 6 en suite, S £50 D £65–90 Parking: 10 **Notes:** ⊗ on premises ⊗ on premises
No children under 10

Anne and Tony Millan's home is truly memorable for its comfort, good food and relaxing atmosphere.
This hospitable couple extend a warm welcome at their whitewashed Georgian house just outside
Llandrindod Wells. On colder days a log fire blazes in the comfortable lounge, where you can make
yourself at home. Tea or coffee can be served here, or a drink from the bar in the evenings. Anne
is a superb cook, and her imaginative meals, combing new and traditional recipes, are made from
fresh local produce – look out for her naughty puddings. The spacious bedrooms are individually
furnished and all rooms are now en suite. One room on the ground floor provides easy access for less
agile guests. Plenty of homely extras are provided in all rooms, and refreshment trays are also
supplied. Situated behind the main house, off a small courtyard, is the recently converted Coach House
suite, a comfortable, well-equipped cottage ideal for two guests, which includes a jacuzzi bath. Guidfa
House is an ideal base for touring the the Brecon Beacons and Welsh borderlands.
Recommended in the area
Elan Valley; RSPB Red Kite feeding station; Scenic drive New Radnor–Aberystwyth; Royal Welsh
Showground, Builth Wells

Cammarch Hotel

◆◆◆◆

Address:	LLANGAMMARCH WELLS, POWYS LD4 4BY
Tel:	01591 610802
Fax:	01591 610807
Email:	mail@cammarch.com
Website:	www.cammarch.com
Map ref:	2, SN94
Directions:	Turn off A483 at Garth signed

Llangammarch Wells

Rooms: 10 en suite S £40–55 D £55–69 Suites £62–82
Parking: 15 **Notes:** ⊗ on premises 🐾 allowed in bedrooms

Set amid beautiful mid-Wales countryside, Cammarch offers a range of rooms and suites that can be used for anything from self-catering or bed-and-breakfast to full-board. The hotel is licensed and all rooms have television, tea-making facilities and are en suite. The building has been extensively modernised, and is set in delightful grounds, with a small lake. The Cammarch also owns fishing rights on the rivers Cammarch and Irfon.

Recommended in the area

Builth Wells; Brecon; Hay-on-Wye

Yesterdays

◆◆◆◆

Address:	Severn Sq, NEWTOWN, POWYS SY16 2AG
Tel/Fax:	01686 622644
Email:	info@yesterdayshotel.com
Website:	www.yesterdayshotel.com
Map ref:	2, SO19
Directions:	Off junct High St & Broad St onto Severn St

to Severn Sq

Rooms: 6 en suite, S £30–35 D £50–60
Notes: ⊗ on premises ⊗ on premises

When it comes to providing exactly what guests want, who better than a pair of seasoned travellers to understand the little niceties that make a stay so special? Hosts Jim and Moyra certainly fall into that category, and their Georgian guesthouse in the centre of Newtown will not disappoint with its home comforts, stylish decor and up-to-the-minute facilities. Free WiFi access is available in all the rooms. The power-showers in the bathrooms are another bonus. Rooms vary in size, from single to family-size, with two on the ground floor. Dinners include local specialities and vegetarian choices.

Recommended in the area

Severn Way; Powis Castle and Gardens; lakes and mountains of mid Wales

Moors Farm B&B

★★★★★ FARMHOUSE

Address: Oswestry Road,
WELSHPOOL,
POWYS SY21 9JR
Tel: 01938 553395
Email: moorsfarm@tiscali.co.uk
Website: www.moors-farm.com
Map ref: 2, SJ20
Directions: 1.5m NE of Welshpool off A483
Rooms: 6 en suite, S £50 D £80
Notes: ⊘ on premises

Once the principal farmhouse of Powis Castle – a medieval castle perched on a rock above 17th-century garden terraces and owned by the National Trust – Moors Farm remains impressive and is well situated on the main A483, between the River Severn and the Montgomery Canal. The farmhouse is still at the heart of a working farm that raises sheep and cattle as well as running a pheasant shoot. The building is full of character, with lots of exposed old beams and log-burning fires that are as warm as the welcome, and has been extensively renovated to provide accommodation that is both spacious and comfortable. Wholesome breakfasts are served in the country-style breakfast room and house party style dinners are available by prior arrangement in the elegant dining room. The luxury Gate House barn conversion offers well-equipped spacious self-catering accommodation suitable for large families or a group of friends. Popular activities in the area inlcude walking, cycling, golf, fishing, horse riding and quad trekking. It is just a mile along the canal tow path into the heart of the bustling maket town of Welshpool where you'll find cafés, restaurants and traditional pubs alongside shops selling quality local produce.

Recommended in the area

Powis Castle and Gardens (NT);Welshpool and Llanfair Light Railway; Offa's Dyke Path; Glyndwr's Way; Glansevern Hall Gardens

Rhossili.

Crescent Guest House

★★★★ GUEST ACCOMMODATION

Address:	132 Eaton Crescent, Uplands, SWANSEA SA1 4QR
Tel:	01792 466814
Fax:	01792 466814
Email:	crescentguesthouse@hotmail.co.uk
Website:	www.crescentguesthouse.co.uk
Map ref:	2, SS69
Directions:	Off A4118 W from centre, 1st left after St James's Church

Rooms: 6 en suite, S £36–40 D £56–65 **Parking:** 6 **Notes:** ⊘ on premises

The Cresent, with its excellent reputation for comfort and courtesy, is within easy reach of the restaurants, bars and shops of Swansea's Uplands area. The Edwardian house provides well-equipped bedrooms with shower rooms and complimentary items such as tea and coffee, an evening paper and toiletries. Breakfast is served in the cosy dining room, and the spacious lounge has impressive views of Swansea Bay. There is a secure car park and easy street parking. Children welcome.

Recommended in the area

Swansea; Gower Peninsula; Mumbles

Caban Coch Reservoir.

MAPS

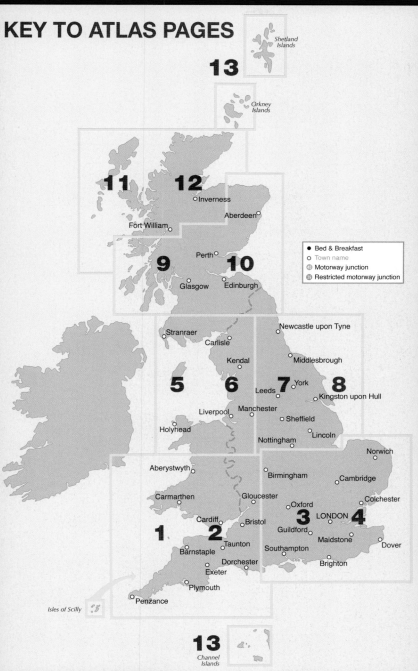

KEY TO ATLAS PAGES

Shetland Islands

13

Orkney Islands

11 **12**

Inverness

Aberdeen

Fort William

Perth

9 **10**

Glasgow Edinburgh

- ● Bed & Breakfast
- ○ Town name
- ⊕ Motorway junction
- ⊖ Restricted motorway junction

Stranraer

Newcastle upon Tyne

Carlisle

Kendal

Middlesbrough

5 **6** **7** York **8**

Leeds Kingston upon Hull

Liverpool Manchester

Holyhead Sheffield

Lincoln

Nottingham

Norwich

Aberystwyth

Birmingham Cambridge

Carmarthen Gloucester Colchester

Oxford

Cardiff **3** LONDON **4**

1 **2** Bristol Guildford

Barnstaple Taunton Southampton Maidstone Dover

Dorchester Brighton

Exeter

Plymouth

Isles of Scilly Penzance

13

Channel Islands

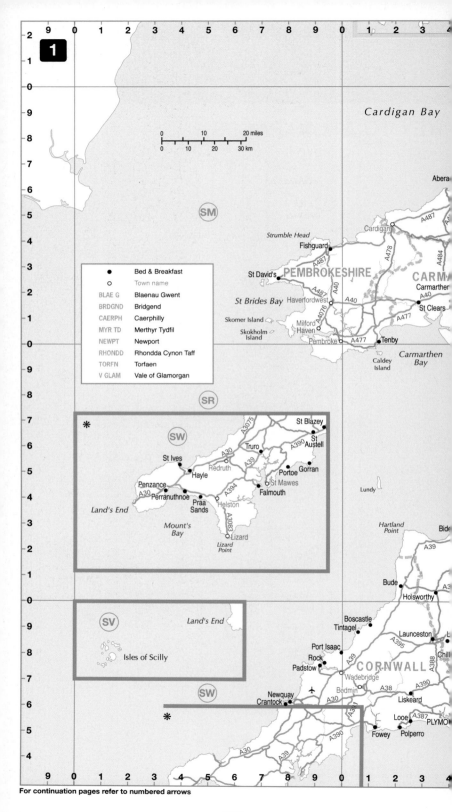

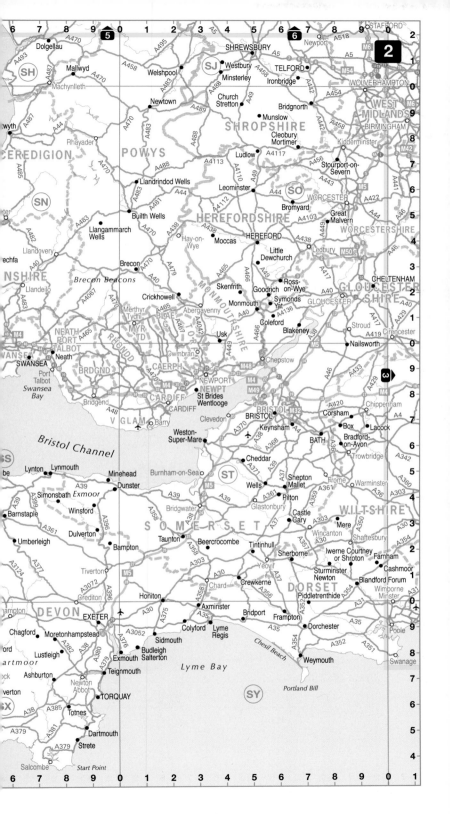

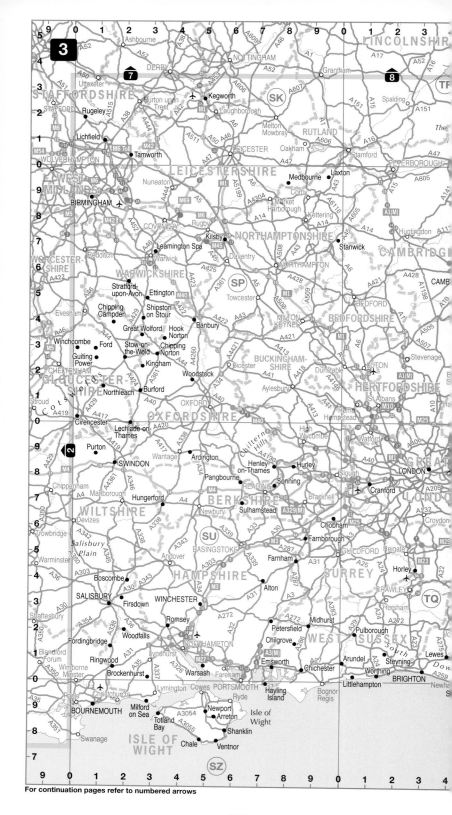

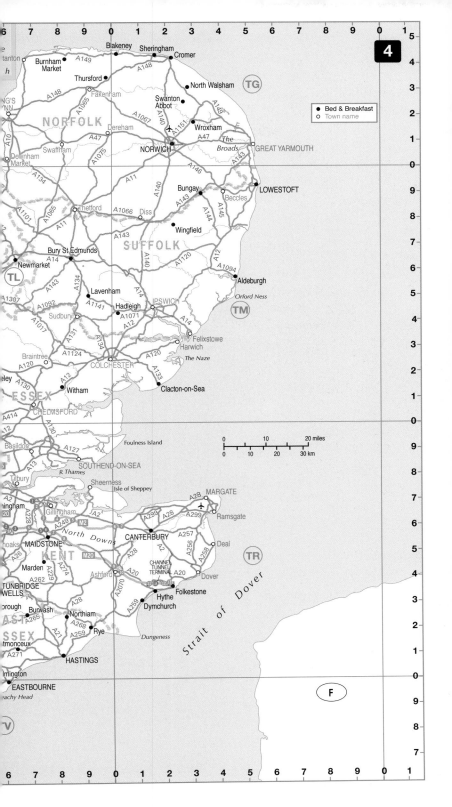

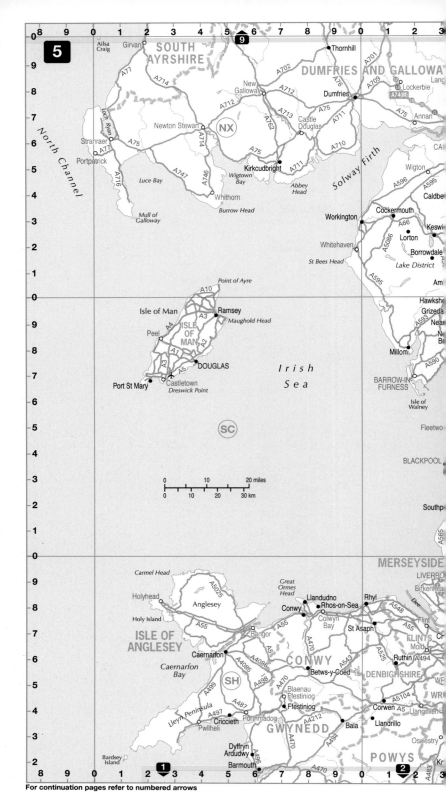

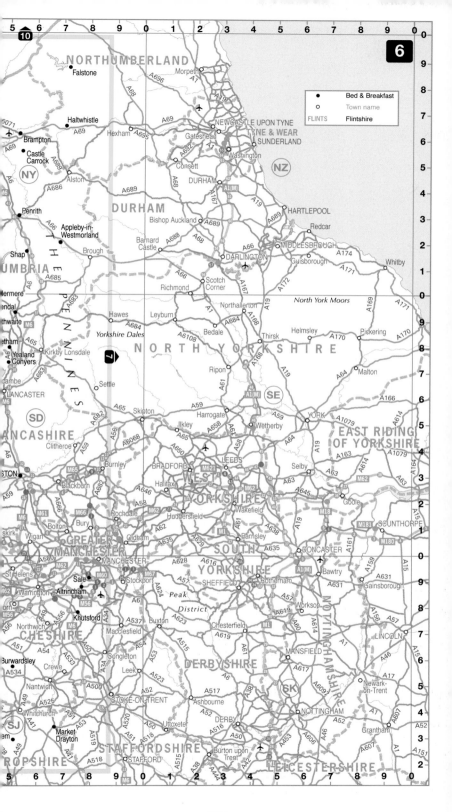

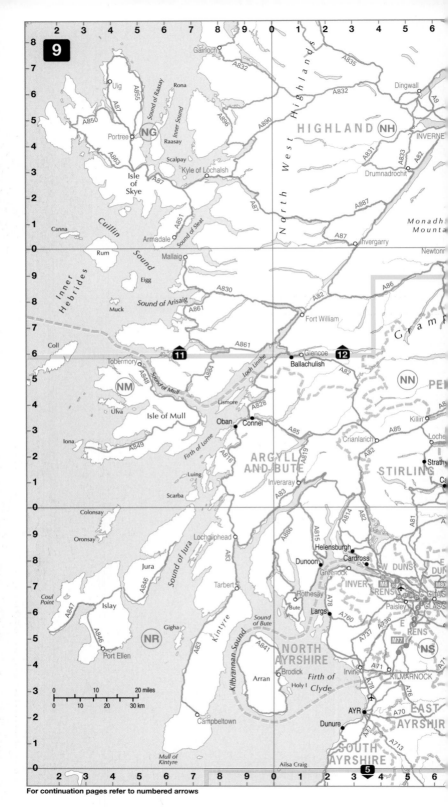

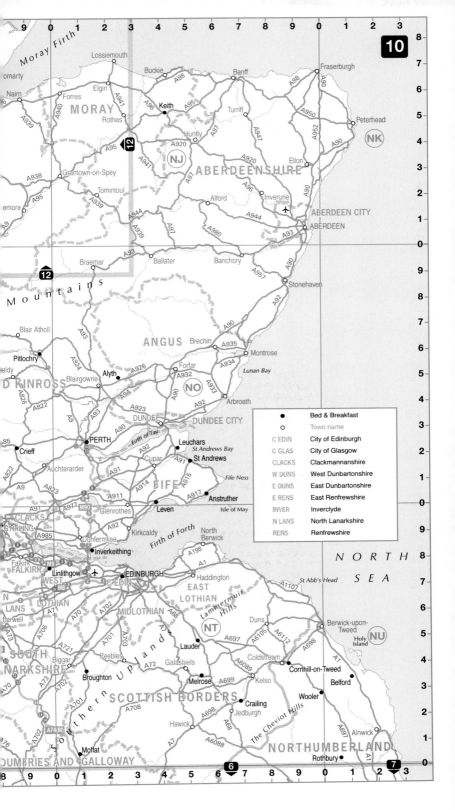

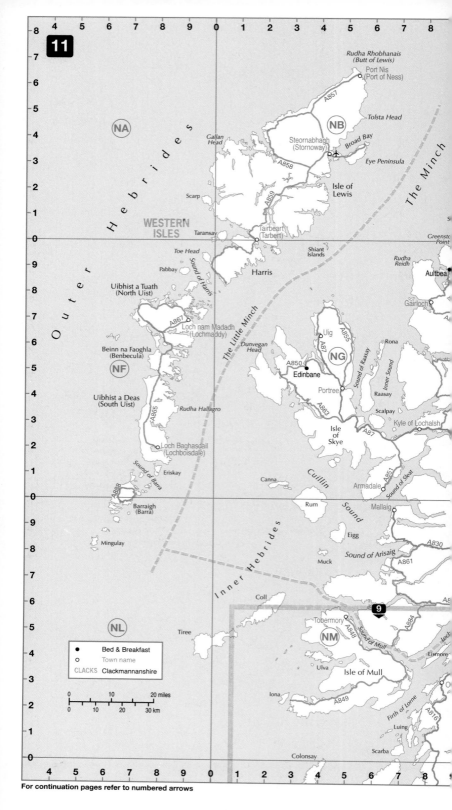

Bed & Breakfast
Town name
CLACKS Clackmannanshire

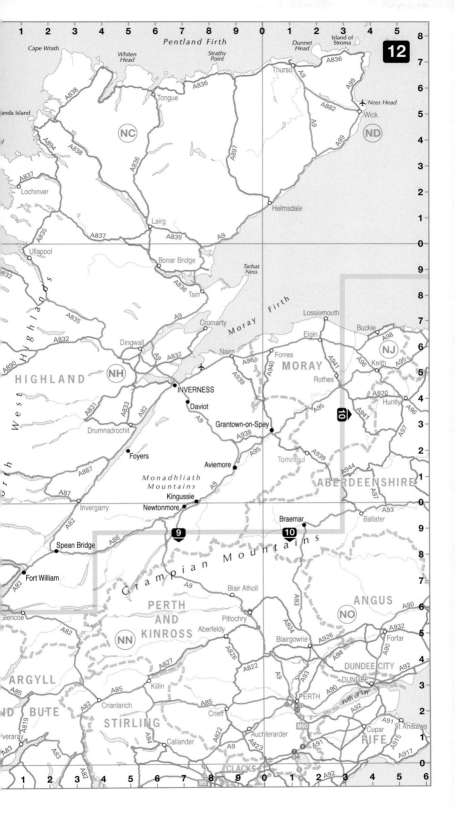

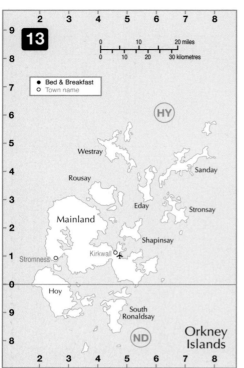

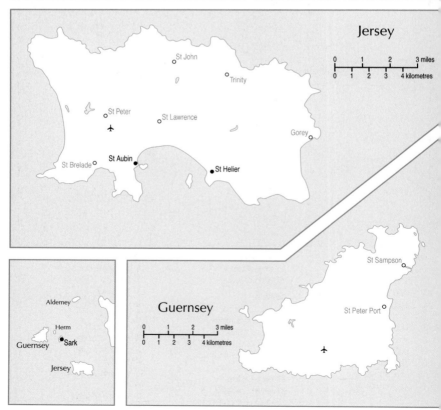

County Map

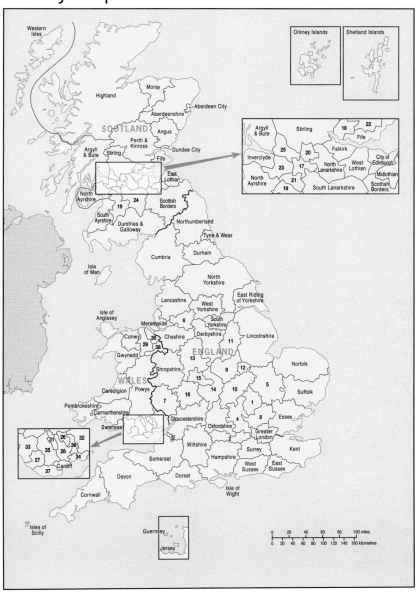

England

1 Bedfordshire
2 Berkshire
3 Bristol
4 Buckinghamshire
5 Cambridgeshire
6 Greater Manchester
7 Herefordshire
8 Hertfordshire
9 Leicestershire
10 Northamptonshire
11 Nottinghamshire
12 Rutland
13 Staffordshire
14 Warwickshire
15 West Midlands
16 Worcestershire

Scotland

17 City of Glasgow
18 Clackmannanshire
19 East Ayrshire
20 East Dunbartonshire
21 East Renfrewshire
22 Perth & Kinross
23 Renfrewshire
24 South Lanarkshire
25 West Dunbartonshire

Wales

26 Blaenau Gwent
27 Bridgend
28 Caerphilly
29 Denbighshire
30 Flintshire
31 Merthyr Tydfil
32 Monmouthshire
33 Neath Port Talbot
34 Newport
35 Rhondda Cynon Taff
36 Torfaen
37 Vale of Glamorgan
38 Wrexham

Location Index

Location Index

Location Index

488

Location Index

Location Index

Location Index

B&B Index

B&B Index

B&B Index

B&B Index

B&B Index

Picture credits

The following photographs are held in the Automobile Association's own photo library (AA World Travel Library) and were taken by these photographers:

5 AA\A Burton; 7 AA\J Beazley; 8 AA\V Greaves; 10 Royalty Free Photodisc; 11 Photodisc; 12 AA\A Burton; 13 AA; 14 AA\T Mackie; AA\14/15 AA\A Mockford & N Bonetti; 16 AA\C Jones; 20 AA\W Voysey; 22 AA\S Day; 24 AA\M Birkitt; 25 AA\L Whitwam; 26 AA\J Mottershaw; 28 AA; 29 AA\R Tenison; 33 AA\C Jones; 38 AA\N Ray; 41 AA\A Lawson; 48 AA\A Besley; 56 AA\J Wood; 61 AA\R Ireland; 67 AA\E A Bowness; 69 AA\T Mackie; 74 AA\E A Bowness; 81 AA\T Mackie; 92 AA\T Mackie; 93 AA\T Mackie; 94 AA\T Mackie; 97 AA\T Mackie; 100 AA\ J Hopkins; 104 AA\N Hicks; 111 AA\A Lawson; 113 AA\N Hicks; 122 AA\N Hicks; 126 AA\C Jones; 129 AA\W Voysey; 132 AA\N Hicks; 141 AA\J Tims; 153 AA\R Coulam; 154 AA\C Lees; 156 AA\C Lees; 157 AA\M Birkitt; 160 AA\R Surman; 161 AA\D Hall; 171 AA\H Palmer; 173 AA\S Beer; 174 AA\S Day; 176 AA\J Mottershaw; 177 AA\S Day; 182 AA\T Souter; 186 AA\A Burton; 187 AA\C Jones; 195 AA\M Short; 196 AA\T Souter; 198 AA\D Foster; 202 AA\D Forss; 204 AA\D Noble; 211 AA\J Miller; 212 AA; 214 AA\M Birkitt; 216 AA\M Birkitt; 217 AA\D Forss; 218 AA\M Birkitt; 222 AA\R Victor; 224 AA\C Sawyer; 226 AA\S McBride; 229 AA\C Sawyer; 231 AA\S Day; 233 AA\A Baker; 240 AA\ Baker; 241 AA\M Birkitt; 244 AA\R Coulam; 245 AA\J Beazley; 250 AA\R Coulam; 251 AA\M Birkitt; 252 AA\R Newton; 253 AA\J Tims; 256 AA\S Day; 259 AA\C Jones; 260 AA\M Haywood; 264 AA\C Jones; 271 AA\C Jones; 272 AA\C Jones; 274 AA\E Meacher; 276 AA\C Jones; 278 AA\C Jones; 284 AA\R Czaja; 290 AA\J Tims; 292 AA\N Moss; 296 AA\W Voysey; 297 AA\T Mackie; 301 AA\J Welsh; 302 AA\T Mackie; 308 AA\M Birkitt; 310 AA\M Trelawny; 312 AA\M Trelawny; 315 AA\J Miller; 322 AA\D Forss; 329 AA\J Miller; 331 AA\P Brown; 337 AA\J Miller; 338 AA\M Birkitt; 340 AA\P Baker; 345 AA\J Welsh; 347 AA\B Johnson; 352 AA\S & O Mathews; 354 AA\E Meacher; 355 AA\M Moody; 357 AA\M Kipling; 361 AA\M Kipling; 371 AA\J Mottershaw; 373 AA; 374 AA\S & O Mathews; 375 AA\L Whitwam; 378/379 AA\W Voysey; 381 AA\P Trenchard; 383 AA\P Trenchard; 384/385 AA; 387 AA\N Jenkins; 388/389 S Day; 399 AA\K Paterson; 402 AA\K Paterson; 407 AA\J Smith; 414 AA\E Ellington; 423 AA\S Anderson; 429 AA\D Corrance; 430/431 AA\ Burgum; 433 AA\ Burgum; 437 AA\M Allwood-Coppin; 446 AA\D Croucher; 459 AA\ Burgum; 462 AA; 469 AA\ Burgum; 470 AA\M Adelman

Every effort has been made to trace the copyright holders, and we apologise in advance for any accidental errors. We would be happy to apply the corrections in the following edition of this publication.